Timothy A. Brookins is Assistant Professor of Classics at Houston Baptist University. His research focuses on New Testament backgrounds, with a primary emphasis on the Pauline epistles. He has published articles in numerous journals, including *New Testament Studies*, *The Journal of Theological Studies*, and *Journal for the Study of the New Testament*.

CORINTHIAN WISDOM, STOIC PHILOSOPHY, AND THE ANCIENT ECONOMY

This work reexamines the divisive wisdom Paul addresses in 1 Corinthians. Challenging the recent consensus that the Corinthians' wisdom was rooted primarily in the Greco-Roman rhetorical tradition, Timothy A. Brookins offers a revisionary thesis centered on a striking pattern of discourse similarities between the perspective of the Corinthian "wise" and the Stoic system of thought. Brookins argues that several members of the church, after hearing Paul's initial gospel message, construed that message in terms of Stoic philosophy and began promoting a kind of "Stoic-Christian" perspective that helped precipitate divisions in the church. Being apprised of their views, Paul then exploited the "Stoic" discourse of his opponents in order to sustain common discursive ground. In addition to providing a fresh synthesis of the data in 1 Corinthians, Brookins brings in cutting-edge research on the ancient economy as he explores questions related to philosophical education and social status within the church community.

TIMOTHY A. BROOKINS is Assistant Professor of Classics at Houston Baptist University. His research focuses on New Testament backgrounds, with a primary emphasis on the Pauline epistles. He has published articles in numerous journals, including *New Testament Studies, The Journal of Theological Studies,* and *Journal for the Study of the New Testament.*

SOCIETY FOR NEW TESTAMENT STUDIES

MONOGRAPH SERIES

General Editor: Paul Trebilco

159

CORINTHIAN WISDOM, STOIC PHILOSOPHY, AND THE ANCIENT ECONOMY

SOCIETY FOR NEW TESTAMENT STUDIES

MONOGRAPH SERIES

Recent titles in the series

136. *The Judaean Poor and the Fourth Gospel*
TIMOTHY J. M. LING
137. *Paul, the Stoics and the Body of Christ*
MICHELLE LEE
138. *The Bridegroom Messiah and the People of God*
JOCELYN McWHIRTER
139. *The Torn Veil*
DANIEL M. GURTNER
140. *Discerning the Spirits*
ANDRÉ MUNZINGER
141. *The Sheep of the Fold*
EDWARD W. KLINK III
142. *The Psalms of Lament in Mark's Passion*
STEPHEN P. AHERNE-KROLL
143. *Cosmology and Eschatology in Hebrews*
KENNETH L. SCHENCK
144. *The Speeches of Outsiders in Acts*
OSVALDO PADILLA
145. *The Assumed Authorial Unity of Luke and Acts*
PATRICIA WALTERS
146. *Geography and the Ascension Narrative in Acts*
MATTHEW SLEEMAN
147. *The Ituraeans and the Roman Near East*
E. A. MYERS
148. *The Politics of Inheritance in Romans*
MARK FORMAN
149. *The Doctrine of Salvation in the First Letter of Peter*
MARTIN WILLIAMS
150. *Jesus and the Forgiveness of Sins*
TOBIAS HÄGERLAND
151. *The Composition of the Gospel of Thomas*
SIMON GATHERCOLE
152. *Paul as an Administrator of God in 1 Corinthians*
JOHN K. GOODRICH
153. *Affirming the Resurrection of the Incarnate Christ*
MATTHEW D. JENSEN
154. *Riches, Poverty, and the Faithful*
MARK D. MATHEWS
155. *Paul and the Rhetoric of Reversal in 1 Corinthians*
MATTHEW R. MALCOLM
156. *The Genre of Acts and Collected Biographies*
SEAN A. ADAMS
157. *The Eschatology of 1 Peter*
KELLY D. LIEBENGOOD
158. *The Hermeneutics of Christological Psalmody in Paul*
MATTHEW SCOTT

Corinthian Wisdom, Stoic Philosophy, and the Ancient Economy

TIMOTHY A. BROOKINS

CAMBRIDGE
UNIVERSITY PRESS

CAMBRIDGE
UNIVERSITY PRESS

32 Avenue of the Americas, New York, NY 10013–2473, USA

Cambridge University Press is part of the University of Cambridge.

It furthers the University's mission by disseminating knowledge in the pursuit of education, learning, and research at the highest international levels of excellence.

www.cambridge.org
Information on this title: www.cambridge.org/9781107046375

First published 2014

Printed in the United States of America

A catalog record for this publication is available from the British Library.

Library of Congress Cataloging in Publication Data
LanBrookins, Timothy A.
Corinthian wisdom, stoic philosophy, and the ancient economy / Timothy A. Brookins.
pages cm. – (Society for New Testament studies ; Volume 159)
Includes bibliographical references and index.
ISBN 978-1-107-04637-5
1. Bible. Corinthians, 1st – Criticism, interpretation, etc. 2. Stoics. 3. Corinth (Greece) – Economic conditions. I. Title.
BS2675.52.B76 2014
227′.2067–dc23 2013044946

ISBN 978-1-107-04637-5 Hardback

To Mary Mac
who has shown me daily that love is more excellent than human wisdom
Amor omnia vincit

CONTENTS

List of tables — *page* xi
Acknowledgments — xiii
List of abbreviations — xv

1 Introduction — 1

2 Rhetoric versus philosophy and 1 Corinthians — 8
1 Corinthians 1–4 in recent scholarship — 13
Assessment of recent scholarship — 17
Conclusion — 58

3 Method — 62
Studies in epistolary reconstruction — 64
Synthesis — 78
Reconstructing 1 Corinthians — 81
Conclusion — 103

4 The Corinthian social world — 104
Socioeconomic considerations — 104
Religio-cultural considerations — 124
An educated "elite"? — 132
Church relations — 147
Conclusions — 151

5 The "wise man" among the Corinthians — 153
Stoicism — 154
1 Corinthians and Stoicism — 157
Conclusion — 198

6 Loose ends — 201
The question of Apollos — 201
The role of Paul — 204

The divisions and 2 Corinthians 209
Alternative theses 211
Conclusion 220

7 Conclusion 225

Bibliography 231
Index of passages 249
Index of modern authors 261

TABLES

1. Occurrences of the σοφ-/*sapient*– root in contemporary literature *page* 36
2. Occurrences of σοφός/*sapiens* as a substantive in contemporary literature 37
3. Reference and reliability according to Sumney 71
4. Corinthian slogans according to commentators up to 1965 92
5. Corinthian slogans according to commentators from 1965 to the present 92
6. Friesen's (2004) poverty scale 120
7. Elite and middling group percentages 122
8. Corinthian church members of the middling group 123
9. The Athenian ephebate, 119 BC–AD 200 144

ACKNOWLEDGMENTS

This book is a revised version of a doctoral dissertation defended at Baylor University in February 2012. It would be impossible to estimate how deeply indebted this project has been to the astute minds of teachers, colleagues, scholars, and friends who have engaged with me over the many years of its completion. Immense thanks are due professors Bruce Longenecker and Mikeal Parsons, who read or heard presented, in several stages of production, each and every chapter of the book. Throughout my time at Baylor they – along with Charles Talbert, Lidija Novakovic, and the rest of the Religion faculty – served as the refining fire for all my academic work. From Baylor's Classics department, Jeffrey Fish was involved from the earliest stages of the project, and proved to be a constant source of guidance and profound encouragement along the way. I also owe a debt of gratitude to David Armstrong from the University of Texas–Austin, who invested an exceedingly generous share of his time musing over earlier drafts of my thesis.

I thank my parents and grandparents for their undying support, both spiritual and material, throughout my many years of graduate school. I am grateful to Josh Stout, Peter Reynolds, Eric Gilchrest, and my other studymates in the graduate program at Baylor for their much-needed companionship during some difficult years. I also thank Philip and Nicole Donnelly, and countless others who offered me and my family warm hospitality, spiritual nourishment, and sincere friendship during our time in Waco.

I thank my colleagues at Houston Baptist University for providing the circumstances needed to bring this project to completion in its final stages. Thanks must go to *Neotestamentica* for allowing me to incorporate reworked material from one of my earlier articles.

Most of all I thank my wife, Mary Mac, whose contribution to my success, happiness, and livelihood over the last ten years (spent almost entirely in graduate school) has been inestimable. Words cannot express the gratitude she is owed. It is to her, with great love, that this volume is dedicated.

ABBREVIATIONS

AE	*Archaiologike Ephemeris*
Brev. vit.	*De Brevitate Vitae*
Corinth VIII	*Corinth: The Inscriptions 1926–50*. Edited by J. H. Kent. Princeton, 1966.
D. L.	Diogenes Laertius
De diff. puls.	*De differentia pulsuum*
IGRR	*Inscriptiones Graecae ad res Romanas pertinentes*. Edited by R. Cagnat. 3 vols. Paris, 1906–27; repr. Chicago, 1975.
ISmyrna	*Die Inschriften von Smyrna*. Edited by G. Petz. Bonn, 1982–90.
IStratonikeia	*Die Inschriften von Stratonikeia*. Edited by Sahin. Bonn, 1981–90.
IvO	*Die Inscrhiften von Olympia*. Edited by W. Dittenberger, K. Purgold. Berlin, 1896.
LS	Long, A. A. and D. N. Sedley, eds. *The Hellenistic Philosophers*. 2 vols. Cambridge: Cambridge University Press, 1988.
Mor.	*Moralia*
NT	New Testament
Or.	*Orationes*
PAA	Traill, John S. *Persons of Ancient Athens*. Vol. 7: ERAGINOS TO EON-. Toronto: Athenians, 1998.
TAM	*Tituli Lyciae linguis Graeca et latina conscripti*. Edited by E. Kalinka. Vienna, 1920–44.

All other abbreviations follow the Society of Biblical Literature *Handbook of Style*.

1

INTRODUCTION

In at least one respect, the subject of this book is one on which scholars have shared practically universal agreement: "wisdom" (σοφία), as it was understood by some in the Corinthian church, was critical to the problem of division that threatened to topple that fledgling church into ruin (1 Corinthians 1–4).[1]

But over the last 200 years, this subject has also made cause for great disagreement, as scholarly assessments of this wisdom have varied widely. (1) In 1831, F. C. Baur published his programmatic essay arguing that the church's four putative "parties" (1 Cor 1:10–12) could be reduced to two: Paul's Hellenistic-Jewish faction, which extolled grace, and Peter's Palestinian Jewish faction, which extolled the Law and human wisdom.[2] (2) From the early to mid-twentieth century, wisdom came to be understood in terms of Greek Gnosticism, whereby certain ones in the church were thought to have demeaned the material realm and to have

[1] This has been the common judgment from one generation of interpreters to the next: e.g., A. T. Robertson and A. Plummer, *A Critical and Exegetical Commentary on the First Epistle of St. Paul to the Corinthians*, ICC (Edinburgh: T & T Clark, 1914), 15; F. Grosheide, *Commentary on the First Epistle to the Corinthians* (Grand Rapids: Eerdmans, 1954), 42; J. C. Hurd, *The Origin of 1 Corinthians* (New York: Seabury, 1965), 76, 77; R. Funk, "Word and Word in 1 Cor 2:6–16," in *Language, Hermeneutic, and Word of God* (New York: Harper & Row, 1966), 277; C. K. Barrett, *A Commentary on the First Epistle to the Corinthians* (London: Adam and Charles Black, 1971), 275–6; G. Fee, *1 Corinthians*, NICNT (Grand Rapids: Eerdmans, 1987), 64; S. M. Pogoloff, *Logos and Sophia: The Rhetorical Situation of 1 Corinthians*, SBLDS 134 (Atlanta: Scholars, 1992), 105; R. E. Ciampa and B. S. Rosner, *The First Letter to the Corinthians*, Pillar (Grand Rapids: Eerdmans, 2010), 120; cf. 20–1; M. T. Finney, *Honour and Conflict in the Ancient World*, LNTS 460 (London: T & T Clark, 2011), 80. Otherwise, M. V. P. Branick ("Source and Redaction Analysis of 1 Corinthians 1–3," *JBL* 101 [1982]: 251–69) has stood alone in finding no connection between wisdom and the divisions.

[2] F. C. Baur, "Die Christuspartei in der korinthischen Gemeinde, der Gegensatz des paulinishcen und petrinischen Christentums in der ältesten Kirche, der Apostel Petrus in Rom," *Tübinger Zeitschrift für Theologie* 4 (1831): 61–206; followed by "The Epistles to the Corinthians," in *Paulus, der Apostle Jesu Christi* (Stuttgart: Becker & Muller, 1866), 268–320.

boasted in the spiritual salvation ostensibly achieved through baptism.[3] (3) Beginning in the final third of the twentieth century, scholars began to liken Corinthian wisdom to either "over-realized eschatology" or the wisdom of Hellenistic Judaism, both of which could be described, if not in terms of Gnosticism, at least in terms of incipient or "proto-gnosticism."[4] (4) Also gaining traction during this period – though still continuing as the dominant perspective today – were social-historical theories that connected the Corinthians' wisdom with elite, and especially rhetorical, education.[5]

[3] First, W. Lütgert, *Freiheitspredigt und Schwarmgeister in Korinth* (Göttingen: C. Bertelsman, 1908); followed by a few others, but famously revived by W. Schmithals, *Die Gnosis in Korinth: Eine Untersuchung zu den Korintherbriefen* (Göttingen: Vandenhoeck & Ruprecht, 1969); ET, *Gnosticism in Corinth: An Investigation of the Letters to the Corinthians* (Nashville: Abingdon, 1971).

[4] Over-realized eschatology: A. C. Thiselton, "Realized Eschatology at Corinth," *NTS* 24 (1978): 510–26; reaffirmed but qualified in ibid., *The First Epistle to the Corinthians*, NIGTC (Grand Rapids: Eerdmans, 2000), esp. 40. Hellenistic-Judaism: Richard Horsley, "Pneumatikos vs. Psychikos: Distinctions of Spiritual Status among the Corinthians," *HTR* 69 (1976): 269–88; "Wisdom of Words and Words of Wisdom in Corinth," *CBQ* 39 (1977): 224–39; "How Can Some of You Say That There Is No Resurrection of the Dead? Spiritual Elitism in Corinth," *NovT* 20 (1978): 203–31; "Consciousness and Freedom among the Corinthians (1 Cor 8–10)," *CBQ* 40 (1978): 574–89; "Gnosis in Corinth: 1 Cor 8:1–6," *NTS* 27 (1981): 32–51; as well as his commentary, *1 Corinthians*, 33–36; and his collection of essays, *Wisdom and Spiritual Transcendence at Corinth: Studies in First Corinthians* (Eugene: Cascade, 2008); also B. A. Pearson, "Hellenistic-Jewish Wisdom Speculation and Paul," in R. L. Wilken (ed.), *Aspects of Wisdom in Judaism and Early Christianity* (Notre Dame: Notre Dame University Press, 1975), 43–66; and J. A. Davis, *Wisdom and Spirit: An Investigation of 1 Cor 1:18–3:20 against the Background of Jewish Sapiential Traditions in the Greco-Roman Period* (New York: University Press of America, 1984). Jerome Murphy-O'Connor demonstrates just how closely the "over-realized eschatology" and Hellenistic-Jewish theses relate in labeling the wise Corinthians "Spirit people": *Paul: A Critical Life* (Oxford: Oxford University Press, 1996), 275ff; and *Paul: His Story* (Oxford: Oxford University Press, 2004), 163–5.

[5] J. Munck was a harbinger: "Menigheden uden Partier," *Dansk Teologisk Tidsskrift* 15 (1952): 215–33; ET, "The Church without Factions," in *Paul and the Salvation of Mankind* (London: SCM, 1959), 135–67; but the thesis was more fully developed beginning with B. Winter; "Philo and Paul among the Sophists: A Hellenistic Jewish and a Christian Response," PhD dissertation, Macquarie University (1988); published in *Paul and Philo among the Sophists* (Cambridge: Cambridge University Press, 1997); 2d edn. (Grand Rapids: Eerdmans, 2002); others taking the rhetorical line have included: Pogoloff, *Logos and Sophia*; A. Clarke, *Secular and Christian Leadership in Corinth: A Socio-Historical and Exegetical Study of 1 Corinthians 1-6* (New York: Brill, 1993), 102–7; D. Litfin, *St. Paul's Theology of Proclamation: 1 Corinthians 1–4 and Greco-Roman Rhetoric*, SNTSMS 79 (Cambridge: Cambridge University Press, 1994); and L. L. Welborn, *Politics and Rhetoric in the Corinthian Epistles* (Macon: Mercer University Press, 1997). D. Martin (*Corinthian Body* [New Haven: Yale University Press, 1995]) sees the Corinthians as having knowledge of "popular philosophy" bordering on elite-level education (pp. 61–68), but he also finds in them an obsession with the high status associated with rhetoric (pp. 47–66). Studies focusing on social conventions more generally include: P. Marshall, *Enmity in*

Of these trends, the first two have been effectively demolished.[6] Baur's thesis has long been regarded as reductive, if at all accurate. Gnosticism, as was shown in the 1970s, apparently did not exist before the early or mid-second century, much less in Paul's day.[7] Moreover, interpretations of the third sort have been blackened by association. In their recent review of Corinthians scholarship, Edward Adams and David Horrell subsume under one heading theses based on "religious and philosophical parallels," which include not only the Gnostic thesis but also theses related to Hellenistic Judaism, Greco-Roman philosophy, and popular philosophical thought.[8] The difficulty they find with such theories reflects a common sentiment at present: "When parallels are found in Gnosticism, Hellenistic Judaism, Stoicism, Cynicism, Epicureanism, and so on, we are bound at least to ask whether the Corinthians can ever be clearly located in relation to one movement or another."[9] This objection, sensible as it seems, has generally led in either of two directions. Many scholars, bracketing the question of the Corinthians' wisdom, have now shifted focus from the putative background *behind* the letter to the task of examining Paul's own side of the conversation – what *his* theology of wisdom was, what kind of rhetoric he used in treating the exigencies, and so on. The second solution has been to address the Corinthians' wisdom, but with the understanding that it cannot be characterized by any single system of thought: it is rather the wisdom acquired from elite education and therefore must pertain to *rhetorical* eloquence or sophistry, not any readily definable set of religious or philosophical beliefs. Both of these

Corinth: Social Conventions in Paul's Relations with the Corinthians, WUNT 2:23 (Tübingen: Mohr Siebeck, 1987); and J. K. Chow, *Patronage and Power: A Study of Social Networks in Corinth*, JSNTSup 75 (Sheffield: JSOT, 1992).

6 Even if their specters still show themselves from time to time. Baur's thesis has been revived and further elaborated in recent years by Michael Goulder in "σοφία in Corinthians," *NTS* 37 (1991): 516–34; and *Paul and the Competing Mission in Corinth* (Peabody: Hendrickson, 2001). One still finds mention of "Gnosticism" as well: e.g., M. Taiwo, *Paul's Rhetoric in 1 Corinthians 10:29b-30* (Saarbrücken: Müller, 2008), 54; and G. Theissen, "Social Conflicts in the Corinthian Correspondence: Further Remarks on J. J. Meggitt, *Paul, Poverty and Survival*," *JSNT* (2003): 389–90; cf. T. E. Klutz, "Re-Reading 1 Corinthians after *Rethinking 'Gnosticism*,'" *JSNT* 26 (2003): 193–216.

7 Credited with the exposé is Edwin M. Yamauchi, in *Pre-Christian Gnosticism* (Grand Rapids; London: Eerdmans, 1973); and "Pre-Christian Gnosticism Reconsidered a Decade Later," in *Pre-Christian Gnosticism: A Survey of the Proposed Evidences* (Grand Rapids: Baker Book House, 1983), 187–249.

8 E. Adams and D. Horrell, *Christianity at Corinth: The Quest for the Pauline Church* (Louisville: Westminister John Knox, 2004), 16–23. Studies to note here include the following – on Epicurean philosophy: G. Tomlin, "Christians and Epicureans in 1 Corinthians," *JSNT* 68 (1997): 51–72 – on Cynic philosophy: F. G. Downing, *Cynics, Paul, and the Pauline Churches* (London: Routledge, 1998) – on Stoic philosophy, see later in the book.

9 Adams and Horrell, *Christianity at Corinth*, 22.

approaches have reinforced the recent trend of widening investigation to examination of the broader social milieu and consideration of the *general* secular attitudes that the Corinthians might have imbibed from it. Accordingly, most would now consider attempts to locate the Corinthians' wisdom in relation to particular systems of thought to be beyond the pale of what is currently acceptable.

Few, if any, would deny that these trends have marked a significant advance from the ideas of Baur and proponents of the Gnostic thesis. Yet, it should be asked whether the flow of present scholarship is one simply to be *entered into*, or whether – as at any juncture in the history of interpretation – it too may be in need of some redirection. To be sure, social-historical approaches to the text will remain indispensable for a full appreciation of what is taking place in 1 Corinthians. But such approaches, I hope to show, need not lead us to the conclusion that the Corinthians' wisdom cannot be understood primarily in terms of particular systems of thought (controversial as that may sound), nor to the now dominant perspective that the Corinthians' wisdom is best understood in terms of Greco-Roman rhetoric or sophistry.

In the light of present circumstances, the thesis proposed on the following pages, in many respects, appears to buck the trend. Nonetheless it is a thesis that, at least in inchoate form, has precedent as old as any and, once an opportunity has been given for the full breadth of evidence to be assessed, I hope, will be recognized among the most cogent proposals to be forwarded to date, accounting as it does for both a broader range of the internal evidence of 1 Corinthians on the one hand and the social situation of first-century Corinth and its church community on the other. Without denying the role played by social stratification and other secular social forces, I argue that the divisive "wisdom" of the Corinthians, *qua wisdom*, can be accounted for as a *Christian development of Stoic philosophy*, arguably without remainder.[10] Conspicuous in

[10] Earlier articulations of this thesis have generally been limited to select passages within the letter. Stoic connections in 3:21, 3:22, 4:8, and 6:12 are noted as far back as J. B. Lightfoot (*Notes on the Epistles of St. Paul* [London: Macmillan, 1895], 195, 200) and J. Weiss (*Der erste Korintherbrief* [Göttingen: Vandenhoeck & Ruprecht, 1910], 89–91, 157–9). R. Grant ("The Wisdom of the Corinthians," in *The Joy of Study* [New York: Macmillan, 1951], 51–55) believed the Corinthians were self-styled Stoic-Cynic wise men. S. Stowers ("A 'Debate' over Freedom: I Corinthians 6:12–20," in E. Ferguson (ed.), *Christian Teaching: Studies in Honor of Lemoine G. Lewis* [Abilene: Abilene Christian University, 1981], 59–71) says the Corinthian slogans of 6:12, 13, 18 are to be seen against the background of "a popular form of Cynic and Stoic ethics" (p. 67). M. Lakey (*Image and Glory of God: 1 Corinthians 11:2–16 as a Case Study in Bible, Gender and Hermeneutics*, LNTS 418 [London: T & T Clark, 2010], 80) assumes the presence of an underlying Stoic

most of the problems in the letter, this perspective has been adopted among a small but influential minority in the church. While they have not committed to Stoicism slavishly, they are nonetheless deeply indebted to its discourse and superstructure for their interpretation of Paul's message.

The lack of attention this thesis has received over the years owes, I think, less to a dearth of evidence than it does to the irresistible draft of the collective scholarly agenda, which, though set by a few, sweeps nearly all into its powerful current. For some fifty years prior to the ascendancy of social-historical approaches, NT scholarship exhibited an all-time low in interest for how Greek philosophy might illuminate the text,[11] which meant that Stoicism received little attention in investigations of 1 Corinthians.[12] At the end of that period, when the Gnostic thesis suffered its decoronation and social-historical approaches were presented as a sort of replacement, all theses that might have been supported on the basis of comparative religious or philosophical material were collectively crushed, with scarce regard for their independent merits. This has allowed what little treatment the Stoic thesis has received in recent years to fall through the cracks: the thesis has been passed over *on principle* rather than by any sort of direct rebuttal. With "religious" and "philosophical" theses out of the picture, the "rhetorical" thesis then seemed the natural road to take. This direction seemed to be confirmed by a simultaneous shift of opinion regarding first-century Corinth, namely that it was

perspective in several Corinthian catchwords (2:6, 10; 3:1) and slogans (6:12a/10:23a; 6:13a; 8:4, 8). M. Pascuzzi (*Ethics, Ecclesiology, and Church Discipline* [Rome: Editrice Pontificia Universita Gregoriana, 1997]) argues that the problem in 1 Corinthians 5–6 was influenced by the Stoic view that incest was "indifferent." R. Hays ("Conversion of the Imagination," *NTS* 45 [1999]: 391–412) sees the Corinthian position as a hybrid of Stoicism, Cynicism, and charismatic fervor. A. J. Malherbe ("Determinism and Free Will in Paul: The Argument of 1 Cor 8 and 9," in Troels Engberg-Pedersen (ed.), *Paul in His Hellenistic Context* [London: T & T Clark, 1995; London: Continuum, 2004], 231–55) understands the Corinthians' "knowledge" and denigration of the "weak" in Stoic terms. A. Garcilazo (*The Corinthian Dissenters and the Stoics* [New York: Peter Lang, 2007]) notes a number of texts in which Stoicism rears its head, but focuses on the denial of the resurrection in 15:12–58. T. Paige offers the closest thing to a full treatment of the letter, but his analysis is limited to a single article: "Stoicism, *Eleutheria* and Community at Corinth," in M. J. Wilkins and T. Paige (eds.), *Worship, Theology and Ministry in the Early Church* (Sheffield: JSOT, 1992), 180–93.

[11] See A. J. Malherbe, "Graeco-Roman Religion and Philosophy and the New Testament," in E. J. Epp and G. W. McRae (eds.), *The New Testament and Its Modern Interpreters* (Philadelphia: Fortress, 1989), 3–26; and "Hellenistic Moralists and the New Testament," *ANRW* 26.1:267–333.

[12] Of those studies noted earlier, only Robert Grant ("The Wisdom of the Corinthians") wrote during this period, and he emphasized a *pre-Christian Jewish appropriation* of the Greek philosophical categories.

"Roman, not Greek" (again serving to shunt aside theories related to Greek religion or philosophy). With that, the new agenda for Corinthian studies was set: as we hear in the current literature, the divisions of the Corinthians were "social, not theological" in nature, their wisdom was that of "rhetoric, not philosophy," and their city was "Roman, not Greek." Next to such sharp dichotomies, the Stoic thesis has been a nonstarter. As it is, one either follows the consensus willingly or is dragged.

Perhaps the current consensus has also stemmed from our despair at the great diversity of meanings that σοφ- language was capable of carrying in the first century. Such difficulties are not to be denied. Yet, the corollary observation that Paul's discussion of "wisdom" in 1 Corinthians 1–4, too, admits of a wide variety of usages,[13] and wisdom must therefore be nonspecific, seems to involve a non sequitur. Arguably, it confuses the *occasion behind* the letter on the one hand, and Paul's ad hoc *response to it* on the other. Indeed, much could be clarified in Corinthian studies if we would take more seriously the (widely accepted) methodological observation that *not* everything Paul says constitutes the antithesis of some opposite position held by his "opponents," as if the text were an immaculately polished mirror. Rather, historical occasions act as *springboards* for Paul's theologizing: he begins with a *particular* set of circumstances – and many have supposed, in 1 Corinthians, with a particular kind of wisdom – and then expatiates more broadly on "human wisdom" in all its dangerous forms. Just how this set of historical circumstances might be isolated if not through "mirror-reading," however, will have to be considered in our present investigation.

My main aim here is to provide the first sustained treatment for the Stoic thesis, assessing 1 Corinthians from beginning to end,[14] with conscientious attention to methodology, and – marking an advance from the old Gnostic thesis – *within proper social and economic context.* This requires special attention to a broad range of counter theses, most of all the new rhetorical one. As we shall see in Chapter 2, the rhetorical thesis has been taken for granted on the word of a few dominating monographs;

[13] For the varied meanings of σοφία within this discourse and a guess at their meanings, see J. D. G. Dunn, *1 Corinthians* (Sheffield Academic, 1995; T & T Clark, 2004), 43.

[14] In spite of those few earlier studies that challenged the unity of 1 Corinthians (J. Weiss, *The History of Primitive Christianity* [New York: K. W. Wilson-Enckson, 1937], 356–7; J. Hering, *The First Epistle of Saint Paul to the Corinthians* [London: Epworth, 1962], xiii–xv; and W. Schmithals, "Die Korintherbrief als Briefsammlung," *ZNW* 64 [1973]: 87–113), the consensus since Margaret Mitchell's *Paul and the Rhetoric of Reconciliation: An Exegetical Investigation of the Language and Composition of 1 Corinthians* (Louisville: Westminster John Knox, 1993) has been overwhelmingly in favor of the letter's full integrity. See Finney, *Honour and Conflict in the Ancient World*, 69, for recent scholars who have taken this position.

though a closer, and fuller, look at the evidence reveals that their case finds far less support in the ancient sources than recent literature has suggested. Chapter 3 canvasses the state of the issue with regard to methodology and attempts on this basis to distill a set of methodological principles for the present pursuit. In Chapter 4, I undertake an investigation of the Corinthian social world, addressing especially questions related to the socioeconomic configuration of the Corinthian church, the religio-cultural character of their city, and potential philosophical influences within the community. Chapter 5 sets forth the Stoic thesis, with an eye not simply to 1 Corinthians 1–4 – the usual locus of attention – but rather to the *pattern* of issues found throughout the letter as a *whole*. Many observations will have been noted in previous studies,[15] but it will also become apparent that past studies have left some ponderable stones unturned. Chapter 6 ties together the loose ends, attempting to answer how the present thesis lines up with insights from other studies, past and present. In the end, the composite evidence should tell a different story from that told in recent years: the "wise man" among the Corinthians is less the "sophist" than he is the "Stoic."

[15] In such cases, I cite the relevant literature.

2

RHETORIC VERSUS PHILOSOPHY AND 1 CORINTHIANS

Long before the first scholars showed us the parallels between 1 Corinthians and Philo's brand of Hellenistic-Judaism, and still before anyone sought to convince us of Gnosticism in Corinth, many interpreters were pointing to a different form of wisdom as the source of the Corinthians' troubles – the Greco-Roman rhetorical-philosophical tradition.[1] Now, nearly a century later, we are said to have come full circle. The Gnostic and Hellenistic-Jewish theses have been found either impossible or inadequate, and we have arrived back at rhetoric.

Since the new rhetorical thesis hit the presses in force in the early 1990s, few have expressed doubt as to its conclusions. In the first place, it was immediately heralded as a retrieval of the old and widely accepted "rhetorical" thesis that had circulated among scholars prior to the middle of the twentieth century, when it was temporarily – and wrongfully – eclipsed by the Gnostic and Hellenistic-Jewish arguments. Moreover, rhetorical wisdom – closely associated with high social status in Greco-Roman antiquity – has seemed to connect naturally with the insights made in the 1970s and 1980s (though still considered basically valid) by Gerd Theissen, Wayne Meeks, and others regarding social stratification in the Corinthian church. Add to this our recent rediscovery of ancient rhetorical theory and its warm reception by biblical scholars in the form of rhetorical criticism of the NT, and the rhetorical thesis appears a perfect fit for the times. Indeed, current conditions tell us that the rhetorical thesis is here to stay.[2]

Despite this apparent security, the rhetorical thesis has some weaknesses that have yet to be given close attention. First, while exponents have been quick to remind us that their thesis is an old one, they have also

[1] Lightfoot, *Notes on the Epistles of St. Paul*, 170; Weiss, *Der erste Korintherbrief*, 23; U. Wilckens, "Σοφία, σοφός, σοφίζω," *TDNT* 7:522, recalling the consensus of older scholarship.

[2] Though we have met with occasional dissenters: e.g., R. D. Anderson, *Rhetorical Theory and Paul*, CBET 18 (Leuven: Peeters, 1999), 245–76.

been suspiciously reticent as to the fact that, in the older treatments, philosophy had been given an important place alongside – or even prominence over – rhetoric. Duane Litfin, for instance, tells us that "until recent times exegetes *consistently* interpreted the phrase σοφία λόγου (1.17) with *primary reference* to Greco-Roman rhetoric."[3] Here he footnotes, among other sources, Ulrich Wilckens's article from *TDNT*, whom he quotes as saying that "most exegetes" have held the rhetorical explanation to be the "customary interpretation." Turning to Wilckens's article, however, we find that Litfin's statement does not give us an entirely accurate perspective of the issue:

> *Most exegetes* in expounding the whole discussion in 1 C. 1:18–2:5 concentrate on the phrases σοφία λόγου in 1:17, ὑπεροχὴν λόγου ἢ σοφίας in 2:1, and ἐν πειθοῖς σοφίας λόγοις in 2:4. It thus seems that in this section the Chr. preacher is opposing *any philosophical or rhetorical presentation* of the Gospel acc. to the standards of *Gk. philosophy*.[4]

Wilckens classically goes on to demur from "most exegetes," suggesting that Paul's opponents are "Gnostics" – that is, as he says, "Gnostics, not *Gk. Philosophers*" (emphasis added). Thus, far from supporting Litfin's suggestion that exegetes have for a long time "consistently" interpreted 1:17 with "*primary* reference" to Greco-Roman rhetoric, Wilckens instead places the emphasis of "most exegetes" on the other side – that of philosophy. A look at some of the most prominent interpreters on 1 Corinthians around the dawn of the twentieth century only confirms the accuracy of this claim.[5]

If Litfin's error owes, in part, to his unique conception of the relationship between rhetoric and philosophy in the first century (discussed later), this cannot be said of Lawrence Welborn, who claims: "The σοφία that Paul fears will undermine the community is *nothing other than rhetoric*. This interpretation," Welborn says, "was the view of an older generation of scholars more familiar with Greek and Latin authors."[6] As we shall see, such simple disregard for philosophy will not be limited to Litfin and Welborn.

[3] Litfin, *St. Paul's Theology of Proclamation*, 3; emphasis added.

[4] Wilckens, *TDNT* 7:522; emphasis added.

[5] See, e.g., Lightfoot, *Notes on the Epistles of St. Paul*, 170; and Weiss, *Der erste Korintherbrief*, 23, 158–9.

[6] L. L. Welborn (*Politics and Rhetoric in the Corinthian Epistles* (Macon: Mercer University Press, 1997), 30; emphasis added.

Tied with the disappearance of philosophy from the old thesis is the question of Paul's dominating emphasis in the discourse. That the Corinthians' divisive wisdom was merely "*human*" is stated plainly in the text (2:5, 13; cf. "wisdom of the world," 3:19), but whether that wisdom was more "formally" or more "substantively" problematic is left uncertain. In antiquity, the conflict between the "form" and "content" of wisdom was often framed in terms of a clash between rhetoric and philosophy – rhetoric was about the form of expression, or mere *words* (*verba*/λόγος), whereas philosophy was about the content, or real *things* (*res*/πράξεις). The separation is an artificial one, but it is one that was regularly insisted on in the ancient sources. Even among those who believed that philosophy could make *use* of rhetoric, it was maintained that "rhetoric" was its own art, reducible to its own system, and distinct from philosophy and other forms of speech. In that regard, which of these two areas – rhetoric or philosophy – could rightly lay claim to wisdom was a matter of perennial and often heated debate.

In light of the ancient dispute, NT scholars have exerted themselves in trying to discern whether Paul was concerned more with the *form* or more with the *content* of the Corinthians' σοφία – or, as the debate is usually framed, more with "rhetoric" or more with "philosophy." In this regard, three main text units have come to the fore – 1:17–31, 2:1–5, and 2:6–16. Within these units, four phrases in particular have become the center of attention:

> 1:17 – οὐκ ἐν σοφίᾳ λόγου – "not with eloquent wisdom" (NRSV); "not in cleverness of speech" (NAS)
>
> 2:1 – οὐ καθ' ὑπεροχὴν λόγου ἢ σοφίας – "not with lofty words or wisdom" (NRSV); "not with superiority of speech or of wisdom" (NAS)
>
> 2:4 – οὐκ ἐν πειθοῖ[ς] σοφίας [λόγοις] – "not with plausible words of wisdom" (NRSV); "not with persuasive words of wisdom" (NAS)
>
> 2:13 – οὐκ ἐν διδακτοῖς ἀνθρωπίνης σοφίας λόγοις – "words not taught by human wisdom" (NRSV)

Conclusions regarding Paul's focus of attention have remained fairly diverse. Most studies consider 1:17 to be concerned entirely with the form of wisdom,[7] although almost as many detect a dual concern

[7] Robertson and Plummer, *First Epistle of St. Paul to the Corinthians*, 15–16; E.-B. Allo, *Première épître aux Corinthiens* (Paris: Gabalda, 1934), 12; Funk, "Word and Word in 1 Cor 2:6–16," 281; C. Senft, *La Premiere Epitre de Saint Paul aux Corinthiens*, CNT; 2d edn.

for form and content, with alternating emphases.[8] A few have concluded that the full emphasis is on content.[9] Likewise, most interpreters take 2:1, 4 in connection with form or rhetoric,[10] even though many believe it

(Geneva: Labor et Fides, 1990), 36; B. Witherington, *Conflict and Community in Corinth: A Socio-Rhetorical Commentary on 1 and 2 Corinthians* (Grand Rapids: Eerdmans, 1995), 82, 85; R. Hays, *1 Corinthians* (Louisville: John Knox Press, 1997), 24; R. Collins, *1 Corinthians*, SP (Collegeville: Liturgical, 1999), 85, citing Pogoloff; A. Lindemann, *Der erste Korintherbrief*, HNT (Tübingen: Mohr Siebeck, 2000), 43; A. C. Thiselton, *The First Epistle to the Corinthians*, NIGTC (Grand Rapids: Eerdmans, 2000), 143; C. Talbert, *Reading Corinthians: A Literary and Theological Commentary* (Macon: Smyth & Helwys, 2002), 17; D. E. Garland, *1 Corinthians*, BECNT 1 (Grand Rapids: Baker Academic, 2003), 56, following Litfin and Pogoloff; J. Fitzmyer, *1 Corinthians: A New Translation with Introduction and Commentary* (New Haven; London: Yale University Press, 2008), 148; and Ciampa and Rosner, *The First Letter to the Corinthians*, 86. Lightfoot (*Notes on Epistles of St. Paul*, 157) sees form as the concern, although he says it could be either "rhetorical" or "dialectical." Some say that Paul is taking the side of wisdom's content over against that of form, with which the Corinthians are infatuated: e.g., E. Krentz, "Logos or Sophia: The Pauline Use of the Ancient Dispute between Rhetoric and Philosophy," in J. T. Fitzgerald, T. H. Olbricht, and L. M. White (eds.), *Early Christianity and Classical Culture: Comparative Studies in Honor of Abraham J. Malherbe* (Leiden: Brill, 2003), 280.

[8] Form and content: H. Conzelmann, *1 Corinthians: A Commentary on the First Epistle to the Corinthians*, Hermeneia (Philadelphia: Fortress, 1975), 46; F. Lang, *Die Briefe an die Korinther*, NTD; 2d edn. (Göttingen: Vandenhoeck & Ruprecht, 1994), 22; C. Wolff, *Der erste Brief des Paulus an die Korinther* (Leipzig: Evangelische Verlagsanstalt, 1996), 33 – rhetoric and philosophy: Horsley, *1 Corinthians*, 46–47 – emphasis on content: J. Moffatt, *The First Epistle of Paul to the Corinthians* (London: Hodder & Stoughton, 1938), 14–16; Schmithals, *Gnosticism in Corinth*, 142–3; Fee, *1 Corinthians*, 65, 66, 68 – emphasis on form: Weiss, *Der erste Korintherbrief*, 23; Barrett, *First Epistle to the Corinthians*, 49; W. Schrage, *Der Erstebrief an die Korinther*, EKK 7 (Zürich; Düsseldorf: Benziger Verlag, 1991), 1:158 – emphasis on rhetoric, though without excluding philosophy: C. Keener, *1–2 Corinthians*, NCBC (Cambridge: Cambridge University Press, 2005), 28, 36 – Witherington (*Conflict and Community in Corinth*, 87, 96, 103, 104, 142) and Hays (*1 Corinthians*, 27) note that 1:18–25 is also about both form and content.

[9] Content: Anderson, *Rhetorical Theory and Paul*, 276 – philosophy: Grosheide, *First Epistle to the Corinthians*, 40–41; H. Schlier, "Kerygma und Sophia: zur neutestamentlichen Grundlegung des Dogmas," in *Die Zeit der Kirche: Exegetische Aufsätze und Vorträge* (Freiburg: Herder, 1956), 206–32; D. H. Lietzmann, *An Die Korinther I, II* (Tübingen: Mohr, 1969), 9. Cf. on 1:18–25, M. Bullmore, *St. Paul's Theology of Rhetorical Style: An Examination of 1 Corinthians 2:1–5 in the Light of First-Century Rhetorical Criticism* (San Francisco: International Scholars Publications, 1995), 221.

[10] Form: Barrett, *First Epistle to the Corinthians*, 63 – rhetorical ability: Robertson and Plummer, *First Epistle of St. Paul to the Corinthians*, 32; Moffatt, *The First Epistle of Paul to the Corinthians*, 22–23; Allo, *Première épître aux Corinthiens* , 25–6; Funk, "Word and Word in 1 Cor 2:6–16," 282; Schrage, *Der Erstebrief an die Korinther*, 224–35; Witherington, *Conflict and Community in Corinth*, 121–3; Wolff, *Der erste Brief des Paulus an die Korinther*, 49; Hays, *1 Corinthians*, 35; J. Kremer, *Der erste Brief an die Korinther* (Regensburg: F. Pustet, 1997), 52; Collins, *1 Corinthians*, 116–20; Horsley, *1 Corinthians*, 53; Thiselton, *The First Epistle to the Corinthians*, 208; Keener, *1–2 Corinthians*, 35; Fitzmyer, *1 Corinthians*, 169–73; Ciampa and Rosner, *First Letter to the Corinthians*, 112–19 – social status connected with rhetorical ability: Garland, *1 Corinthians*, 82; cf. Keener, *1–2 Corinthians*, 39.

could refer to either form or content,[11] or even to content alone.[12] Finally, almost all agree that 2:6–16 refers again to wisdom's content, whereas 2:13 alone could refer to either content or form.[13]

Thus, as far as our select phrases go, most – though by no means all – recent interpreters have regarded either "form" or "rhetoric" as the winning emphasis in the discourse. Interpreters, however, show less agreement regarding Paul's overall emphasis from one unit of thought to the next. In this regard, it is generally thought that Paul's movement shifts, after 1:17, from content (1:18–25), to form (2:1–5), and finally back to content (2:6–16).

Such disagreement notwithstanding, the four phrases noted – 1:17, 2:1; 2:4, and 2:13 – have enticed a slim majority of interpreters over the decades to identify form or rhetoric as Paul's leading concern in 1:17–2:5. Whether these phrases have been interpreted rightly – and more importantly, *with due emphasis* – is a matter for consideration in what follows.

At the outset, it should be said that the rhetorical thesis has in many ways deserved the following it has commanded. As we shall see, much about it is plausible, and advocates are to be commended both for their diligent attention to Greco-Roman urban culture and for their creativity in sorting out certain pieces of evidence afforded by the letter. Nonetheless, in those texts that have been invested with critical importance, our survey so far – and the considerable disagreement it has revealed among commentators – has indicated that Paul is anything but explicit in identifying the Corinthians' wisdom with "rhetoric." Moreover, even an emphasis on the "form" of σοφία in certain verses need not point to Greco-Roman rhetoric *in particular*, much less rhetoric as the main issue that contributed to the divisions. Without these verses at the foundation (1:17;

[11] Form and content: Conzelmann, *1 Corinthians*, 54; Lindemann, *Der erste Korintherbrief*, 56 – form and content, emphasis on form, either philosophical or rhetorical: Lightfoot, *Notes on Epistles of St. Paul*, 170; Senft, *La Premiere épître de Saint Paul aux Corinthiens*, 45–7; Lang, *Die Briefe an die Korinther*, 35–7 – rhetoric and philosophy: Allo, *Première épître aux Corinthiens*, 23; Hering, *The First Epistle of Saint Paul to the Corinthians*, 14 – rhetoric and philosophy, though primarily rhetoric: Witherington, *Conflict and Community in Corinth*, 121–3. Fee (*1 Corinthians*, 89–90) takes 2:1–2 in relation to content and 2:3–4 in relation to form, but the whole of 2:1–5 primarily in relation to form. Bullmore (*St. Paul's Theology of Rhetorical Style*, 209, 221) takes 2:2 to indicate form and 2:4 to indicate content, but he sees the main emphasis in 2:1–5 as being content.

[12] Grosheide, *First Epistle to the Corinthians*, 61.

[13] 2:6–16 in relation to wisdom's content: Moffatt, *The First Epistle of Paul to the Corinthians*, 25; Horsley, "Wisdom of Words and Words of Wisdom in Corinth," 224; Fee, *1 Corinthians*, 101; Litfin, *St. Paul's Theology of Proclamation*, 213; Krentz, "Logos or Sophia," 281. Still, Fee (*1 Corinthians*, 114), for instance, notes that v. 13 refers to both form and content.

2:1, 4, 13), we shall see that the evidence actually begins to mount up quite differently.

Demonstration of these observations is the task of the present chapter. In short, it is argued that the divisive wisdom of the Corinthians can be explained in terms of Greco-Roman rhetoric only with difficulty, only with selective attention to the full facts of the letter, and only by discounting the alternative explanation that is readily available in that other ancient champion of wisdom – philosophy. To this end, we turn next to an assessment of the current dominant argument, with especial attention to the landmark studies associated with Stephen Pogoloff, Duane Litfin, and Bruce Winter.

1 Corinthians 1–4 in recent scholarship

The first monograph to expound the new rhetorical thesis in detail was Stephen Pogoloff's *Logos and Sophia* (1992). Pogoloff cleared the way by noting that past scholarship had mistakenly understood ancient rhetoric as nothing more than "mere form." In correction, he noted that "the leading theorists of rhetoric treated their subject as concerned with far more than the ornaments of style. ... The unity of form and content they espoused was, in large measure, lived out in the wider rhetorical culture."[14] Thus, far from being blusterers of empty speech, rhetors in Paul's day were experts in both the techniques of formal adaption *and* the content of a wide variety of liberal arts subjects. In a word, a rhetor was "one who could speak well on any subject."

Pogoloff's recognition of the synthesis of form and content in rhetorical education should not, however, be taken as an indication that he sees substantial overlap between the wisdom of rhetoric and that of philosophy. Rather, Pogoloff contends that rhetoric and philosophy "conflicted and competed social and verbally .... *[N]ever* did philosopher become rhetor or vice-versa, for their approaches were radically different."[15] He continues: "Just as the philosophers did not become rhetors, the rhetors did not become philosophers."[16] And again, rhetoric and philosophy "remained distinct and competitive cultures."[17] For all these reasons, he says, "we must be especially cautious about any close linkage between rhetoric and philosophy in Paul's Corinth."[18] In sum, we "have no

[14] Pogoloff, *Logos and Sophia*, 48.
[15] *Ibid.*, 57; emphasis added.
[16] *Ibid.*, 58.
[17] *Ibid.*, 62.
[18] *Ibid.*, 64.

evidence that in Paul's Corinth one whose speech was considered wise would *necessarily* have been expected to speak philosophically."[19] Therefore, thinks Pogoloff, if rhetorical education included a heavy dose of "content," still that content was scarcely philosophical in nature, and we can conclude that, when Paul spoke of σοφία λόγου (1:17), he was referring to the wisdom of a cultured rhetor who could speak on *any* subject – just probably not philosophy.

It is within this context that Pogoloff understands the divisions in Corinth. The "wise" person was *not* the philosopher, but the rhetor, the person who spoke in such a way as reflected a typical upper-class education. The culpable Corinthians were among the nouveau riche, those struggling with status dissonance because they possessed money but lacked other status symbols. These Corinthians perceived Paul and Apollos as high-status rhetors and rallied around the leader of their choosing, hoping to boost their own status through association. To counter the Corinthians' claims, Paul attributed to himself the rhetoric of *weakness* (e.g., 1:25–27; 2:3; 4:10; 8:7–12; 9:22; 12:22). In sum, Pogoloff's reconstruction integrates earlier sociological treatments of 1 Corinthians with his new insights concerning the relevance of Greco-Roman rhetoric: what the Corinthians value, specifically, is the high status of the rhetor, and it is this, in turn, that Paul repudiates.

Duane Litfin provides a similar assessment of the situation in *St. Paul's Theology of Proclamation* (1994). Litfin begins with a lengthy summary of the rhetorical tradition, tracing its history from Athens in the fifth century BCE down to Rome in the first century AD. Throughout this period, he maintains, the essential concern of rhetorical theory remained the same: to explore how the orator might adapt his speech in such a way as to successfully persuade his audience. While they may have parted ways when it came to epistemology, the sophists, Plato, Aristotle, Isocrates, Cicero, and Quintilian were all alike in their understanding of rhetoric as *persuasion*. As Litfin puts it, "it was as if the orator worked with a grand equation in which everything was fixed except his own contribution. . . . Only the orator's own efforts were completely under his control."[20] Thus, whereas Pogoloff focuses on rhetorical wisdom in relation to *social status*, Litfin underscores Paul's opposition to rhetoric as *a means of persuasion*. Litfin takes 1:17–25 as Paul's "theology of proclamation," his declaration that faith comes not by the clever manipulation of human rhetoric, but by the power of the Spirit. This passage, then, is Paul's apology against those

[19] *Ibid.*, 65.
[20] Litfin, *St. Paul's Theology of Proclamation*, 133.

Corinthians who have faulted him for substandard display of rhetoric. Opposing Paul is Apollos, whose rhetorical abilities the Corinthians regard quite highly. Between these two men the church is divided, in accordance as each leader has been judged for his rhetorical aptitude.

Despite certain similarities, Litfin differs from Pogoloff in conceiving of the relationship between rhetoric and philosophy as one not of contrariety, but of synthesis. For Litfin, rhetoric always united form and content, eloquence (λόγος) and wisdom (σοφία) so that, to the public eye, the distinction between the rhetorician and the philosopher would have been difficult to discern. Even in the first century, when the Greek world sat at the cusp of the Second Sophistic and the scales of oratory tipped toward the side of empty form, the untrained masses would have been incapable of differentiating the two: "[T]o the vast majority of people in antiquity wisdom and eloquence together must have appeared to be what philosophy was about."[21]

The third major monograph to forward the rhetorical thesis was Bruce Winter's *Philo and Paul among the Sophists* (1997), now in its second edition (2002).[22] Winter builds on the old proposal of Johannes Munck[23] – for decades overshadowed by the Gnostic thesis – that in 1 Corinthians 1–4 Paul articulates an anti-sophistic modus operandi. But whereas Munck had relied almost exclusively on evidence from Philostratus (from the late second century AD), Winter has been able to locate several sources that point to a sophistic presence in Corinth nearer the time of Paul. Spanning the period between about AD 90 and the mid-second century, these sources include two speeches of Dio Chrysostom (AD 89–96), a diatribe of Epictetus (AD 92–93), the Corinthian oration of Favorinus (reign of Hadrian), Plutarch's *Questiones Conviviales* (AD 99–116), and an inscription commemorating Herodes Atticus (b. AD 101, d. AD 177). These sources, along with Paul's Corinthian correspondence (i.e., 1 Corinthians 1–4; 9; 2 Corinthians 10–13), are used to prove Winter's larger thesis that the Second Sophistic, traditionally thought to have emerged in the second century, was already in full swing in Corinth in the second half of the first century.

After presenting in detail the extrabiblical evidence for the sophistic movement in first- and second-century Corinth, Winter undertakes to

[21] *Ibid.*, 123.

[22] Though this was based on his earlier doctoral dissertation: "Philo and Paul among the Sophists: A Hellenistic Jewish and a Christian Response," PhD dissertation, Macquarie University (1988).

[23] J. Munck, "Menigheden uden Partier," *Dansk Teologisk Tidsskrift* 15 (1952): 215–33; ET, "The Church without Factions," *Paul and the Salvation of Mankind* (London: SCM, 1959), 135–67.

prove that this is the background against which the divisions in the Corinthian church are to be understood. As such, Winter surmises that the Corinthians have seen Christianity as a kind of wisdom, the church's leaders as sophists, and themselves as students (ζηλῶται/μαθήται) of these teachers and, therefore, as wise men. The Corinthians are "behav[ing] in secular fashion" by "measur[ing] their instructors by the same canon as do the secular Corinthians."[24] It is such secular attitudes – which are, specifically, sophistical in nature – that Paul repudiates in 1 Corinthians 1–4, 9 and 2 Corinthians 10–13.

Such are the views of Pogloff, Litfin, and Winter. As a kind of triple-braided cord, these three scholars have ably hoisted the mainsail of an interpretive vessel that has sailed the seas of Corinthians scholarship proudly and smoothly for the last twenty years. Based largely on their work, it is now taken for granted that the wisdom with which the Corinthians were enamored, and which Paul in turn eschewed, was primarily that of rhetoric. Select almost any recent article, monograph, or commentary in which the Corinthians' wisdom is addressed, and that is the basic perspective likely to be assumed, without further assessment.[25]

[24] Winter, *Philo and Paul among the Sophists*, 175.

[25] In addition to those studies named in notes 3–11 to this chapter, we may identify the following – C. Mihaila, *The Paul-Apollos Relationship and Paul's Stance toward Greco-Roman Rhetoric*, Library of New Testament Studies 402 (New York: T & T Clark, 2009), who names Pogoloff, Winter, and Litfin as the foundations of his study (pp. 2–3); Clarke (*Secular and Christian Leadership in Corinth*, 102–7), citing Litfin and Winter (i.e., Winter's 1988 dissertation); Hays ("Conversion of the Imagination," esp. 402), expressly relying on Pogoloff; S. Grindheim ("Wisdom for the Perfect: Paul's Challenge for the Corinthian Church [2:6–16]," *JBL* 121 [2002]: 689–709), drawing from Winter, Litfin, Pogoloff, and others; V. H. T. Nguyen (*Christian Identity in Corinth: A Comparative Study of 2 Corinthians, Epictetus, and Valerius Maximus* [Tübingen: Mohr Siebeck, 2008], 125–9), citing both Pogoloff and Winter; Collins (*1 Corinthians*, 85), citing Pogoloff; Garland (*1 Corinthians*, 56), following Litfin and Pogoloff; Ciampa and Rosner (*First Letter to the Corinthians*, 104–12), citing Winter; Finney, *Honour and Conflict in the Ancient World*, 80–1, citing Pogoloff. Witherington (*Conflict and Community at Corinth*, 74n9) says Pogoloff's understanding of the issue in 1 Corinthians "is essentially the same as mine" (cf. Pogoloff, *Logos and Sophia*, 237ff). Martin (*Corinthian Body*, 47–66) says that Paul rejects the rhetorical values attached to high social status. Oh-Young Kwon, "A Critical Review of Recent Scholarship on the Pauline Opposition and the Nature of its Wisdom (σοφια) in 1 Corinthians 1–4," *Currents in Biblical Research* 8 (2010): 386–427, says that the Corinthians' obsession with rhetoric is one aspect of their problematic, secular perspective. Bullmore (*St. Paul's Theology of Rhetorical Style*, 220–1, passim) says that rhetoric is a significant problem, but does not rule out philosophy. Winter's work has also insinuated itself into recent assessments of the Second Sophistic: e.g., I. Henderson, "The Second Sophistic and Non-Elite Speakers," in T. Schmidt and P. Fleury (eds.), *Perceptions of the Second Sophistic and Its Times – Regards sur la Seconde Sophistique et son époque* (University of Toronto Press, 2011), 29–31.

I may mention here one further permutation of the argument, set forth in an article by Edgar Krentz.[26] Krentz situates Paul's interplay between form and content within the context of the classical controversy between "words" and "things," as embodied in the debate between rhetoricians and philosophers. Stemming from Platonic thought, the two dimensions distinguish the unreal from the true – "words" or rhetoric reflect the former, "things" or philosophy the latter. In this connection, Krentz proposes that 1:17 and 2:4 present Paul's rejection of the Corinthians' love of "persuasive rhetoric," while 2:6–16 offers his own understanding of wisdom in terms of content. Thus, Paul opposes "words," or *form*, and prefers "things," or *content*, as if advocating a form of "philosophy" over rhetoric. As such, 1 Cor 2:6–16 focuses on the true *content* of wisdom and stands "antithetical to the wisdom that comes via good speaking or persuasive rhetoric alone," that is, wisdom via *form*.[27]

Each of these studies stands as a specimen of fine scholarship. They show a great deal of creativity in working with the internal evidence, and, unlike the Gnostic studies of the mid-twentieth century, have been especially sensitive to the sociological matrix of first-century Corinth, where the ability to speak well was, it seems, the coveted pursuit of every educated person, and the enjoyment of hearing it the fondest obsession of almost everyone else. In spite of it all, I hope to show that evidence for the rhetorical thesis is actually much weaker than has been imagined. Thus, true as it is that a triple-braided cord is not easily broken, we shall undertake it here to test the rule.

Assessment of recent scholarship

Rhetoric and philosophy in the first century[28]

In three of the four studies surveyed in the preceding section, a putative separation between rhetoric and philosophy plays a critical role. Pogoloff is explicit that rhetoric and philosophy "remained distinct and competitive cultures,"[29] and that we must therefore "be especially cautious about any close linkage between rhetoric and philosophy in Paul's

[26] E. Krentz, "Logos or Sophia," 277–90.

[27] *Ibid.*, 282. Keener (*1–2 Corinthians*, 9) follows the same formulation.

[28] With the permission of *Neotestamentica*, this section has incorporated modified material from T. Brookins, "Rhetoric and Philosophy in the First Century: Their Relation with Respect to 1 Corinthians 1–4," *NeoT* 44 (2010): 233–52. Where changes have been made, the present argument supersedes the earlier one.

[29] Pogoloff, *Logos and Sophia*, 62.

Corinth."[30] Hence, he says, although rhetors could speak well on any subject, we have no reason to believe that they necessarily spoke on philosophical issues.[31]

Even though Winter avoids making such overt claims, it becomes immediately evident that this dynamic is operative in his analysis as well. Indeed, in his discussion of sophism in Alexandria, he spends close to thirty pages sketching the split between rhetoric and philosophy, the withdrawal of the philosophers from the public sphere, and the dominance of the rhetoricians.[32] Moreover, it seems to be on these grounds that he omits any discussion of philosophical wisdom and the possibility that this could explain the language of "wisdom," the "wise man," and the values associated with him in 1 Corinthians (e.g., "powerful" and "well-born" in 1:26, "rich" and "kings" in 4:8). Indeed, it is striking that Winter writes not so much as a word to rule out philosophy as an explanation. We may perhaps presume that he means for the first-century dominance of rhetoric, and its (ostensibly) complete separation from philosophy, to be explanation enough.

Krentz's essay has shown a similar dynamic. For Krentz, Paul's apparent shifting between discussion of wisdom's form in 1:17–2:5 and its content in 2:6–16 is resolved in the thesis that Paul opposes the former in favor of the latter, in the manner of the philosopher taking the side of true content over the rhetorician's mere form. In that regard, the historic philosophy-rhetoric dispute again supplies the framework for sorting out the data.

Although Litfin avoids separating rhetoric and philosophy, his understanding of their relationship nonetheless leaves rhetoric entirely dominant. He fills some one hundred pages making the point that there had been a tradition of synthesis between the two, only to reveal at last that, in first-century rhetoric, "the scales tipped to form over content."[33] At that time, he maintains, the role of the rhetorician became that of the mere persuader, whose chief aim was not truth, but the fulfillment of audience expectations for delight. What Litfin's formulation really amounts to, then, is the absorption of philosophy into rhetoric – to the point of philosophy's essential annihilation. Thus Litfin's proposed "synthesis" between rhetoric and philosophy seems practically equivalent to what others have meant by rhetoric: call "wisdom" a matter of mere form, or

[30] *Ibid.*, 64.
[31] *Ibid.*, 65.
[32] Winter, *Philo and Paul among the Sophists*, 16–25, 44–58.
[33] Litfin, *St. Paul's Theology of Proclamation*, 89, 114, 119.

call it the well-expressed knowledge of the liberally educated speaker, but it does not really fit what the ancients would have thought of as philosophical truth or "content."

It seems to me that the issue here is not simply which direction the internal evidence of the letter has naturally taken interpreters – toward rhetoric or toward philosophy – nor simply a matter of how the social milieu has helped illuminate the text. In all of this it is evident that conceived *relationship* between rhetoric and philosophy in the first century – or the external evidence, formulated in terms of a rigid *model* – has been *laid over* the internal evidence of 1 Corinthians, in some formulations determining, almost a priori, in which direction the evidence can be taken. But either formulation – whether the absolute separation model followed by Pogoloff or the "synthesis" model of Litfin – relies on a theoretical construct that hardly holds true in first-century reality. Hence, in an embodied historical situation such as that behind 1 Corinthians, such rigid hermeneutical frameworks will be of very limited value. What is needed is a more nuanced understanding of the relationship between rhetoric and philosophy, one that pays attention to the theoretical strictures provided by the sources, but that is flexible enough to account for actual first-century phenomena.

Thus, even though the rhetoric-philosophy relationship has already been sketched in detail elsewhere – and most fully by Litfin himself – it will profit us to canvass it again here. In the section that follows, we trace this relationship at both the theoretical and practical levels, focusing on, but not limiting attention to, the first century AD. Even our brief survey should be sufficient to show that the categories of rhetoric-rhetorician-sophist and philosophy-philosopher are relatively flexible labels, understood in different ways by different ancient authors – and sometimes in different ways even within the same author's oeuvre – though on the whole resisting conflation with each other.

Separation?

Although the controversy itself was much older, our first sources to recount the ancient debate in detail come from the hand of Plato. Two of his dialogues are of note.

In the *Gorgias*, Socrates dialogues with the eponymous figure, the renowned Sicilian sophist who for years dazzled Athens with his brilliant speeches. Here Socrates tells us that rhetoric must aim at a higher end than mere persuasion: it must aim at knowledge of virtue. Moreover, only the good and noble orator could benefit the public with his oratory – for example, by exonerating the good or punishing the wicked. Thus the telos of rhetoric was knowledge of the true and good, and not, as the sophist would have it, mere persuasion.

In the *Phaedrus*, Plato presents a theory of rhetoric as it would have to be in order to be considered a true "art" (τέχνη). As Plato informs us, Socrates and the sophists agree that rhetoric aims at persuasiveness, but they disagree as to whether it requires actual knowledge (ἐπιστήμη). The sophists maintain that to prevail on one's audience, one needed only the appearance of probability, not real knowledge of the truth. Socrates remonstrates that only the man who knows the truth can know what will seem probable. Truth, therefore, must be the end of rhetoric.

Thus ran the dispute between rhetoricians and philosophers according to Plato. From his perspective, the one aimed at empty "words," the other at actual "things" (e.g., *Resp.* 2.362A), the one at "seeming," the other at "being" or "doing" (e.g., *Resp.* 521D, 527B, 601B).

From Plato throughout antiquity, the conflict persisted.[34] By the Roman era, Plato's dichotomies continued, and philosophers and rhetoricians remained as far from rapprochement as ever. From the side of the philosophers, Plato's basic views continued to be promoted. The Stoic Seneca (AD 1–65), for instance, maintained that audiences should be "roused to the content (*rem*), and not to the words (*verba*)" of a discourse (*Ep.* 52.14 [Gummere, LCL]; cf. 45.5–6; 52.14; 75.7). Like Plato, he contrasts "saying" and "doing" (*dicere* and *facere*; *Ep.* 20.2; 108.39), "speaking" and "living" (*loqui* and *vivere*; *Ep.* 88.42), "seeing" and "hearing" (*videre* and *audire*; *Ep.* 75.4). Rhetoric, he believed, was concerned with mere words – words full of tricks and craftiness – and aimed only at popular approval (*Ep.* 20.2; 45.8; 48.5; 75.4; 108.12). Philosophy, on the other hand, with its concern for real content, aimed to transform lives (*Ep.* 108.35–37; 95.13; 88.4).

Others agreed. Whereas philosophers sought to foster love of virtuous living, rhetoricians were wont to entrap their listeners with clever and deceitful words (Dio, *Or.* 12.13; 33.14) and maintained no regard for the truth (Dio, *Or.* 22.4–5). The rhetorician was concerned with words, but the philosopher with deeds (Musonius Rufus, *Diatr.* 5.26–37; 6.7–10), and especially that one's words and deeds should be in agreement (Dio, *Or.* 18.17; Philo, *Jos.* 230; *Mos.* 1.29, 283; 2.48, 66, 130, 140, 150).

But recriminations were made from the other side – rhetoricians against philosophers. In Cicero we hear that by the time of the late Roman

[34] For a basic summary, see S. Ijsseling, *Rhetoric and Philosophy in Conflict: An Historical Survey* (The Hague: M. Nijhoff, 1976), 1–40.

Republic, "philosophers looked down on eloquence (*eloquentiam*) and the orators on wisdom (*sapientiam*), and never touched anything from the side of the other study except what this group borrowed from that one, or that one from this" (*De or.* 3.72 [Rackham, LCL]). Philosophers, moreover, had acquired a reputation for uselessness; they had immured themselves in their studies to pursue interests far removed from the concerns of the state (Cicero, *De or.* 3.5–58; Quintilian, *Inst.* 12.2.6; Dio, 34.52). Not only were philosophers useless; they themselves failed to meet the standards they exacted of others. Quintilian lamented, "Very great vices have been concealed under this name [philosopher] in many persons," for they neglect "by virtue or learning to be regarded as philosophers; instead, they put on a gloomy face and an eccentric form of dress as a cover for their immorality" (*Inst.* 1.pr.14–15).[35] Accordingly, he said, "[P]hilosophy can be counterfeited," but "eloquence cannot" (*Inst.* 12.3.12). The philosophers, moreover, had become "disdainful of the precepts of rhetoric" and attempted to establish their own authority against that of the rhetoricians (*Inst.* 12.3.12). Where philosophers were of practical value, they were often considered nothing more than moral pedants (Horace, *Sat.* 1.14.103–29; Quintilian, *Inst.* 11.1.33). The gravamen of the charges was that the philosophers were of little profit to the state, whereas the eloquence of the rhetorician served it well.

Far from being isolated comments, these remarks from the Roman period reflect a cross-section of what seems to have been a persistent conflict between philosophers and rhetoricians, which in Quintilian's day had reached a fever pitch. Perhaps, as Quintilian notes, rhetoricians and philosophers had *at one time* been taken to be the same (1.pr.13, 17–19; 2.15.34; cf. 2.21.13), but among Roman orators, that old, philosophical rhetoric was "very rare" (*paucissimos*, 10.1.123). In his own day, "rhetoric" and "philosophy" stood quite apart, each with its own practitioners – as we shall see, the "eloquent" and "wise men," respectively – and each with its own proper material (*propria*; 12.2.5; cf. 10.1.36). This, he notes, was the first-century reality, whether it was in keeping with his wishes or not (see discussion later in the book).

The theoretical separation between rhetoric and philosophy is also apparent in alleged "conversions" to philosophy, which we hear of during this era. These sometimes implied a clean break from the pursuits of sophism. A well-known case was Dio Chrysostom, who allegedly converted from sophism to philosophy during his years in exile under Domitian. Even in the second century, when rhetoric and philosophy

[35] All translations of Quintilian are from Russell, LCL.

had become less distinguishable, Lucian of Samosata claimed to have undergone a similar conversion (*Bis acc.* 32).[36]

It is apparent, then, that the opposition between rhetoric and philosophy seen in Plato persisted in some form through the end of the first century. This is evident from the polemical language waged from both sides of the dispute, as well as from attestations of conversion from one realm of study to the other. Nonetheless, we should question how far the separation could be pressed, even in theory. Blinded amid the fury of the ancient fracas, it is easy for us to lose sight of the fact that there was, in reality, no united view as to how the two ought to relate: there were also dissenting perspectives. Cicero's dialogue *De Oratore* shows this to have been the case in his day (mid-first century BC), and arguably in the generation before him, where the dialogue is historically situated. In that work, Crassus presents the ideal, and Cicero's position – that rhetoric and philosophy be wedded. Anthony presents the counterargument – that the orator need not study philosophy. Both claim to present positions that find support in their day. The very existence of this dialogue signifies that rhetoricians, at any rate, had reached no full agreement as to the value of philosophy.

Union?

As just suggested, Plato's jaundiced perspective was not the only one that found acceptance. Indeed, amid the tumult of rhetoric and philosophy's intense rivalry stood a stout tradition of concord. Plato's coeval Isocrates had insisted on the synthesis of wisdom and eloquence (*Antid.* 89; 170–214). And within the tradition of Isocrates fell the later rhetoricians Cicero and Quintilian. Cicero noted that, from the time of Socrates, there had occurred a "reprehensible severance between the tongue and the brain" – or between eloquence and wisdom (*De or.* 3.49). In Cicero's view, "wisdom without eloquence (*sapientiam sine eloquentia*) does too little for the good of states, but . . . eloquence without wisdom (*eloquentiam sine sapientia*) is generally highly disadvantageous and is never helpful" (*Inv.* 1.1; cf. 1.2; 1.5; 2.178 [Hubbell, LCL]). Quintilian expressed a similar sentiment, calling oratory "the best gift of the gods to man"

[36] Others had similar experiences of conversion to philosophy. C. Cassius Longinus converted to Epicureanism in the first century BC (Cicero, *Fam.* 15.16.3; 17.3); the Epicurean system was usually considered to be hostile to what was called "display" rhetoric (see C. Chandler, *Philodemus on Rhetoric: Translation and Exegetical Essays* [Routledge, 2006]). For further examples of such "conversions," see H. Marrou, *A History of Education in Antiquity* (New York: The New American Library, 1956), 206.

(*Inst.* 12.11.30), since, *in combination with "Reason,"* one may use it to "defend friends, guide the senate, and lead a people or an army" (12.16.14–15). He lamented that the moral concerns of philosophy should never have been wrenched from the orators. Rather, oratory ought always to have been concerned with both eloquence *and* wisdom, and in fact, with all the parts of philosophy – rational, natural, and moral. Indeed, to be a good orator one needed also to be a good man (*Inst.* 1.pr.9–20; 12.2.1–23). In short, Cicero, Quintilian, and others[37] affirmed that wisdom and eloquence – or, as it were, philosophy and rhetoric – often did not, but nonetheless *ought* to, go together.

If in theory rhetoricians did not reject philosophy outright, neither did philosophers entirely reject rhetoric. Epictetus said explicitly that he did not disparage the study of rhetoric (*Diatr.* 2.23.46–7), and called it the gift of God and a benefit to others (2.23; 2.24.1–3). Seneca spoke to the same effect: "Even philosophy does not renounce the company of cleverness. . . . If . . . you can attain eloquence (*eloquentia*) without painstaking, and if you either are naturally gifted or can gain eloquence at slight cost, make the most of it and apply it to the noblest uses" (*Ep.* 75.3–5; cf. 79.9–10).

This fusion of rhetoric and philosophy in theory is noteworthy. Perhaps more significant, however, was how things worked out in practice. Indeed, we find both rhetoricians interloping onto the territory claimed for the philosophers, and philosophers encroaching on the ground claimed for the rhetoricians. In Philo we find those labeled "sophists" engaging in "philosophical" activity, such as discussing the "facts of nature" (*Her.* 246–7), naming the elements (*Contempl.* 4), and delivering "philosophical discourses" (*Det.* 74). Conversely, Epictetus chastises philosophers for sharing in all the vices of the orators: overvaluing eloquence, and coveting praise, money, and large crowds (*Diatr.* 3.23, especially §10, 19, 24). The younger Seneca finds similar fault with student-philosophers of his day, charging that a great number of them have "sat for many years at the feet of a philosopher and yet have not acquired the slightest tinge of wisdom," concerned as they were only with enjoying and parroting their teachers' rhetoric , rather than with receiving any moral profit (*Ep.* 108.5–6). He goes on to say that such pupils of philosophy "come to their teachers to develop, not their souls, but their

[37] Theon's *progymnasmata* also follows in the tradition of Cicero and Quintilian, as seen in his discussion of theses (*Prog.* 120). Further references to the role of philosophy in rhetorical education include: Cicero, *De or.* 3.65–66; *Fin.* 3.3; 4.4; *Rhet. Her.* 1.1.1; Quintilian, *Inst.* 1.pr.13–15; 2.15.24–31; 4.44.57; 12.2.29; 12.10.52.

wits" (108.23). Instead, he would have them become "practical" philosophers, and not "just to entertain [their] listeners with a *clever display of language*" (*Ep.* 104.22; emphasis added).[38] Elsewhere he expresses dissatisfaction regarding "how much superfluous and unpractical matter the philosophers contain," who "*know more about careful speaking* than about careful living" (*Ep.* 88.42–43; emphasis added).

It therefore seems that many philosophers had picked up some of the rhetoricians' ostensibly disreputable habits. At any rate, their avowal of rhetoric, in practice, was inescapable.[39] Even Plato, who so derided the art of the sophists, is said to have displayed great eloquence in the very process of refuting them (Cicero, *De or.* 1.47; cf. 1.137–145; 2.75–76; 3.59–61; 3.70–73), a charge to which Seneca was no less liable (e.g., Suetonius, *Cal.* 53.2).

Thus many who were called philosophers were deemed guilty of the worst alleged vices of the rhetorician. Consequently it became incumbent to distinguish between the "real" philosopher from his mere counterfeit. In that regard, just as we find Plato speaking of the "spurious" versus the "true" philosopher (*Resp.* 485D), so we find later philosophers denying the label to those they considered unworthy of it. Musonius Rufus advised students to consort "with men who were philosophers not in name only but in truth (οὐκ ὀνόματι μόνον ἀλλ' ἀληθῶς φιλοσόφοις)" (*Diatr.* 17.14–16 [Lutz]). Dio Chrysostom on one occasion said that the "philosophers" with whom his audience had grievance were not *really* philosophers, for "no one is a philosopher who belongs among the unjust and wicked" (*Or.* 31.3; cf. 34.3). In several places he refers to this class of people as "those who are called philosophers (τῶν καλοῦμενων φιλοσόφων)" (*Or.* 13.11; 31.8; 34.3; cf. 31.8–12, esp. 10). He notes that unfitting habits had led to a certain ambiguity of identity: "The disease is already affecting, not only public speakers, but some philosophers as well – though it would be more correct to say that public speakers are no longer easy to recognize" (*Or.* 32.68 [Cohoon, LCL]). Epictetus, like Dio, simply narrowed the qualifications: to be a "genuine philosopher" (οἱ γνησίως φιλοσοφοῦντες), one should live like Socrates, Diogenes, or Cleanthes (*Diatr.* 3.26.23).

Despite these protestations, there must have been a vast difference between the "ideal" philosopher and the reality. Indeed, the circle of

[38] Quoted from R. Campbell, *Seneca: Letters from a Stoic* (London: Penguin Books, 2004), 190.

[39] On the use of rhetoric in philosophical prose of the Hellenistic period: D. Schenkeveld, "Philosophical Prose," in Stanley E. Porter (ed.), *Handbook of Classical Rhetoric* (Leiden: Brill, 2001), 195–264.

"true philosophers" could have been tightened until the only individuals that fit within it were the purest specimens – a Socrates or a Diogenes – but this obviously would have done no justice to the way the designation was being applied.

Clearly, classifying the rhetorician and philosopher could be thorny business. G. R. Stanton observes, "Educated Greeks with literary and philosophical interests who lived and traveled in the eastern provinces of the Roman Empire have proved difficult to classify, particularly in terms of the contrast between sophists and philosophers."[40] Stanton considers, for example, Plutarch, Dio Chrysostom, and Aelius Aristides, who have been placed in either camp, in ancient and modern literature alike. How, then, does one decide what is the appropriate designation for the would-be "rhetorician" or "philosopher"? In Stanton's assessment of Plutarch, Dio, Aristides, and Marcus Aurelius, he finds that there was a tendency "to want to be regarded as philosophers and not as sophists."[41] That is, in their own minds, philosopher and sophist were of two different species, not one. Here it should be added, however, that each of these authors was active several decades after the time of the Corinthian correspondence, and squarely within the period we know as the Second Sophistic, by which time the boundaries between rhetorician and philosopher had indeed worn thin.[42] In this regard, while I cannot accept Pogoloff's full conclusion on this point, I must agree with his basic contention that the more ambiguous philosopher-rhetorician dynamic that characterized the Second Sophistic cannot be appropriately retrojected into Paul's day. For, as he observes:[43]

1. One finds only a few examples of "philosophical sophists" between the fourth century BC and the late second century AD.

[40] G. R. Stanton, "Sophists and Philosophers: Problems of Classification," *AJP* 94 (1973): 350.

[41] Stanton, "Sophists and Philosophers," 364.

[42] Nowhere is this thinning more evident than in Lucian. His satires are replete with ostentatious and morally bankrupt philosophers; see esp. *Icar.* 29; 30; *Par.* 31–7; 43; 56; *Men.* 4–5; *Fug.* 13; 16–20; *Eunuch.* 7; as well as the works *Philosophies for Sale*; *The Dead Come to Life, or The Fisherman*; *The Lover of Lies*; and *Nigrinus*. Frequently philosophers are even called "sophists"; e.g., *Iupp. conf.* 19, 27, 30, 32; *Par.* 43; *Fug.* 10–11; *Eunuch.* 13. Even if meant only in a pejorative sense, the association with sophism illustrates the heightened similarity. On the pejorative use of σοφίστης, see P. Chantraine, *Dictionnaire étymologique de la langue grecque: Histoire des mots* (Klincksieck, 2000), 1031. On the relationship between rhetoric and philosophy in the Second Sophistic, see also Marrou, *A History of Education in Antiquity*, 206–12.

[43] Summarized from Pogoloff, *Logos and Sophia*, 66.

2. The Second Sophistic, in full bloom, postdated Paul's Corinth by a century.[44]
3. The philosopher and the sophist, though often overlapping in character, were distinguishable even in the Second Sophistic.

We can summarize our discussion so far by saying that not only did many rhetoricians in Paul's day recognize the necessity of philosophy, but all of the major philosophical schools, in general, conceded to the value and usefulness of rhetoric, even if their polemical contexts sometimes compelled them to denigrate it. In that regard, our sources present a certain tension on the subject. On the one hand, rhetoricians and philosophers tended to disassociate from the other, each claiming that their own realm of study was preeminent and that the others' was degenerate. Yet, on the other hand, we have seen that the separation was far from absolute. Neither could easily deny the value of the other. This point they grudged in theory, and proved in practice.

All of this reveals that the ancient typology carried a certain range of flexibility. The categories, which were not entirely empty but which perhaps lacked hard-and-fast lines of distinction, were "rhetoric-rhetorician-sophist" and "philosophy-philosopher" – a critical question to answer will be where "wisdom" and the "wise man" fits in. Tension between those in these opposing spheres ran high enough to belie any claim that there was no real difference between them. Even where the distinction was blurred in the hurly-burly of everyday life, as we shall see shortly, a categorical distinction seems to have been maintained at the theoretical or *semantic* level. On the other hand, enough ambiguous characters apparently occupied the streets and lecture halls of antiquity to cast doubt on the notion that the philosopher *never* played the "rhetor," or the rhetor the "philosopher." We therefore ought to employ the given distinctions – rhetoric versus philosophy and rhetorician versus philosopher – but with the realization that they are artificial, theoretical constructs reinforced in a polemical situation by the most stalwart proponents within each sphere. In this way we should grant each one the designation he professes, mindful that, in practice, a professing rhetorician may at times have played the philosopher, and a philosopher the rhetorician.

[44] In relation to this point, see discussion of Winter's (*Philo and Paul among the Sophists*) counter thesis later in the chapter.

A clarification on "form" versus "content"

The dichotomy between rhetoric and philosophy, form and content, seen in the ancient sources may appear somewhat problematic. Indeed, from a modern linguistic perspective, a divorce between form and content is entirely unsustainable: for *there is nowhere that "rhetoric" is not.* We must realize, however, that the semantic range of the English term "rhetoric" does not map precisely onto that of its ancient equivalents (*oratoria*, *rhetorica*, ῥητορική). It would be a mistake, for instance, to import our modern notion of "New Rhetoric," where "rhetoric" is conceived in terms of the patterns of speech universally exhibited in persuasion, self-consciously or not – rather than, as most ancients apparently understood it, as the studied speech of the professional orator – into the ancient debate as just outlined. While some ancient thinkers may have conceived of the term in this way (Aristotle would be the nearest example), we have seen that among many thinkers, both philosophers and rhetoricians, the term was conceived in a much more limiting sense. "Rhetoric" was a certain *kind* of speaking, which was, ostensibly, not always operative in speech, and was in that sense distinct from certain other types of discourse. Quintilian's work exemplifies this framework quite clearly: he maintained explicitly that not everyone who speaks is an orator (2.17.11); that rhetoric is an "art" which must be *learned* (2.17.2); that some speech, far from reflecting this art, can be considered a "non-art" (*atechnica*, 2.20.2); and that what is called "dialectic" constitutes a different kind of argumentation, distinct from the art of "rhetoric" (2.20.7; see also LS 31). In a word, said Quintilian, there was that which was "*truly* rhetoric (*vere rhetorice*)" (2.20.5), and then there was everything else. For present purposes, it is this conception of rhetoric that counts, not some modern philosophical notion of the ontological "unity of form and content" or the theoretical "pervasiveness of rhetoric" in human speech.

Artificial as this distinction might seem, then, it will have to be born in mind in our examination of 1 Corinthians, for as widely as it was insisted upon in the ancient sources, it is a distinction that Paul, as part of that milieu, is only too likely to have shared. Moreover, it is a distinction that has also been insisted on in some important secondary literature (though perhaps to a more exaggerated degree than the ancient sources warrant): "wisdom," it is claimed, semantically designates rhetoric-not-philosophy. What we shall find is that the ancients *did* in fact have specialized, and in many respects conceptually exclusive, terminology to designate the spheres of "rhetoric" and "philosophy." Evidence for the usage of that terminology, however, flies quite directly into the face of the conclusions of recent secondary literature.

Rhetoric and philosophy in recent scholarship

Having surveyed the ancient debate between rhetoric and philosophy, let us now return to Pogoloff. To begin, it has become apparent that Pologoff's assumption that "philosophers did not become rhetors" and vice versa, and his argument on these grounds that rhetors were not speaking on philosophical topics, actually comes short of the mark. Worse, however, are the implications his perspective has had for exegesis of 1 Corinthians. His assumed wedge between rhetoric and philosophy has made it so that rhetoric, which perhaps plausibly explains select elements in Paul's discourse, has been enlarged to form a total explanation in which rhetoric does not actually do justice to the evidence. We return to this point later in the chapter, and more fully in Chapter 5. For now, it is enough to note that any approach that appeals to a theoretical rhetoric-philosophy divorce as grounds for removing philosophical wisdom from consideration, as Pogoloff has explicitly done, already starts us off on the wrong foot.

To a lesser extent, this criticism applies to Winter as well. It has been observed that, although Winter avoids *explicitly* ruling out philosophy on the basis of its (from one point of view) estrangement from rhetoric, he does give us reason to believe that the split-dynamic has played an important role in directing him to his conclusions. For not only does he fill nearly thirty pages discussing the split, but, thereafter, the possibility that some sort of philosophical wisdom could constitute the focus of Paul's attention in 1 Corinthians 1-4 is not so much as mentioned. Are we not to believe that he considers the separation of rhetoric and philosophy, and the hegemony of the former in the broader culture, to be reason enough for the omission?

To Litfin, we may put the question whether the available evidence really supports his claim that "the vast majority of people" could not distinguish a philosopher from a rhetorician. If cultivation of rhetorical skill was indeed the beginning and end of the entire school curriculum (as in many ways it was), then surely parents knew the difference between sending their children to philosophers and sending them to rhetoricians or sophists. Add to this that we are not talking about the "vast majority of people" but about a real historical situation dealing with a very specific, and by Litfin's own admission, status-conscious group of people in the Corinthian church, who were apparently exceptionally interested in this sort of wisdom.[45] Would these not have known the difference? Most importantly, we are missing the whole nub of the first-century debate over σοφία if we think that wisdom was a thing so amicably shared: as we shall see, it was scarcely considered common property.

Finally, it should be said regarding Krentz's theory – that Paul presents the gospel's wisdom of content over against the Corinthians' wisdom of form, as if preferring philosophy over rhetoric – that we are missing any of the dichotomies that would ordinarily have attended this debate. Paul conjures up no antitheses between "words" and "things," "speaking" and "doing," or "seeming" and "being." Nor does he associate the Corinthians' wisdom with "empty" words, "clever tricks," or the courting of applause. Not that this in itself renders Krentz's thesis invalid. But it does immensely decrease its likelihood, especially given that, as our survey of the commentaries has shown, it is already less than clear that σοφία λόγου must refer to rhetoric.[46] Moreover, it may be just as likely that Paul is pitting *his own type of content* – the wisdom of the cross – against *other content*. We can only conclude that the form-versus-content framework that Krentz employs is more imposed on the text from without, than it is drawn from within.

Needless to say, none of what has been said so far renders the rhetorical thesis impossible. But I hope to have shown that the extraneous rhetoric-versus-philosophy *dynamic* constructed by these scholars has been used *misleadingly* as a sort of grid through which to push the material found in 1 Corinthians 1–4. In many cases, and most unequivocally in Pogoloff, wisdom has been conceived as an either-or deal, so that once certain features in the text seem to be identified in relation to rhetoric, the counter-wisdom of philosophy must be sidelined from consideration (a far cry from the philosophical-rhetorical thesis we see subscribed to early in the twentieth century). Of course, a matter for later consideration will be whether "wisdom" in the first century is really as appropriately identified with rhetoric as it is with philosophy – that is, wisdom may in fact have been considered exclusive to one group as far as the contemporary discussion was concerned. For now, I should simply like to emphasize that the imposition, *ab extra*, of a theoretical "separation" *model* to discount philosophy is in itself a less than satisfactory use of the external

[45] True, Litfin (*St. Paul's Theology of Proclamation*, 166) notes that "the average member" of the congregation could not claim to have been a "finished" orator, but he also notes that some may have been such, and that there were others "on the fringe" of circles of status, influence, and sophistication in Corinth.

[46] Despite Krentz's assertion ("Logos or Sophia," 280) that 1:17 constitutes an "explicit" rejection of wisdom conveyed by rhetoric.

evidence. But our main concern is over how such an external scheme may have skewed our examination of the text itself. It is to these matters that we now turn.

Λόγος and σοφία

As an internal foundation for the rhetorical thesis, advocates have adverted attention to the four disputed phrases mentioned earlier: (1) 1:17 – οὐκ ἐν σοφίᾳ λόγου – "not with eloquent wisdom" (NRSV); (2) 2:1 – οὐ καθ' ὑπεροχὴν λόγου ἢ σοφίας – "not with lofty words or wisdom" (NRSV); (3) 2:4 – οὐκ ἐν πειθοὶ[ς] σοφίας [λόγοις] – "not with plausible words of wisdom" (NRSV); and, to a lesser extent, (4) 2:13 – οὐκ ἐν διδακτοῖς ἀνθρωπίνης σοφίας λόγοις – "words not taught by human wisdom" (NRSV). Explanations for the syntax are many, depending partly on which substantive is taken to be the governing term. In 1:17, for instance, λόγου may be regarded as an *attributed* genitive if λόγου serves as the governing noun (i.e., "wise words), but *attributive* if governance belongs to σοφίᾳ (i.e., "the wisdom characterized by rational argumentation," or, "*logical* wisdom").[47] Nonetheless, many have concluded that the appearance of λόγος with σοφία must point specifically to the art of rhetoric as *distinct* from philosophy, allegedly as in the ancient debate. Hence, Winter takes liberty in rendering οὐκ ἐν πειθοὶς σοφίας λόγοις (2:4) "persuasive rhetoric."[48] Wolff translates the same expression "Weisheitsrhetoric."[49] Pogoloff is able to say of 1:17, 2:1, 4 that "*any Hellenistic reader* would have taken [Paul's] disclaimers to refer to rhetorical practice,"[50] and of 2:13 that the rhetorical meaning is "unmistakeable."[51] Mihaila is equally confident, concluding that "the evidence adduced by Litfin and Winter is *overwhelmingly* in favor of understanding σοφία when used in juxtaposition with λόγος as rhetoric (i.e., cleverness in speaking), not the least because when the two are used together they appear in the context of preaching (cf. 1 Cor. 1.17;

[47] A similar problem presents itself in 2:4. If λόγοις governs, σοφίας is mostly likely *attributive* ("with *wise* words"); if σοφίας itself governs, it could be *attributed* (i.e., "persuasive *wisdom*"), or else a genitive of content ("words *full of wisdom*") or source ("words *which arise out of wisdom*"). Daniel Wallace's categories (*Greek Grammar Beyond the Basics: An Exegetical Syntax of the NT* [Grand Rapids: Zondervan, 1996]) simply will not settle the issue.

[48] B. Winter, "Rhetoric," in G. F. Hawthorne and R. P. Martin (eds.), *The Dictionary of Paul and His Letters* (Downers Grove: IvP, 1993), 821.

[49] Wolff, *Die erste Brief des Paulus an die Korinther*, 49.

[50] *Logos and Sophia*, 7; emphasis added.

[51] *Logos and Sophia*, 140.

2.1, 4, 13)."[52] Kwon follows on the heels Pogoloff, claiming that the reference of 1:10–4:21 to Greco-Roman rhetoric is "is *clearly evident* in Paul's frequent use of rhetorical terminology such as σοφία and its equivalents (which appear 26 times in chs. 1–4) and λόγος (nine times)."[53]

Unfortunately, an excess of confidence does not provide sufficient compensation for slapdash treatment of the evidence. Indeed, either the rhetorical interpretation of these texts is truly "unmistakeable" and so "clearly evident" that no examination of counter-explanations is necessary – a conclusion that our survey of the commentary literature renders unwarranted – or we should expect some painstaking lexicographical analysis and extensive demonstration that the rhetorical meaning is in fact superior among the options. Kwon's statement seems to convey that the mere *appearance* of σοφία and λόγος ends the discussion. Pogoloff is more conscientious, though hardly more accurate. He speaks repeatedly of the "ordinary" or "common" usages of σοφία and λόγος.[54] Putting the two together, he then concludes that the "most common and least specialized or esoteric meaning" is "sophisticated speech."[55] Upon closer examination, however, on neither count is the meaning Pogoloff is actually demanding the "ordinary" one. Let us trace his argument.

First, he solicits LSJ on σοφία, interweaving its entries with his own comments:

> The original meaning of σοφία, '*cleverness* or *skill* in handicraft and art,' continued throughout antiquity. It could also mean '*skill* in matters of common life, *sound judgement, intelligence, practical wisdom*, etc. ... *cunning shrewdness,* ... *learning.*' Less frequently, it meant *'speculative wisdom,'* including knowledge of divine matters, or 'natural philosophy.'[56]

Presumably on the basis of the given entries, he then concludes that the ordinary usage of σοφία "suggested nothing of philosophical or religious speculation," but was rather "a matter of learning applied to *practical* accomplishment."[57] To undergird this claim, he selects a portion of

[52] *The Paul-Apollos Relationship*, 92; emphasis added.

[53] Kwon, "A Critical Review of Recent Scholarship on the Pauline Opposition and the Nature of its Wisdom (σοφια) in 1 Corinthians 1–4," 420; emphasis added. Cf. Krentz, "Logos or Sophia," 280, where he calls 1:17 an "explicit" rejection of wisdom conveyed by rhetoric.

[54] Pogoloff, *Logos and Sophia*, 109, 112 (twice). Cf. also his claim that συζήτητης (1:20) refers "most naturally" to the rhetorician (160).

[55] *Ibid.*, 109.

[56] *Ibid.*, 109.

[57] *Ibid.*, 109.

TDNT's entry on σοφία referring to the "seven competent wise men" of the Classical period and their activities as statesmen, judges, and legislators. Significantly, however, Pogoloff inserts a footnote here faulting the author of the entry for going on to affirm that the term came, later in antiquity, to refer "only to philosophical ideas and qualities" (Pogoloff's paraphrase). But there is in fact a great deal of truth in the point he denies. Whether or not the term "less frequently" denoted *speculative* wisdom, a broader philosophical meaning had become far and away the dominant one by Paul's day. In the first place, the "seven wise men" whom Pogoloff brings to bear themselves came to be understood in philosophical terms. By the time the canon of seven was forming in the fourth century BC, already they are referred to as "philosophers" (φιλοσοφεῖν; Plato, *Prot.* 343a). More importantly, however, Pogoloff provides no lexicographical, and particularly *diachronic*, evidence to show, against *TDNT*, that σοφία is best – or as he would have it, more "commonly" – understood in terms of rhetoric. In fact, R. Dean Anderson observes that Pogoloff "really only cites one concrete use of this word [σοφία] in a definite rhetorical context, namely, Isoc. 15.199–200."[58] More could be found, no doubt. But even if they were provided (and they are not), mere examples of rhetorical "σοφία," found at some point across antiquity, hardly demonstrate that the rhetorical meaning was the "common" or "ordinary" meaning in the *first century*.

Actually, it is when we begin to undertake a lexicographical analysis of this terminology that the rhetorical interpretation begins to topple. Σοφία could indeed mean "cleverness," "skill," or "practical wisdom," as cited in the first two entries of LSJ. Viewing the term diachronically, however, we notice that, beginning from the late Classical period, the σοφ- word group gradually moved *away* from this range of meaning and indeed eventually came to designate, predominantly, the pursuits of philosophy. So Chantraine's entry on σοφία in his etymological dictionary of the Greek language:

> Mis à part les emplois particuliers que σοφίστης a connus en attique et plus tard pour l'enseignement de la rhétorique, emplois souvent péjoratifs, les débuts de l'histoire des mots σοφός, σοφία, etc., montrent comment les Grecs sont passés d'une connaissance pratique à une connaissance philosophique, les mêmes termes convenant pour ces deux demarches.[59]

[58] Anderson, *Rhetorical Theory and Paul*, 270.

[59] Chantraine, *Dictionnaire étymologique de la langue grecque*, 1031. We should also note here that LSJ's entries tend to be ordered chronologically. The first two entries,

This movement can be demonstrated in one way by noting those places where σοφός and δείνος are pitted *against* each other in late Classical and Hellenistic usage, where the one referred to *philosophical wisdom*, the other to *practical cleverness*. For instance: "Our proof will be unconvincing to merely clever men (δείνοις) but convincing to wise men (σοφοίς)" (Plato, *Phaed.* 245C [Fowler, LCL]; cf. *Thaet.* 164D). Or again: "And in no other way will the wise man (σοφόν) approve himself acute, nimble-witted, and generally skilful (δεινὸν) in argument" (D. L. 7.48 [Hicks, LCL]). The same conceptual distinction can be found in Latin literature around the first century.[60] On the other hand, when these two words are paired in more or less a synonymous sense, the association comes to be predominantly negative, not positive.[61] For example, in Dio Chrysostom, σοφούς τε καὶ δεινοὺς refers to "pettifogging lawyers, who pledge their services to all alike for a fee, even to the greatest scoundrels," and so on (*Or.* 7.123 [Cohoon, LCL]). Incidentally, Pogoloff claims that in the first century σοφία, in conjunction with δείνος ("clever or skillful"), often refers to the rhetorician (but in a positive sense?), although he provides only one example, and that missing any reference to σοφία![62] No matter; σοφία is *not* used in conjunction with δείνος in 1 Corinthians.

Furthermore, we have definitive lexicographical evidence that by the first century the wider public had indeed yielded the rights of "wisdom" – at least in name – to the sole proprietorship of Philosophy.

Sources from the Roman era routinely speak of the "pursuit of wisdom" as a technical expression for *philosophy* and of "wisdom" as a technical term for philosophy's content. Here Paul's affirmation that "Greeks desire wisdom" (1:22; Ἕλληνες σοφίαν ζητοῦσιν) – which in no place to my knowledge finds parallel with reference to rhetorical eloquence – comes to bear. We frequently find parallel statements referring to philosophy or the philosopher, and these emanating not only from

"cleverness"/"skill" and "practical wisdom," thus name meanings that prevailed in earlier times, whereas the third meaning, "wisdom"/"learning," including philosophical speculation, came to prevail during the Classical and Hellenistic periods.

60 Seneca often contrasts the wisdom of the philosopher with the cunning of the sophist (e.g., *Ep.* 111, esp. §3). Cicero speaks of cunning dissembling for wisdom (e.g., *Off.* 3.72; 3.96).

61 When viewed in their contexts, other examples of this pairing are arguably negative as well; cf. Dio, *Or.* 32.2; 72.15.

62 *Logos and Sophia*, 112–13. In the context we do find σοφιστείαν. But whether "sophistry" was commonly, and favorably, referred to as "wisdom" (σοφία) in the first century is precisely what is under debate. Pogoloff (*Logos and Sophia*, 114) does cite one more passage where σοφία and δεινότης are in fact conjoined (Plutarch, *Mor.* 148D). However, they are conjoined there in reference not to a rhetorician but to a small girl. Moreover, the pairing in the context seems to indicate that σοφία's *negative* sense of "cleverness" was best clarified by association with δεινότης.

the mouths of philosophers but also of rhetoricians. Seneca, for instance, defines philosophy as the "love and pursuit of wisdom" (*sapientiae amor est et adfectatio*; *Ep.* 89.4); philosophy is "that which seeks," wisdom "that which is sought" (*quod adfectatur*; *Ep.* 89.6). Strikingly, we find similar statements in Quintilian. He regrets that philosophers in his day held exclusive claim to the title *studiosi sapientiae*, or "seekers of wisdom" (*Inst.* 1.pr.14). Later, he uses an analogous phrase with reference to philosophy itself: *studia sapientiae*, or "the pursuit of wisdom" (*Inst.* 12.2.8). Cicero confirms that Quintilian's usage of this language with reference to philosophy was also more widely accepted, for he states: "Those who seek wisdom are called philosophers, and philosophy is no other thing – if I may be allowed to translate it into our own idiom – than the *pursuit of wisdom* (*studium sapientiae*)" (*Off.* 2.5). In another place, Cicero speaks of "the pursuit of wisdom (*studio sapientae*), which is also called philosophy" (*Tusc.* 1.1).

Time and again we find this expression as a circumlocution for philosophy.[63] But might this expression also refer to the art of rhetoric? I have found no evidence for it. Rather, even though we find certain authors advocating a conjunction between the two, the "pursuit of wisdom" seems to have been one thing, and "eloquence" another. To this even the rhetoricians bear witness. We have already seen how Cicero, in speaking of the regretful severance that certain people had perpetrated between the "tongue and the brain," or as it were, "eloquence and wisdom," had stated that, when those at the state's helm possessed eloquence (*eloquentia*) but had neglected the pursuit of wisdom (*sapientia*), disaster had ensued (*Inv.* 1.1–3). Quintilian too, much as he desired synthesis between the two, also bore witness to their separation in common usage. He customarily refers to "rhetoric" and "philosophy" using the respective labels *eloquentia* and *sapientia*, or "eloquence" and "wisdom" (*Inst.* 12.6.7; cf. Tacitus, *Agr.* 4), and he tells us explicitly that *eloquentia* is the preferred translation for the Greek term ῥητορική (2.14.1–3). We find analogous usage when it comes to the practitioners themselves: there are "the eloquent" (*eloquentes*) and there are the "philosophers" or "wise men" (*sapientes*) (*Inst.* 1.pr.3).

This last observation brings us to a crucial point that we have yet to discuss, and that is the usage of the term σοφός or *sapiens* ("wise man") in the Hellenistic and Roman periods. There has been relative neglect for the significance of this substantive (as distinguished from the attributive)

[63] For additional examples, see: Cicero, *Tusc.* 4.3; 5.8; Seneca, *Vit. beat.* 24.4; Tacitus, *Agr.* 4; cf. Lucretius, *De Rer. Nat.* 5.7–12, 18–21; 1.635–44.

designation in 1 Corinthians. In the first four chapters it appears at least five times as a definite substantive (1:19, 20, 27; 3:19, 20; cf. 3:18), as well as once, arguably, as an indefinite substantive (3:18).[64] It also appears as a substantive in 6:5, a text that, next to 3:18, provides the most probative evidence that the title was one in use by some who were still among the Corinthians, and indeed by some of the Corinthians themselves:

> "If anyone among you thinks he is a *wise man* . . . " (3:18)
>
> "Is there no *wise man* among you . . . ?" (6:5)

Twice Paul inserts the title into OT quotations, where no known text type actually includes it (3:19/Job 5:13; 3:20/Ps 93:11). Should we assume, as Winter and others do, that this is the sophist or rhetorician?

Like σοφία, σοφός had undergone a considerable semantic shift between the Archaic period and Hellenistic and Roman times. Even though the term continued to carry some of its earlier meanings (that is not to be denied), by the first century philosophical associations had in fact come to dominate. The "wise man" as a technical class had first been elaborated in Plato's *Republic*, and was further developed in each of the major philosophical schools thereafter. By the first century, we find that, even when the term did not refer specifically to the philosopher, its meaning was often colored by philosophical usage – as it was in Hellenistic Judaism, and in its more generalized usage as the person with good moral judgment.[65] By contrast, scarcely was it used in connection with the rhetorician.

All of what has been said so far is compellingly supported by a deeper examination of first-century usage of "wisdom" language in rhetorical

[64] The NRSV obscures the technical nature of this designation by rendering it "the one who is wise" (e.g., 1:20).

[65] On earlier, Classical usage of the σοφ- word group, see A. W. H. Adkins' "Review of Burkhard Gladigow's *Sophia und Kosmos: Untersuchungen zur Frühgeschichte von σοφός und σοφίη*," *The Classical Review*, New Series 21 (1971): 391–93; also, W. Burkert, "Platon oder Pythagoras? Zum Ursprung des Wortes 'Philosophie,'" *Hermes* 88 (1960): 159–77. For the dominance of the philosophical meaning after Plato, see G. B. Kerferd, "The Sage in Hellenistic Philosophical Literature," in J. G. Gammie and L. G. Perdue (eds.), *The Sage in Israel and Ancient Near East* (Winona Lake: Eisenbrauns), 320: "One might say in general that the concept of the wise man must be interpreted from Plato and Aristotle onward in terms of the various systems of philosophy within which the concept is positioned." On its usage in Hellenistic Judaism, see M. Kolarcik, S. J., "The Sage behind the Wisdom of Solomon," in L. Purdue (ed.), *Scribes, Sages, and Seers: The Sage in the Eastern Mediterranean World* (Göttingen: Vandenhoeck & Ruprecht, 2008), 245–57. For a generalized moral usage indebted to the philosophical tradition, see Cicero's *De Officiis* (e.g., 1.159; 3.29, 38, 89–93), which was based on the writings of the Stoic Panaetius (2.60; 3.7).

Table 1. *Occurences of the σοφ-/*sapient– *root in contemporary literature*

Author	Occurrences
Seneca	**550+**
Quintilian	60
Ad herennium	17
Theon	12

and philosophical writings. In my own comprehensive examination of four authors – Seneca, Quintilian, and Theon from the first century AD, and the author of the anonymous *Rhetorica ad Herennium* from the century before – not only is wisdom language exceedingly more prevalent in the philosopher (Seneca), but even when it is used by the *rhetoricians*, still it refers routinely to philosophers, and apparently in a standard technical sense – and we shall presently discover the reasons for any exceptions.[66] By my count, the total appearances of the σοφ-/*sapient-* root[67] in these authors are as indicated in Table 1.

That there are far fewer occurrences of this language in *Ad Herennium* and Theon is as expected, given their brevity in comparison with the other authors. But one is struck by the paucity of wisdom language in Quintilian when set next to the works of Seneca, which are of comparable length.[68] It should go without saying that, almost exclusively, Seneca uses the terms "wisdom" (*sapientia*) of philosophy (e.g., *Ep*. 89.4–6), and "wise man" (*sapiens*) of the philosopher (e.g., *Ep*. 9; 41; 109; *Vit. beat.* 16.3), and specifically of the *Stoic* philosopher. I have yet to find an example where he uses "wise man" to mark someone out as a rhetorician.

What is noteworthy, however, is not just that the three rhetorical works exhibit markedly fewer uses of wisdom language than do the works of Seneca, but that even in the rhetorical works such language, when it does appear, occurs still as technical language for philosophy/philosophers, and not for rhetoric/rhetoricians (see Table 2). It should be noted that *not*

[66] From Seneca, I considered the moral epistles and moral essays; from Quintilian, the *Institutio Oratoria;* and from Theon, the *Progymnasmata*.

[67] Including the noun σοφία/*sapientia*; the adjective σοφός/*sapiens*, whether attributive, predicative, or substantival; and, though rare, the adverb σοφῶς/*sapienter*.

[68] I may add that this terminology appears more than twice as often in Cicero's philosophical work *De Finibus* than it does in his rather longer, rhetorical work *De Oratore* – some 150 times in comparison with 60.

Table 2. *Occurences of σοφός/*sapiens *as a substantive in contemporary literature*

Source	Philosopher	Rhetorician
Quintilian	12	[2]
Ad Herennium	0	0
Theon	1 [7]	0

one occurrence of *sapiens*/σοφός ("wise man") in either *Ad Herennium* or Theon refers to the rhetorician, although in Theon at least 1, and perhaps as many as 7, refer to the philosopher specifically (*Prog*. 126.16; cf. 123.7, 9, 14, 20, 24; 124.9).[69]

Quintilian provides still further evidence for the philosophical usage, while also helping us understand any exceptions to the rule. In his treatise on rhetoric, at least 12 occurrences of *sapiens* refer clearly to the philosopher, without discussion or qualification, while in only 2 cases does it refer to the rhetorician. Moreover, both of these exceptions, as we shall see, explicitly constitute attempts to *redefine* the term.[70] Thus, in Quintilian, as in Seneca, *sapiens* is the default term not for the rhetorician, but for the philosopher. For the rhetorician he uses a separate term – *eloquentes*. He notes, for instance, that in earlier times "philosophers and orators (*sapientes atque eloquentes*) were taken to be the same" (1.pr.13 [LCL, Russell]). Not so in his own day, however, when the two had come to be seen as separate. I have already pointed out that the same goes for his usage of *sapientia*: this is the accepted name for philosophy, as opposed to rhetoric, which goes by the name of *eloquentia* (12.6.7; cf. 2.15.33). In the two instances where *sapiens* does refer to the rhetorician, Quintilian betrays that he is not following common acceptation. In the first of these texts, he mentions "the orator, who *ought to be* a wise man (*qui debet esse sapiens*)" (1.10.6). Thusly articulated, it apparently does not go without saying that the orator was expected to be *thought* a wise man. Even more revealing is the second text. Here, Quintilian laments the withdrawal of philosophers from public life and asks urgently for that vacancy to be filled by others (12.2.7):

[69] Line numbers follow L. Spengel, *Rhetores Graeci*, 2 vols. (Leipzig: Teubner, 1854; repr. 1966), 2:59–130.

[70] Of the philosopher: 1.pr.13; 1.1.4; 1.10.15; 2.17.27, 28; 6.3.109; 10.1.68; 11.1.10; 12.1.4; 12.1.18; 12.1.39; 12.7.9; cf. 1.10.5; 11.1.35; of the rhetorician, with qualification: 1.10.6; 12.2.7.

> Hence this exhortation of mine does not mean that I want the orator to be a philosopher, for no other way of life is more remote from the duties of a citizen and the task of an orator generally. ... What philosopher has ever been active in the government of the state, the very subject on which so many of them give so much advice? All the same, I should like the orator I am training to be a sort of Roman Wise Man (*Romanum quondam velim esse sapientem*), able to play the part of the real statesman not in private seminars but in the experience and activity of real life.

Quintilian's remarks reflect the old debate about whether the philosopher should engage in politics. Most had declined the path recommended by Aristotle, and had preferred withdrawal. Accordingly, what Quintilian is again suggesting is that the "wise man" in generally accepted usage was the *philosopher* – or as it were, the one who had withdrawn from the public sphere. *This* sort of wise man, whom he finds wanting, he hopes to *replace* with another – "a sort of Roman Wise Man" (*Romanum quondam velim esse sapientem*) – the orator trained for statesmanship (see also 11.1.35). Thus, true as it may have been that in pre-Socratic times "wise men" received their name from their eloquent speech, by Quintilian's day the wise man as *philosopher* was the one people knew; the old, wise man as *orator* was one Quintilian could only hope to recreate. Let me reiterate: *we have not understood Quintilian's treatise on rhetoric if we have not understood this point*. He is sketching a picture of what the *ideal orator* might look like *if he existed* (*id quod quaerimus*; 2.4.17; 9.1.41; 10.2.28; cf. 1.9–27; 1.10.8, 24; 12.1.24),[71] such a one as might *re*claim the "wisdom" content that had since become consigned, at least in name if not also in matter, to the domain of philosophy (see 1.pr.9–20; 12.2). As it is, it is clearly not the orator who was known as a "wise man." It was the philosopher.

The upshot of all this is that the "wise man" was indisputably a standard technical designation for the philosopher, as seen in both philosophical and rhetorical works, and must have referred to the rhetorician exceedingly infrequently, and then (apparently) only when an attempt to redefine current usage was being undertaken. Therefore, true as it was that Quintilian wished to create a "wise man" in his orator, his actual usage

[71] One might object that it was also debated whether many philosophers had ever reached the ideal of "wise man" status. Nonetheless, "wise man" status remained at least the *expectation* for philosophers, while, as we have seen, in Quintilian's day it evidently was *not* for orators.

reveals that he presented an ideal that did not reflect the common opinion, or for that matter, the reality (cf. 1.pr.17), in his own day. (Based on my preliminary observations, an examination of Cicero's philosophical and rhetorical treatises only confirms this.)[72]

So far, then, we have seen that a more calculated examination of wisdom language around the first century – in the works of both philosophers and rhetoricians – reveals that both the term "wisdom" (σοφία/*sapientia*) and the substantive designation "wise man" (σοφός/*sapiens*) were used more – one may now say "commonly" – in connection with philosophy or the philosopher than with rhetoric or the rhetorician. If Pogoloff's judgment that a rhetorical meaning was the "common" or "ordinary" one cannot, then, be sustained in light of either contemporary philosophical or rhetorical literature, and in spite of the judgment of more than one etymological dictionary (so far, *TDNT* and Chantraine), then we must ask on what precisely it is based, or whether it is simply being declared.

What then of λόγος? Should it be taken for granted that "rhetoric" is the ordinary meaning? In a suspiciously shifty paragraph, Pogoloff tells us that it is:

> The third [intersection of λόγος and σοφία] includes one of the most common, everyday meanings of λόγος as 'speech.' From the papyri we can gather that λόγος developed from its ordinary sense of 'word' or 'saying' to its developed meanings as 'speech in progress.' Thus, in both koine and literary texts, λόγος was commonly understood to mean speech. In particular, it was used to mean a '*speech* delivered in court, assembly, etc.'; in other words, it meant the product of *rhetoric*.[73]

Should this paragraph not give us serious pause? Notice that, by sheer sleight of hand, the "common, everyday meaning" of λόγος has slipped from the rather generalized "speech," to "speech in progress," to "speech delivered in court," to none other than "rhetoric," without regard to context. In just such a way, Pogoloff concludes that "σοφία λόγου would mean clever or skilled or educated or rhetorically sophisticated speech."[74]

In all this – from σοφία to λόγος – the astute reader will not miss what Pogoloff has done. Without a transparent show of the evidence, he has

[72] "Wisdom" and the "wise man" are to philosophy and the philosopher, as "eloquence" and "the eloquent" are to rhetoric and the rhetorician.

[73] Pogoloff, *Logos and Sophia*, 110.

[74] *Ibid.*, 110.

made us believe that the "least specialized" meaning of σοφία λόγου is "rhetorically sophisticated speech," when his renderings of λόγος and σοφία are in fact both specialized. On the contrary, the *least* specialized usages would leave us with something like "wisdom/learning" and "word/speech," which when combined would give us some general expression like "wisdom of word." The rest is a matter of interpretation – and in this matter contemporary usage of σοφία cannot be so easily brushed aside.

But as Pogoloff himself points out, other interpretive options do present themselves. He notes, for instance, the possibility that λόγος could indicate "reason" or "philosophical dialogue," so that, when combined with σοφία, the expression could refer to the process of dialectical reasoning. He even notes that "[t]his has been a popular alternative throughout the history of exegesis, and it fits well theologically with much of what Paul says in the rest of the chapter." The reader who expects a rebuttal of this option will be disappointed, however. None is forthcoming. We are merely told that the third option, which he prefers, "is so compelling that few commentators can avoid taking it into account."[75] Unfortunately, as we have seen, a mere declaration that a particular interpretation is "compelling" or that its rendering of the text represents the most "common" meaning in the first century, hardly makes it so. We can no longer avoid attending to actual first century usage.

In fact nothing about the context of 1:17–2:16 would prevent us from taking λόγος and σοφία and their associated phrases in terms of the process of *rational argumentation generally* – which might include what Quintilian calls "unartful" speech (2.20.2, 4), along with "dialectic," a mode of argumentation theoretically distinguished from rhetoric in the ancient sources (see Quintilian 2.20.7; LS 31). In the first place, it should be said that "rational argumentation," rather than "speech," is often the better rendering of λόγος, even when the term appears alone. According to the Stoics, the "logical" (λόγικα) part of philosophy, which embraced both "dialectic" and "rhetoric," was concerned with all forms of λόγος, or rational discourse. Isocrates attested that λόγος – or reasoned argumentation – was what separated rational humans from the irrational beasts (*Nic.* 5–9; cf. Plato, *Phaedr.* 259e-261a). Aristotle used the term similarly, noting, besides, that it was "designed to indicate the advantageous and the harmful, and therefore also the right and the wrong" (*Pol.* 1253a14 [LCL, Rackham]). In earlier days, Parmenides had spoken of rational discourse, such as the philosophers employed, using the expression

[75] *Ibid.*, 110.

πιστὸν λόγον, or "probable speech" (*Nature* fr. 8.50). In the same way, Plato spoke of the philosopher's πειθοῖ διὰ λόγων, "persuasion by speech" (*Resp.* 411D), and πίθανος λόγος, "persuasive argument" (*Phaedo* 88D; *Leg.* 839B). And in the first century Dio Chrysostom, in his famous Alexandrian discourse, lauded the one who assuaged the souls of the people through "persuasion and *reason* (λόγου)" (*Or.* 32.18). What all this means is that a similar field of terminology – including words like σοφία, λόγος, πείθος, πίθανος, and πίστις, for instance – surrounded rational argumentation generally as surrounded the art of "rhetoric" specifically.

Many of the same criticisms apply to Litfin and Winter. Like Pogoloff, Litfin takes no pains to demonstrate that the σοφ- word group, and especially the substantive σοφός, is best understood in relation to rhetoric. The sparse examples he provides derive almost exclusively from Dio (in the late first or early second century), and not one of them refers to the rhetorician or sophist with the substantive designation "wise man."[76] Furthermore, we must ask how Litfin can justify repudiating the idea that σοφία λόγου in 1:17 refers to wisdom's content, indeed calling such an interpretation "tendentious," when he himself says that matters of content "will arise soon enough in Paul's argument" – that is, by his own admission, as early as v. *18*![77]

Neither does Winter provide any diachronic analysis to prove that wisdom language is best understood in connection with rhetoric. Moreover, he seems to contradict important evidence from one of his chief sources, Philo of Alexandria. Indeed, Philo's works bear witness that wisdom is to be associated, not with the sophist (as Winter would have it), but with the *philosopher*. In this regard, Philo frequently pits wisdom and the sophist *against each other*, preferring to associate wisdom with the "wise man" or philosopher instead. Philo, for instance, states that the sophists had "given the name of wisdom" (that is, σοφία, the root seen in the name σοφ-ίστης) "to their rascality, conferring on a sorry work a divine title" (*Post.* 101 [Colson and Whitaker, LCL]). From this, and many other examples,[78] it is evident that, as far as Philo was concerned, wisdom was the property of the philosopher and *not* the sophist. Of course, Philo's statements to this effect *could* indicate that the title σόφος (in addition to σοφ-ίστης) was at times claimed for the

[76] Litfin, *St. Paul's Theology of Proclamation*, 121–3.

[77] Cf. *Ibid.*, 188, 205.

[78] On the philosopher as wise man over against the sophist, see also Philo, *Cher.* 1.10; *Sobr.* 1:9; *Q.G.* 3.33; Dio, *Or.* 10.32; *Or.* 4.32.2; Plutarch, *Mor.* 999E.

sophist, which fact Philo then felt he had to combat; but Winter cites no positive evidence of such an application. What we have instead is further explicit evidence of this (substantive) title's attachment to the philosopher. Further examples support this point. For instance, Winter observes that Philo speaks favorably of Moses as the "the wise man par excellence" (πάνσοφος).[79] Yet, in contradiction, Winter's work has set out to argue that "the wise man" was the *sophist*, whom Philo *opposed*, and whom Paul had set his face *against* in his letters to the Corinthians. Again, Winter later refers to Dio Chrysostom, when he played the role of the *philosopher* in his thirty-second discourse (*Or.* 32.11.8), as "the protypical wise man."[80] Is Winter not inadvertently demonstrating that, in Philo, the wise man as philosopher was more standard usage than the wise man as sophist?

None of these points has escaped the notice of the lexicons (nor, I might add, of the translators of our Classical texts). In fact, the lexicons are so surprisingly clear on the semantics at issue here that one wonders whether they have simply not been consulted. They give us little reason to believe that either σοφία or λόγος was used as a technical designation for rhetoric or eloquence. Woodhouse gives as the Greek equivalents for "rhetoric" ῥητορική and ῥητορεία, and for "eloquence" δεινότης, εὐγλωσσία, πειθώ, ῥητορική and ῥητορεία – but in neither case is σοφία or λόγος given. In LSJ, one does find "eloquence" as a more specialized gloss for λόγος, under the meaning "expression," "utterance," "speech" (meaning #9), but it is also noted that this meaning (besides depending on contextual modifiers) obtains only in the plural, which we find in neither 1 Cor 1:17 nor 2:1 (the plural in 2:4 is based on a doubtful variant; and "eloquence" does not work as the meaning in 2:13). BDAG offers only one example of σοφία as "cleverness in *speaking*," and it comes from 1 Cor 1:17 (σοφία λόγου), one of the very texts being called to count. On the contrary, Woodhouse gives σοφία as the Greek rendering, not for "rhetoric" or "eloquence," but for "*philosophy*."[81] The Latin term *sapientia* ("wisdom") is explicitly given to mean "philosophy" in the *OLD* (meaning #3). The entry in *Brill's New Pauly* on "Wisdom," discussing this concept in the Hellenistic and Late Antique periods, is confined entirely to a discussion of philosophy, and makes no mention of rhetoric

[79] Additionally, Philo frequently uses the uncompounded form σοφός in reference to Moses and other "philosophers": in reference to Moses, *Gig.* 1.48; *Ebr.* 1.37, 1.100; *Migr.* 1.201; in reference to others, *Dec.* 1.1.

[80] Winter, *Philo and Paul among the Sophists*, 47.

[81] S.C. Woodhouse, *English-Greek Dictionary: A Vocabulary of the Attic Language* (London; New York: Routledge, 1998).

at all. We have already discussed the entries on σοφία from LSJ, *TDNT*, and Chantraine, which all confirm its technical associations with philosophy. The terms in 1 Corinthians of course have to be treated within their specific semantic contexts. But short of exceptionally explicit contradictory evidence – and of that we fall quite short – on what grounds can we defy what is clearly the accepted contemporary usage, defaulting instead to one that neither lexicography nor the historical dictionaries nor standard translations commonly recognize?

All of this simply confirms what we have seen from Quintilian and others about first-century usage of wisdom terminology. Without denying that the first-century rhetorician could be called "wise," it has been shown that, at that time, wisdom language was associated in a technical way with philosophy in a way that it apparently was not with rhetoric. Accordingly, it is found predominantly in connection with the former. Those who have told us otherwise have been satisfied merely to drop in a few unexamined examples, with no regard for diachronic considerations and without dealing with (or being unaware of) the exceedingly greater prevalence of the terminology in relation to philosophy. Thus they show no recognition that σοφία/*sapientia* was a technical designation for philosophy, and the substantive σοφός/*sapiens* a technical designation for the philosopher, in the parlance of philosophers and rhetoricians alike. That λόγος is occasionally added in Paul's references to σοφία need hardly compel us to take them in connection with rhetorical eloquence, for as we have seen, this term often denotes rational discourse more generally, and moreover, usually indicates "eloquence" only when it occurs in the plural, and when contextual factors make such a rendering absolutely necessary.

Therefore, no longer can the rhetorical meaning of 1:17 and 2:1, 4 be presumed the "obvious" one, or indeed so "overwhelmingly" plain that other explanations, such as those related to philosophy or rational argumentation, can either be dismissed without reason (Pogoloff) or passed over entirely (Winter). Quite the contrary, contemporary evidence regarding σοφία/σοφός points compellingly in the direction of philosophy. Of course, the context of the letter must serve as the final arbiter for interpretation of such language in 1 Corinthians – "wisdom" does not *have* to denote philosophy. But surely we can see that if we are to take the Corinthians' understanding of wisdom in a way that runs against the grain of prevailing usage in first-century Greco-Roman culture, then we must have extraordinarily good reasons for doing so. Moreover, we have seen that there is more to 1 Corinthians 1–4 and what Paul divulges about the Corinthians' wisdom there than the language of 1:17; 2:1, 4, 13. I have drawn attention so far not only to Paul's frequent references to the "wise man" (1:19, 27; 3:19, 20; 1:20; cf. 6:5), but also to his repeated references to wisdom generally and his specific remark that Greeks "seek" it (1:22).

Nonetheless, those advocating the rhetorical thesis do have other evidence to show forth, evidence that must be considered before we can cast a verdict on the whole argument. We look next at another major piece, one found in a cluster of terminology appearing alongside λόγος and σοφία in 2:1–5.

Supporting internal evidence

1. Several other terms in 2:1–5 could be meant to conjure up associations with ancient rhetoric. These include: ὑπεροχή (v. 1), ἀπόδειξις (v. 4), δύναμις (vv. 4, 5), πείθος (v. 4), and πίστις (v. 5).[82] If a case can be made for a rhetorical background of the Corinthians' wisdom, it stands its best chances on the basis of the dense cluster of language in these few verses, much of which, along with λόγος and σοφία, can be found in other literature in connection with rhetorical eloquence.

Here it must be confessed that, in repudiating the use of persuasive human argumentation of that kind which precludes reliance on the power of the Spirit (2:4–5), Paul surely means to *include* in his repudiation certain uses of rhetoric (even in the term's more restrictive ancient usage). However, that need not mean that Paul is disavowing the eloquence of the *rhetorician* specifically. To begin, there is little inherent in ὑπεροχή to denote rhetoric per se. The term carried a range of very generalized meanings, from "projection, prominence" or "preeminence, superiority," to "excess," "supremacy, authority, dignity," or "prolixity" (LSJ). Ἀπόδειξις, to be sure, could be used of a rhetorical "demonstration," but at least equally often it was used – in fact in a technical sense (Cicero, *Luc.* 26) – to refer to "demonstrations" in *philosophical* persuasion (e.g., D. L. 7.44, 52, 79; Sextus Empiricus, *Pyrr.* 2.135–43; Strabo, *Geogr.* 2.3.5; Lucian, *Eunuch.* 13). Regarding δύναμις, it is hardly to be denied that the term was an important one in rhetorical theory. But once again, we have mitigating factors. Never mind that this term too had wide application, and could refer to any natural capacity or faculty, not just that of speech or rhetorical eloquence: what is more, even Socrates, of all people – the supposed enemy of rhetoric – was said to have possessed the "*power* of speech" (τοὺ στόματος δυνάμει; Plato, *Symp.* 215C; cf. 216C). As for πιστός and πείθος/πίθανος, I have already pointed out that these terms could be used of persuasion in philosophical or more

[82] Winter (*Philo and Paul among the Sophists*, 149–50) lists all of these.

generalized contexts and need not have referred to the tricks of rhetoricians (e.g., πιστὸν λόγον, "probable speech" in Parmenides, *Nature* fr. 8.50; πειθοῖ διὰ λόγων, "persuasion by speech" in Plato, *Resp.* 411D; πίθανος λόγος, "persuasive argument" in Plato, *Phaed.* 88D; *Leg.* 839B; πειθοῦς καὶ λόγου, "persuasion and reason" in Dio Chrysostom, *Or.* 32.18; cf. πίστις, "firm conviction" in D. L. 10.85).

I hope to be fair. With the foregoing, I do not say that rhetoric, in its narrower sense, was *excluded* from the embrace of Paul's disavowal of wisdom in 2:1–5, but I do suggest that Paul does not here repudiate rhetorical wisdom *specifically*.[83] Rather, he is denying reliance on any natural human argumentation as the sole instrument of persuasive success. This *could* include wisdom associated with rhetorical eloquence, or that associated with philosophical or rational argumentation generally.

And yet, the non-rhetorical usage of this terminology is, for all that, somewhat off the point. What we should really be asking is why, even on the assumption that 2:1–5 *did* single out the wisdom of the rhetorician, we must see this as a reflection of the peculiar perspective of the *Corinthians*. Indeed, a *rather* striking parallel to this text appears *outside* 1 Corinthians, in Paul's First Letter to the Thessalonians. Compare 1 Thess 1:5 with 1 Cor 2:3–5:

> Our message of the gospel *came* to you *not* in *word* only, *but also* in *power* and in the Holy *Spirit* and with full *conviction*.
> (1 Thess 1:5, NRSV; cf. 2:1–12; Gal 1:10)

> 3 And I *came* to you with weakness and fear and much trembling,
> 4 and my *speech* and my proclamation were *not* with plausible *words* of wisdom, *but* with a demonstration of the *Spirit* and of *power*,
> 5 so that your *faith* might rest not on human wisdom but on the *power* of God. (1 Cor 2:3–5)

A "coming" (ἐγενόμην/ἐγενήθην), the "Spirit" (Πνεῦμα), the "word" (λόγος), "power" (δύναμις), faith/conviction (πλροφορία/πίστις), the "not … but" construction (οὐ … ἀλλά) – it is all there in 1 Thessalonians 1:5, just as in 1 Corinthians 2. We lack only σοφία (added to meet the occasion). Why then have we been so confident that 1 Cor 2:1–5 must directly address the views of the Corinthians? Do these similarities not, rather, betray Paul's general concern for personal reputation, a concern that transcended specific occasions and localities? If this is right, the

[83] *Pace* Welborn: "The σοφία that Paul fears will undermine the community is *nothing other than rhetoric*" (*Politics and Rhetoric in the Corinthian Epistles*, 30).

terminology of 2:1–5 unfortunately proves little, if anything, about the Corinthians' own views.

2. But advocates of the rhetorical thesis have also looked to some material outside 2:1–5. Some have found significance in the appearance of κρίνω ("judge") in 4:5. It has been propounded that Paul has been "judged" on the basis of the criteria used to evaluate eloquence and the high status associated with it.[84] In particular, the Corinthians are said to have "judged" Apollos superior, and Paul inferior. While this interpretation is not impossible, one must, however, face the fact that this is at best based on a speculative "mirror-reading" of the situation – although we might more accurately call it an a priori assumption. Indeed, we are given not a hint of the actual charges, nor necessarily is there any indication that specific charges had been made. At all events, other, equally plausible explanations for this single reference are likely to be at hand.

3. Adding a further argument, Winter capitalizes heavily on sophistic parallels related to the Corinthians' "quarrels" (ἔριδες, 1 Cor 1:11) and "factionalism" (ζῆλος, 1 Cor 3:3).[85] He observes that the students of sophists could be called μαθηταί, or, if they were zealous for the reputation of their teachers, ζηλωταί. Among especially zealous students, rivalries, or ἔριδες, could develop on behalf of competing teachers. This, Winter proposes, is what is happening in the Corinthian church. Some of the converts have begun to perceive themselves as μαθηταί/ζηλωταί of their Christians teachers – some of Paul, and others of Apollos – and have formed factions around them. They are now judging their teachers in accordance with the "secular attitudes" of the sophists – they are acting like mere worldlings (cf. σάρκινος, νήπιος, σαρκικός, κατὰ ἄνθρωπον; 3:1–3). Winter's theory appears to rest on solid ground, until we recognize (and this he does not mention) that the same language can be found with reference to students of philosophers. The students of philosophers too could be called, not only μαθηταί (e.g., Dio, *Or.* 55.1–6) but also ζηλωταί. Diogenes Laertius speaks of the emulators of the Skeptic Pyrrho as ζηλωταί (9.63), and of Theophrastus as a ζηλωτής of Parmenides (8.55). Epictetus encouraged his students to become ζηλωταί of Socrates (*Diatr.* 3.7.34). Josephus recalls how he submitted himself to the way of life of each of the three major Jewish "sects" of his day – each of which he likens to one of the three major Greco-Roman philosophies (*J.W.* 2.119; *Ant.* 18.11) – noting that he became a ζηλώτης of his Essene

[84] Litfin, *St. Paul's Theology of Proclamation*, 229–33; Witherington, *Conflict and Community in Corinth*, 137.

[85] Winter, *Philo and Paul among the Sophists*, 172–8.

teacher (*Vit.* 1.10–12).[86] The term could also be used in the sense of a philosophical rivalry (Lucian, *Peregr.* 15.17). And we can find instances where ἔρις arises over philosophy (Lucian, *Symp.* 1).

4. Paul's discussion of Apollos in 1 Corinthians 3–4 has also played an important role. The argument here, however, really depends on what can be gleaned from material outside 1 Corinthians: because Acts calls Apollos λόγιος ("learned," or possibly, "eloquent"; 18:24), it is surmised that some Corinthians saw him as a rhetor superior to Paul, who, according to 2 Corinthians, was "contemptible in speech" (ὁ λόγος ἐξουθημένος; 10:10). Interestingly, Litfin enlists both Acts and 2 Corinthians 10 to his cause, despite the fact that he deliberately refrains from treating 1 Corinthians material outside 1:17–2:5, *and* claims to be upholding Dahl's methodological principle that "information from other Pauline epistles, Acts, and other early Christian, Jewish, Greek, or Gnostic documents should not be brought in until the epistolary situation has been clarified as far as possible on the basis of internal evidence."[87] As we shall see in Chapter 6, however, contrary to common perception Paul does not give any clear indication in 1 Corinthians that Apollos actually played a major role in the divisions. Why we have made Apollos the whipping boy if 1 Corinthians is silent (or at best murky) on the matter is a question that must be further addressed. In any case, had Apollos been involved, could it not have been as a conduit of certain *philosophical* knowledge,[88] for which his native city (Alexandria) was also renowned?

5. Other supporting arguments include the appearance of συνζητήτης in 1:20 – whom some have identified as a rhetorician[89] – and the possible association of the "high-status" terms of 1:26 (σοφοί, δύνατοι, εὐγενεῖς) and 4:8–10 (ἐβασιλεύσατε, ἐπλουτήσατε, φρόνιμοι, ἰσχυροί, ἔνδοξοι) with "sophistic values."[90] Again, in each case the material is open to multiple possible interpretations. Some have quite plausibly argued that the (rare) term συνζητήτης is more likely the philosopher,[91] if not simply generalizing. And the "sophistic values" of 1:26 and 4:8–10 can all be

[86] Other references to ζηλωταί of philosophers include: Lucian, *Herm.* 14.7; *Dem.* 48.6.

[87] He says that he is not obliged to say how his thesis relates to material outside 1:17–2:5 (*St. Paul's Theology of Proclamation*, 148–50), and then later quotes Dahl (p. 236).

[88] As indeed has been argued in the past: R. M. Grant, "The Wisdom of the Corinthians," in S. E. Johnson (ed.), *The Joy of Study* (New York: Macmillan, 1951), 51–5.

[89] Pogoloff, *Logos and Sophia*, 160.

[90] Winter, *Philo and Paul among the Sophists*, 192, 198–9.

[91] So Fee, *1 Corinthians*, 71; and Fitzmyer, *First Corinthians*, 156, who provides solid primary source evidence.

found in other contexts in relation to spiritual or intellectual values, not least in philosophical literature,[92] where they may, in fact, more properly belong.

In the end, the linchpin for the rhetorical argument has remained the language of 1:17 and 2:1–5 and the underlying inference that, in employing this language, Paul is denying the very thing that lies at the heart of the Corinthians' problems – their high estimation of eloquent speech. But as we have seen, any and all of the evidence adduced in chapters 1–4 for the rhetorical thesis is subject to multiple interpretations, and our survey of philosophers and rhetoricians has shown that Paul's "wisdom" language is undoubtedly better taken in another direction. What can be gathered from the remaining twelve chapters of the letter will be paramount in adjudicating which direction we should take.

The popularity of rhetoric

Pogoloff, Litfin, and Winter rightly emphasize the dominance of rhetoric in first-century Greco-Roman education and in popular culture more broadly. But we must be careful not to allow this dominance to predetermine the way in which we sift the internal evidence of the letter. Winter is keenly aware of this: "even when the extrabiblical evidence of the sophistic movement has been assembled, it cannot be assumed *ipso facto* that this provides the actual background to the problems in the church discussed by Paul in 1 Corinthians 1–4, 9 and 2 Corinthians 10–13."[93] This conclusion, he says, must be assembled from the text itself.

Nonetheless, the dominance of rhetoric has been used as a supporting argument. Winter, for instance, bringing to bear Theon's statement that students of his day were "far from the knowledge of philosophy," remarks: "[P]resumably they were not interested or had not been trained in it."[94] Elsewhere he says that the people had "voted with their feet and were only too anxious to enroll their sons in the sophists' schools. Alas, for the philosophers of his day, they no longer held centre stage in the public's estimation."[95] Litfin notes that rhetoric was "ubiquitous in the Greco-Roman culture," even "endemic, an inherent part of life."[96] Pogoloff is more explicit, reminding us that Greco-Roman education

[92] See, e.g., Horsley, *1 Corinthians*, 31–32, 51–52, 69.
[93] Winter, *Philo and Paul among the Sophists*, 13; cf. 140, 159.
[94] *Ibid.*, 21.
[95] *Ibid.*, 219.
[96] Litfin, *St. Paul's Theology of Proclamation*, 125.

was "almost exclusively education in rhetoric,"[97] but that philosophers tended to be only "marginal" members of society.[98]

Yet, Winter's caveat must hang constantly before us: that rhetoric was immensely popular in the first century is no guarantee that it lay at the heart of the problems in Paul's Corinthian community. And indeed, just as rhetoric was by no means the only so-called wisdom of the first century, neither was it the only option for those seeking higher education. One could procure a philosophical education in any number of ways – at the gymnasium; by private tutors, at home or abroad; or by attending popular lectures.[99] Its practitioners even considered philosophy to be the true capstone of education, that for which the liberal arts and sciences were only preparation (e.g., Philo, *Congr.* 1.79). In that regard, the claim that a rhetorical education was a high-status indicator could be made equally of a philosophical education, for a tertiary education almost always indicated a person of means. As we shall see in Chapter 4, the chances that there may have been some in the Corinthian church who had a fair acquaintance with philosophy is well within the realm of possibility.

At this point, we shall also need to remark on what seems to be a defect in Winter's argumentation. *Paul and Philo among the Sophists* is, of course, about Paul *and* Philo and how they furnish evidence for the sophistic movements in first-century Corinth and Alexandria respectively. Or is it? The Corinthian sources on which Winter relies include Dio Chrysostom, *Or.* 6 and 8 (AD 89–96), a diatribe of Epictetus (AD 92–93), the Corinthian oration of Favorinus (reign of Hadrian), Plutarch's *Questiones Conviviales* (AD 99–116), an inscription commemorating Herodes Atticus (b. AD 101, d. AD 177), and, along with these, Paul's Corinthian letters. Here arises what seems to me a vexing question: are these other Corinthian sources, which were written between AD 90 and the late second century, being used to bolster Winter's thesis about the sophistic problem behind the Corinthian correspondence, which

[97] *Logos and Sophia*, 49.

[98] *Ibid.*, 62–3.

[99] Private tutors, at home or abroad: see M. Joyal, I. McDougall, and J. C. Yardley (eds.), *Greek and Roman Education: A Sourcebook* (Milton Park: Routledge, 2009), 193, 207–8, 224–5 – the gymnasium: see R. Dutch, *The Educated Elite in 1 Corinthians: Education and Community Conflict in Graeco-Roman Context*, JSNTSup 271 (London: T & T Clark, 2005). See also J. T. Townsend, "Ancient Education in the Time of the Early Roman Empire," in J. Benko and S. O'Rourke (eds.), *The Catacombs and the Colosseum* (Valley Forge: Judson Press, 1971), 314–15, as well as Teresa Morgan's comments on secondary literature's oversight of philosophy in the ancient school curriculum, in *Literate Education in the Hellenistic and Roman Worlds*, CCS (Cambridge: Cambridge University Press, 1998), 193.

occurred some 40 to 100 (plus) years earlier? Or is the sophistic background of the Corinthian correspondence being argued on its own terms and then used in support of his argument about the larger sophistic movement in Corinth?

Inasmuch as Winter is doing the latter – as the volume's primary thesis suggests – he leads us to believe that he is *also* doing the former (hence a noticeable circularity). Indeed, he states, several times, that he has relied on the extrabiblical sources as evidence that the "[s]ophists were a major force in first-century Corinth" – although these sources actually occur decades *subsequent* to the time of the Corinthian correspondence (AD 90–180) – and says that he intends, from this point of departure, to flesh out his argument about the Corinthian correspondence using internal evidence.[100] But then is the cart not to some extent coming before the horse? It has not yet been shown that the Second Sophistic *was* in fact in full swing *at the time of the Corinthian correspondence*. Rather, the Corinthian correspondence would still stand alone as an example of this movement in mid-first-century Corinth. Yet one suspects that Winter's continual affirmation that sophists were a major force in first-century Corinth is meant to prepossess us toward the sophistic interpretation of the *letter*.

Moreover, given Winter's conclusions we cannot pass over the book he produced between the first (1997) and second (2002) editions of the present one – *After Paul Left Corinth* (2001). This work uses, among others, Epictetus and Favorinus – two of the authors he uses in his 1997/2002 book to argue for the emergence of the Second Sophistic as early as the middle of the first century, and indeed as early as the Corinthian correspondence – as evidence for a "cultural watershed" in Corinth, wherewith the city, formerly entrenched in *Roman* customs and ideals, became transformed into a city zealous to revive the glories of its Classical *Greek* past.[101] But this combination of arguments could not be more puzzling. First, it means that the same evidence that is used in 1997/2002 to support a sophistic background behind 1 Corinthians is *also*, in 2001, being used to demonstrate a cultural *shift* that Winter insists

[100] Winter, *Philo and Paul among the Sophists*, 13; cf. 140, 159. That being so, one wonders why he has arranged the book as he has. We may conclude that the book is not *really* about how Paul contributes to our understanding of the sophistic movement in the first century (as the title and inclusion of Philo seem to indicate), but about how the presumed sophistic movement of the first century contributes to our understanding of the Corinthian correspondence. But to say it is both is surely circular.

[101] B. Winter, *After Paul Left Corinth: The Influence of Secular Ethics and Social Change* (Grand Rapids: Eerdmans, 2001), 18–19.

happened decades *after* 1–2 Corinthians, and which somehow changes how we are to interpret the letters. Or are we to believe that Epictetus and Favorinus simultaneously establish *and* cut across this cultural watershed? Second, if with time Corinthian culture did drift from Roman to Greek orientation, according to Winter's (2001) argumentation this would mean that the other sources attesting to sophism in Corinth (Dio, Epictetus, Favorinus, and so forth), which he uses in the 1997/2002 book, have been undermined and are no longer very helpful to his thesis regarding the background to the Corinthian correspondence – for they occur after the supposed watershed. Thus, Winter's contradictory manipulation of the evidence ends in a zero-sum game, and we must conclude that his argument in *Philo and Paul among the Sophists* is not much aided by the (late) external sources he names. Having pulled the rug out from under himself, his case must be made from the letter itself.

Methodological approach

We now come to the crucial issue of methodology. Though we shall explore this issue in more detail in the Chapter 3, it will be apposite here to address the question briefly in relation to the rhetorical thesis. Indeed, the rhetorical thesis has relied largely on a method of interpretation that has long since fallen into disrepute, at least in principle. It has been more than twenty years since John Barclay, in a now-classic essay, warned us of the dangers of "mirror-reading,"[102] that technique whereby the interpreter reads every attack made by the author of an epistle as an indication that the repudiated behavior or belief somehow characterized or was shared by the original audience. Frequently, this involves the οὐ ... ἀλλά construction ("not ... but"). As it happens, this is precisely the construction we find in those verses that scholars have pinpointed as the foundation for the rhetorical thesis: "*not* with lofty words or wisdom" (2:1), "*not* with persuasive words of wisdom ... *but* with a demonstration of the Spirit and of power" (2:4); "words *not* taught by human wisdom ... *but* taught by the Spirit" (2:13; cf. "*not* with eloquent wisdom," 1:17). This methodological point has critical implications. Suppose it can be established that the wisdom referred to in these verses is that of rhetoric: even so, we have then only ascertained that the rhetorical wisdom involved was something that Paul *himself* repudiated, *not* necessarily that what he repudiated was specifically at the root of the *Corinthian* understanding of wisdom. Indeed, Paul seems everywhere to want to distance himself

[102] "Mirror-Reading a Polemical Letter: Galatians as a Test Case," *JSNT* 31 (1987): 73–93.

from the sort of argumentation alluded to in these texts, which is why we often find him making parallel statements elsewhere. I have already drawn attention to the almost identical statement that appears in 1 Thess 1:5 ("Our message of the gospel *came* to you *not* in *word* only, *but also* in *power* and in the Holy *Spirit* and with full *conviction*," NRSV; cf. 1 Cor 2:3–5; 1 Thess 2:1–12); its likeness also appears elsewhere (Gal 1:10).

At times interpreters seem aware of what they are doing. Litfin, for instance, states: "Because we cannot fully appreciate what Paul is affirming unless we *reconstruct the opposite member of the contrast*, we have taken pains to describe the relevant aspects of the Greco-Roman rhetorical tradition."[103] Ciampa and Rosner are even more explicit: "A mirror-reading [of 1:17] would imply that Paul has been criticized, or unfavorably compared with leaders like Apollos."[104] At other times mirror-reading seems to be employed unwittingly, as when Litfin, dropping the οὐκ, says, "[Paul] perceived these Corinthians as wanting him to preach ἐν σοφιᾳ λόγου, that is, in eloquent words."[105] Mihaila provides a subtler example. He argues that we can take the expression "not with σοφία λόγου" as a clear renunciation of the Corinthians' views on *rhetoric* on the basis that it appears "in the context of preaching":[106] what is implied here is that what Paul says about his own preaching can be set in direct antithesis to the Corinthian's own views about speaking, and thus their obsession with rhetoric.[107] This approach crops up also in interpretations of that small quantity of material that has been considered outside 1 Corinthians 1–4, as for example, when Winter surmises that Paul uses the rhetoric of weakness in 9:15–23 and 11:17–34 in order to counter the *sophistic* values of the Corinthians.[108] (Why they must be sophistic values remains a mystery.)

Of course, this is not to say that mirror-reading paves us a sure road to error – actually it can be both necessary and helpful, when practiced responsibly – it is simply to recognize that there is potential difference between what Paul says about *his own* beliefs and behavior on the one hand and what we can take to be the views *of the Corinthians* on the other. In this regard, Dale Martin is more judicious:

[103] *St. Paul's Theology of Proclamation*, 245; emphasis added.
[104] Ciampa and Rosner, *The First Letter to the Corinthians*, 87.
[105] Litfin, *St. Paul's Theology of Proclamation*, 193.
[106] Mihaila, *The Paul-Apollos Relationship*, 92.
[107] But Mihaila's remark implies another fallacious assumption as well: that speaking is not involved when, say, a *philosopher* presents an argument.
[108] *Philo and Paul among the Sophists*, 214ff, 252ff.

> There is no evidence that Paul is being directly attacked by anyone in Corinth at the time he wrote 1 Corinthians. He does sound apologetic sometimes, as when he defends his decision to accept no money from the Corinthian Christians. ... Elsewhere in 1 Corinthians Paul sometimes sounds as if he is defending himself, as when he says repeatedly that he is *not* using skillful rhetoric. But mock apologies and demurrals ... were not unusual in Greco-Roman speeches; they served to disarm potential critics and predispose the audience to be more favorably inclined toward the speaker.[109]

Abraham Malherbe confirms this observation in his earlier study "Gentle as a Nurse," where he demonstrates that negative and antithetic formulations were routinely employed by Cynic philosophers to distinguish themselves from charlatans, even when no specific charges had been made against them.[110]

In drawing attention to the precariousness of the mirror-reading method, I do not mean to imply that we are now forced to restrict attention to the text and what can be made of Paul's own views *within* in, and to abandon the quest for the reconstructed situation and the opposing perspectives that stood *behind* it. I simply propose that we must base our reconstructions on more secure footholds than on some notion of conjectural contrariety between Paul's expressed views and the historical realia embodied in the Corinthian church. More specifically, the approach I am proposing would involve a set of methodological principles that enable us to make more reasoned judgments regarding the difference between the Corinthian perspective and problems on the one hand and Paul's theological or kerygmatic *response* on the other. Once we come to terms with this difference, we can more fully appreciate that not everything Paul says in 1 Corinthians 1–4 can be taken to mirror the specific wisdom he finds so problematic. Rather, it becomes evident that he may begin by confronting the problem at hand – a problem that may indeed have involved wisdom of a more *particular* sort – and from there takes the opportunity to widen his assault so as to demolish human wisdom *in all its forms* (largely accounting for his varying uses of σοφία in these chapters). Thus, we begin with the historical anchors. We end with Paul's theology. My proposal is developed more fully in Chapter 3.

[109] Martin, *The Corinthian Body*, 52. For a similar argument, see Anderson, *Rhetorical Theory and Paul*, 274–5.

[110] Abraham J. Malherbe, "'Gentle as a Nurse': The Cynic Background to 1 Thess II," *NovT* 12 (1970): 204–5, 214–15, 217.

The scope of the rhetorical thesis

So far we have seen that the internal data of 1 Corinthians 1–4 admits of, and in some respects speaks loudly in favor of, interpretations other than the rhetorical one. The argument up to this point may be summarized as follows:

1. In the recent past, attempts to push the controversy seen in 1 Corinthians through a social-scientific grid structured around the ancient *relationship* between rhetoric and philosophy has led to a distortion of the internal evidence of the letter.
2. *Semantically*, wisdom/wise man terminology was used around the first century as technical language for "philosophy/philosopher," whereas rhetoric/sophist terminology was usually designated with the language of "eloquence/the eloquent."
3. Paul's discussion of wisdom in 1 Corinthians may be born out of a conflict in the community over philosophy, even if that discussion is enlarged in the course of his response in order to include *all* forms of "human" wisdom in its sweep, including that of "plausible argumentation" or even "rhetoric."

Before developing our alternative thesis, however, it will be important to advert attention to another aspect of the rhetorical argument – just how much of the letter does it claim to explain?

With 1 Corinthians 1–4, exponents of the rhetorical thesis have taken a reasonable point of departure. Indeed, there can be no grounds for locating the central factor in the church's divisions in some problem other than wisdom, of whatever kind we decide it was. That the divisions were most closely associated with this has been the consistent conclusion of interpreters from decade to decade of critical scholarship.[111]

Beyond this, whether all the issues in the letter can be traced to a common cause is doubtful. Most interpreters, however, have sought out common threads before taking recourse to the conclusion that we have a mere miscellany of disconnected topics or – worse – a pastiche of several Pauline letters. Anthony Thiselton has emphasized this point repeatedly:

> I stand by my conclusion of 1978 that the topics addressed in 1 Corinthians do not represent an almost random set of pastoral and ethical problems in relation to which Paul adopts a merely reactive stance, but that a 'systematic and coherent' dimension characterizes *both* theological themes in Corinth *and* Paul's

[111] See ch. 1, n. 1.

> reproclamation of grace, the cross, and resurrection instantiated and actualized in terms of these contingent problems.[112]

Others have concurred. Some certain thing, or a pattern of things, binds the otherwise disparate parts of the letter together.[113]

Advocates of the rhetorical thesis share this basic impulse for unity, although each has configured the data a little differently. Pogoloff notes that after 1:10–12 "the issues of the cross, proclamation, wisdom, boasting, and division remain major themes for the rest of chapters 1–4," and that the reader is "constrained to relate all these factors when constructing a narrative of the rhetorical situation."[114] Elsewhere he says that the *ethos* of σοφία λόγου is "intimately tied to issues of social status, boasting, and rivalries."[115] For Winter, the main problems Paul deals with are "status/inferiority," "imitation," and "boasting."[116] Litfin, however, deliberately limits attention to 1:17–2:5, announcing that he is in the "happy position of not having to decide" how chapters 1–4 relate to the rest of the Corinthian correspondence because he is concerned only with a single aspect of Paul's thought (i.e., his theology of proclamation). For Litfin, then, the question of the relationship of chapters 1–4 with the rest of the epistle can "remain an open question."[117]

Almost any argument, however, can be "proven" if we are selective enough with the data. Indeed, the very thing that makes Litfin "happy" turns out to be a crippling weakness for the rhetorical thesis, for when he fails to address what chapters 1–4 (or, the small selection of verses treated in 1:17–2:5) have to do with the remaining fourteen or fifteen chapters of the letter (adding to chapters 1–2), one has to wonder whether we do not simply have a case of "exegetical gerrymandering." Are parts not best understood in the light of the whole? On the other hand, while

112 Thiselton, *First Epistle to the Corinthians*, 40 (emphasis added).

113 Grosheide (*First Epistle to the Corinthians*, 16) names as unifying themes lasciviousness, spiritual pride, and abuse of Christian liberty; Fee (*1 Corinthians*, 6, 10) locates the connecting thread in what the Corinthians think it means to be "spiritual"; W. Baird ("'One against the Other': Intra-Church Conflict in 1 Corinthians," in R. T. Fortna and B. R. Gaventa (eds.), *The Conversation Continues: Studies in Paul and John in Honor of J. Louis Martyn* [Nashville: Abingdon, 1990], 131) suggests that "the most common feature" is "pride"; Ciampa and Rosner (*First Letter to the Corinthians*, 120) note that a lack of true wisdom leads to the ethical problems of chs. 5–6, 7, 8–10, and 11–14; Davis, *Wisdom and Spirit*, 145; P. W. Barnett, *The Corinthian Question: Why Did the Church Oppose Paul* (Nottingham: Apollos, 2011), 84, argues that the dominating theme is the Corinthians' refusal to recognize Paul's leadership.

114 *Logos and Sophia*, 105.

115 *Ibid.*, 54.

116 *Philo and Paul among the Sophists*, ch. 9.

117 *St. Paul's Theology of Proclamation*, 148–50.

Winter and Pogoloff seem aware that their argument is more convincing with a greater quantity of the text within its compass, it turns out that they too actually take little of the letter in hand, even *within* chapters 1–4. Pogoloff admits as much, noting in his conclusion that "the issue of rhetoric does not explicitly reappear in the rest of the letter."[118] It is for this reason that he (no less than Winter) is compelled to slip over from wisdom to *social status* after the first four chapters, as if the latter actually took center stage. When that is done, he is able to add the dispute in 11:17–34, where status-related tensions seem to be spoiling church dinners, and then a few verses where Paul is said to characterize himself as a person of weakness (9:15–23; 12:22), presumably, because his "opponents" valued those of opposite character.[119]

Of course, to a certain extent Pogoloff does get it right: we can no longer deny that social stratification was a problem in the Corinthian church, and a considerable one at that. But at least two observations come to bear here. First, it is not most clearly social status, under which fall wisdom and other problems, that *Paul* marks out as the keynote issue, but rather *wisdom*, to which are (apparently) related problems of social status and so on. On the surface, Pogoloff seems to recognize this – after all, he tells us it is the high status associated specifically with *rhetoric* that is the problem. But he would then have us reverse the order in effect, granting social status primacy and supposing that the problem of rhetorical wisdom is somehow embedded in it. What then results is a thesis so loosely constructed that it falls apart as soon as it is prodded: if social status is really the primary issue, it must be asked what point it serves to isolate *rhetoric* – as opposed to any number of other status symbols – as the chief issue involved; on the other hand, if rhetoric is the chief symbol, it must be asked why later chapters (and, one might add, much of chapters 1–4) reveal no connection with it whatsoever. Neither horn of the dilemma is grasped to Pogoloff's advantage. And so the tension becomes best ignored.

This moves us to a second point: even when Pogoloff reverses the emphasis, placing social status above wisdom rather than vice versa, we are still left with an explanation that compasses little material outside 1 Corinthians 1–4. Again, it may be that the problems behind the divisions are so miscellaneous and disconnected that no comprehensive explanation can be admitted. But other solutions should be sought before settling with a minimalist conclusion. Boasting, divisions, and social

[118] *Logos and Sophia*, 271.

[119] See *Ibid.*, 147–55, 196, 214ff, 252ff; Winter, *Philo and Paul among the Sophists*, 141.

status are only a few of the many problems touched upon in the letter. We also need to reckon with how their views on wisdom might tie in with the issues of sexual immorality (5:1–13; 6:12–20), litigation (6:1–11), abstinence (7:1–40), eating meat sacrificed to idols (8:1–13; 10:1–11:1), freedom (9:1–27), spiritual gifts and the order of worship (11:2–16; 12:1–14:14), practices surrounding their celebration of the Lord's Supper (11:17–34), and denial of a general resurrection (15:1–58). It should also be asked what *other* unifying threads these might share. Indeed, if the parts are best understood in the light of the whole, such efforts at synthesis can not be disregarded.

The said alternatives

When the new rhetorical thesis sprang to life in the early 1990s, it was presented to us as the replacement for moribund alternatives. Winter was aware that the Gnostic thesis was already in its death throes when he penned his dissertation in 1988, and thus presented his thesis as the new solution.[120] Similarly, Litfin contrasted the rhetorical thesis with contemporary treatments that "depend heavily upon the concepts of wisdom as found in the Greek mystery religions and Gnosticism, or the syncretistic Jewish-Hellenistic philosophy exemplified by Philo."[121] He allows that these other wisdom traditions may have played a part in the Corinthian exigencies, but concludes that the Greco-Roman rhetorical tradition "was eminently closer to hand and forms a sounder, more complete, and less fanciful key for unlocking the Apostle's meaning in this important passage [1:17–2:5] than these other popular options."[122]

Left with the choice between the rhetorical thesis and the older Gnostic one, on balance we should have little difficulty judging the former superior. Nonetheless, it remains curious that those who have advocated the rhetorical argument have neglected, and in some cases explicitly repudiated, philosophical wisdom as a live alternative. As we have noted, in earlier treatments of 1 Corinthians, most of those emphasizing Paul's condemnation of rhetorical wisdom either mentioned philosophy in the same breath or deemed it the leading concern. Moreover, articles and books proposing certain Hellenistic philosophical systems as the dominating "wisdom" of the Corinthians have continued to appear in

[120] See Winter, *Philo and Paul among the Sophists* (Cambridge: Cambridge University Press, 1997), cf. xiv, 245–6.
[121] *St. Paul's Theology of Proclamation*, 172.
[122] *Ibid.*, 173.

the latest decades, even if they have received less attention.[123] Here, it has been shown that, in keeping with a larger diachronic trend, the semantic scope of "wisdom" and, especially, the "wise man" in the first century fell more properly within the realm of philosophy and the philosopher than of rhetoric and the rhetorician. All said, one can only surmise that the ancient rhetoric-philosophy dynamic, as it has been framed by recent advocates of the rhetorical thesis, has played a major role in sidelining the latter element.

While Litfin is right to allow a place for "other wisdom traditions" alongside rhetoric in the background of 1 Corinthians (though he does not mention philosophy),[124] I should now like to reverse his emphasis: Paul may indeed have taken rhetoric to task in his sweeping condemnation of human wisdom, but I have begun making the case that rhetoric was probably *not* the primary "wisdom" that proved so problematic in the Corinthian church. Again, even if in certain verses Paul does single out eloquent speech over against other forms of argumentative discourse (and that may now be doubted), we still have a responsibility to determine whether that condemnation addresses the chief problem at hand, or whether it constitutes only an *extension* within Paul's larger *theological response* to it.

Therefore, if twenty years ago Litfin could say that "ignoring or slighting the rhetorical dimensions" of Paul's argument will "no longer do,"[125] surely we can now say as much for philosophy. The possibility that at the heart of the Corinthians' divisions lurked some form of Greco-Roman philosophy is a thesis that has yet to be responsibly reckoned with.

Conclusion

For all their subtle differences, Pogoloff, Litfin, and Winter have stood together in affirming that the problematic wisdom behind the divisions in 1 Corinthians was related primarily to Greco-Roman rhetoric. With these three figures in the vanguard, the rhetorical thesis has now become the dominant one in NT scholarship. It is hoped, however, that this chapter has laid the axe at this argument's root.

[123] Epicurean philosophy: G. Tomlin, "Christians and Epicureans in 1 Corinthians," *JSNT* 68 (1997): 51–72 – Cynic philosophy: F. Gerald Downing, *Cynics, Paul, and the Pauline Churches* (London: Routledge, 1998) – "Stoic-Cynic" philosophy: R. Hays, "Conversion of the Imagination," *NTS* 45 (1999): 391–412, esp. 395–6 – Stoic philosophy: See ch. 1, n. 10.

[124] Litfin, *St. Paul's Theology of Proclamation*, 173.

[125] *Ibid.*, 253.

To begin with, how scholars have transformed the *philosophical*-rhetorical thesis of the early twentieth century into the rhetoric-but-*not-philosophy* thesis of today, in which the Corinthians' wisdom is characterized as "nothing other than rhetoric," and that under the guise of a "return" to the thesis that exegetes had "consistently" posited, remains a mystery. But plain documentation reveals that this amounts to a distortion of the facts. Moreover, despite declarations that the "wise man" was the rhetorician, and "wisdom" was "unmistakeably," "overwhelmingly," or "clearly" a reference to rhetoric, a less superficial examination of first-century sources has shown not only that these terms were standard technical designations for the philosopher and philosophy respectively – in the usage of both philosophers and rhetoricians alike – but also that they apply to the latter very rarely, and then, as the evidence seems to attest, only where an attempt is being made at *re*-definition. Indeed, neither Pogoloff, nor Litfin, nor Winter provides even one example from the first century (BC or AD) in which the rhetorician was called by the name "wise man" without qualification, and together provide only a *single* example in which the title was so used even *with* qualification (Quintilian, *Inst.* 12.2.7). From the present analysis, it has become apparent that, if the rhetoricians could claim victory in the public sphere, it had come at a cost. In exchange for hegemony, they had only to relinquish their claim on wisdom. Much as Quintilian and others deplored, even actively resisted this, they bore witness that in first century acceptation, the right to the title "wise man" had been won by the philosophers. Such as it is, we would need exceptional internal evidence – nay, perhaps the complete inadequacy of a philosophical explanation – to construe wisdom in Paul's Corinth against this prevailing usage.

Equally critical, however, is the fact that the "rhetorical" thesis embraces so little, if properly any, 1 Corinthians material outside chapters 1–4. Somehow Acts 18 and 2 Corinthians 10 have risen to a greater level of importance than chapters 5–16 of the letter actually under consideration. Moreover, exponents of the thesis have remained desperately dependent on their interpretations (!) of the terminology of 1:17 and 2:1–5. Like diggers assembling the scattered remains of a skeleton, they have built up around these core pieces the finer details of the situation – evidence of "worldly" values here (1:26; 4:8), an allusion to Apollos' "eloquence" there (Acts 18:24) – until they thought they could envision a complete specimen of Paul's opponent – flesh, sinew, and all – none other than the rhetorician or sophist.

But if wisdom was in fact the leading stimulant that caused divisions to fester in the church, we should expect further connections in the letter, and if such can be afforded in some first-century wisdom tradition other than that of rhetoric, Gnosticism, the mystery religions, or Hellenistic Judaism, then we may be on our way to a better alternative. It will be my contention that such an alternative, alive and quite popular in first-century Corinth, and hereto un-refuted as an option in modern scholarship, is indeed at hand – at least in adapted form – in Stoicism. Conversely, we have seen that the rhetorical thesis has relied on an extraneous, and questionable, framework regarding the ancient relationship between rhetoric and philosophy as a way of sidelining philosophical wisdom from the discussion. But neither the affirmation that rhetoric and philosophy were "separate," nor the assertion that rhetoric was dominant in the first century, provide acceptable grounds for pushing aside philosophical wisdom as the underlying problem. Our conclusions must be based as much on a responsible, and complete, treatment of the *internal* evidence as it has been on broader sociological investigation.

At this juncture it may be apposite to circle back to what seems a telling coincidence in recent scholarly trends. As Pogoloff observes in his introduction, the rhetorical thesis owes its return in large part to the rediscovery and renewal of interest in ancient rhetoric.[126] One of the forms this renewal has taken is that of rhetorical criticism of the NT. It seems no coincidence that, only shortly after George Kennedy's seminal book *New Testament through Rhetorical Criticism* (1984) appeared on the scene, articles and essays advocating the rhetorical thesis for 1 Corinthians began to fill the presses[127] and monographs elaborating the thesis in detail were published in spate.[128] For my part, I believe that turning our gaze to rhetorical criticism has proved immensely helpful for illuminating the meaning of the NT documents, not least the epistles of Paul. However, I think we should reflect on whether we have not been so dazzled by this new light of rhetoric that we are no longer seeing clearly. Burned into our vision, handbook-rhetoric has begun to appear everywhere we turn – even where it is not.[129] In this regard, while rhetoric, or

[126] *Logos and Sophia*, 1.

[127] E.g., H. D. Betz, "The Problem of Rhetoric and Theology according to the Apostle Paul," in A. Vanhoye (ed.), *L'Apotre Paul in Personalité, Style et Conception du Ministère*, BETL 73 (Leuven University Press, 1986), 16–48; T. H. Lim, "Not in Persuasive Words of Wisdom, but in the Demonstration of the Spirit and Power (1 Cor 2:4)," *NovT* 29 (1987): 137–49; and J. R. Levison, "Did the Spirit Inspire Rhetoric?," in D. F. Watson (ed.), *Persuasive Artistry* (Sheffield: Sheffield Academic, 1991), 25–40.

[128] Beside Pogoloff (1992), Litfin (1994), and Winter (1988/1997/2002), I may mention Bullmore, *St. Paul's Theology of Rhetorical Style* (1995); and Welborn, *Politics and Rhetoric in the Corinthian Epistle* (1997).

[129] E.g., in the center of the Corinthian controversy!

the wisdom of "form," may be *included in Paul's critique* of human wisdom, I maintain that far too much has been made of it in reconstructing the occasion behind 1 Corinthians, and that as a consequence we have turned our eyes from what seems to be the more burning issue.

In closing, I should reiterate that Pogoloff, Litfin, and Winter have put together well-written and clearly – as far as recent scholarship has been concerned – compellingly argued theses in favor of a rhetorical background behind 1 Corinthians. But it should now be clear that the rhetorical argument is far more impressive in the support it has garnered among contemporary scholars than it is in the support it can find from the ancient evidence. Wherever the future of Corinthian studies lies, it can no longer be with the rhetorical thesis. That ship has now sailed.

3

METHOD

In Chapter 2 we discussed the popular opinion among recent interpreters that the "wisdom" of the Corinthians is best understood in connection with Greco-Roman rhetoric. It was shown, first, that the thesis is not, as some have claimed, a "return" to the "consistent" opinion of scholars shared at the beginning of the twentieth century, but that it rather constitutes a departure from an equal, or even dominating, emphasis on *philosophical* wisdom found in earlier studies. Moreover, the leading advocates of the rhetorical thesis have relied on a questionable construct concerning the relationship between rhetoric and philosophy in the first century as a way of sidelining the latter from discussion; have overlooked the predominance of the terms "wisdom" and "wise man" as technical language connected with philosophy, and its striking paucity in connection with rhetoric; have engaged little of the actual material in the letter, instead depending heavily on select verses (1:17; 2:1–5), on "rhetorical" descriptions of Paul and Apollos outside 1 Corinthians (2 Cor 10:10; Acts 18:24), and on generalized first-century social trends; and in all of this have essentially made "mirror-reading" their methodological starting point (again, 1:17; 2:1, 4, 13).

We now turn to the issue of methodology at greater length: Is mirror-reading an acceptable *starting point* when dealing with Paul's letters? If not, how does one pursue reconstruction of his letters, when our interpretation is almost entirely at the mercy of Paul's own, limited depiction of the exigencies? From Gnosticism to Jewish-Hellenism to over-realized eschatology, and more, reconstructions over the years have apparently remained too disparate to reconcile with one another. Therefore, in more recent decades, scholars have grown increasingly sceptical about the possibility of precise historical reconstruction. Years ago Conzelmann had recognized the difficulty when he proposed that "[t]he position in Corinth cannot be reconstructed on the basis of the possibilities of the general history of religion."[1] This sentiment is shared by scholars today more than ever, for we have seen that many at present are more apt to see the Corinthians' divisions in terms of general secular or social values, especially those associated with sophistry, than in terms of any specific religious or philosophical system.[2] The fact is that we see "through a glass darkly":[3] we can make out only outlines of what hides on the other side of the murk, and even that is subject to interpretation.

Owing to the difficulties involved in such endeavors, some have condemned interpretations which "read between the lines."[4] Most, however, remain aware that such efforts are unavoidable. Ben Witherington, among others, has been explicit on this point:

> Since we have access to Paul's letters but not to their social contexts, it is natural to give primary attention to the texts themselves. Sociological analysis of Paul's communities *requires reading between or behind the lines* of the letters to reconstruct their social contexts. Despite the conjectural nature of such reconstructions, they are both necessary and extremely valuable, especially for understanding texts like 1 and 2 Corinthians.[5]

That is, unless we remain content to confine attention to Paul's own thought rather than retaining an interest in what his thought was developed in response *to*, or wish to focus solely on what the text "means to us," we must look as much to what seems to stand *behind* the text, as to what is happening *in* and *in front of* it. In the process, however, we must lay a firmer methodological foundation than that of mirror-reading. To that end, this chapter seeks out a set of methodological principles for interpretation of 1 Corinthians. In the first part of the chapter, I make an overview of recent studies in epistolary reconstruction, looking at issues related to the use of literary parallels, the practice of mirror-reading, reconstruction of Paul's "opponents," how to identify Corinthian language, and the use of social history. In the remaining sections, I offer a

[1] Conzelmann, *1 Corinthians*, 15.

[2] Raymond Collins (*1 Corinthians*, 97) is representative: it was "the wisdom as it was taught in the rhetorical schools and exploited by popular rhetoricians." As he continues, "At best one can speak of a popular philosophical trend ... in which knowledge was highly valued and matter was demeaned"; but there were "a variety of philosophical influences."

[3] As many have reminded us – e.g., Barclay, "Mirror-Reading a Polemical Letter," 79; Hays, *1 Corinthians*, 2.

[4] Litfin, *St. Paul's Theology of Proclamation*, 167, 186.

[5] Witherington, *Conflict and Community in Corinth*, xii (emphasis added). For like remarks, see Barclay, "Mirror-Reading a Polemical Letter," 73–74; Talbert, *Reading Corinthians*, 11; and Garland, *1 Corinthians*, 13.

synthesis, which is then used to distill a set of dominating topics in the letter, from which, in Chapter 5, we shall begin a new reconstruction.

Studies in epistolary reconstruction

Context and function

The practice of using parallels from extrabiblical literature to help illuminate the NT stretches back several hundred years. Beginning in the seventeenth and eighteenth centuries, scholars began noting parallels in terminology and phraseology between the NT writers and rough contemporaries such as Polybius, Josephus, and Philo, operating with an underlying assumption that only years later would be widely recognized as problematic – that parallel language necessarily indicated parallel meaning. It was this "philological" approach that brought us Wettstein's monumental collection in the eighteenth century and the history of religions productions of the late nineteenth and early twentieth centuries.

By the mid-twentieth century, however, this approach had come under severe criticism. In his classic presidential address at the 1961 SBL meeting, Samuel Sandmel described this approach as "parallelomania," or "that extravagance among scholars which first overdoes the supposed similarity in passages and then proceeds to describe source and derivation as if implying literary connection flowing in an inevitable or predetermined direction."[6] This was not to say that Sandmel denied the existence, or even the usefulness, of genuine parallels. What he eschewed was "*extravagance*" in claims of similarity and literary dependency.

The latter half of the twentieth century contributed greater methodological clarity to these issues. In terms of *literary dependency*, at least two conclusions have come to be accepted: first, that in a world in which ideas flowed freely between systems, communities, and subcultures, and underwent unique transformation in each, *whether* literary dependence is involved in a given case is notoriously difficult to establish; and second, that even where some direct literary relationship may seem likely, it is scarcely possible to determine *in which direction* dependence ought to be construed. As part of a larger movement that began in the 1960s, the solution followed by Abraham Malherbe and his students was to remove attention from literary dependency between authors and to focus instead on *topoi* or "commonplaces" shared in the thought world of Hellenistic

[6] S. Sandmel, "Parallelomania," *JBL* 81 (1962): 1–13.

authors more broadly.[7] In that regard, rather than asking whether the NT writers "borrowed" specific expressions from particular ancient authors, scholars have begun to speak more clearly in terms of how writers may have shared and adapted material inherent to the broader Greco-Roman matrix of ideas.

In terms of *formal similarity*, it is now generally recognized that parallel usage does not necessarily amount to equivalent meaning. It *may*, of course, but that must be established on the basis of a close comparison of social and linguistic context. For Paul and reconstructions of his letters, this means that a "parallel" can only be established as such on the basis of a similar conceptual framework and plausible sociological connections.[8]

Mirror-reading

In the 1980s, yet another methodological tendency was called to account – that of mirror-reading. In 1985, George Lyons mounted a fierce attack on this practice in Pauline studies.[9] As he explained, the practice consisted in the assumption that Paul's autobiographical remarks respond apologetically to specific accusations or allegations made against himself, his office, or his message. Put differently, it assumes that "what Paul denies, his opponents have asserted and/or that what he asserts, they have denied."[10] As noted earlier, very often it works backward from Paul's antithetical "not … but" formulation (οὐκ … ἀλλά; cf. 1 Cor 1:17; 2:1, 4, 13).

Since the 1980s, scholarly evaluations of the practice have remained predominantly negative, although the extent of dismissal has varied. Hans Betz noted that "not everything that Paul denies is necessarily an accusation by his opponents."[11] Margaret Mitchell denounces

[7] E.g., A. J. Malherbe, "Hellenistic Moralists and the New Testament," and "Graeco-Roman Religion and Philosophy and the New Testament," in E. J. Epp and G. W. MacRae (eds.), *The New Testament and Its Interpreters* (Atlanta: Scholars, 1989), 3–26. We find similar approaches in Johannine scholarship of the 1960s: C. H. Dodd, *The Interpretation of the Fourth Gospel* (Cambridge: Cambridge University Press, 1968); and in Hebrews scholarship: F. F. Bruce, "'To the Hebrews' or "To the Essenes,'" *NTS* 9 (1963): 217–52; and J. Coppens, "Les analogies qumrâniennes de l'Épître aux Hébreux," *NRT* 84 (1961): 128–41.

[8] For such observations, see L. M. White and J. T. Fitzgerald, "*Quod est comparandum*: The Problem of Parallels," in *Early Christianity and Classical Culture*, 13–39; and J. Sumney, "Studying Paul's Opponents: Advances and Challenges," in S. E. Porter (ed.), *Paul and His Opponents* (Leiden: Brill, 2005), 87–94.

[9] G. Lyons, *Pauline Autobiography*, SBLDS 73 (Atlanta: Scholars, 1985), 79–120.

[10] *Ibid.*, 81.

[11] H. D. Betz, *Galatians: A Commentary on Paul's Letter to the Churches in Galatia*, Hermeneia (Philadelphia: Fortress, 1979), 6.

"mirror-reading" from Paul's self-references.[12] Others, including Lyons, reject the method altogether. For Lyons, mirror-reading constitutes "an inappropriate, if not entirely fallacious, method for identifying either Paul's opponents or the function of his autobiographical remarks."[13] Likewise, W. C. Van Unnik has declared that it seems "a wrong historical method . . . to reconstruct the unknown ideas of the Christians there [in Corinth] by reverting Paul's words to the opposite and by thinking that everything the apostle wrote was prompted by the necessity of contradicting very explicitly ideas held by them."[14]

In Lyons' favor, it must be said that many Pauline denials simply cannot be understood as answers to charges. I quote Lyons regarding several instances from 1 Corinthians:

> Is it conceivable that . . . God allows one to be tempted beyond his strength (1 Cor 10:13)? . . . Or should 1 Cor 3:7 be taken to suggest that it had been charged that God mattered little by comparison to his servants? Or does 1 Cor 1:17 require the presumption that Paul had been charged with having been called only to baptize and not to preach?[15]

Moreover, Lyons questions whether the formulation functions primarily to *deny*, or whether it actually performs the more rhetorical purpose of *affirmation*. That is, Paul's antithetical statements may be more "epexegetical" than "polemical" in purpose, serving to amplify the meaning of a point rather than to deny the stance of his opponents.[16] As such, "Paul's 'rhetoric' rather than his 'opponents' may be responsible for these statements."[17] Rhetorical practices from Paul's day confirm Lyons' suspicions: as already noted (Chapter 2), antithetic formulations made by a speaker scarcely required that specific charges had been made.[18]

Though countless others have voiced a negative estimation of mirror-reading,[19] scholars generally advocate caution rather than outright

[12] M. Mitchell, *Paul and the Rhetoric of Reconciliation* (Louisville: Westminster John Knox, 1991), 54–55.

[13] Lyons, *Pauline Autobiography*, 96.

[14] W. C. Van Unnik, "The Meaning of 1 Corinthians 12:31," *NovT* 35 (1993): 144.

[15] Lyons, *Pauline Autobiography*, 111.

[16] *Ibid.*, 120.

[17] *Ibid.*, 120.

[18] Malherbe, "'Gentle as a Nurse,'" 204–5, 214–15, 217.

[19] E.g., C. H. Cosgrove, *The Cross and the Spirit: A Study in the Argument and Theology of Galatians* (Macon: Mercer University Press, 1988), 31–38; W. Baird, "'One against the Other': Intra-Church Conflict in 1 Corinthians," 119; N. K. Gupta, "Mirror-Reading Moral Issues in Paul's Letters," *JSNT* 34 (2012): 361–81.

rejection of the practice. Indeed, for the majority of scholars today, the problem with mirror-reading is not that it constitutes an "inherently fallacious" method of interpretation, but that it leads to precarious conclusions when it is practiced "injudiciously," "incautiously," or "over-confidently."[20] This is the more balanced assessment of John Barclay in what is perhaps the most thoroughgoing treatment of the subject to date – his article "Mirror-reading a Polemical Letter: Galatians as a Test Case."[21] Acknowledging that Paul's letters are very often polemical in tone, Barclay nonetheless recognizes that if we are to understand the nature of the relevant disputes, we must make every possible effort to reconstruct the stance of those on the other side of the debate, and this from the text itself, because we have no additional witnesses to the specific occasions addressed. Hence, although the practice is problematic, it is also essential: "we must use the text which answers the opponents as a *mirror* in which we can see reflected the people and the arguments under attack."[22]

Therefore the trick, Barclay says, is to delineate criteria whereby mirror-reading might be practiced *responsibly*. Practiced *ir*responsibly, mirror-reading would involve undue selectivity (e.g., focusing only on Paul's defensive statements), over-interpretation (e.g., assuming that Paul's rebuttals were each matched by counter-statements made by his opponents), and/or the hanging of an entire thesis on dubious verbal or phraseological pegs. A responsible approach, on the other hand, would be moored by considerations such as the following:

1. What type of utterance is Paul making? Is it a statement? A denial? A command? A prohibition?
2. What is Paul's tone? Is it emphatic? Urgent? Polemical?
3. How frequently is the matter broached in the letter?
4. How clear is the meaning of the statement?
5. Is the language unfamiliar in Paul's writings and therefore likely to stem instead from his opponents?
6. Does Paul betray perspectives so diverse that we must imagine multiple opponents and viewpoints?
7. How plausible is the reconstruction historically?

[20] So Garland, *1 Corinthians*, 13; cf. Hays, *1 Corinthians*, 8; Clarke, *Secular and Christian Leadership in Corinth*, 6–7.

[21] J. M. G. Barclay, "Mirror-reading a Polemical Letter: Galatians as a Test Case," *JSNT* 31 (1987): 73–93.

[22] *Ibid.*, 73.

Taken together, it could be said that clear and frequent statements made in non-polemical contexts, and conveying atypical Pauline language, would be more likely to represent the positions of Paul's opponents than other sorts of material would, particularly if the reflected behavior or stance is plausible within the social context. Nonetheless, as Barclay points out, mirror-reading should not be made the "cornerstone" of any reconstruction. It must remain supplementary to other reconstructive considerations. Were we to follow this recommendation, we would have to exercise caution toward any attempt to reconstruct 1 Corinthians that was predicated upon Paul's "denial of rhetoric" in 2:1–5. Other considerations must remain primary.

Reconstructing Paul's "opponents"

At this point in the discussion, a terminological clarification is in order. I have been using the customary label "opponents" in speaking of those whom Paul blamed for the problems that transpired among his addressees. While this is a helpful label when dealing with many of Paul's letters, however it does not best characterize the culpable party in 1 Corinthians. Indeed, ordinarily when we speak of Paul's "opponents," we refer to antagonists who beleaguer the community *from the outside*. In 1 Corinthians, however, the agitators seem to stem from *within* the community itself. That is, they are not antagonistic *outsiders* but rather ill-behaved *insiders*. Because the methodological principles used to identify the positions of such people remain essentially the same, however, we shall continue to have recourse to the term "opponents" in what follows. Thus this label will be used as a temporary catchall, for methodological purposes, and should not be taken to imply that Paul had Christian "opponents" per se in the Corinthian church.

In beginning this discussion, a distinction needs to be drawn between "reconstruction" and "mirror-reading." The two are not synonymous. Properly speaking, *mirror-reading* is the practice of assuming that what Paul denies his opponents have asserted, or vice versa. But this is only one of several means that can be used to formulate a full picture of his opponents. *Reconstruction* – a larger category – involves the additional examination of material actually quoted from opponents, assessment of the nature of the ethical or theological problems clearly narrated or elaborated, and consideration for the wider social-historical context in which the dispute seems to have taken place.

Reconstructions have often begun by trying to identify what *types* of discourse are likely to convey material about Paul's opponents. Charles

Cosgrove proposes that the "first unit" that gives specific and direct information about the opponents should act as the starting point of reconstruction, since it is likely to introduce the main occasion of the letter.[23] Mark Nanos, taking a slightly different angle, has suggested that we begin with Paul's "situational discourse" (i.e., that written directly to the addressees, especially using ironic rebuke, so as to persuade them toward or dissuade them from certain courses of action), as opposed to "narrative discourse" (i.e., that drawn from "other experiences or stories to support the lines of argument taken up in the situational discourse").[24]

Other have sought out a more comprehensive methodology. Years ago, Nils Dahl enumerated several guiding principles for interpreting 1 Corinthians 1–4, principles that now more than three decades later, continue to resound with judiciousness.[25] His five principles may be summarized as follows:

1. The interpreter must try to understand both Paul and the Corinthian reaction to him.
2. Reconstruction must be based mainly on information contained within the relevant section of the letter (i.e., 1 Corinthians 1–4), beginning with the clearest and most objective statements.
3. The integrity of 1 Corinthians may be assumed as a working hypothesis, and can be confirmed if thematic unity can be shown to cut across chapters 1–4 to material in 5–6 and beyond.
4. Information from other Pauline epistles, Acts, and extrabiblical comparative material should not be brought in until the epistolary situation has been clarified as far as possible on the basis of the internal evidence.
5. Any reconstruction is at best a reasonable hypothesis, though the more likely to the degree that it accounts for the total argument and details within 1 Corinthians 1–4.

Years earlier, Johannes Munck, in an attempt to correct the errors of the Tübingen School, had also advocated assessing each of Paul's letters, and the occasions behind them, independently of each other.[26]

[23] Cosgrove, *The Cross and the Spirit*, 38.

[24] M.D. Nanos, *The Irony of Galatians: Paul's Letter in First-Century Context* (Augsburg: Fortress, 2002), 62.

[25] N. Dahl, "Paul and the Church at Corinth According to 1 Corinthians 1:10–4:21," in *Studies in Paul: Theology for the Early Christian Mission* (Minneapolis: Augsburg, 1977), 44–45.

[26] J. Munck, *Paulus und die Heilsgeschichte* (Copenhagen: E. Munckgard, 1954); ET, *Paul and the Salvation of Mankind* (London: SCM, 1959), 85.

More recently, Jerry Sumney has offered a lengthy treatment of methodology in Pauline reconstructions. His 1990 monograph devotes nearly fifty pages to the question of how to reconstruct Paul's opponents.[27] It will profit us here to briefly summarize his conclusions.

His first chapter on the issue ("Historical Reconstructions") concludes that (1) sources written later than the relevant letter should not be used; (2) a priori reconstructions (e.g., Baur's Peter-Paul dialectic) cannot be imposed on the letter; and (3) we cannot presume to know the situation better than the author (i.e., Paul) did himself.

The second chapter ("Sources Other than the Primary Text") concludes that (1) each letter must be interpreted individually; (2) parallels can only be established as such if they share a similar conceptual framework; and (3) parallels illuminate rather than determine the meaning of a passage.

The third chapter ("Assessing Passages within the Primary Text") is Sumney's most rigorous. It considers four kinds of contexts for Pauline statements: (1) polemical sections, (2) apologetic sections, (3) didactic sections, and (4) conventional periods (i.e., greetings, thanksgivings, hortatory material, and closings). Within each context, he considers three types of statements: (a) explicit statements about opponents, (b) allusions to opponents, and (c) affirmations. He then ranks each type of text according to both its *certainty of reference* to Paul's opponents and its *reliability* in its depiction of Paul's opponents. Levels of *reference* range from 1 to 5, with 1 constituting the highest level of certainty and 5 the lowest; levels of *reliability* range from 1 to 4, with 1 indicating the most reliable information and 4 the least. His conclusions are summarized in Table 3.

As shown, on the whole there seems to be surprisingly little difference whether the context is polemical, apologetic, didactic, or conventional. According to Sumney's analysis, what matters most is Paul's explicitness: references to his opponents can be identified most certainly in explicit statements, less so in allusions, and *least* of all in his own affirmations.

Corinthian language

When treating the question of epistolary reconstruction, several factors distinguish 1 Corinthians from the other Pauline letters. First, this particular letter includes a unique quantity of *quoted* material from the agitators

[27] J. Sumney, *Identifying Paul's Opponents: The Question of Method in 2 Corinthians* (Sheffield: JSOT, 1990), 76–113.

Table 3. *Reference and reliability according to Sumney*

Context	Type of Statement	Subcontext	Certainty of Reference	Reliability
polemical	explicit		1	3
	allusions		3	3
	affirmations		3	2
apologetic	explicit		1	3
	allusions		2	3
	affirmations		3	2
didactic	explicit		1	1
	allusions		3	1
	affirmations		5	–
conventional	explicit	greeting	1	3
		thanksgiving	1	1
		hortatory	4	4
		closings	1	3
	allusions	thanksgiving	3	1
	affirmations	thanksgiving	5	–

in the church. Second, it *names the sources* from which Paul derived this information – an oral source (1:11; cf. 5:1; 11:18) and a written one (7:1, likely delivered by the delegation named in 16:17). And third, it speaks directly *to* the agitators rather than speaking to a third party *about* them. Together, these factors allow for a much clearer and fuller picture of the agitators than is permitted with Paul's other letters, and with a rather higher likelihood that the relevant individuals are being represented fairly – since under these circumstances Paul is far less likely to have publically attributed to them words or positions that were not their own, and since his representation of them is based in large part on quotations from a letter they themselves had written.

As has long been noted, Paul's sources conveyed to him not only certain catchwords and phrases, but also a number of "slogans" in currency in the church. Because their words are not always formally introduced, however, we must rely on a convergence of criteria for disambiguating them from the distinctive voice of Paul.

In this regard, scholars have usually relied on a combination of mirror-reading and arguments from lexical usage or style. Richard Horsley remarks that the language of Paul's opponents can be discerned through noting those aspects to which he responds negatively (i.e., an argument from mirror-reading), and can be confirmed when such contexts involve language that is either absent from or relatively insignificant in Paul's other letters (i.e., an argument from style or lexical usage).[28]

David Hall treats the question in more detail. He lists five types of statements that may be suspected of interacting with Corinthian language:[29]

1. *Quoted statements*, as when Paul says that "some say" (e.g., 3:4, 18; 8:2; 14:37; 15:12).
2. *Modified statements*, as when a statement is made and then immediately modified (e.g., 6:12; 7:1; 8:1; 10:23; possibly 8:3–4).
3. *Untypical* [sic] *language*, as when a cluster of language infrequent or otherwise absent in Paul appears (e.g., 2 Cor 2:1–7; 7:8–11).
4. *Unexplained ideas*, as when Paul suddenly introduces a word or phrase that is unexplained and not immediately germane to the context (e.g., 2 Cor 6:12; 7:2).
5. *Apologetic contexts*, as when Paul defends himself (e.g., 1 Cor 4:1–5; 9:3).

These are all helpful guidelines, though some will be more determinative than others. In the end, no hard-and-fast rules for discerning Corinthian language can be devised. Instead, judgments must be based on the context of the unit under consideration, using a combination of formal, stylistic, logical, syntactical, and other contextual indicators for assistance. That is, is a particular phrase or clause explicitly attributed to the Corinthians? Does it create syntactical tension within the immediate context? Does it present logical tension with positions otherwise associated with Paul in the present letter? Does the language present a lexical or stylistic anomaly within the Pauline corpus? Moreover, after examples of Corinthian language have been clarified and a hypothesis as to the letter's occasion begins to take shape, we should ask whether other, less conspicuous examples of Corinthian language can be identified on the basis of coherence or fit with the situation, if other factors have already made such attribution likely.[30]

Finally, the opinions of commentators should be enlisted, not as a means of definitive arbitration, but as a means of confirmation on

[28] Horsley, "How Can Some of You Say That There Is No Resurrection of the Dead," 204.

[29] Summarized from D. Hall, *The Unity of the Corinthian Correspondence*, JSNTSup 251 (Continuum, 2003), 201–4.

[30] For a recent synthesis on criteria for locating Corinthian slogans, see J. E. Smith, "Slogans in 1 Corinthians," *BSac*167 (2010): 74–86.

arguments made from existing internal evidence. As we shall see, commentators share an extraordinary level of agreement on most of the language under consideration in 1 Corinthians, and we shall have little trouble establishing this material as genuine Corinthian language.

Social history

Beginning in earnest with Gerd Theissen, Abraham Malherbe, and Wayne Meeks in the 1970s and 1980s,[31] scholars began to consider whether the divisions in Corinth might have had more to do with the broader social values of the Roman Empire than with specific systems like Gnosticism or the Hellenistic mystery religions. Thus the strong emphasis on linguistic parallels that characterized much scholarship in the nineteenth and early twentieth centuries has given way in recent decades to broader social-historical considerations. Now less weight is given to comparative literary evidence focused on religious parallels and more to a combination of literary, inscriptional, archaeological, and other sociocultural data. This shift has ushered in a welcome corrective to scholarship that often showed too little regard for the particularities of social and political context. Indeed, the Corinthian church was not an embodiment of some typical Greco-Roman religious "idea," but a particular community with its own social idiosyncrasies and peculiar influences.[32]

This sensitivity to social history has shifted the direction of Corinthians scholarship considerably. We have become more aware of the potential role of social stratification in issues such as the eating of "meat sacrificed to idols" (1 Cor 8, 10) and the disorderly observance of the Lord's Supper (11:17–34), as well as of the Corinthians' apparent embrace of "secular" values such as wealth, patronage, honor – and even wisdom itself (1:26; 2:1–5; 4:8–10; chs. 5–6).[33] But perhaps most importantly, the study of social history has set much needed restraints on what kinds of

[31] Although we find rudimentary sociological analyses of 1 Corinthians as early as C. Heinrici, *Der erste Brief an die Korinther*, KEK5:6 (Göttingen: Vandenhoeck & Ruprecht, 1896).

[32] With the permission of the *Journal of Theological Studies*, this paragraph has been revised from T. Brookins, "The Wise Corinthians: Their Stoic Education and Outlook," *JTS* 62 (2011): 51–76, esp. 52. Where changes have been made, the present argument supersedes the earlier one.

[33] On chs. 8, 10 and 11:17–34, see G. Theissen, "Social Integration and Sacramental Activity: An Analysis of 1 Cor. 11:17–34," in *The Social Setting of Pauline Christianity* (Philadelphia: Fortress, 1982), 145–74. On the role of patronage, see Chow, *Patronage and Power*. On the role of social stratification in the divisions discussed in chapters 1–4, see W. Baird, "'One against the Other,'" 116–36.

interpretations can be regarded as the most probable, or even possible. As Andrew Clarke has observed:

> The problems inherent in mirror-reading the social situation ... can be diluted by using the relevant and available evidence which can place ... 1 Corinthians within its social context. The information gleaned largely from 'one end of a telephone conversation' can be carefully added to what is already known about the circumstances in order to reconstruct the other side of the conversation.[34]

In a word: for a particular interpretation of the internal evidence to be plausible, that interpretation first needs to be *possible* vis-à-vis the mores and circumstances of first-century Corinth.

Indispensible as social-historical considerations continue to be, however, I wish to register some misgivings at how this paradigm has sometimes been used. When Theissen and others made their foray into the social sciences decades ago, they did not mean to rule out "theological" factors in the Corinthians' divisions, but merely wished to *emphasize* what had long been *under*emphasized in explaining them – secular social values.[35] Many who have followed Theissen's approach continue to recognize theological factors even while placing new emphasis on other sociological considerations.[36] Some, however, have seemed to pose false dichotomies. Pogoloff states that in 1 Corinthians 1–4, "Paul is addressing an exigence of the ethical dimensions of division, *not doctrinal divergence*."[37] Likewise, Laurence Welborn says that "[i]t is a power struggle, *not a theological controversy*, that motivates the writing of 1

[34] Clarke, *Secular and Christian Leadership in Corinth*, 6–7.

[35] See, for example, Theissen ("Social Integration and Sacramental Activity," 123): "The sociological analysis of a theological quarrel does not, in my opinion, mean reducing it to social factors." So also Malherbe (*Social Aspects of Early Christianity*, 84): "The history of research does reveal a neglect of the sociological aspects of the Corinthians' problems, but it equally reveals that theological issues have been identified and explored successfully. Therefore Theissen's work provides a welcome new perspective from which to view those discussions, but it cannot be regarded as an alternative."

[36] Chow (*Patronage and Power*) notes that he "does not take theological matters to be of minor importance" (p. 12), though his express aim is to turn attention to sociological explanations (esp. pp. 133–66). Marshall (*Enmity in Corinth*) says: "Much success has been achieved in identifying the theological issues but I suggest that any such interpretation is incomplete without an adequate social understanding of the problems in Corinth" (vii). John Hiigel (*Leadership in 1 Corinthians: A Case Study in Paul's Ecclesiology*, Studies in the Bible and Early Christianity 57 [Lewiston, N.Y.: E. Mellen, 2003], 3) says: "the divisions in the Corinthian church are rooted both in secular social competition and in a theology which fostered individual spiritual ambitions."

[37] Pogoloff, *Logos and Sophia*, 104; emphasis added.

Corinthians 1–4."[38] Going farther, Ben Witherington says that "every problem" addressed in the letter, except "perhaps" the resurrection, was "social, *not* theological in origin."[39] Andrew Clarke is similar, suggesting that the Corinthians' acceptance of secular perceptions of leadership constituted the "single, dominant problem in the community," a thesis he follows throughout, but does not limit to, 1 Corinthians 1–6.[40] In tracing the history of scholarship on 1 Corinthians, Adams and Horrell observe how Corinthians scholarship has "shift[ed] in focus from religious or theological ideas to social and political ones"; however, several essays in the same volume put things in starker terms. James Dunn notes that the problems of 1 Corinthians 11 were "*not theological but social*" (his emphasis).[41] Bengt Holmberg extends this point to the whole letter: "[W]hat may look at first like theological and ethical problems and discussions are actually caused more by social factors like stratum-specific behavior patterns operative in the everyday life of these Christians than by differing religious perspectives or theological traditions."[42] Then, speaking in more dichotomous terms are Ciampa and Rosner:

> Numerous religious and philosophical parallels with the putative behavior and beliefs of the church there (inferred from a mirror reading of 1 and 2 Corinthians) have been adduced. . . . However, in recent years a rough consensus has begun to emerge in which scholars agree that the problems Paul addresses in 1 Corinthians reflect the infiltration of Corinthian social values into the church.[43]

Intended or not, Ciampa and Rosner clearly leave the impression that they regard "religious or philosophical" explanations, on the one hand, and "social" explanations, on the other, as being somehow categorically opposed.

For all they may get right, statements such as these also manifest several problems. In the first instance, they pose dichotomies that cannot be sustained in reality, depending as they do on an artificial distinction between "religion" or "theology" on the one hand and the "social" patterns of everyday life on the other. Upon more careful reflection, it

[38] Welborn, *Politics and Rhetoric in the Corinthian Epistles*, 7; emphasis added.
[39] Witherington, *Conflict and Community at Corinth*, 74n9; emphasis added.
[40] Clarke, *Secular and Christian Leadership in Corinth*, xiii.
[41] J. D. G. Dunn, "Reconstructions of Corinthian Christianity," in *Christianity at Corinth*, 303.
[42] B. Holmberg, "Methods of Historical Reconstruction," in *Christianity at Corinth*, 261.
[43] Ciampa and Rosner, *First Letter to the Corinthians*, 4.

must be said that religious values and beliefs are part and parcel of the general social systems that comprise people's symbolic universes.[44] "Theology" and "sociology" – or, as it were, "beliefs" and "behavior" – are mutually reinforcing: beliefs drive behavior, behavior in turn modifies beliefs, and the process continues in an endless dialectic. Even supposing that theology and sociology could be disentangled, it surely overstates the case to say, not simply that a problem is *more* social than theological (or vice versa), but that a problem, or indeed "every problem in the letter," is "social *not* theological" in origin. Moreover, we must not make the mistake of limiting the meaning of "theology" to abstract and systematic doctrinal speculation. Indeed, thusly understood, we may doubt not only whether the Corinthians had a theology but also the extent to which Paul had one. Is theology not, in a less limiting sense, simply a matter of how one conceives of the relationship between the human and the divine? Must that process of reflection be conscious, systematic, or a matter of intense abstract speculation in order to qualify? Indeed, the Corinthians had a theology, and they were quite moved by it, even if they could not have written books about it.

Second, these statements seem to reveal that an older error has simply been replaced with a new one: rather than reducing the divisions to "theological" differences as they were before Theissen, for many the problem in Corinth has now become "socio-economic, *not theological*" in nature.

Third, the banner of "sociology" as an explanation for the divisions could be said to constitute mere "settlement" with generic explanations in the place of more exact ones. One notices that reconstructions of 1 Corinthians have moved from specific *religious* systems such as Gnosticism or Hellenistic Judaism now to general Hellenism and broader *secular* values. To be sure, many of the texts from 1 Corinthians once thought to find their closest parallels in one of these specific systems have now been shown to reflect values shared widely in secular society. For example, references to the "well-born" (1:26), "carnal" (3:3), or "prudent" (4:10) need not be tied with the spiritual values of Philo's Judaism, or whatever, but may simply reflect the literal external values – or vices – of the secular world. It may be doubted, however, whether *secular* social values can explain all of the material found in these

[44] For a fuller proposal as to how these might be fitted together, see D. Horrell, *The Social Ethos of the Corinthian Correspondence: Interests and Ideology from 1 Corinthians to 1 Clement*, Studies of the New Testament and Its World (Edinburgh: T & T Clark, 1996), 18–22, 113–23.

same contexts – the distinction between the "spiritual" and "unspiritual" (2:6–16; 3:1–3), which seems to be connected with the Corinthians' views on spiritual gifts (chs. 12, 14), comes to mind. It may also be doubted whether this best accounts for material that seems to be more figurative in nature – for example, when Paul asks, "are you *kings*?" (4:8). And it may be doubted still *how much* of the letter this explanation can account for with a high degree of probability, without *over*generalization, and with attention to the *full complexity* of the phenomena (one thinks, for example, of chs. 8–10).

In response to these issues, several points should be highlighted. First, "social" may be a better modifier of the general values standing behind the Corinthians' behaviors than what is sometimes termed "*secular* social." Second – to hazard stating the obvious – we should expect *general* social values also to be integrated into *specific* religious or philosophical ideologies. Thus, identifying the root of the Corinthians' divisions as "social" in nature does not rule out the presence of more specific systems. Third, preferring the general explanation to the specific is only advisable if more specific explanations have in fact been ruled out – which, in my opinion, is yet to be settled. Fourth, we must reject the idea that religion or philosophy, on the one hand, and social values, on the other, are somehow categorically opposed.

In all of this, it is evident that we have been entangled in a morass of ill-defined categories. "Theology" has been pitted now against "sociology," now against "secular values," with as little regard for whether sociology might include theology as for whether there is any difference between *social* and *secular* values. The waters have been muddied still further by those who have used the term "theology" to embrace both "religion" *and* "philosophy."[45] Equivocation added to equivocation has thus allowed us to view a "sociological" explanation for the divisions as exclusive not only of a "theological" explanation, but then *also* of a "philosophical" one. We can then see how our swift careen toward "sociology" as a replacement for the Gnostic thesis has allowed us to look almost completely past Hellenistic philosophy.

In concluding this section, let it be emphasized, first, that I affirm the fact that consideration for social history remains an essential part of our task, for it provides some necessary restraints on the range of possible interpretations. In that regard, we may continue to follow Theissen, Malherbe, Meeks, Stanley Stowers, Bruce Longenecker, David Horrell,

[45] This is how Adams and Horrell (*Christianity at Corinth*, 17–23), for instance, organize the data.

and a whole host of others, who, to our great benefit, have used "sociology" to thicken our knowledge of the first-century cross-section of that broader category we call "history." However, given that methodology often constructs one's reality (confused as such a procedure is), we perhaps need to be more careful in defining what social history really is. We must regard it either as embracing all aspects of first-century life and practice, religion and all, *or* if it is thought exclusive of theology, as only one angle from which the divisions in Corinth can be viewed.[46] Otherwise "social history" as a methodological approach leads us, *as a matter of course*, to an exclusively non-"theological" set of possible conclusions, regardless of the full complexity of the issues.

Synthesis

Based on our methodological survey, we can now draw together some guiding principles for the present pursuit.

1. *Reliance on Paul.* We must continue to trust Paul as a sufficiently reliable source for what is going on in Corinth. He did not know the situation perfectly, but he did know it better than we do.
2. *Rejection of a priori reconstructions.* A priori reconstructions, such as the postulate that Paul's opponents were invariably Judaizers, regardless of the letter under consideration, should be rejected. Reconstructions must be made from within each letter, rather than imposed from without.
3. *Cautious use of mirror-reading.* It has been observed that mirror-reading lays a precarious foundation for the task of epistolary reconstruction. Assuming, as a general rule, that in each of Paul's denials is reflected a Corinthian affirmation, or vice versa, indeed involves a kind of hermeneutical fallacy. Without proper restraints, such a maneuver presents the risk of foisting upon the Corinthians views that Paul never intended to attribute to them, and that they never held. Paul's own apparent disavowal of "rhetoric," for instance (if that is what is happening in 2:1–5), need not indicate that the wisdom of the Corinthians was that of rhetoric and that rhetoric in turn was the central cause of the divisions; such a claim would need to be established on

[46] In this regard, "historical" approaches cannot be set against "sociological" ones; rather the latter serve to *broaden* our understanding of the former (so Horrell, *The Social Ethos of the Corinthian Correspondence*, 30). Accordingly, Theissen says, "The sociological perspective itself is but one among others" (*The Social Setting of Pauline Christianity*,195).

other grounds. Nonetheless, mirror-reading can still be useful, if undertaken with caution and as a tool subordinate to other means of analysis.

4. *Separation of occasion and response.* As an extension of the previous point, care must be taken to distinguish properly between the *occasio*n behind the letter, reflected in the views and language that Paul clearly attributes to the Corinthians, and Paul's own theological *response* to that occasion, in which he may expatiate more broadly.
5. *Initial sequestering of 1 Corinthians.* We must treat 1 Corinthians separately before taking recourse to evidence deemed expedient from other sources, be it Acts, 2 Corinthians, or other ancient literature.
6. *A "simple" view of the agitators.* In keeping with the spirit of Ockham's razor, we should assume only one main group of agitators within the letter *unless explanatory potential is lost in doing so.* (See later discussion on the recent consensus on the "party slogans" of 1:10–12.)
7. *Assumed unity of letter contents.* Assuming the integrity of the letter, we should be able to find unifying threads, if not an overarching explanation, for its various parts, allowing us to account not only for the material in chapters 1–4, but also for that in chapters 5–16. The more material a hypothesis can satisfactorily account for across the letter, the more likely it becomes.
8. *Preferment of certain types of evidence.* Any hypothesis should be based on the clearest, most explicit, and most objective statements Paul makes about the agitators. Where they can be identified, quotations are among the most reliable material. Topics addressed clearly or frequently, or both, are more likely to be at issue in the church than those mentioned seldom or without lucid narration.
9. *Identification of Corinthian language.* Corinthian slogans must be identified as such on contextual grounds, on the basis of formal, logical, syntactical, stylistic, and broader contextual indicators. Arguments for Corinthian vocabulary can be made from "typical" Pauline style or lexical stock and known Pauline theology, but only with due caution. A dense cluster of consistently atypical vocabulary, especially if it is related to Corinthian language already established on other grounds, is more likely to issue from the Corinthians than terms that seem atypical of Paul but that stand alone.

10. *Use of outside sources and "parallels."* If outside sources are used to help clarify the internal evidence, we must rely chiefly on contemporary sources, less so on earlier sources, and on later sources only if we have demonstrable grounds for concluding that they accurately reflect earlier thought or practice. The postulation of parallels in thought on the basis of parallels in language is only justifiable if certain conditions are met. The more selective the use of the sources and the more restricted one's focus within the letter, the more questionable the connections become. Probable connections rather rely on a "total" examination of the outside sources and the evidence provided *across* the letter. Where one finds consistency – *multiple* points of contact or *patterns* of correspondence –and within a similar social context, one is likely to have met with a genuine set of parallels. Parallels, however, are more likely attributable to a common thought world than to literary dependency.
11. *Constraints from social history.* Social-historical considerations provide the parameters for possible interpretations. Nonetheless, such considerations remain ancillary to the internal evidence of 1 Corinthians.
12. *Confirmation from interpreters.* Wide agreement among interpreters may be used to confirm, but not alone to establish, a particular interpretation that has been shown valid on other grounds.

In sum, we must deal with the internal evidence of 1 Corinthians in its entirety, first relying on the clearest, most objective, and most explicit statements from Paul regarding the Corinthians, before taking recourse to material found in Acts, 2 Corinthians, the other Pauline letters, or extra-biblical material. As already suggested, the clearest and most explicit information regarding the Corinthians is to be found in the matters specifically identified throughout the letter as areas of disagreement or doubt in the community; in the Corinthian slogans quoted by Paul; and, to a lesser extent, in allusions to and Pauline reappropriations of Corinthian language; but little, if at all, in Paul's apologetic *denials* or polemical affirmations. Only after we have dealt with this material can we broaden the scope of investigation to other NT material, extra-biblical literature, and social-history generally. We therefore turn next to an examination of the internal evidence, with primary attention to two types of data: (1) the specific problems that seem to have occasioned the letter, and (2) identifiable Corinthian slogans, catchphrases, and catchwords.

Reconstructing 1 Corinthians

Problems addressed

Following an exordium on the Corinthians' divisions and its relation to wisdom in chapters 1–4, Paul treats a number of other issues, some related to Corinthian misconduct or misunderstanding, others to queries they wanted answered, and others to both. Many of these issues certain Corinthians had brought to Paul's attention by letter (7:1). Perhaps the rest was conveyed through Chloe's people (1:11).[47] Thus, in the case of 1 Corinthians, we are fortunate enough not to have to resort to mirror-reading – from vice lists or hortatory material, for example – to identify what the issues were. In many cases Paul identifies them explicitly, either by quoting the Corinthians or by narrating their problems. We may identify the following as the issues that occasioned the letter, offering for the present as little interpretation as possible.

1. *Divisive human wisdom* (1:10–4:21). A number of Corinthians have espoused some form of "human" wisdom, which has led to boasting; this wisdom, above all else, is integrally connected with the divisions in the church.
2. *Sexual immorality* (5:1–13; 6:12–20). An unidentified man in the church is living with his father's wife, and the church has condoned it (5:1–13). Either the Corinthians, or the man himself, or both, have sought to justify lax sexual conduct (6:12–20), whether categorically or with specific reference to the case discussed in 5:1–13.
3. *Litigation* (6:1–11). Certain individuals in the church are litigating against others, relying on the secular law courts rather than settling the disputes among themselves.
4. *Abstinence* (7:1–40). The Corinthians have inquired about abstinence by way of letter to Paul.
5. *Freedom and eating meat sacrificed to idols* (8:1–13; 10:1–11:1; 9:1–27). Certain individuals have asserted their freedom to eat meat sacrificed to idols. Their judgment to do so somehow arises out of their presumed knowledge. The "weak," who do not

[47] At one time it was assumed that Paul's περὶ δέ formula invariably introduced material quoted from the Corinthians' letter to Paul. As such, the material in chapters 1–6 derived from his oral source, and that in chapters 7–16 from the Corinthian letter. However, it is now acknowledged, on the basis of rhetorical theory, that this formula may mark no more than a change of topic. On this see M. Mitchell, "Concerning *peri de* in 1 Corinthians," *NovT* 31 (1989): 229–56.

share this knowledge, are in danger of being wounded in conscience on account of the former's stance. Elaborating on these issues, Paul discourses on his rights as an apostle. He states *both* that this is a "defense" (9:3) *and* that he is setting himself up as an example for the Corinthians to "imitate" (11:1), insofar as he relinquishes his freedom for the well-being of his fellow believers.

6. *Spiritual gifts and the order of worship* (11:2–16; 12:1–14:14; 13:1–13). Paul treats various questions of church order. The assembly experiences disturbances related to head covering, prophesying, and speaking in tongues. Paul intercalates a parenthesis on the supremacy of love to the spiritual gifts of knowledge, prophecy, and tongues.
7. *Practices surrounding the Lord's Supper* (11:17–34). When the church gathers for the Lord's Supper, they are divided. Some batten themselves before others have arrived. Others are left with nothing to eat at all.
8. *Denial of a general resurrection* (15:1–58). Paul responds to those who say, "there is no resurrection of the dead" (15:12).

Corinthian slogans quoted

Paul punctuates his discussion of the aforementioned issues with several full-sentence quotations, or "slogans," from the Corinthians.[48] In most cases, attribution is easily established, whether because the slogan is attributed explicitly (15:12), or because it contains other formal markers indicative of a quotation (7:1; 8:1, 4), or because we have a combination of logical, syntactical, stylistic, and contextual indicators (see later discussion). The following texts are those most frequently identified as Corinthian quotations.

2:15 – "The spiritual man (πνευματικός) judges all things, but is judged by no one." Though this statement lacks the earmarks of a quotation and fits smoothly within its immediate context, several factors provide evidence that it was, if not in fact a Corinthian slogan, at least reflective of the Corinthian viewpoint: (1) it is consistent with and occurs amid a cluster of related, but non-Pauline, vocabulary (2:6–16); (2) it

[48] I share Smith's ("Slogans in 1 Corinthians," 82) definition of a Corinthian "slogan" as "a motto [or similar expression that captures the spirit, purpose, or guiding principles] of a particular group or point of view at Corinth, or at least a motto that Paul was using to represent their position or attitudes."

defies known Pauline thinking in implying a spiritual status distinction between two types of Christians, viz. the πνευματικός ("spiritual") and the ψύχικος ("unspiritual"); (3) Paul later implies that certain Corinthians have in fact claimed to be πνευματικός (cf. 7:40, "I think that I *too* [κἀγὼ] have the Spirit of God"; 14:12, 37, see below); (4) the statement resembles another status distinction, which seems also to stem from the Corinthians, namely that of the "strong" (or better, "knowledgeable") versus the "weak" (8:1–13).

Paul of course would not have entirely disagreed with the slogan, but he was apparently inclined to qualify it: the truly spiritual man indeed judges all things and is judged by no one, but only because he, like *all* believers, has *the mind of Christ* (v. 16).

6:12a – "All things are permissible for me." The context provides ample evidence that this assertion issued from the Corinthians. First, it is corrected as soon as it is asserted ("'All things are permissible for me,' *but* not all things are beneficial. 'All things are permissible for me,' *but* I will not be dominated by anything."). Second, it provides the requisite counterpoint to Paul's present argument that the body is not meant for fornication/belongs to the Lord/is a temple of the Lord. Third, it is consistent with the *Corinthian* claim to behavioral "freedom" evident in the near context (5:1–13), and then later in the matters of eating meat sacrificed to idols (chs. 8–10) and several other issues. Fourth, use of the first-person pronoun in 6:12b (ἐγώ), which is grammatically unnecessary, becomes syntactically nonsensical if Paul is merely qualifying his own statement: Why emphasize the first person in a qualification to a statement that was supposedly being made by the same person? The pronoun is indeed present to lend the first person greater prominence, but that prominence is intended to bring into focus a *contrast* (a common use of the explicit pronoun; e.g., ὑμεῖς vs. ὁ θεός in 1 Cor 5:12–13; ἐγω vs. σύ in Mark 14:36; ἐγώ vs. υἱοί in Luke 11:19), not between *Paul and Paul*, but between *Paul* (ἐγώ) and the *Corinthian(s)* (μοί). The negative (οὐ) is then placed next to ἐγώ – rather than, as usual, next to the verb – for the same reason: to highlight the contrast between *persons*.[49]

There is little strength in the counter arguments. Indeed, not infrequently does Paul quote material without introduction or attribution,[50]

[49] For this function of the negative, see H. W. Smyth, *Greek Grammar* (Cambridge, MA: Harvard University Press, 1956), §2690.

[50] Garland (*1 Corinthians*, 226) argues that this is not a Corinthian slogan on this basis. Though elsewhere he seems to affirm that it was; e.g., "The Corinthians understand freedom in terms of the slogan 'All things are permissible for me [6:12; 10:23]'"(p. 404), and, "Their attitude could have been bolstered by the maxim 'All things are permitted'" (p. 488).

whether that material is from Scripture (2:16; 5:13; 10:26; 15:27; 15:32; allusions in 5:7–8; 10:1–13), from the sayings of Jesus (4:8 = Matt 5:3, 6; Luke 6:20–21), or from pagan literature (15:33).[51] How much less would his quotations of the Corinthians require introduction, when the words were their own? The words are already introduced abruptly enough. Nor is it of any consequence that slogans appearing later in the letter are generally introduced with the περὶ δέ formula ("now concerning," discussed later). Indeed, the absence of the formula here seems to be in keeping with a larger pattern, in which quotations from *the Corinthians' letter to Paul*, discussed from 7:1 on, are introduced with this formula, while quotations presumably gathered from *Chloe's oral report* (1:11; cf. 5:1; 11:18) are not.[52]

6:13a – "Food is meant for the stomach and the stomach for food, and God will destroy both one and the other." If this is a Corinthian quotation, we must also answer how far it extends, for its limits are disputed. In favor of the view that we have quoted material here, it may be said, on the basis of examples already cited, that Paul is not obligated to attribute quotations explicitly, not least those which the Corinthians would easily have recognized as their own. Moreover, we know from other texts in the letter that certain Corinthians had disparaged the body: Paul says explicitly in 15:12 that some of them have denied the general resurrection, at which point their objection seems to have been related to the problem of *somatic* post-mortem existence.[53] Conversely, in a context where Paul is already pressed to convince them of the relevance and ongoing importance of the body (6:12–18), it would hardly aid his case to broach its limited range of significance ("Food is meant for the stomach and the stomach for food") and its transience ("God will destroy both one and the other"). Indeed, this would counteract his repeated insistence on the relevance of the body found not only in the immediate context (6:19, "your body is the temple of the Holy Spirit"), but also elsewhere in this letter (7:34, "holy in body and in spirit"; 9:27, "I punish my body and enslave it"; 15:12–58, the resurrection of the body; see also 1 Thess 5:23; 2 Cor 7:1). These arguments apply equally to the possibility that the quotation terminates after "food is meant for the stomach and the stomach for food": for Paul then to add an editorial comment about the imminent destruction of the physical could

[51] Consider also Douglas Campbell's (*The Deliverance of God: An Apocalyptic Re-Reading of Justification in Paul* [Grand Rapids: Eerdmans, 2009], 541–2) excursus on "multiple textual voices" and "hidden transcripts" in ancient texts.

[52] Alternatively, Will Deming ("The Unity of 1 Corinthians 5–6," *JBL* 119 [1996]: 311) sees the slogan as a Pauline parody of the Corinthian position.

[53] See the excellent summary in Thiselton, *First Epistle to the Corinthians*, 1174–5.

only weaken his case.[54] Moreover, to concede Paul's emphasis on the *body* while then ascribing to him the statement about the *belly* would drive too great a wedge between the belly and the body,[55] and would probably require a μὲν ... δὲ construction; as such:

> "For the *stomach* (μὲν) is food meant, and likewise the stomach for food, and God will destroy both one and the other ..."
>
> "But the *body* (δὲ) is not for fornication but for the Lord, and the Lord for the body."

Ultimately, the structure of vv. 13–14 provides our surest clue for resolving the question of the slogan's extent, as I believe Jay Smith has shown definitively. According to Smith's reconstruction, 6:13–14 "consists of a two-part Corinthian slogan (v. 13a and v. 13b) and a corresponding two-part response by Paul (v. 13c and v. 14)."[56] Thus, Paul responds in v. 13c to the Corinthian slogan of v. 13a, and again in v. 14 to the Corinthian slogan of v. 13b:

13a	τὰ βρώματα τῇ κοιλίᾳ, καὶ ἡ κοιλία τοῖς βρώμασιν (Corinthian slogan #1)
13b	ὁ δὲ θεὸς καὶ ταύτην καὶ ταῦτα καταργήσει (Corinthian slogan #2)
13c	τὸ δὲ σῶμα οὐ τῇ πορνείᾳ ἀλλὰ τῷ κυρίῳ, καὶ ὁ κύριος τῷ σώματι (Paul's response to Corinthian slogan #1)
14	ὁ δὲ θεὸς καὶ τὸν κύριον ἤγειρεν καὶ ἡμᾶς ἐξεγερεῖ διὰ τῆς δυνάμεως αὐτοῦ (Paul's response to Corinthian slogan #2)

Consistent with both the immediate and broader context of the letter, "Food is meant for the stomach and the stomach for food, and God will destroy both one and the other" would thus constitute a further example of the Corinthian tendency toward the subordination of the physical to the spiritual: not only sex but also matters of diet were regarded as mere matters of the body. The Corinthians could therefore boast special freedom in these things.

6:18b – "Every wrong a person commits is outside the body." Greater disagreement has surrounded this text. St. Augustine's despair that he did

[54] Against the NRSV and NIV, which so divide the material. Actually, many notable interpreters are now preferring the longer version of the slogan: e.g., Collins, *1 Corinthians*, 244–5; Wolff, *Erste Brief an die Korinther*, 1:126; Witherington, *Conflict and Community at Corinth*, 168; and Hays, *1 Corinthians*, 102–3.

[55] As Garland does (*1 Corinthians*, 230).

[56] J. E. Smith, "1 Corinthians 6:13–14: Isolating Slogans, Rethinking Soma, 'Correcting' Translations," (paper presented at the annual meeting of the Southwest Commission of Religious Studies, Irving, TX, March 10, 2012), 2.

"not know if the difficulties in this text can be completely cleared up" seems to be shared by more recent interpreters, whose solutions have multiplied with staggering diversity.[57] If the words here are Paul's, they would seem to imply some qualitative or quantitative distinction between sexual sin and other types of sin – in the one case meaning that sexual sin is in a class of its own, because it is the only sin carried out exclusively by means of the body, and in the other case meaning that sexual sin is somehow graver or more detrimental than other sins. Besides raising logical problems, however, such explanations, in all their varieties, ultimately depend on the insinuation of the gloss "other" into the Greek text (i.e., "Every *other* wrong a person commits is outside the body"). But the difficulties remain only as long as we insist on attributing the expression to Paul. An alternative, which does not resort to such an emendation, is to take the text as a Corinthian citation that, consistent again with both the immediate and broader context of the letter, bespeaks subordination of the physical to the spiritual. As such, the assertion would mean that the body is morally irrelevant: sin occurs only on the spiritual level.

The lexical context in fact provides further support for this conclusion. Indeed, most have passed over the peculiarity of the term used here for sin/wrong – ἁμάρτημα. The term appears otherwise in Paul only *once* (Rom 3:28). His usual word for sin is ἁμαρτία, which by striking contrast occurs some *fifty times within the major Pauline epistles alone*.

Thus 6:18 seems both incoherent with respect to the discursive sequence and inconsistent with Paul's preferred idiom. Along with 6:12a and 6:13a, this is better taken as a Corinthian quotation, with which the surrounding context stands in dialogue.

7:1 – "It is good for a man not to touch a woman." Across the history of interpretation this text has remained a notorious crux. On the one hand, the view that this is Paul's position could perhaps be supported with an argument from "Pauline style" – as Conzelmann notes, καλὸν (7:1) appears also in 7:8, 26.[58] Moreover, it was the virtual consensus of (later) patristic interpreters that these words were Paul's own, spoken in advocacy of an ascetic lifestyle. For a host of reasons, however, this view has not held sway in recent years. Gordon Fee remarks that, for one thing, Paul nowhere else appears to be an ascetic, whether on food, drink, or

[57] For Augustine's remarks see J. Kovacs, *1 Corinthians*, The Church's Bible 53 (Downer's Grove: InterVarsity, 1999), 100. Fee (*First Epistle to the Corinthians*, 261) notes that already in 1956 Allo could cite twenty or thirty solutions. For an overview of modern interpretations, see Thiselton, *First Epistle to the Corinthians*, 470–4.

[58] As does Conzelmann, *1 Corinthians*, 115n10.

marriage;[59] at any rate, he suggests, such a position on marriage would have been out of place for a Jewish man in Paul's day.[60]

But more can be said from the immediate context. First, the text is introduced in such a way as would mark a quotation: "Now concerning the things which you wrote about (Περὶ δὲ ὧν ἐγράψατε) – 'It is good for a man not to touch a woman.'" While, it is true that we can no longer be certain that the introductory περὶ δέ ("now concerning") *must* serve as a citation formula,[61] we should probably take it as such here, for several reasons. Indeed, the formula is the same as the one that introduces 8:1,[62] which, by unanimous agreement, constitutes a quotation of the Corinthians (see later discussion). Second, unless the statement that follows – "'It is good for a man not to touch a woman'" – is itself that "which" (or at least one of the things "which") the Corinthians wrote in their letter, then the relative, ὧν, remains undetermined, and we, along with the Corinthians themselves, are left wondering what Paul is talking about. Third, Paul does not use the term ἅπτω ("touch") in any of his extant letters, save in a quotation in 2 Cor 6:17. Fourth, the assertion promptly contrasts with the contrapuntal injunction that "each man should have his own wife and each woman her own husband" (7:2). Fifth, the assertion contradicts a biblical principle with which Paul himself is sure to have agreed: "it is *not* good (καλόν) for the man to be alone" (LXX Gen 2:18).[63] Sixth, the "concession" (συγγνώμη) that Paul mentions in 7:6 makes most sense as referring not to marriage, but to the "temporary agreed *abstinence*" of the previous verse. Seventh, Paul acknowledges that marriage is a *gift* (χάρισμα) from God (7:7), not something to be condemned with such a simple slogan as 7:1a. All said, the flatness of the initial statement in 7:1 contrasts sharply with the subtle qualifications Paul makes of it in his subsequent discussion (vv. 2–40).[64]

[59] Fee, *First Epistle to the Corinthians*, 276.

[60] *Ibid.*, 332.

[61] See n47, referencing Mitchell, "Concerning *peri de* in 1 Corinthians."

[62] The structural similarities are striking: in both cases περὶ δὲ is followed, first, by an object (relative pronoun in 7:1, noun in 8:1), and then by an epexegetical or appositive independent clause. Thus:

"Now concerning	the things which you wrote about	'It is good for a man not to touch a woman.'"
"Now concerning	meat sacrificed to idols	'We know that we all have knowledge.'"

[63] See S. J. Kistemaker, *1 Corinthians* (Grand Rapids: Baker, 1993), 209.

[64] Garland (*1 Corinthians*, 244), for instance, notes the prevalence of qualifying language like "I wish," "I do not command," "I think," etc.

For all these reasons, this text is best taken as a quotation from the Corinthians' letter to Paul, with which Paul's agreement can only have been partial.

8:1 – "We know that we [all] have knowledge." That this is a quotation from the Corinthians' letter is almost certain. To begin, the statement is immediately corrected: γνῶσις "puffs up," and the one who thinks he has knowledge "does not yet know as he ought to know" (8:2). Second, this interpretation dovetails nicely with the context of chapters 8, 10, where the Corinthians seem to have drawn a spiritual status distinction between those thought to possess "knowledge" and therefore the freedom to eat meat sacrificed to idols, and those who are ignorant of this freedom and therefore "weak" (ἀσθενεῖς) or inferior. Third, γνῶσις ("knowledge") was almost undoubtedly a Corinthian catchword. It occurs 10 times in 1 Corinthians alone, but only 13 times in the remaining twelve letters of the Pauline corpus.[65] In chapters 12–13, as in 8:2, Paul lists it among the spiritual gifts that contrast with love (12:8; 13:2, 8), indicating that the Corinthians may have seen it as a charism of sorts.[66] Once he seems to attribute it to the Corinthians explicitly ("If anyone thinks he *knows* something, he does not yet *know* as he ought to know," 8:2). Twice he says to them, "I do not want you to be *ignorant* (ἀγνοεῖν)" (10:1; 12:1). The question "do you not *know* that ..." appears no less than *ten times* in this epistle (3:16; 5:6; 6:2, 3, 9, 15, 16, 19; 9:13, 24) and only *once* in all of his other epistles combined (Rom 6:16); and not only does the syntax of this expression mirror that of 8:1, but, framed as a rhetorical question, the expression implies that the addressees have in fact made some claim to knowledge. Compare:

> οἴδαμεν ὅτι . . . (8:1)
> οὐκ οἴδατε ὅτι . . . (3:16; 5:6; 6:2, 3, 9, 15, 16, 19; 9:13, 24)

This would suggest that the quotation begins not with πάντες, but with οἴδαμεν. That is,

> Not: "We [wise Corinthians and Paul] know that 'We all have knowledge'"
>
> But: "'We [wise Corinthians] know that we all have knowledge.'"

[65] And then only six times in the remaining NT writings.

[66] For a sustained argument on this point, see P. D. Gardner, *The Gifts of God and the Authentication of a Christian: An Exegetical Study of 1 Corinthians 8–11* (Lanham: University Press of America, 1994).

Perhaps Paul could have agreed that "all have knowledge," provided their understanding of knowledge were qualified. But as it is, he seems to set himself against their claim, for v. 7 blatantly contradicts v. 1:

> "We know that we all have knowledge" (8:1)
> "But knowledge is not in everyone" (8:7)

Alternatively, it is possible that the original Corinthian slogan was "We know that we ... have knowledge," and Paul is responsible for adding the "all." If so, he would be employing one definition of "knowledge" in 8:1, and another in 8:7. Thus:

> "We know that we *all* have knowledge" (8:1; where Paul has added the "all" so that he can agree with the statement)
>
> "Your '*knowledge*' is not in everyone" (8:7; where Paul means knowledge only as the Corinthians understand it).

Whichever solution we prefer, 8:1 is one of our clearest examples of a Corinthian assertion. Certain ones have undoubtedly said, "We know that we [all] have knowledge."

8:4 – "An idol is nothing in the world; there is no God but one." 8:4 structurally parallels both 7:1 and 8:1. Περί reintroduces the topic of eating meat sacrificed to idols, broached first with a quotation from the Corinthian letter in 8:1. Οἴδαμεν plus the ὅτι recitative follows, also as in 8:1, before the assertion, "An idol is nothing in the world; there is no God but one."[67] With strong arguments for a Corinthian origin of 8:1, these structural similarities, in conjunction with the consistency of content, generate a high level of probability that the two statements introduced by the ὅτι clause here constitute Corinthian assertions as well.

Yet there are further arguments. While it is true that these statements express principles consonant with biblical monotheism and its stance against idols (e.g., Deut 6:4; 32:39; Isa 44:6), which will undoubtedly have resonated with Paul, still in the context, it makes far more sense for

[67] Although οὐδέν ("nothing") could be taken attributively (i.e., "There is *no* idol in the world"), at least two points favor the *predicative* translation. First, the attributive rendering would create an assertion that would seem to be simply false, from the perspective of both Paul and the Corinthians, for both would have affirmed that idols in fact *did* exist in the world. Second, the predicative rendering makes more sense of the contrapuntal statement made in 10:19; compare:

> "An idol is *nothing* (οὐδέν)" (8:4).
> "What do I say? ... that an idol is *anything*(τί)?" (10:19).

The question, then, is not about the existence of idols, but rather their value – a point captured by the predicative rendering.

the Corinthians to have said "an idol is nothing, because there is only one God," as a way of justifying indiscriminate eating of idol-meat, than it does for this to have been a fresh assertion of Paul. Indeed, is he not here at pains to *deter* the Corinthians from eating idol-meat, and that largely on the grounds that he finds it *perilous* to do so (10:14, 19–21)? Such statements from his own mouth could only weaken his case. More likely, these are Corinthian assertions, with which Paul could agree only with qualification.

8:8 – "Food will not bring us close to God. We are no worse off if we do not eat, and no better off if we do." This verse bears none of the structural marks of a quotation. Yet, we have a sudden shift from the third person singular to the first person plural. And once again, the citation makes more sense as a Corinthian quotation than it does as an assertion of Paul. On the one hand, it conveys a sort of indifference toward eating that countervails Paul's point in chapters 8–10, namely that what one eats matters a great deal, as regards one's relation with fellow believers (8:11) as well as one's relations with divine entities, whether Christ or demons (8:12–13; 10:19–21). On the other hand, the assertion is remarkably consistent with the Corinthian assertion of ἐξουσία ("freedom") seen not only in 6:12–13, but also distinctly highlighted throughout chapters 8–10, and most explicitly in 10:23, where the essential quotation of 6:12 is repeated. If the Corinthians have boasted the freedom to do as they wish with their bodies, for them this evidently has implications for food just as much as it does for sex.

10:23 – "All things are permissible." Paul repeats the quotation of 6:12, minus μοι ("for me"). Thus, consistent with other Corinthian slogans, 10:23 appeals to freedom in matters pertaining to the physical. In 6:12 it is sex, here it is food.

15:12 – "There is no resurrection of the dead." This statement is one of only two places where Paul explicitly attributes speech to the Corinthians apart from a conditional: λέγουσιν ἐν ὑμῖν τινες ὅτι ("some of you say that . . ."). Here we have no reason to believe that the statement is anything but a quotation, or at the very least a paraphrase, of what some of the Corinthians were in fact saying.

1:12 (cf. 3:4) – "Each of you says, 'I am of Paul,' and 'I of Apollos,' and 'I of Cephas,' and 'I of Christ.'" I treat the "party slogans" last, because most interpreters now see these as Paul's own formulations, rhetorically representing a divided church, rather than as verbatim quotations;[68] this view reaches back at least as far as Chrysostom

[68] Some agree with patristic sources (cf. G. L. Bray, *1–2 Corinthians*, ACCS [Downers Grove: InterVarsity, 1999] on 1 Cor 1:12; cf. *1 Clem.* 47:1–7) that the parties were *indistinct*: e.g., Barrett, *First Epistle to the Corinthians*, 46; Conzelmann, *1 Corinthians*, 14; Lang, *Die*

(*Hom. 1 Cor.* 3.1). As evidence, it has been noted that Paul leaves no further indication that there were four distinct parties in the church, equipped with their own theologies, nor any inkling that the named persons lent support to the putative parties that claimed them for their leaders. In sum, while the so-called party slogans are sure to depict real fissiparous tendencies in the church, we may not be able to regard them as "slogans" in the sense that the others are such. Moreover, this text represents the *resulting* community problem, and not, as the other slogans, the *underlying* problems that were aggravating it.

Such are the texts most likely to represent Corinthian slogans.[69] Over the last several decades, commentators have shown considerable agreement regarding their attribution. In 1965, J. C. Hurd tabulated the views of twenty-four contemporary commentators and found that they almost unanimously affirmed 6:12/10:23, 8:1, and 8:4 as Corinthian slogans, and a near majority affirmed 7:1 and 8:8 (see Table 4). The material from 2:15 Hurd omitted from consideration because he regarded all the Corinthian quotations as originating from the letter Paul had received from Corinth, which he thought was introduced only after chapter 6 (though the slogan of 6:12 anticipated that of 10:23). The saying in 6:18 he passed over as well. The Corinthian origin of 15:12 was never subject to question.

In effort to move beyond Hurd's earlier summary, I have undertaken it to tabulate the views of 20 more recent commentators (see Table 5).[70] In accord with his tabulation, I have found that virtually no one questions whether 6:12/10:23, 6:13, 8:1, and 8:4 (as also 15:12) represent Corinthian slogans. Furthermore, a majority are now taking 7:1 and 8:8

Briefe an die Korinther, 20–21; Collins, *First Corinthians*, 73, 81; Lindemann, *Der erste Korintherbrief*, 39; Helmut Koester, "The Silence of the Apostle," in *Urban Religion in Roman Corinth*, 342; Keener, *1–2 Corinthians*, 24 – Others say there were no parties at all: e.g., Munck, "Menigheden uden Partier"; Fee, *First Epistle to the Corinthians*, 5, 47, 59; Horsley, *1 Corinthians*, 44 – Mitchell (*The Rhetoric of Reconciliation*, 84) says that the slogans of 1:12 merely caricature childish behavior – Still others say that there were parties, though apart from the consent of the leaders named: e.g., Hering, *The First Epistle of Saint Paul to the Corinthians*, 5. For a summary of the current consensus, see Garland, *1 Corinthians*, 50–51. Stanley Porter ("Paul of Tarsus and His Letters," in S. E. Porter [ed.], *Handbook of Classical Rhetoric* [Leiden: Brill, 2001], 582) identifies the slogans as an example of *sermocinatio*, or the practice of speaking dramatically in the first person for someone else, and for rhetorical purposes, attributing to the represented person language that is appropriate to his or her character.

[69] A couple of others have been proposed over the years – i.e., 11:19; 14:33b-34; 15:19 – but these have, rightly, never been widely entertained.

[70] Included are those of Barrett, Lietzmann, Conzelmann, Fee, Senft, Schrage, Witherington, Murphy-O'Connor, Collins, Hays, Horsley, Kremer, Wolff, Lang, Lindemann, Thiselton, Talbert, Garland, Fitzmyer, and Ciampa and Rosner. See also Smith's tabulation ("Slogans in 1 Corinthians," 88fig2) of modern biblical translations and their signaling of Corinthian slogans.

Table 4. *Corinthian slogans according to commentators up to 1965*

Verse	Corinthian Slogan	Not Corinthian Slogan
6:12/10:23	22	2
6:13	15	9
7:1	10	14
8:1	24	0
8:4	19	5
8:8	10	14

Table 5. *Corinthian slogans according to commentators from 1965 to the present*

Verse	Corinthian Slogan	Not Corinthian Slogan
2:15	5	15
6:12	19	1
6:13/10:23	18	2
6:18	6	14
7:1	17	3
8:1	20	0
8:4	20	0
8:8	12	8
15:12	20	0

as Corinthian as well – 17 for the one and 12 for the other. Although passed over by Hurd, 2:15 and 6:18 have also begun to receive a fair amount of support – 5 and 6, respectively.

Commentators are representative of recent interpreters generally. Verses 6:12/10:23; 6:13; 8:1; 8:4; and 15:12 are virtually unquestioned as Corinthian slogans. Verses 6:18 and, to an even greater extent, 8:8 command a great deal of support, though not a unanimous consensus.[71]

[71] Besides the commentaries already tabulated, see, for example, on 6:18: R. L. Omanson, "Acknowledging Paul's Quotations," *BT* 43 (1992): 201–13; L. Morris, *The First Epistle of Paul to the Corinthians*, TNTC (London: Tyndale, 1985), 103; J. Murphy-O'Connor, "Corinthian Slogans in 1 Cor 6:12–20," *CBQ* (1978): 391–6; C. F. D. Moule, *An Idiom Book of New Testament Greek* (Cambridge: Cambridge University Press, 1959), 196–7; M. E. Thrall, *The First and Second Letters of Paul to the Corinthians*

And almost all agree that 2:15 picks up Corinthian language, even if it is not an actual slogan (see later discussion).

In the light of our analysis and accompanying tabulation of interpreters, it is now possible to state some tentative conclusions. For most of the texts in question, Corinthian attribution can be established with a high level of probability on the basis of the immediate context alone. In other cases, we have suggestive contextual indicators, but also rely to some extent on support from our more secure fixtures. Therefore, we should keep in mind that our initial judgments are based largely on immediate logical and structural indicators in the text; probability may increase for particular texts once we consider additional catchwords and -phrases, discussed later, and as an overarching thesis begins to take shape.

Most probable. Verses 6:12, 13; 7:1; 8:1, 4; 15:12 reflect Corinthian slogans almost without question. Verses 7:1, 8:1, and 8:4 share structural indicators that seem to indicate quotations, and 15:12 is explicitly introduced as Corinthian material. Moreover, all six texts arguably reflect a departure from Pauline style or thought, a contradiction with the discursive flow of Paul's present argument, a closer affinity with the apparent Corinthian position, or some combination of these. And in all cases, it can be said, based on *actual calculation*, that an overwhelming majority of commentators has confirmed our judgment.

Probable. Though 6:18 and 8:8 involve no telltale structural signs of quotation, they pose enough tension with Paul's own logic or perspective, and cohere closely enough with texts that we have seen are more certainly of Corinthian origin, to establish a level of high probability that they too represent Corinthian slogans. Verse 6:18 offers the added, arresting evidence of un-Pauline terminology for an otherwise dominating Pauline concept (ἁμάρτημα for ἁμαρτία). We have, in any case, seen that formal introduction is not required, for almost everyone has accepted 6:12 and 6:13 as Corinthian without it. Moreover, 6:18 and 8:8 have

(Cambridge: Cambridge University Press, 1965), 49; R. Kempthorne, "Incest and the Body of Christ: A Study of 1 Corinthians 6.12," *NTS* 14 (1967–68): 568–74; R. E. Brown, *An Introduction to the New Testament*, ABRL (New Haven; London: Yale University Press, 1997), 527; J. E. Smith, "The Roots of a 'Libertine' Slogan in 1 Cor 6:18," *JTS* 59 (2008): 63–95 – on 8:8: J. Murphy-O'Connor, "Food and Spiritual Gifts in 1 Cor. 8:8," *CBQ* 41 (1979): 297; Gardner, *The Gifts of God and the Authentication of a Christian*, 48; Morris, *The First Epistle of Paul to the Corinthians*, 128; Khiok-Khing Yeo, *Rhetorical Interaction in 1 Corinthians 8–10*, BibIntMon 9 (Leiden: Brill, 1995), 192–3; J. Fotopoulos, "Arguments Concerning Food Offered to Idols: Corinthian Quotations and Pauline Refutations in a Rhetorical *Partitio* (1 Corinthians 8:1–9)," *CBQ* 67 (2005): 618; Campbell, *The Deliverance of God*, 541; Michael Lakey, *Image and Glory of God*, 80; Thiselton (*First Epistle to the Corinthians*, 647) lists eight further writers who support this view of 8:8.

increasingly been regarded as Corinthian slogans within the last thirty years of interpretation.

Possible. The two remaining texts, 1:12 (cf. 3:4) and 2:15, can be said with some confidence to reflect the Corinthian viewpoint, if not their actual words. Verse 1:12 is less important for our purposes because it encapsulates the community problem itself rather than the perspectives or behaviors underlying it. Verse 2:15 is difficult because it lacks the formal earmarks of a quotation and seems to express a thought with which Paul would in a certain respect have agreed; as such, it could simply be an assertion of Paul. Nonetheless, 2:6–16 abounds with terminology and accompanying ideas uncharacteristic of the apostle, and, from other material in the letter, we have good reason to believe that certain Corinthians did style themselves "spiritual" in a sense meant to set them apart from the "unspiritual." All of this renders it likely that *either* 2:15 is a simple Corinthian slogan which Paul has repeated, *or* he has appropriated a Corinthian slogan and either conceded it to the Corinthians tongue in cheek or filled it with new content in the light of his own thinking. We shall revisit this question further below.

Other Corinthian language

Besides the full-sentence slogans just examined, 1 Corinthians also preserves several terms or phrases that seem to have been in currency among the Corinthians.

Σοφία and *σοφός*. As already noted, interpreters have long understood "wisdom" (σοφία) to be the principal factor that stimulated divisions in the church. The term σοφία appears already *16 times* in the first *three chapters* of the letter,[72] but only *11 times* in the remaining *twelve letters* of the Pauline corpus. Given the centrality and frequency of the word, and Paul's singularly negative evaluation of it in 1 Corinthians (he speaks positively of it elsewhere), we can reasonably conclude that it was in popular usage in Corinth.

It would be a mistake, however, to read Paul's every negative usage *as a photo-negative of the Corinthian understanding of the concept*. Undoubtedly Paul expatiates on the notion in a way that moves beyond the Corinthian usage, widening his assault so as to demolish not only the Corinthians' brand of wisdom but also "human wisdom" in all its varieties.

[72] The complete list of its occurrences in 1 Corinthians is as follows: 1:17, 19, 20, 21 (x2), 22, 24, 30; 2:1, 4, 5, 6 (x2), 7, 13; 3:19; 12:8.

The centrality of the theme of wisdom in Corinth is thrown into relief by Paul's repeated use of σοφός, or "wise" person.[73] The term appears either as an adjective or as a substantive no less than 11 times in 1 Corinthians – more than twice as often as it appears in the rest of the Pauline corpus together, and more frequently than it occurs in the entire NT outside 1 Corinthians. At least twice Paul implies that the Corinthians have applied the label to themselves, using either a conditional or a leading rhetorical question: "If anyone among you thinks himself wise (σοφὸς) . . . " (3:18); and "Is there no wise man (σοφός) among you who is able to judge between his brothers?" (6:5). And twice he inserts the term into OT citations, where apparently no text type originally included it (3:19/Job 5:13; 3:20/Ps 93:11).

That σοφία and σοφός were Corinthian catchwords is often noted by interpreters explicitly,[74] but it is always assumed in actual analysis. Along with the consensus, we may conclude with a high degree of confidence that both σοφία and σοφός were catchwords in Corinth, and that certain Corinthians considered themselves "wise men" possessed of extraordinary "wisdom."

Γνῶσις. This term appears more often in the Corinthian correspondence (16 times) than it does in the entire remainder of the NT (15 times).[75] Moffatt observes that, chronologically speaking, 1 Corinthians is the first NT writing to use the word.[76] Moreover, we have already seen that it appears in 8:1 – which is almost certainly a Corinthian slogan – and that it plays a central role in the debate over eating in chapter 8. We have also noted that Paul classes it among the spiritual gifts (12:8), subordinates it to love (13:2, 8), and all but says that the Corinthians have predicated it of themselves ("If anyone thinks he has knowledge," 8:2). Interpreters agree: γνῶσις was undoubtedly a special word for the Corinthians.[77]

Λόγος. In terms of sheer numerical comparison, λόγος is a rather unexceptional word in 1 Corinthians. It does occur nine times in the first four chapters of the letter,[78] but it is equally frequent in most of the

[73] Found in 1:19, 20, 25, 26, 27; 3:10; 3:18 (x2), 19, 20; 6:5.

[74] Publications affirming this explicitly include, for example: *TDNT* 7:522; Barrett, *The First Epistle to the Corinthians*, 60, Conzelmann, *1 Corinthians*, 37; Fee, *The First Epistle to the Corinthians*, 48; Barclay, "Thessalonica and Corinth," 61; Finney, *Honour and Conflict in the Ancient World*, 80.

[75] It occurs in 1 Corinthians in 1:5; 8:1 (x2), 7, 10, 11; 12:8; 13:2, 8; 14:6.

[76] Moffatt, *First Epistle of Paul to the Corinthians*, 6.

[77] E.g., Fee, *First Epistle to the Corinthians*, 39, 367; Barclay, "Thessalonica and Corinth," 61; and Winter, *Philo and Paul among the Sophists*, 184.

[78] The complete list of its occurrences in 1 Corinthians is as follows: 1:5, 17, 18; 2:1; 2:4 (x2), 13; 4:19, 20; 12:8 (x2); 14:9, 19 (x2), 36; 15:2, 54.

NT letters, Pauline and non-Pauline. Its uniqueness in this letter derives from how it is *combined* with other Corinthian concepts. On one occasion it is conjoined with γνῶσις (1:5); six times, however, it is conjoined with σοφία (1:17; 2:1, 4 [x2], 13; 12:8). This latter combination, together with Paul's repeated repudiation of "wisdom of argumentation/word," has led many to conclude that the combination σοφία λόγου might have been a Corinthian catchphrase.[79]

"Freedom" language. Evidently, the problems in Corinth involved abusive claims of "freedom." In treating these abuses, Paul employs an array of cognate terminology, including ἔξεστιν, ἐξουσία, ἐξουσιάζω, ἐλεύθερος, and ἐλευθερία. That the Corinthians had made use of some of these is hardly to be doubted. We have already noted that ἔξεστιν appears in the Corinthian slogan of 6:12. Verse 8:9 implies that they have used ἐξουσία as well, for Paul speaks there of "that freedom (ἐξουσία) of yours." Together these terms appear in almost every major issue in the letter. In sum, while we may be unable to determine whether the Corinthians had used *all* of these terms, the conclusion that, in their assertions of freedom, they had made use of some of them can be established beyond reasonable doubt.

Contrasts in 2:6–16, 3:1–3. These verses involve a series of contrasts that seem to have been employed by the Corinthians.[80]

πνευματικός	ψύχικος
τέλειος	νήπιος
	[σάρκινος]

That Paul is repeating Corinthian terminology here is suggested by several pieces of evidence. First, 2:6–16, just as 2:15 earlier, appears to promote a system of spiritual elitism nowhere else articulated by Paul: that wisdom is only for the "perfect," that the "spiritual man" alone can fathom the deep things of God, and that he is exempt from the judgment of others, all imply, in the presence of contrasting terms (ψύχικος, νήπιος, σάρκινος), a spiritual hierarchy uncharacteristic of Pauline thought. Second, the terms themselves are exceptionally rare in the NT, and in Paul in particular. Πνεύματικος is attributed to a person on only one other occasion in the NT (Gal 6:1, where the reference *could* be ironic); τέλειος appears elsewhere in Paul, though almost as infrequently; outside

[79] Grosheide, *Epistle to the Corinthians*, 41; Fee, *First Epistle to the Corinthians*, 64; Lindemann, *Der erste Korintherbrief*, 43; Fitzmyer, *1 Corinthians*, 148.

[80] Πνευματικός and ψύχικος (cf. 2:13 [x2], 14, 15; 3:1; 9:11; 10:3; 10:4 [x2]; 12:1; 14:1, 37; 15:44, 46); τέλειος and νήπιος (cf. 2:6–3:3; 13:10, 11; 14:20); σάρκινος (3:1).

1 Corinthians, ψύχικος is attributed to a person only in Jude 19; νήπιος and σάρκινος are equally rare. Third, although appearing nowhere else in the Pauline corpus, the τέλειος-νήπιος contrast emerges still two further times in 1 Corinthians (13:10–11; 14:20), once in reference to the Corinthians themselves (14:20). Fourth, that the most frequent and overt contrast, πνευματικός versus ψύχικος, is paralleled in no extant literature prior to 1 Corinthians – Jewish, Christian, or otherwise – and only here in Paul, suggests that it is probably a new coinage.[81] In that regard, we should also note that Paul later seems to place πνευματικός in the Corinthians' very mouths ("Anyone who claims to be ... spiritual [πνευματικός] ... " 14:37; cf. 14:12, "since you are zealots for spiritual things," ἐπεὶ ζηλωταί ἐστε πνευμάτων). Fifth, all of these terms (minus σάρκινος) reemerge in contexts where Paul is at pains to check the Corinthians' overemphasis on the spiritual, or to correct their de-emphasis on the physical (cf. 13:10, 11; 14:20; 15:44, 46) – which again would suggest that they were thinking of themselves as "spiritual," "mature," or perhaps beyond the paltry matters of the body. For all of these reasons, most interpreters have concluded that, in 2:6–3:3, Paul picks up this Corinthian language for the sake of argument, but adapts it to his own purposes.[82]

Contrast between the knowledgeable and the "weak." In 1 Corinthians 8, 10 we find a contrast between the person who has "knowledge" and the person who is said to be ἀσθενῆς, or "weak."The contrast is starkest in 8:10–11: "If someone sees *you who have knowledge* (σὲ τὸν ἔχοντα γνῶσιν) eating in the temple of an idol, will not the conscience of *the person who is weak* (ἀσθενοῦς) be encouraged to eat idol meat? In that case, *the weak person* (ὁ ἀσθενῶν) is destroyed by your *knowledge* (γνώσει)." We have already noted that γνώσις was a Corinthian catchword. While the term "weak" could have been Paul's own formulation,

[81] Horsley, *1 Corinthians*, 57.

[82] E.g., Moffatt, *First Epistle of Paul to the Corinthians*, 25; Funk, "Word and Word in 1 Cor 2:6–16," 300n107; J. D. G. Dunn, "1 Corinthians 15:45 – Last Adam, Life-Giving Spirit," in B. Lindars and S. S. Smalley (eds.), *Christ and Spirit in the New Testament: Studies in Honour of Charles Francis Digby Moule* (Cambridge: Cambridge University Press, 1973), 129; Conzelmann, *1 Corinthians*, 58; Fee, *First Epistle to the Corinthians*, 99–100, 737, 779, 785; Barclay, "Thessalonica and Corinth," 61; Wolff, *Die erste Brief des Paulus an die Korinther*, 63; Hays, *1 Corinthians*, 42; Collins, *1 Corinthians*, 124, 128–9, 136, 139–40; Horsley, *1 Corinthians*, 57–61; Thiselton, *First Epistle to the Corinthians*, 224; Talbert, *Reading Corinthians*, 18; Fitzmyer, *1 Corinthians*, 183; Garland, *1 Corinthians*, 153, 558 (cf. 93–94, 107, 735); cf. Lightfoot, *Notes on the Epistles of St. Paul*, 174; Senft, *La Premiere Epitre de Saint Paul aux Corinthiens*, 48, 54; Schrage, *Der erste Brief an die Korinther*, 1:240–1; Kremer, *Der erste Brief an die Korinther*, 57–62, 67; Finney, *Honour and Conflict in the Ancient World*, 100.

seeing that the first term, "knowledge," belonged to the Corinthians, that there were divisions in the church, and that they had chiefly to do with wisdom and knowledge, it would seem natural to infer that those who ostensibly possessed this knowledge were in fact disparaging those who did not. We could then reasonably suppose that "weak" was the term they had used to do so. No more can be said with certainty. Nonetheless, that both terms and not just the first one belonged to the Corinthians seems to be taken for granted by most interpreters.[83]

"Rich ... kings." One further text deserves mention. In 4:8, Paul formulates two clauses as if they reflected indirect discourse: "Are you already rich (ἐπλουτήσατε)? Are you already kings (ἐβασιλεύσατε)?" He follows in v. 10 with a series of contrasting predicates, one set characterizing the Corinthians (φρόνιμοι, ἰσχυροί, ἔνδοξοι), the other himself (μωροί, ἀσθενεῖς, ἄτιμοι). Inasmuch as 4:8 is framed in terms of implied indirect discourse, I am inclined to take the language of Paul's rhetorical questions as that of the Corinthians themselves, but my reasons for doing so become more apparent in Chapter 5. In terms of 4:10, we may not be able to take these predicates as Corinthian language, but we will not go astray in taking them as an accurate depiction of the Corinthians' self-understanding.

With a high degree of confidence, we can add most of this terminology to the Corinthian language encapsulated in the slogans discussed earlier. It is *most probable* that the Corinthians' catchwords included σοφία, σοφός, γνῶσις, perhaps a variety of terms for "freedom," and a contrast between the πνευματικός ("spiritual") and ψύχικος ("unspiritual") person. It is now worth adding that most of these are implicitly attributed to the Corinthians at key points in the letter, using a consistent formula:

> "If anyone thinks he is wise [σοφός] ..." (3:18)
>
> "If anyone thinks he knows [ἐγνωκέναι] something ..." (8:2)
>
> "If anyone thinks he is spiritual [πνευματικός] ..." (14:37)

If λόγος too was a catchword, it needs to be understood in connection with, and probably in subordination to, σοφία and σοφός, given the

[83] Representative are W. Meeks, *First Urban Christians: The Social World of the Apostle Paul* (New Haven: Yale University Press, 1983), 179; S. K. Stowers, "Paul on the Use and Abuse of Reason," 276; Malherbe, "Determinism and Free Will in Paul," 235; Collins, *1 Corinthians*, 326; and J. Fotopoulos (*Food Offered to Idols in Roman Corinth: A Socio-Rhetorical Reconsideration of 1 Cor 8:1–11:1*, WUNT 2:151 [Tübingen: Mohr Siebeck, 2003], 188–90), who provides a list of predecessors who agree as well. Though some, such as Garland (*1 Corinthians*, 353–95), believe the distinction was a hypothetical one introduced by Paul.

greater predominance and independence of the latter two and the frequent conjunction of these with λόγος. The fact that the contrast between τέλειος and νήπιος is analogous to that between πνευματικός and ψύχικος, appears in the same passages, is equally anomalous in Paul, and is elsewhere in the letter applied to the Corinthians renders it *probable* that this too was a Corinthian contrast. Finally, it remains at the very least *possible* that certain Corinthians were claiming to be "rich" and "kings," since Paul attributes this language to them indirectly, although in combination with considerations to be discussed later, we may very well take it as a *probable* reflection of their very words.

Conclusions on Corinthian language

Interpreters have long been aware that Paul quotes the Corinthians throughout the letter. If reconstruction should be based first and foremost on material that gives the most objective and explicit information about Paul's opponents – or, in our case, agitators – then these quotations are of cardinal importance.

Of course, the matter is not entirely cut and dry, for not only do some of these quotations lack formal markers, but some of them also voice perspectives with which Paul might to some extent have agreed. Despite these complications, however, it can be said that 1 Corinthians affords us with information about the troublemakers that is, among Paul's letters, quantitatively and qualitatively unique. Through a combination of written and oral sources, Paul has been apprised of catchwords and catchphrases as well as of a number of (verbatim?) slogans in currency among the Corinthians. For us, these remain some of the most explicit – if not *the* most explicit – indicators of the Corinthians' views, even if attribution is not in every case definitively clear. Paul of course does not set off these slogans with inverted commas, as if to anticipate a later audience, not privy to attributions that the Corinthians would have had no trouble making. Nonetheless, we have seen that several slogans are surrounded by telling formal markers, and that all of the candidates identified present enough tension with Paul's argument, style, or thought to establish Corinthian attribution with some confidence. Indeed, in almost every case, an impressive majority of commentators has confirmed our conclusions.

It should be reiterated that we have examined these texts more or less as autonomous units (as we should always begin, if we wish to avoid selective or procrustean procedures), divorced from the clarifying light of an overarching thesis. Such an approach allows us to identify "anchor" texts that can be identified as representative of the Corinthian viewpoint on almost independent merits, before turning to arguments from data coherence. These foundational texts may then be used to moderate how we understand those of less certain origin. Thus, our certainty that texts such as 2:15, 4:8, 6:18, and 8:8 reflect the views of the Corinthians, whether in spirit or to the letter, may solidify as we build our thesis on the bedrock of firmer examples such as 6:12, 6:13, 8:1, 8:4, and 15:12, and the community problems clearly spelled out in the letter.

We can now summarize our discussion of Corinthian language as follows:

Most probable
"wisdom" (σοφία)
"wise man" (σοφός)
"knowledge" (γνῶσις)
"spiritual" vs. "unspiritual" (πνευμάτικος vs. ψύχικος)
"freedom" language (a variety of terms)
"All things are permissible for me." (6:12)
"Food is meant for the stomach and the stomach for food, and God will destroy both one and the other." (6:13)
"It is good for a man not to touch a woman." (7:1)
"We know that we [all] have knowledge." (8:1)
"An idol is nothing in the world; there is no God but one." (8:4)
"All things are permissible." (10:23)
"There is no resurrection of the dead." (15:12)

Probable
"perfect" vs. "immature" (τέλειος vs. νήπιος)
"weak" (ἀσθενῆς) vs. "knowledgeable" (cf. γνῶσις)
"Every wrong a person commits is outside the body." (6:18)
"Food will not bring us close to God. We are no worse off if we do not eat, and no better off if we do." (8:8)
["word/argument/reason" (λόγος)]
["The spiritual man judges all things, but is judged by no one." (2:15)]
["rich . . . kings" (4:8)]

Possible
["word/argument/reason" (λόγος)]
["The spiritual man judges all things, but is judged by no one." (2:15)]
["rich . . . kings" (4:8)]

Besides the "explicit" information supplied from quoted Corinthian language, it has been said that we can rely on the foundation of the explicit and, in general, *transparent* information conveyed from Paul's discussion of the various issues mentioned in the letter. In this regard, we have identified the following:

1. *Divisive human wisdom* (1:10–4:21)
2. *Sexual immorality* (5:1–13; 6:12–20)
3. *Litigation* (6:1–11)
4. *Abstinence* (7:1–40)
5. *Freedom and eating meat sacrificed to idols* (8:1–13; 10:1–11:1; 9:1–27)
6. *Spiritual gifts and the order of worship* (11:2–16; 12:1–14:14; 13:1–13)
7. *Practices surrounding the Lord's Supper* (11:17–34)
8. *Denial of a general resurrection* (15:1–58)

Recurring domains

It is on these two pegs – quoted Corinthian language and the behavioral or ideological problems elaborated in the major units of the letter – that we can begin to hang a thesis. These problems, together with identifiable Corinthian language, lay bare a number of recurring topical domains that must be said to have appertained to the *Corinthian* position, and not simply *Paul's* theological response or personal apology. These topics include:

1. *Wisdom and the wise man.* This topic, and its relation to the divisions, stands front and center in chapters 1–4. It seems to bear some relation to personal status and boasting (also important themes in this section), as well as to λόγος (perhaps *qua* rational speech or argumentation), and to γνῶσις, which becomes salient from chapter 8 onward.

2. *A strong emphasis on freedom.* Finding expression with an array of terminology (i.e., ἔξεστιν, ἐξουσία, ἐξουσιάζω, ἐλεύθερος, ἐλευθερία), an appeal to freedom or individualism underlies the justification of loose sexual conduct in 5:1–13 and 6:12–20, of sexual abstinence in chapter 7, and of lax dietary practices in chapters 8, 10, and seems to play some role in the divisions that beset the church's assemblies for worship (11:2–16; chs. 12, 14) and their meetings for the Lord's Supper (11:17–34).
3. *The notion of "indifference."* The Corinthian cry for freedom is apparently shored up by a principle of "indifference" applied toward material reality: as contingencies of the physical realm, matters of food and the human body have become morally irrelevant. As such, whether we "eat or do not eat," and so forth, is treated as a matter of indifference (cf. 6:13, 18; 8:8).
4. *Subordination of the physical to the spiritual/intellectual.* The previous two items relate closely with a Corinthian tendency toward "dualism." If for the Corinthians the physical realm was inferior to the spiritual/intellectual, not only would food and bodily matters have become morally irrelevant (6:12a, 18a; 8:8), but the Corinthians may no longer have been able to accept the notion of a somatic post-mortem existence – thus also their denial of a bodily resurrection, as seen in chapter 15.
5. *Contrasting intellectual/spiritual status indicators.* The Corinthian "wise" seem to have thought of themselves as "spiritual," "perfect," or "knowledgeable" over against the "unspiritual," "immature," or "weak" (2:6–16; chs. 8, 10). Moreover, if they thought of their wisdom and spiritual achievement as that which set them apart from their more jejune counterparts, this could also explain their charismatic fervor, against which Paul inveighs in chapters 12–14.

While I have no intention of *reducing* the church's problems to these five domains, it is evident that these topics – which obviously overlap with each other conceptually – suffuse most of the material found in the letter. It should also be noted that several of these topics may be operative in certain issues only beneath the surface, so that they are not immediately obvious. For instance, the possible effacement of gender distinctions at play in the issue of head covering and hair length (11:2–16) may very well relate to the over-spiritualizing tendency inherent in items (4) and (5); and the inappropriate consumption of the elements of the Lord's Supper may easily have gained impetus from (3) or (4). As I argue in Chapter 5, the single remaining issue in the letter (6:1–11) could have been influenced, at least in part, by some of the same tendencies.

If the parts are best understood in the light of the whole, then our present efforts to formulate a topical synthesis *on the basis of all the issues and Corinthian language identifiable in the letter* should enable greater precision in reconstructing the letter's background than attempts that are more compartmentalized in focus.

Conclusion

In this chapter, we have aimed to devise a set of methodological principles for use in reconstructing the background behind 1 Corinthians. It was concluded that our most reliable information about the Corinthian perspective is to be gleaned not primarily from mirror-reading, nor even – initially – from social history, but by dual attention to quoted Corinthian language – which can be identified with varying levels of probability – and to the *pattern* of the problems discussed throughout the *whole* of the letter. In this regard it was emphasized that "parallels" with the Corinthian perspective can be established only on the basis of *multiple points of contact, consistency*, and larger *patterns* of congruency.

This information was then distilled into a set of five dominating topical domains: wisdom and the notion of the wise man, a strong emphasis on freedom, a principle of "indifference," subordination of the physical to the intellectual/spiritual, and distinctions in intellectual/spiritual status. It is my contention not only that these topics, when viewed together, commend Stoicism as the nearest source of the Corinthians' wisdom, but also that the particular *forms* in which their perspectives were articulated betray this school of thought with striking consistency. To make this proposal more plausible, however, it will first be necessary to address the sociocultural situation of first-century Corinth and its church.

4

THE CORINTHIAN SOCIAL WORLD

So far we have examined the problems inherent in the recently popular rhetorical interpretation of the Corinthians' wisdom (Chapter 2) and have attempted to lay a methodological foundation from which to provide an alternative reconstruction (Chapter 3). In the present chapter, our concern is to shed light on the social world in which the Corinthian church was enmeshed. Indeed, with the death knell of the old Gnostic thesis still ringing in our ears, we are reminded of the crucial importance of a chapter such as this one: before demonstrating the plausibility of the Stoic thesis exegetically, one must first be able to show that Stoicism was both a force to be reckoned with in the Corinthians' present environment, and a system of thought to which they were likely to have had meaningful exposure.

To this end, the present chapter treats a number of issues related to Corinthian social history. I begin with socioeconomic considerations, focusing especially on evidence related to the socioeconomic level of certain Corinthian Christians. Next, I canvass issues related to the religio-cultural orientation of the church and its environment: Was the Corinthian church of a more "Gentile" or more "Jewish" orientation? Was first-century Corinth "Greek," "Roman," or a complex hybrid of the two? Finally, in the light of our socioeconomic analysis, I address whether any people in the Corinthian church might have had a literate or philosophical education within reach. In that regard our main concern will be to determine, based on what we know of their socioeconomic positions, what level of exposure the Corinthians might be expected to have had with Stoic philosophy. As we shall see, for some the prospects looked promising.

Socioeconomic considerations

Social stratification

In the first half of the twentieth century, scholars widely agreed that the primitive church was a movement of the lower classes – poor artisans, peasants, and slaves.[1] In 1960, however, a slender volume from E. A. Judge, focused on the contribution of the social sciences to the NT, broadened our attention to Christianity's wider social spectrum: it was made up of a "broad cross-section of society," including a poor majority, but also a small number of influential and relatively high-status people.[2] By 1977, Abraham Malherbe could report an "emerging consensus" regarding the economic profile of Pauline church communities: they represented a "cross-section of most of Roman society."[3] About that time, Gerd Theissen published a collection of earlier essays which had served as a major impetus for Malherbe's remarks.[4] Wayne Meeks then ratified the consensus decisively in his exhaustive study *The First Urban Christians* (1983): "The 'emerging consensus' that Malherbe reports seems to be valid: a Pauline congregation generally reflected a fair cross-section of urban society."[5] The perspective of Meeks and his predecessors, often designated collectively as the "new consensus," has now been accepted by a majority of scholars,[6] with only slight revision.

As a consequence of this new understanding of early church composition, scholars have begun to explore how issues such as social stratification might have affected early church communities. For a number of reasons, the Corinthian correspondence has stood at the center of the discussion.

To begin, Corinth had always been a wealthy city (Pindar, *Paean*. 122; Thucydides 1.13.2, 5; Strabo, *Geogr*. 8.6.23). This had to do in large part with its location. Ensconced on the isthmus between Achaea and the Pelopponese, the city controlled two major harbors, one leading straight to Asia and the other to Italy (Strabo, *Geogr*. 8.6.20). This location generated a steady flow of trade, commerce, and incoming tourists

[1] The best-known champion for this view was Gustav Adolph Deissmann, in L. R. M. Strachan (trans.), *Light from the Ancient East: The New Testament Illustrated by Recently Discovered Texts of the Graeco-Roman World* (1927; repr., Peabody, MA: Hendrickson, 1995).

[2] *The Social Pattern of Christian Groups in the First Century* (London: Tyndale, 1960), 59–61, 69, 127–34.

[3] A. J. Malherbe, *Social Aspects of Early Christianity* (Philadelphia: Fortress, 1983), 86–87, finding precedent in Judge, *The Social Pattern of Christian Groups in the First Century*, 49–61.

[4] *The Social Setting of Pauline Christianity: Essays on Corinth* (Philadelphia: Fortress, 1982).

[5] *The First Urban Christians: The Social World of the Apostle Paul* (New Haven: Yale University Press, 1983).

[6] Justin Meggitt's monograph, *Paul and Poverty*, Studies of the New Testament and its World (Edinburgh: T&T Clark, 1998), is an exception. Though provocative, it has found little acceptance. Meggitt argues that "over 99% of the Empire's population could expect little more from life than abject poverty" (p. 50), a "bleak material existence" to which Paul and his communities were equally subject (p. 99).

(cf. Aelius Aristides, *Or*. 46.22–23; Plutarch, *Mor*. 831a; Dio, *Or*. 37.8). Both in earlier days and in Paul's lifetime, the city was home to the biennial Isthmian Games, the largest celebration of Greek athletics in the ancient world (Pausanias, *Descr*. 2.2.2; Dio, *Or*. 8.5–10; Aelius Aristides, *Or*. 46.23). The games, along with Corinth's flourishing bronze industry, further contributed to its wealth (Pliny, *Nat. Hist*. 34.1.6–8; Josephus, *Vit*. 68; Pliny, *Ep*. 3.6). In sum, with its profitable location, regular tourist attractions, and coveted wares, Corinth was by far one of the wealthiest cities of its time.[7]

But the importance of the Corinthian correspondence in this discussion has more to do with the evidence of the Corinthian letters themselves. In 1 Corinthians, Paul makes several passing references that seem to represent some within the Corinthian church as people of high means. Theissen's remarks on 1:26 have become almost proverbial: "If Paul says that there were not many in the Corinthian congregation who were wise, powerful, and wellborn [1:26], then this much is certain: there were some."[8] Rightly or wrongly most recent scholars have taken the terms "wise," "powerful," and "of noble birth" literally, as socioeconomic indicators.[9] Many conceive of 4:8–10 in similar terms: Paul is describing their economic standing when he calls certain Corinthians "rich," "kings," and "honored." In 2 Corinthians, moreover, Paul seems to imply that some church members possessed the wherewithal to finance the travel and ministry of Christian missionaries (2 Cor 8:14).

Additionally, many of the problems seen in 1 Corinthians are said to have been precipitated by socioeconomic disparity in the church. (1) It has often been said that some had hopes of elevating their social position by claiming the patronage of "powerful" Christian leaders such as Paul or Apollos (1 Corinthians 1–4). (2) The question of idol-meat in chapters 8, 10 arguably reflects class tensions between the "strong/wealthier" (so-called) and the "weak/poorer," where the former took a liberal stance toward its consumption and the latter an overly restrictive one. It has been presumed that the difference is explained by the fact that the "strong/ wealthier" were accustomed to eating meat regularly and in all kinds of

[7] See S. E. Alcock, *Graecia Capta: The Landscapes of Roman Greece* (Cambridge: Cambridge University Press, 1993), 158–61. See also D. Engels, *Roman Corinth: An Alternative Model for the Classical City* (Chicago: University of Chicago Press, 1990), who argues that Corinth was a "service city" which earned considerable income from production and trade.

[8] Theissen, *The Social Setting of Pauline Christianity*, 72.

[9] E.g., *Ibid*., 70–3; Clarke, *Secular and Christian Leadership in Corinth*, 43–5; Horrell, *The Social Ethos of the Corinthians Correspondence*, 95; Murphy-O'Connor, *Paul*, 271.

contexts, whereas the "weak/poorer" were probably not prosperous enough to have afforded it often, and thus associated it strictly with the pagan dedications they knew from cultic meals. Social stratification may also help explain (3) the divisions at the Lord's Supper in 11:17–34 (e.g., the wealthy dining in one room and the poor in another) and (4) the litigation of some church members against others in 6:1–11 (i.e., the rich litigating against the poor?). (5) It may even be that the guilty man in 5:1–13 had staved off judgment by playing *patron* to the community. In each of these issues, the potential socioeconomic dimensions have been rehearsed too many times over the years to bear repeating in any detail.[10] Suffice it to say that the argument that social stratification played *some* part in the church's divisions has continued to stand up to scrutiny,[11] even if this perspective has sometimes been stretched beyond its due limits.

In discussing Corinthian stratification, we must also address the socioeconomic profile of individual Corinthian church members, for several of these people people are described in the NT with detail sufficient to tell us something of their social standing. We now address these individuals at greater length.

Socioeconomic profiling

Between Acts and the Pauline epistles, we have the names of seventeen persons from the Corinthian church. Theissen's early analysis had assessed their wealth on the basis of several criteria: the ownership of houses and slaves, the holding of public offices, the means to travel, and the rendering of services to the Christian community.[12] From a coalescence of multiple criteria,[13] Theissen concluded that nine of the seventeen known persons belonged to the "upper classes."[14]

Despite the precursory nature of Theissen's work, subsequent prosopographic analyses have differed only marginally. We are still working with basically the same, limited evidence, even if the way in which that

[10] They are summarized, among other places, in J. D. G. Dunn, *1 Corinthians*, New Testament Guides (Sheffield: Sheffield Academic, 1995), 43–65; Horrell, *The Social Ethos of the Corinthians Correspondence*, 101–17.

[11] Theissen has defended his earlier views more recently in "The Social Structure of Pauline Communities: Some Critical Remarks on J. J. Meggitt *Paul, Poverty, and Survival*," *JSNT* (2001): 65–84; and "Social Conflicts in the Corinthian Correspondence: Further Remarks on J. J. Meggitt, *Paul, Poverty and Survival*," *JSNT* (2003): 371–91.

[12] Theissen, *The Social Setting of Pauline Christianity*, 72.

[13] *Ibid.*, 92.

[14] *Ibid.*, 95. See also Meeks's assessment of the Corinthians in *The First Urban Christians*, 51–73.

evidence has been interpreted has continued to vary. Let us look briefly at each of those Corinthians for whom evidence of wealth has been claimed, before turning to the most recent attempts to place these individuals on an economic scale.

"Wealthy" Corinthians?

Gaius. Gaius is thought to have owned a larger-than-average house, sizeable enough to have accommodated several house churches at once. This inference is drawn from the fact that several different house churches seem to have existed (1 Cor 11:18; 14:23; cf. 10:20), while in his house "the whole church" (ὅλης τῆς ἐκκλησίας) was able to come together (Rom 16:23). On such occasions, he may also have had to accommodate the church of Phoebe from the neighboring town of Cenchrea (Rom 16:1).

Peter Oakes's recent analysis of houses from first-century Pompeii corroborates the feasibility of this scenario. Few urban houses were commodious enough to fit forty people (probably the minimum number of individuals in the Corinthian church). Homes spacious enough to have accommodated this number, or more, would need to have been much larger, indeed large enough to place the householder in the top 15 percent or so of society.[15]

Phoebe. Phoebe also has been noted for her means. She not only had the ability to travel but also served as Paul's προστάτης (Rom 16:2). While some debate has surrounded this term, most have agreed that it designates a "benefactor" or "patron" (Latin: *patrona*) rather than a mere "helper."[16] Moreover, contemporary usage affords abundant examples where the title applied to women.[17] Phoebe, therefore, in being a "benefactor" not only "of many" (πολλῶν) but also of Paul himself (ἐμοῦ αὐτοῦ), can probably have had nothing less than a moderate surplus of wealth.

Priscilla and Aquilla. Priscilla and Aquilla are among the few individuals in Romans 16 whose names do not suggest slave origins.[18]

[15] Cf. Peter Oakes's discussion (*Reading Romans in Pompeii* [Minneapolis: Fortress; London: SPCK, 2009], 80–9) of a hypothetical house church in the home of a Pompeian "cabinet-maker," who maintained a space large enough (310 sq. m.) to place him at such a position on the socioeconomic scale (cf. p. 61, table 2.2).

[16] See Meeks (*The First Urban Christians*, 60), citing Judge, *The Social Pattern*, 128f; also Witherington, *Conflict and Community at Corinth*, 34; and B.W. Longenecker, *Remember the Poor: Paul, Poverty, and the Greco-Roman World* (Grand Rapids: Eerdmans, 2010), 241.

[17] Witherington, *Conflict and Community at Corinth*, 34–5.

[18] Peter Lampe, *Christians at Rome during the First Two Centuries* (Continuum, 2006), 182.

At various points in Paul's ministry they either owned or, more likely, rented homes in Ephesus (1 Cor 16:19), Rome (Rom 16:5), and Corinth (Acts 18:18–19), and hosted churches in perhaps all of them. Even if they did not maintain all these properties simultaneously, their ability to move between three different cities, separated by substantial distances, would imply some store of wealth. Acts tells us that they were tentmakers, and prosperous enough to have offered Paul and others hospitality (18:2–3).

Stephanus. Stephanus is said to have been head of his "household" (οἶκος, 1 Cor 1:16; οἰκία, 16:15), which means that he probably also possessed slaves; however, less than prosperous householders might have owned slaves as well. Additionally, he enjoyed the leisure and the means to travel with the delegation mentioned in 1 Cor 16:15–17.

Crispus. That Paul names Crispus alongside Gaius and Stephanus (1 Cor 1:16–17), two other individuals of possible means, may indicate that Crispus too was a person of distinction. Acts tells us he was the ἀρχισυνάγωγος (18:8), or "head of the synagogue." Judging from epigraphical references, the ἀρχισυνάγωγος was – in most cases, if not always – a person of moderate to significant wealth.[19]

Erastus. Most controversial of all is the figure of Erastus, whom Paul describes in Romans (16:23) as οἰκονόμος τῆς πόλεως, or as it is often rendered, "treasurer of the city." Hot debate has surrounded the status of this man ever since the 1929 discovery of an ancient inscription bearing his name. Two portions of a paving slab situated east of the stage building of the Roman theatre together contain the inscription: "Erastus in return for his aedileship laid (the pavement) at his own expense (*Erastus pro aedilitate s.p. stravit*)" (*Corinth VIII* 232). Upon its discovery, the inscription immediately roused the interest of biblical scholars. If this was the same man as the Corinthian Christian spoken of by Paul, this could have seismic ramifications for our understanding of the socioeconomic composition of the earliest church, for the aedileship was one of the highest municipal offices in Corinth.

The earliest treatments on the subject showed no reservations in separating the two Erasti. Assuming the reliability of the Vulgate rendering of οἰκονόμος as *arcarius civitatis*, it was maintained that Erastus must have been only a menial or a slave, not one of the highest elites in the city, that is, an aedile.[20] Thus, for decades after the inscription's discovery, the question of the relationship between these two Erasti remained basically a dead issue. All that changed in the 1970s, however. In 1974, Gerd

[19] Theissen, "The Social Structure of Pauline Communities," 81.
[20] H. J. Cadbury, "Erastus of Corinth," *JBL* 50 (1931): 42–58.

Theissen reset the agenda with his proposal that the two Erasti were in fact one and the same, and Paul's Erastus was therefore a man of high social and economic standing – a municipal *quaestor* at the time of the Epistle to the Romans, and later an aedile. Continual debate has surrounded the Corinthian man ever since.

Three questions remain central to the debate: the date of the inscription, the nature of the office of οἰκονόμος, and the frequency of the name Ἔραστος in antiquity.

Until 2010, it was virtually undisputed that the inscription dated to the middle of the first century AD, precisely during the time of Paul's ministry. A new proposal from Steven Friesen, however, has given us reason to question this conclusion.[21] Friesen rightly notes that there is no firm archaeological evidence to establish a first-century date. Moreover, he demonstrates definitively that the inscription is not in its original location, but that it was moved there in the late third or early fourth century as part of the foundation for a wall that ran along the south end of the plaza where the block was found.[22] As Friesen acknowledges, reuse of the inscription in the foundation clearly sets the late third century as a *terminus ad quem* for the original inscription. Friesen, however, doubts that it dates as far back as the first century. Based on a series of conjectures (which he admits cannot presently be proven),[23] he concludes that the inscription probably dates to the mid-second century, perhaps late in the reign of Hadrian. Apparently further details supporting this dating are forthcoming.[24] At present, however, none of the evidence rules out the continuing viability of a first-century date. Meantime, all that can be said is that we cannot yet *close the book* on the question whether Paul's Erastus can be identified with the aedile.

The second major issue is the precise meaning of the term οἰκονόμος (Rom 16:23). Here we need give little notice to Meggitt's suggestion that it refers to Erastus' "office within the *church*," for Paul plainly calls Erastus the οἰκονόμος "of the *city*."[25] Nonetheless, much ambiguity regarding the political office has remained. Indeed, the term carried a wide variety of meanings in antiquity, ranging in reference from low-level

[21] S. Friesen, "The Wrong Erastus: Ideology, Archaeology, and Exegesis," in S. J. Friesen, D. N. Schowalter, and J. C. Walters (eds.), *Corinth in Context: Comparative Studies on Religion and Society* (Leiden: Brill, 2010), 231–56.

[22] *Ibid.*, 239.

[23] *Ibid.*, 242. Moreover, see the questions raised by J. K. Goodrich, in "Erastus of Corinth (Romans 16.23): Responding to Recent Proposals on his Rank, Status, and Faith," *NTS* 57 (2011): 588.

[24] Says Goodrich, "Erastus of Corinth," 588.

[25] Meggitt, *Paul, Poverty, and Survival*, 136.

bureaucrats or slaves, on the one hand, to eminent municipal officers, including ἀγοράνομοι or colonial aediles, on the other.[26] Latin equivalents of οἰκονόμος included *actor*, *dispensator*, *vilicus*, and *aedilis coloniae*.[27]

Confusion over the term has recently been clarified by John Goodrich, who, in his recently published doctoral dissertation, has conducted the only exhaustive study of the term to date, having extensively investigated its usage from the Hellenistic through the early Roman period.[28] Importantly, he distinguishes *three different types* of οἰκονόμοι: *regal*, *municipal*, and *private*. In the Roman era, *municipal* οἰκόνομοι "*normally* functioned as financial magistrates and possessed considerable socio-economic status within their respective communities."[29] The *private* οἰκονόμος, by contrast, was "normally" a *freedman or slave*.[30] Clearly, as "οἰκονόμος *of the city*," Paul's Erastus was an οἰκονόμος, not of the private type, but of the *municipal* type.

Goodrich's distinction goes a long way in explaining the confusion that has swirled around the term in the Erastus debate: interpreters have, quite mistakenly, been throwing both the *private* and the *municipal* οἰκονόμοι into the same mix and then taking the sort of economic "average."[31] This seems to me to be the only way to explain Friesen's claim – diametricaly opposite to the conclusion of Goodrich's more exhaustive study – that the οἰκονόμος was "*normally* a subordinate financial manager" and "*usually* a slave" (emphasis added). While the inscriptional evidence cited by Friesen does include reference to municipal οἰκόνομοι, unfortunately he

[26] For examples in which οἰκονόμος refers to a high-ranking magistrate, see H. J. Mason, *Greek Terms for Roman Institutions: A Lexicon and Analysis* (Hakkert, 1974), 71, 175f. Goodrich ("Erastus of Corinth [Romans 16.23]," 588), further notes *CIG* 2811; *IAphrodMcCabe* 275; SEG 26.1044; *TAM* 5.743; *ISmyrna* 24.761; 24.771; 24.772; *IStratonikeia* 22.1; and (on p. 592n41) another, disputed, reference – *IGRR* 4.813.

[27] Mason, *Greek Terms for Roman Institutions*, 71; as ratified in B. H. Mclean, *An Introduction to Greek Epigraphy of the Hellenistic and Roman Periods from Alexander the Great down to the Reign of Constantine (323 BC–AD 337)* (Ann Arbor: University of Michigan Press, 2002), 342.

[28] J. Goodrich, *Paul as an Administrator of God in 1 Corinthians*, SNTSMS 152 (Cambridge: Cambridge University Press, 2012), 27–102. Earlier studies include P. Landvogt, *Epigraphische Untersuchungen über den ΟΙΚΟΝΟΜΟΣ: Ein Beitrag zum Hellenistischen Beamtenwesen* (Strassburg: M. Dumont Schauberg, 1908); D. B. Martin, *Slavery as Salvation: The Metaphor of Slavery in Pauline Christianity* (New Haven: Yale University, 1990), 174–77; G. H. R. Horsley (ed.), *New Documents Illustrating Early Christianity: A Review of Greek Inscriptions and Papyri Published in 1979* (Grand Rapids: Eerdmans, 1997), vol. IV, §69; 8:50–1; 53–5; 61–2; 9:32, 35, 39, 42, 43, 54, 55.

[29] Goodrich, *Paul as an Administrator of God in 1 Corinthians*, 50; emphasis added.

[30] *Ibid.*, 75.

[31] L. L. Welborn's arrangement of the evidence (*End to Enmity: Paul and the "Wrongdoer" of 2 Corinthians* [Berlin: de Gruyter, 2011], 261–4) leaves this impression as well, although he comes to a different conclusion than Friesen does.

is able to cite only three examples (*IGR* 4.813; SEG 24: 174 no. 496; SEG 1988, 214 no. 710), of which – we find upon inspection – only *one* instance securely upholds his point (i.e., SEG 24 1969: 174 no. 496). Indeed, there were a great number of slave οἰκόνομοι. But such were usually οἰκόνομοι of the *private*, not the municipal, sort.

Yet, if Paul's Erastus was the same man as the one named in the inscription, then why did Paul not at least call him by what is said to be the more *common* Greek equivalent for the Latin aedile – ἀγοράνομος? Several reasonable answers have been submitted. Possibly, it was because the aedile in Corinth undertook duties slightly different from the aediles in other cities, and Paul uses the term he thinks most suited to his audience.[32] Others, however, have pointed out that, prior to the second century AD, ἀγοράνομος does not appear in the sources at all, so Paul could not have used it in any case.[33] Furthermore, cities across the empire showed no uniformity in the nature of the Greek offices themselves,[34] which helps explain why there were several possible Greek equivalents for the names of *many* Roman offices.[35]

Or, it is just possible that Paul indeed does *not* mark out Erastus as an aedile, but rather as the holder of some other high municipal office, roughly equivalent to the Greek office of οἰκονόμος. According to one form of this argument – put forth years ago by Theissen and revived more recently by Goodrich – Paul's Erastus, οἰκονόμος τῆς πόλεως, might have been a *quaestor*, who only later climbed to the (somewhat higher) post of aedile.[36] While not impossible, however, neither is this hypothesis provable, as Roman Corinth has left no record that it had *quaestores*.[37]

Whatever the term's equivalent, many interpreters have found significance in the fact that Erastus is the *only* named Corinthian to whom Paul attaches a secular title (again, οἰκονόμος "of the city" is not a church

[32] Mentioned by Theissen, *The Social Setting of Pauline Christianity*, 81.

[33] Clarke, *Secular Leadership and Christian Leadership in Corinth*, 50. Moreover, Goodrich (*Paul as an Administrator of God in 1 Corinthians*, 62–63) has shown that οἰκονόμος could also be used as a distinct office from that of the ἀγοράνομος.

[34] McLean, *An Introduction to Greek Epigraphy of the Hellenistic and Roman Periods*, 318.

[35] Theissen, *The Social Setting of Pauline Christianity*, 79.

[36] G. Theissen, "Soziale Schichtung in der Korinthische Gemeinde: Ein Beitrag zur Soziologie des hellenistischen Urchristentums," *ZNW* 65 (1974): 232–72; Theissen, *The Social Setting of Pauline Christianity*, 81–82; also picked up by Meeks, *The First Urban Christians*, 59; and revived by J. Goodrich, "Erastus, Quaestor of Corinth: The Administrative Rank of ὁ οἰκονόμος τῆς πόλεως [Rom 16:23] in an Achaean Colony," *NTS* 56 (2010): 90–115.

[37] Thus Alexander Weiss's response to Goodrich: "Keine Quästoren in Korinth: zu Goodrichs (und Theissens) These über das Amt des Erastos (Röm 16.23)," *NTS* 56 (2010): 576–81.

office).[38] This fact seems more easily explained on the postulate that the title distinguished the man socially than by the dubious hypothesis that Erastus was not actually a Christian.[39]

In the end, it should be said that Goodrich's thorough study of the term "οἰκονόμος" gives us a solid basis for concluding that Erastus, as a *municipal* οἰκονόμος, was a man of no small standing. While Friesen's argument that Erastus could have been merely a low-level bureaucrat or even a slave might remain a possibility, given the odds suggested by the evidence, this is far less likely than the common view. Indeed, following Goodrich, we may conclude that the sort of "average" οἰκονόμος τῆς πόλεως found himself in a higher swath on the socioeconomic scale.

The third major consideration in the debate has been the currency of Erastus' name in antiquity. In this regard, Justin Meggitt tosses into the discussion two arguments that he thinks militate against the possibility that Paul's Erastus was also the aedile of the inscription (granting, for the sake of argument, the possibility that Paul's οἰκονόμος was in fact an aedile). First, he notes that Erastus is not as rare a name as has usually been thought.[40] He claims to have found twenty-three epigraphic attestations of the Greek personal name (Ἔραστος) and fifty-five examples of the Latin cognomen (Erastus).[41] As such, he thinks that we should not assume that there was not another aedile named Erastus in mid first-century Corinth.

Meggitt then gives what he calls "another reason" for doubting the relevance of the Erastus-aedile inscription: given that the upper left corner of the inscription is missing, it is possible that the inscription originally contained not "Erastus," but rather the compound "Eperastus."[42]

With these two arguments Meggitt has, of course, not actually given us *multiple* reasons for doubting, just two alternative and independent possibilities (i.e., they cannot both obtain at the same time). Moreover, neither argument retains its force upon examination.

The possibility that the name was "Eperastus" rather than "Erastus" is unlikely owing to the size and spacing of the letters on the inscription, as

[38] As both Theissen (*The Social Setting of Pauline Christianity*, 76) and Murphy-O'Connor (*Paul*, 268–9) have noted.

[39] On this point at least, Goodrich ("Erastus of Corinth," 589–90) has the upper hand against Friesen ("The Wrong Erastus," 249–55).

[40] Clarke (*Secular Leadership and Christian Leadership in Corinth*, 139), for instance, calls the name "uncommon."

[41] Meggitt, *Paul, Poverty, and Survival*, 139. Actually, he lists twenty-two Greek inscriptions and (mistakenly?) one papyrus (in which the correct reading is not Ἔραστος, but Ἔρατος).

[42] Meggitt, *Paul, Poverty, and Survival*, 140.

the original report of the excavator attests.[43] "Erastus" is clearly the more natural fit. I do not see why, apart from ideological considerations, we should prefer what is simply conceivable to what seems most probable.

Second, while Meggitt's research into the frequency of the name has made an important contribution to the discussion, here too he is ultimately less than convincing. The fact is that "78" occurrences of the name Erastus over the course of several centuries *would* make the name rare. For one thing, only a tiny percentage of these occurrences actually date to the first century, and a Late Antique date can be established for a great number of the others.[44] Furthermore, Meggitt's total is shown to be remarkably *low* when compared with what would have been considered even moderately popular names in Erastus' day. For instance, several of the names invoked alongside Erastus in Romans 16 appear to have been exceedingly more popular than the latter. The *Lexicon of Greek Personal Names* lists only thirty-two distinct individuals named Ἔραστος over the course of approximately 500 years (ca. 300 BC– AD 200), but of individuals named Τιμόθεος, 285; Ἀριστόβουλος, 292; Ἀνδρόνικος, 299; and Ἑρμῆς/Ἑρμᾶς, 315. Στέφανος, of which we find the variant Στεφανᾶ in 1 Corinthians (cf. 1:16; 6:15, 17), has 303 entries. More popular still are Greek names that we have attested closer to a thousand times: e.g., Ἀρτεμίδωρος, 642; Διογένης, 670; Ἡρακλείδης, 773; and Φίλιππος, 941. Then there are names for which we have one to several thousand distinct individuals attested: for example, Ἀρίστων, 1063; Ἀλεξάνδρος, 1443; Ἀπολλώνιος, 1774; Δημήτριος, 1838; and Διονύσιος, 3024. The figures are much larger when we count, not simply the number of distinct individuals attested, but the aggregate number of epigraphical and literary witnesses that attest to them.

Moreover, Meggitt's inscriptions do not actually refer to seventy-eight different Erasti, nor even, in every case, to a man named "Erastus." In at least two of the inscriptions, "Erastus" is a doubtful reading (probably Eperastus in *CIL* V 7232; merely Tiberius Claudius E[] in *AE* [1984]: 625). In seven cases, "Erastus" is not there at all (nothing resembling "Erastus" in *CIL* VI 1300; *CIG* 1249; *IG* IV 1488; "Aerastus" in *CIL* VI 7513 and XIV 4562, 4; not "Erastus" but "Eratus" in *CIL* VI 24452; not Ἔραστος but Ἔρατος in P. Heid. Bi. 7 [IIa]). When it comes to his literary

[43] J. H. Kent, *Corinth*, Vol. VIII, part III, *The Inscriptions 1926–1950* (Princeton, NJ: American School of Classical Studies at Athens, 1966), 100.

[44] Less than twenty of these definitely date to the first century, and even less to the middle years of that century.

references, every instance refers to the same individual: Ἔραστος of Skepsis, pupil of Socrates (Plato, *Ep.* 6.322–3; D. L. 3.46; Strabo, *Geogr.* 13.608). In a few instances, multiple inscriptions refer to the same person as well. (1) SEG 11:622 and *CIG* 1241 both refer to Erastus the father of Apollonius (Ἀπολλώνιος Ἐράστου), from Sparta, and date to the second century AD. (2) Several inscriptions bear the name Tiberius Claudius Erastus (Rome in *CIL* VI 15031; 15325; 15439; Salernum in *CIL* X 527; Formia in *CIL* X 6144; Dacia in *CIL* XVI 33), with three of these instances coming from Rome, presumably under the emperor Claudius, who had granted the individual(s) manumission. (3) A single inscription repeated in two corpora (SEG 25:194 = IG II^2 2323,221) is, erroneously, counted twice. (4) One Erastus can probably also be established for *CIL* 4.4614 and *CIL* 4.4641, where a proud literate has twice scrawled his name on the wall.

Another, more interesting case of common identity involves *IG* II^2 1945, 1990, 1968, and 1985.[45] Each of these not only dates to the very middle years of the first century, and to the city of Athens, but all of them pertain to the gymnasium there, an institution of athletics and higher learning for the Greek "elite." Likely, these four inscriptions refer to a total of only two different people. *IG* II^2 1945 dates to AD 45/6, and names Ἐράστο[υ . . . . 9 . . . .]ου Ἀναφλυστίου as a gymnasium official, viz., the ὑπηρετής. Here the personal name, Ἐράστο[υ, is apparently accompanied by the patronymic – at which point we have a lucuna in the inscription – and then by the demotic Ἀναφλυστίου. It is the demotic that enables us to distinguish this Erastus from that of *IG* II^2 1990, who belonged to the deme of Besa – Ἔραστος Βη<σ>αι<ε>ύς. *IG* II^2 1990, moreover, dates to AD 61/2 and has Erastus filling the role of παιδεύτης, or literary instructor of the ephebes, an unlikely course of life for one who had risen to the rank of ὑπηρετής some fifteen or sixteen years earlier.[46]

The other two inscriptions, *IG* II^2 1968 and 1985, both date to the reign of Claudius (AD 41–54) and list an Erastus among the "ephebes," the approximately eighteen-year-old youths who trained in the gymnasium under its affiliated officers and staff. Ordinarily we would not expect the same individuals to be attested as ephebes more than once, for ephebic

[45] Once dated to the middle of the first century AD, *IG* II^2 1973 is now more accurately dated to the middle of the second century. For the new dating, see R. Hitchman and F. Marchand, "Two Ephebic Inscriptions: *IG* II^2 1973A and 1973B," *ZPE* 148 (2004): 165–76.

[46] However, Erastus the literary instructor must have been a man of some standing, for his son (Δημοκράτης Ἐράστου Βησαιεύς) is listed as an ephebe in the same inscription.

inscriptions were usually undertaken by the state on an annual basis, and training lasted only one year. On the other hand, the lack of patryonomic and demotic with the personal name reveals that *IG* II^2 1968 and *IG* II^2 1985 were not officially sanctioned inscriptions, but were rather informal honorary monuments, funded (likely) by the ephebes themselves.[47] As such, both ephebic inscriptions *could* refer to the same man. Unfortunately, the fragmentary nature of the texts renders an exhaustive comparison between the two ephebic lists impossible.

What then is the relationship among these four Athenian gymnasium inscriptions? At least two individuals are represented, for the two officers are distinguished by their demes. If – as is probably the case – the two ephebes are to be distinguished as well, these could, however, be the same individuals as the officers. In support, it should be said that advancement from the ephebate to municipal offices was always the expected routine, and it is well attested in the sources.[48] Second, the name "Erastus" was, in the first century, extremely rare – outside the NT (Acts 19:22; Rom 16:23; 2 Tim 4:20), we have *not a single* reference to an Erastus in first-century papyri or literature, in Greek or in Latin. Moreover, since multiple Erasti are attested in inscriptions in every century from 300 BC to AD 200, would it not be strange indeed suddenly to have no Erastus at all, in *any* city in Greece, from AD 1–41 and 61–99 – a period of eighty years – while having four concentrated in the *same* city, and in the same institution, within the span of only twenty? It is easier to believe we have the same men counted twice. The only other inscription mentioning an Erastus at all in first-century Greece would be *Corinth VIII* 232, the controversial inscription mentioning the aedile, and that only if Friesen's new dating is wrong.

Likely, then, we are left with only *two* Erasti in first-century Greece: the first of them a young man active in elite circles a few miles from Corinth in the years just prior to the Corinthian correspondence (being the officer of *IG* II^2 1945 and the ephebe of 1985 or 1965), and the second, if not an ephebe, at least a gymnasium affiliate some fifteen years later (being the officer of *IG* II^2 1990 and possibly the ephebe of 1985 or 1965):[49]

[47] Hitchman and Marchand ("Two Ephebic Inscriptions," 170) note that these were common in the Roman era.

[48] See, for example, *PAA* 7:400525; 402085; 401575; 401480; 422940.

[49] Conversely, if the *traditional* dating for *Corinth VIII* 232 remains valid, it could be noted that the Erastus named would hold a lot in common with the two men from the gymnasium, and the possibility of common identity with one of the others could not be easily dismissed.

Erastus #1: Ἔραστος Ἀναφλυστίος

[IG II^2 1968:	Athenian ephebe, AD 41–54]
[IG II^2 1985:	Athenian ephebe, mid first c. AD]
IG II^2 1945:	**ὑπηρετής in the Athenian gymnasium, AD 45/6**

Erastus #2: Ἔραστος Βησαιεύς

[IG II^2 1968:	Athenian ephebe, AD 41–54]
[IG II^2 1985:	Athenian ephebe, mid first c. AD]
IG II^2 1990:	**παιδεύτης in the Athenian gymnasium, AD 61/2**

Could one of these two Athenian ephebes have gone on to become οἰκονόμος in Corinth and a convert to Christianity by the time Paul wrote Romans in AD 56/7? It cannot be proven, but it is a tantalizing possibility, and one that is lent especial credence by an otherwise unlikely convergence of circumstances: a rare name, unattested in first-century Greece outside this dense cluster of attestations from the very middle years of the century, and in every case tied with the Athenian gymnasium, that elite institution which promised to prepare its members for a career in politics.[50]

What then of Paul's Erastus? Debate clamors on regarding the date of *Corinth VIII* 232, the nature of the office of οἰκονόμος, and the frequency of the name. At stake are the question of Erastus' socioeconomic position and our understanding of early church, and particularly Corinthian, stratification. From Theissen until Friesen's article in 2010, a consensus had been maintained: since *Corinth VIII* 232 was agreed to date from the middle of the first century, since οἰκονόμος could refer to the office of quaestor or aedile, since the name Erastus occurred infrequently, and

[50] The possibility that one of the Erasti of *IG* II^2 1945, 1968, 1985, 1990 might have gone on to be οἰκονόμος in Corinth would depend on the fulfillment of any one of the following three conditions: (1) the οἰκονόμος in Corinth was not a member of the city's *decurial* board, as Roman citizenship (a status that the names in the inscriptions belie) was required for membership; (2) one of these men (more likely the second, given the dates) was granted Roman citizenship at some time subsequent to these inscriptions but prior to filling the office; or (3) one of the two ephebes, whose citizen status cannot be determined from the extant information, was distinct from either of the two officers and *did* possess Roman citizenship, as Athenian ephebes often did (e.g., *PAA* 7:401440; 401445; and examples in S. G. Byrne, *Roman Citizens of Athens* (Studia Hellenistica 40; Leuven: Peeters, 2003), 8 [Publius Aelius Διονύσιος (of tribe Aiantis)]; 149 [Claudius Ἀκυλῖνος of Besa and Claudius Λέων of Besa]; passim).

since no other Erastus of Corinth was known around Paul's day,[51] most[52] were compelled to conclude that the Erastus of the inscription and the "Erastus, οἰκονόμος τῆς πόλεως" mentioned by Paul were one and the same. Yet, with the release of Friesen's new article, the question may now hang in the balance. What remains to be seen is whether any further insights will decisively shift the weight of opinion.

Several points can be made in closing. First, while Friesen may have cast doubt on the traditional, first-century dating of *Corinth VIII* 232, we may retain it as a strong possibility unless he can provide more definitive archaeological support for his alternative. Second, studies have continued to affirm that the term "οἰκονόμος" could refer to a wide range of officers, from relatively menial functionaries to high-level municipal bureaucrats. But for declarations of the term's "usual" meaning and the holder's precise social status to be warranted conclusions need to be based on a significant and representative sample size. As of yet we have been shown exceedingly little proof that, outside of *private* contexts, οἰκονόμος "usually" referred to a slave. The only exhaustive study to date has been that of Goodrich, which has demonstrated that, while there were certainly exceptions to the rule, the *municipal* οἰκονόμος was "normally" a citizen of considerable wealth and social standing. Finally, regarding the frequency of the name Erastus, I have reaffirmed the old conclusion that the name was indeed rare, having added that it was almost entirely unknown in the first century, aside from a few Athenian inscriptions that seem to refer to only *two* separate individuals.

Chloe. Far less can be said regarding the remaining figures. Chloe's membership in the Corinthian church has not gone unquestioned. Murphy-O'Connor tenders the hypothesis that her "people" (1:11) had brought news from Corinth (whither they had gone on some sort of business trip) back to Paul in Ephesus (where they permanently resided). He suggests that her delegation reported on items not mentioned in the Corinthians' letter to Paul, divulging just the sorts of gossipy trifles that *outsiders* would – how the Corinthians are or are not covering their heads,

[51] An Erastus is mentioned three times in the NT (Acts 19:22; Rom 16:23; 2 Tim 4:20), and, as Goodrich ("Erastus of Corinth [Romans 16.23]," 591n38) notes, each time in connection with Corinth/Achaea, Paul, Timothy, Priscilla and Aquila, and perhaps also Ephesus.

[52] Meggitt (*Paul, Poverty, and Survival*, 137) states that "few, if any, resist assuming an association between the two characters"; Garland (*1 Corinthians*, 11) says that "Most assume that he was the same Erastus who paid for paving the plaza . . ."; and Thiselton (*The First Epistle to the Corinthians*, 9) cites several recent studies that have made the case for common identity between the two Erasti. Welborn (*An End to Enmity*, 267), notes that classicists and archaeologist tend to favor identity, as he himself does (273).

who is speaking out in church, and so forth. Paul in turn respects the confidentiality of his sources, thinking it malapropos to name his informants. While this scenario may not be outside the realm of possibility, however, the text leaves us no evidence that Chloe was not a Corinthian, and there are reasons to think otherwise. For one thing, Chloe seems to require no introduction; Paul simply assumes the Corinthians know her.[53] Conversely, if Paul's salutations are any indication, Chloe does *not* belong in Ephesus, for he fails to mention her in his greetings from the church in that city (Rom 16).[54]

Achaicus and Fortunatus. Achaicus and Fortunatus were also a part of the traveling delegation of Stephanus (16:17). Murphy-O'Connnor argues that, while both have slave names, in all likelihood they have now obtained their freedom, for they have the freedom to travel.[55] Yet, slaves could travel on behalf of their masters as well, and travel by itself was not a sufficient guarantee of wealth. Thus, while the possibility that these two men had some measure of wealth cannot be entirely ruled out, neither can it be confidently established.

Tertius. To these nine persons we should also add Tertius, the Corinthian who "wrote" Paul's epistle to the Romans (ὁ γράψας; 16:22). Secretaries could be people of high birth. Yet, literacy and wealth did not always go hand in hand: literacy was found also among freedmen, and occasionally even slaves. In the end, little can be said of Tertius.

Economy scales

Recently, some important studies have continued to sift the data, hoping to refine the binary poor-elite model associated with Theissen and Meeks's earlier work.[56] In the search for a more sophisticated economy scale, Steven Friesen's 2004 article, "Poverty and Paul: Beyond the So-Called New Consensus," deserves credit as a major galvanizing force.[57] Here Friesen constructs a seven-tiered "poverty scale" (PS)

[53] So Horrell, *The Social Ethos of the Corinthians Correspondence*, 98.

[54] So Theissen, *The Social Setting of Pauline Christianity*, 92–3. Of course, it is possible that she goes unmentioned because she was not a Christian. One can arrive at this conclusion, however, only on the *pre*supposition that she was a permanent resident of Ephesus and on that basis would have to have been a member of the local church there. But assuming that she was a member of the Corinthian church would equally explain the facts.

[55] Murphy-O'Connor, *Paul*, 272.

[56] Although Theissen's later work ("The Social Structure of Pauline Communities," 74) expressly applies Alfoldy's *multi*tiered model.

[57] S. Friesen, "Poverty and Paul: Beyond the So-Called New Consensus," *JSNT* 26 (2004): 323–61.

Table 6. *Friesen's (2004) poverty scale*

Scale	Description	%
PS1–3	imperial, regional, and municipal elites, respectively	<3%
PS4	moderate surplus resources	7%
PS5	stable near subsistence level	22%
PS6	at subsistence level	40%
PS7	below subsistence level	28%

for the urban Roman Empire, with each tier being defined relative to human subsistence level, and wealth being made the dominant status variable.[58] As shown in Table 6, Friesen assigns each level its own demographic and a figure indicating the percentage of the total population that, according to his calculations, that demographic must have constituted.[59]

Using the available NT evidence, Friesen is then able to locate several Pauline church members on the scale. He concludes (ostensibly against Theissen and the "new consensus") that Pauline communities included "no wealthy saints," only a majority consisting of slaves, peasants, and poor artisans, larded with a few standout individuals of moderate but nonetheless sub-elite means.[60]

Following Friesen's article, a rapid succession of developments ensued. In 2009, Bruce Longenecker developed his own "economy scale" (ES), using Friesen's "poverty scale" (PS) as a point of departure.[61] Based chiefly on the insights of Walter Scheidel,[62] Longenecker argued that Friesen's percentages needed to be adjusted in order to "allow more 'exposure' to the 'middling groups.'"[63] Consequently, he raised Friesen's "PS4" group percentage from 7 percent to 17 percent.

Longenecker's revisions were short-lived, however. Later that year, Friesen and Scheidel joined efforts to publish an article entitled "The Size

58 As he states ("Poverty and Paul," 343), "'subsistence level' is here defined as the resources needed to procure enough calories in food to maintain the human body. The calorific needs of humans are gauged in various ways by scholars, but they usually range from 1,500 to 3,000 calories per day, depending on gender, age, physical energy required for occupation, pregnancy, lactation and so on."

59 Friesen, "Poverty and Paul," 347.

60 Friesen, "Poverty and Paul," 348.

61 B. Longenecker, "Exposing the Economic Middle: A Revised Economy Scale for the Study of Early Christianity," *JSNT* 31 (2009): 243–78.

62 W. Scheidel, "Stratification, Deprivation and Quality of Life," in M. Atkins and R. Osborne (eds.), *Poverty in the Roman World* (Cambridge: Cambridge University Press, 2006), 40–59.

63 Longenecker, "Exposing the Economic Middle," 46.

of the Economy and the Distribution of Income in the Roman Empire," in which they proposed a highly refined economy scale that took into account the GDP of the entire Roman Empire and the overall distribution of its wealth.[64] The article adduced a range of estimates for the size of the economy, so that the upper middling group (basically equivalent to Longenecker's ES4 and Friesen's old PS4) could have comprised as little as 6 percent and as much as 12 percent of the *overall* population (i.e., city plus hinterlands).[65] Longenecker has taken these developments into account in his 2010 monograph (*Remember the Poor*), where, for a variety of reasons, he has again adjusted the percentages.[66]

Shortly before Longenecker's monograph came off the presses, Peter Oakes was issuing a related work.[67] Based on archaeological excavations at Pompeii, Oakes devised an economy scale based, not on subsistence level or size of income, but on domestic space occupied. With figures startlingly close to those of Friesen and Longenecker, Oakes estimated that *elite* householders would have comprised about 2.5 percent of first-century Pompeiian society, the *destitute* about 67 percent, and *the rest* the middle 30.5 percent.[68] The fact that there was a relatively sizeable percentage of people located in the middle range reveals that significant social stratification was indeed possible within the limits of those who were neither elite nor destitute.

There are, of course, complications with any of these scaling approaches, owing, for one thing, to the nature of the Greco-Roman household (e.g., slaves in the household could be well above subsistence level), and figures in all models obviously generalize across diverse geographic and demographic contexts. These points, however, do not ultimately undermine the scales' heuristic value. Nor are the fluctuations significant to our present aims (see Table 7 for a summary of the percentages). More important is the fact that these developments have advanced us beyond

[64] S. Friesen and W. Scheidel, "The Size of the Economy and the Distribution of Income in the Roman Empire," *JRS* 99 (2009): 61–91.

[65] Friesen and Scheidel, "The Size of the Economy and the Distribution of Income in the Roman Empire," 83–4.

[66] B. Longenecker, *Remember the Poor: Paul, Poverty, and the Greco-Roman World* (Grand Rapids, MI: Eerdmans, 2010), 44–53. He lists the following reasons for adjusting Friesen and Scheidel's percentages: "(1) an 'optimistic' interpretation of the middling groups in the Roman economy is to be preferred over a 'pessimistic' one (see Appendix 1 below); (2) the income of the *Augustales* needs to be attributed primarily to the middling groups rather than the elites (see Appendix 1 below); and; (3) the urban environment had more attraction to the middling group members than rural environments" (p. 53).

[67] P. Oakes, *Reading Romans in Pompeii: Paul's Letter at Ground Level* (Minneapolis: Fortress, 2009).

[68] See Oakes, *Reading Romans in Pompeii*, 61, figure 2.2.

Table 7. *Elite and middling group percentages*

Socioeconomic level	Friesen's 2004 Percentages	Longenecker's 2009 Percentages	Friesen and Scheidel's 2009 Percentages	Longenecker's 2010 Percentages
upper elite	3%	3%	~1%	3%
middling group	7%	17%	6–12%	15%

the rhetorically useful but historically inaccurate dichotomy of "wealthy/elite" versus "poor/non-elite."[69] Longenecker's ES4 and ES5 groups could only qualify as poor in a very relative sense. In fact, the sizeable ES4 group would have contained some who approached elite status (ES4a), with those at the lower end still fortunate enough to have maintained a moderate surplus of income (ES4b).[70] With perhaps some 13–18 percent of the population maintaining *at least* a moderate surplus of funds, then, these percentages could have significant bearing on how we view the social position of some Pauline church members.

Based on these advancements, Friesen and Longenecker have each conducted prosopographic analyses of Pauline Christians for whom we have revealing data. Given the paucity of evidence afforded us by the biblical text, little can be said here beyond what these scholars have already done. Actually, their results differ little from those of the "new consensus";[71] they offer fine-tuning rather than anything radically different. Table 8 summarizes their analyses of Corinthian church members.[72]

[69] For more refined differentiation of economic levels, I hereafter employ Longenecker's "ES" language (though without necessarily committing to his exact figures).

[70] Longenecker, *Remember the Poor*, 55.

[71] As Longenecker (*Remember the Poor*, 252) notes, prosopographic analyses have remained stable "even across the 'consensus' divide." Furthermore, Theissen himself ("The Social Structure of Pauline Communities [2001], 66) anticipated Friesen ("Paul and Poverty," 325) in saying, "The 'new consensus' is neither new nor is it a consensus." Accordingly both John Barclay ("Poverty in Pauline Studies: A Response to Stephen Friesen," *JSNT* 26 [2004]: 363–6) and Peter Oakes ("Constructing Poverty Scales for Graeco-Roman Society: A Response to Steven Friesen's 'Poverty in Pauline Studies,'" *JSNT* 26 [2004]: 367–71) have suggested that Friesen's contribution was less revolutionary than he presented it to be.

[72] From Friesen, "Poverty and Paul," 348–58; and Longenecker, *Remember the Poor*, 220–58.

Table 8. *Corinthian church members of the middling group*[73]

Corinthian Individual	Friesen's PS (2004)	Longenecker's ES (2010)
Erastus	PS4 or 5	ES4 (probably ES4a)
Gaius	PS4	ES4 (maybe ES4a)
Priscilla and Aquilla	PS4 or 5	ES5
Stephanus	PS5 (or PS6)	ES4 (or ES5)
Crispus	–	ES4 (or ES5)
Phoebe	PS5 (or PS4)	ES4
Chloe	PS4	–

As is evident, the two analyses tally closely with each other.[74] Friesen disregards Crispus and seems to rank Stephanus and Phoebe lower than most would.[75] Regardless of which analysis we prefer, however, we can see that several known members of the church appear to have qualified as possessing at least "moderate surplus resources" (PS4/ES4). In addition, most of these individuals are almost certainly heads of their households, perhaps with further children at or beyond maturity. In all cases, moreover, we are dealing with *termini a quibus* as regards their economic level – the evidence prevents that these individuals be placed any *lower* on the scale, while only silence prevents their being put any *higher*.

In sum, it is significant that, even among those few Corinthians who are named and profiled for us in the NT, we are able to identify several individuals who likely fell at the ES4-level. Perhaps there were others. Whether Paul had targeted such people as an evangelistic strategy,[76] or whether such converts are only *mentioned* more often on account of their

[73] Given that the Friesen and Scheidel (2009) percentages for the middling group hardly differ from those of Friesen (2004) – 6–12% in 2009 as compared with 7% in 2004 – we can assume that Friesen's 2004 analysis is still more or less representative of where he stands. That is, "PS4" status would still place the individual within the top 10% or so of society and, accordingly, within the economic "middle."

[74] We may also draw attention to L. L. Welborn's recent analysis (*End to Enmity: Paul and the 'Wrongdoer' of 2 Corinthians* [Berlin: de Gruyter, 2011], 230–82), which agrees that Crispus, Gaius, Stephanas, and Erastus were all "possessed of sufficient resources" and carried strong influence in the Corinthian community (236).

[75] For which Oakes ("Constructing Poverty Scales for Graeco-Roman Society," 367) calls Friesen "unduly pessimistic."

[76] Malherbe, *Social Aspects of Early Christianity*, 75; Theissen, *The Social Setting of Pauline Christianity*, 102; Murphy-O'Connor, *Paul*, 265–73.

greater influence within the church,[77] this prominence of prosperous individuals should not be surprising, especially when we remember the prosperity of Roman Corinth at large.

If any of these "wealthier" members were at the center of controversy in the church, we might expect to find evidence of it, at least beneath the surface, in Paul's mention of these individuals. In this regard it is interesting to note that, while individuals like Stephanus seem to have enjoyed his favor (16:16), he is more ambivalent about Gaius and Crispus,[78] and Erastus gets no mention at all – an interesting point when we bear in mind that Paul, as a rule, never named an opponent.[79]

Religio-cultural considerations

Before exploring the implications of the analysis conducted in our foregoing discussion, some religio-cultural considerations need to be addressed. Here two issues present themselves: the religious or ethnic orientation of the church and the cultural orientation of the city. I treat these in order.

Jewish or Gentile church?

On the question of the church's religious background interpreters have shared wide agreement. Claudius' expulsion of the Jews from Rome in AD 49 (Suetonius, *Claud.* 25.4) was bound to have relocated many of the city's Jews to Corinth. We know that Corinth contained a Jewish community (Philo, *Legat.* 281; Pliny, *Ep.* 5.8), and most probably also a synagogue (Acts 18:8).[80] Accordingly, eight known members of the Corinthian church are said to be of Jewish origin (Aquila, Priscilla, Crispus, Sosthenes, Lucius, Jason, Sosipater, and Apollos), and an occasional remark in 1 Corinthians seems to imply a Jewish presence in the church (e.g., 7:18, NRSV – "Was anyone at the time of his call already circumcised? Let him

[77] The view that a small, prosperous minority enjoyed disproportionate influence in the church is well attested in the secondary literature: e.g., Malherbe, *Social Aspects of Early Christianity*, 72; Theissen, *The Social Setting of Pauline Christianity*, 69, 73, 95–6; Murphy-O'Connor, *Paul*, 271; and Theissen, "Social Conflicts in the Corinthian Correspondence," 377.

[78] Welborn (*An End to Enmity*, 240, 251) quite plausibly argues that Paul's mention of Gaius and Crispus in 1:14 reflects "feigned indifference," designed to separate them from Stephanus, who was in Paul's better favor.

[79] As Welborn notes (*An End to Enmity*, 213), drawing from Judge and Marshall's earlier insights. Paul instead refers to opponents by using τινές, τις, τοῖουτος, and other periphrastic constructions (226).

[80] The synagogue inscription often cited is subject to question; see J. Wiseman, "Corinth and Rome I: 228 BC-AD 267," *ANRW* 7.1:503; Collins, *1Corinthians*, 22; and Fitzmyer, *1 Corinthians*, 31.

not seek to remove the marks of circumcision. Was anyone at the time of his call uncircumcised? Let him not seek circumcision"). On the other hand, at least two prominent church members were of Gentile background (Erastus, Titius Justus), and six other individuals have distinctive Greek (Stephanas) or Roman names (Achaichus, Fortunatus, Gaius, Tertius, and Quartus). Moreover, Paul is explicit that the divisions are grounded in Greek rather than Jewish thought (1:22), and most, if not all, of the problems in the letter are best explained in terms of a pagan background (i.e., appeal to pagan courts, 6:1–11; sexual immorality, 6:12–20; abstinence and sex, ch. 7; pagan temple meals, chs. 8–10; former idolatry, 8:7; 12:2). Fee summarizes the situation best when he says that "[n]othing in the letter cannot be explained in light of its Greco-Roman origins; whereas several items are extremely difficult to explain on the hypothesis of Hellenistic Jewish origins."[81] All said, while the Corinthian church did contain Jews, most agree that Gentile culture predominated.[82]

"Greek" or "Roman" Corinth?

How much the Corinth of Paul's day reflected continuity with the earlier Greek city has remained a matter of debate. In 146 BC, the Hellenistic city had been ravaged by the Romans. Its population devastated and its civic administration dissolved, it lay all but vacant until it was refounded as a Roman colony more than 100 years later (44 BC).[83]

Despite this historical break, older scholarship tended to emphasize cultural continuity between the earlier Greek city and the new Roman colony. In 1940, A. H. M. Jones stated flatly that the Roman emperors "made no attempt to Romanize the Greek-speaking provinces"; their motives "were strictly practical," alleviating an overcrowded Rome and rewarding war veterans with land.[84] This view remained the consensus position for several more decades, so that in 1965 G. W. Bowersock could still write that "Romanization" was "hardly the reason for colonial

[81] Fee, *The First Epistle to the Corinthians*, 14.

[82] As all have agreed – e.g., Baird, "'One against the Other,'" 120; Clarke, *Secular Leadership and Christian Leadership in Corinth*, 101n66; Hays, *1 Corinthians*, 6; Murphy-O'Connor, *Paul*, 273; Horrell, *The Social Ethos of the Corinthian Correspondence*, 91–2; Garland, *1 Corinthians*,18; and Adams and Horrell, "Introduction," in *Christianity at Corinth*, 10.

[83] Reference to its colonization under Caesar can be found in Appian, *Punica* 136; Strabo, *Geogr.* 8.6.23; 17.3.15; Plutarch, *Caes.* 52, 57; Pausanias, *Descr.* 2.1.2; Dio Cassius 43.50.3–5; and Diodorus 32.327.3.

[84] A. H. M. Jones, *The Greek City: From Alexander to Justinian* (Oxford: Clarendon, 1940), 60–2.

foundations" in the east; Caesar, as he said, cannot have had this aim in mind when he "sent so many Greeks back to their old environment."[85]

Only in the last third of the twentieth century did the scene begin to change. According to E. T. Salmon, Roman colonies (though particularly in the west) were indeed intended to act as "centres of Roman influence," serving to introduce the Latin language, to help promote the imperial cult, and to familiarize the indigenous peoples with Roman institutions.[86] In recent decades, the view that Romanization was among the chief purposes of imperial colonization has become a sort of new consensus. Now it is believed that colonization in the east was undertaken as part of a wider imperial strategy to unite the Greek east with Rome. As the capital of the province of Achaea,[87] and home to the biennial Isthmian games, Corinth acted as a "pro-Roman focal point" in Achaean life.[88]

Biblical scholars have applied these new insights to the Corinthian letters, although, I think, with an unfortunate lack of restraint. On the one hand, they have been right to note that, according to Aulus Gellius (*Noct. att.* 16.13), Roman colonies were "little effigies" of Rome, or Rome in miniature; that Roman Corinth was intentionally designed with Italic rather than Greek architecture; that it had a strong imperial cult; and that – judging from the preponderance of epigraphical and numismatic evidence – Latin was the official language of the colony until AD 69.[89] Many have also done well to heed *Pseudo-Julian*, the official petition dispatched from Corinth's neighbors in the mid-first century condemning the city for (allegedly) abandoning its Greek heritage and selling out to *Romanitas*.[90]

And yet I wonder whether we can go as far as Bruce Winter, when he calls Corinth a "*thoroughly* Roman colony" that "*invariably* took its cue from Roman and *not* Greek culture."[91] For Winter, this is not just rhetoric; he does mean *invariably*: "whether rich or poor, bond or free, the cultural milieu which impacted life in the city of Corinth was *Romanitas*."[92] In

[85] G. W. Bowersock, *Augustus and the Greek World* (Oxford: Clarendon, 1965), 66–7.

[86] E. T. Salmon, *Roman Colonization under the Republic* (Ithaca, NY: Cornell University Press, 1970), 148.

[87] Possibly – for the evidence is not entirely clear: cf. Appian, *Hist. rom.* 2.1; Florus, *Epitome of Rom. Hist.* 2.32; and Apuleius, *Metam.* 10.18. For a discussion, see Wiseman, "Corinth and Rome I," 501.

[88] Alcock, *Graecia Capta*, 169.

[89] For such an argument, see for instance D. W. J. Gill, "Corinth: A Roman Colony in Achaea," *BZ* 37 (1993): 259–64; and "In Search of the Social Elite in Corinth," *TynBul* 44 (1993): 323–37.

[90] Winter, *After Paul Left Corinth*, 5, 20; and J. Murphy-O'Connor, *St. Paul's Corinth: Texts and Archaeology* (Collegeville, MI: Liturgical, 2002), 96.

[91] Winter, *After Paul Left Corinth*, 12; emphasis added.

[92] *Ibid.*, 120, 122.

short, so Roman was Paul's Corinth that, in dealing with the Corinthian correspondence, "it would be *inappropriate* to search for ethics, customs, etc. [a tantalizing omission!] in ancient classical Greek or Hellenistic eras rather than the late Republic and early Roman period" (emphasis added).

Winter *is*, of course, extreme, but he is not alone in his essential conclusion. "Roman rather than Greek," "geographically in Greece, culturally in Rome" – frequent statements such as these encapsulate the popular impression given by biblical scholars that, when Mummius marched through in 146 BC, *Romanitas* swept Corinth all but clean of Hellenism.[93]

But seldom are such stark contrasts accurate. Without doubt, the public face of new Corinth looked recognizably "Roman," but this fact need not lead us to the aforementioned conclusions. We need consider not only the differences between public and private, "elite" and "poor," in way of life, but also the ways in which "Greek" and "Roman" culture, for all their differences, in fact blended into one another. The complexity of this relationship has not been fully appreciated in recent biblical scholarship. Whether in the realm of architecture, religion, language, or even culture at large, Roman Corinth, at any social stratum, was not culturally homogeneous, as recent classical studies have agreed.

Margaret Laird has shown that the new city's *Augustales* monument was, like other religious monuments, deliberately built on an old religious site,[94] and with a Greek appearance. In this regard, the monument was designed to elicit a sense of continuity with the city's Greek heritage. Moreover, even if imperial propaganda was an underlying motivation, we cannot, says Laird, assume that the city founders' intentions for this monument necessarily reflected – or would later reflect – the perspective of the populace. More important was how the monument was actually *perceived* during each phase of its history, and perception would have become increasingly "Greek" as time went on. As Laird puts it, "With each passing year, the distinction between Roman commission and Greek form would blur, rooting the monument more firmly in the ancient past."[95]

[93] For the quotations, see Thiselton, *First Epistle to the Corinthians*, 6 (cf. 3–4); Garland, *1 Corinthians*, 3; cf. also Gill, "Corinth," 264; "In Search of the Social Elite in Corinth," 328; Adams and Horrell, *Christianity at Corinth*, 6; V. Nguyen, *Christian Identity in Corinth*, 122–3; and R. M. Grant, *Paul in the Roman World: The Conflict at Corinth* (Louisville, KY: Westminster John Knox, 2001), 19.

[94] M. L. Laird, "The Emperor in a Roman Town: The Base of the *Augustales* in the Forum at Corinth," in S. J. Friesen, D. N. Schowalter, and J. C. Walters (eds.), *Corinth in Context* (Leiden: Brill, 2010), 67–116; in this regard, see also C. M. Thomas, "Greek Heritage in Roman Corinth and Ephesos: Hybrid Identities and Strategies of Display in the Material Record of Traditional Mediterranean Religions," in *Corinth in Context*, 117–49.

[95] Laird, "The Emperor in a Roman Town," 67–116, esp. 110.

Bronwen Wickkiser demonstrates that Corinthian religion was equally convoluted. The Asklepius cult may serve as an example. While this cult was modified in order to evoke parallels between the cult's namesake and the emperor Augustus, in many respects the cult continued to bear the impress of its Greek formulation. In this regard, Wickkiser concludes that the Asklepius of Roman Corinth was "neither a static artifact from the Greek period of the city nor a mere copy of the Roman god, much as the colonists themselves were *neither strictly Greek nor Roman* but were *carving out new cultural identities for themselves*."[96]

The situation is no less complicated when it comes to language in the colony, despite biblical scholars' frequent appeal to the predominance of Latin inscriptions as a clinching factor. Simply counting the Latin inscriptions and setting the total sum next to the total number of Greek inscriptions hardly adds up to the view that Corinth was "thoroughly Roman." Indeed, as Ben Millis has argued, it is imperative to consider the *context* of the inscriptions:

> Greek texts indicate quite clearly that the choice of language used in an inscription of the early colony had little to do with the ethnic or social origins of the colonists and everything to do with the context of the inscription itself . . . One would no more erect an inscription in Latin detailing the officials or victors of the Isthmian games than one would dedicate a building or monument in the Forum using an inscription in Greek.[97]

Beside inscriptions, Millis also investigates other forms of epigraphy: an overwhelming majority of the markings he examines are written in Greek.[98] Little wonder that Greek was the language of the Corinthian correspondence as well.

We may add that Aulus Gellius' oft-cited remark (*Noct. att.* 16.13) – that whereas *municipia* were allowed to retain the laws and customs of the original inhabitants, Roman *colonies* were made to represent "Rome in miniature" – cannot automatically be presumed accurate with respect to Paul's Corinth. Leaving aside the fact that Gellius' remark was penned a century later than the Corinthian letters were, we have plentiful evidence that his characterization of colonies and *municipia* and the differences

[96] B. L. Wickkiser, "Asklepios in Greek and Roman Corinth," in *Corinth in Context*, 37–66, esp. 66; emphasis added.

[97] B. Millis, "The Social and Ethnic Origins of the Colonists," in *Corinth in Context*, 24.

[98] Millis, "The Social and Ethnic Origins of the Colonists," 26–9.

between them admitted of exceptions.[99] Sometimes there seemed no difference at all.[100] Gellius' text therefore hardly warrants the conclusion that Corinth, as a colony, was "entirely" Roman; such a claim would have to be established by careful point-by-point comparison, which, evidently, has not been undertaken carefully enough.

Moreover, extant data reveals that Roman Corinth traveled an unambiguous Hellenizing trajectory. It is no good here to point out that Hellenization began to receive *imperial* endorsement only in Nero's day, in the mid-60s (cf. Suetonius, *Nero* 19ff), and publically to win over the elite still years later, in the time of Hadrian (cf. Dio, *Or.* 37.26). Clearly, if we take seriously what has already been said, it is apparent that a Hellenistic undercurrent had been moving in Corinth *ab initio*, as it did routinely in Roman colonies established on Greek soil. That the population of old, Greek Corinth was left entirely desolate between its ruination in 146 BC and its colonization in 44 BC is now known to be a gross overstatement,[101] and most of the colonizers of the new city were freedmen of Rome, and themselves Greeks.[102] In short, Corinth was loaded for re-hellenization from the start, despite certain public efforts to the contrary.

Beside these issues, we would be remiss to ignore the Romans' debt to the Greeks within the realm of education. Roman education was of course bilingual (taught in both Greek and Latin), and had been taken over from a Greek model in both its form and its essential content.[103] Philosophy, which was taught at the higher levels of learning, had gone across to the Romans almost entirely intact. In the third and second centuries BC, it had arrived in Rome as a "Greek importation," its teachers almost invariably of Greek or eastern provenience.[104] By the first century BC, Cicero and

[99] See K. Lomas, *Roman Italy, 338 BC–AD 200: A Sourcebook* (New York: Routledge, 1996), 88.

[100] Salmon, *Roman Colonization under the Republic*, 155.

[101] For a discussion of the primary sources, see Wiseman, "Corinth and Rome I," 493–6.

[102] Millis ("The Social and Ethnic Origins of the Colonists") argues that they were freedmen and "entirely Greek in origin" (30). The group did not, as has sometimes been said (e.g., J. Walters, "Civic Identity in Roman Corinth and Its Impact on Early Christians," in D. N. Schowalter and S. J. Friesen [eds.], *Urban Religion in Roman Corinth: Interdisciplinary Approaches*, HTS 53 ([Cambridge, MA: Harvard Theological Studies, 2005], 402), consist of both freedmen *and* veterans.

[103] T. Morgan, *Literate Education in the Hellenistic and Roman Worlds* (Cambridge: Cambridge University Press, 1998), 33; Marrou, *A History of Education in Antiquity*, 242–54; and M. Joyal, I. McDougall, and J. C. Yardley (eds.), *Greek and Roman Education: A Sourcebook* (Milton Park, Abingdon, Oxon; New York: Routledge, 2009), 166.

[104] A. A. Long, "Roman Philosophy," in D. N. Sedley (ed.), *The Cambridge Companion to Greek and Roman Philosophy* (Cambridge: Cambridge University Press, 2003), 184.

Lucretius could still speak of the "poverty" of the Latin language as a conduit of philosophy.[105] Accordingly, as a general rule, philosophy was discussed and taught in Greek, rarely if ever in Latin. In fact, A. A. Long notes that "there were no exclusively Roman schools of philosophy, as distinct from the long-established Academics, Peripatetics, Epicureans, and Stoics."[106] To be sure, we know of a few philosophers who wrote in Latin, such as Seneca and Apuleius, but these of course had received their training in Greek.[107] (Moreover, neither of these can rightly be called "teachers" of philosophy, as neither ever served as the head of a school).[108] In short, though studied and practiced by Romans, philosophy remained essentially a Greek enterprise throughout the Hellenistic and Roman eras. Most students of philosophy taught or wrote in Greek, even "Roman" Stoics like Epictetus, Musonius Rufus, and indeed, the Roman emperor himself, Marcus Aurelius. Thus, if philosophy constituted a significant force in first-century Corinth – and as we shall see, it did – it would have added significant "Greek" color to the city, especially, though by no means solely, in elite circles.

In all of this, the wider issue is the extent to which a hard-and-fast line between "Greekness" and "Romanness" can even be drawn. In recent years, the term "Romanization," convenient as it has been, has increasingly fallen out of usage, and for good reason. Rome's expansion and gradual transition into a worldwide empire necessitated a process of reflection on what it meant to be "Roman" in an increasingly cosmopolitan world. Augustus' success in bringing peace and stability to the state owes a great deal to his realization that such a process would have to involve the participation of the provinces and a fusion of the diverse identities they brought to bear. The "Hellenizing" initiative of Nero and later emperors was not, then, some whimsical program introduced against the wishes of a "Roman," and for that reason, antagonistic, ruling class, but a willing acceptance of the fact that the empire – the "Roman" empire – was moving in that direction already.[109]

[105] Long, "Roman Philosophy," 185.

[106] Long, "Roman Philosophy," 184.

[107] Marrou, *A History of Education in Antiquity*, 254.

[108] Long, "Roman Philosophy," 193.

[109] For a discussion of the interplay between "Greek" and "Roman" in the formation of Roman identity, see, for example: A. Wallace-Hadrill, "*Mutatas Formas*: The Augustan Transformation of Roman Knowledge," in K. Galinsky (ed.), *The Cambridge Companion to the Age of Augustus* (Cambridge: Cambridge University Press, 2005), 55–84, esp. 81; N. Purcell, "Romans in the Roman World," in *The Cambridge Companion to the Age of Augustus*, 85–105, esp. 105; G. Woolf, "Provincial Perspectives," in *The Cambridge Companion to Augustus*, 106–29, esp. 109; C. Katsari and S. Mitchell, "The Roman Colonies of the Greek East: Questions of State and Civic Identity," *Athenaeum* 95 (2008):

In concluding this section, I wish to make clear that I am not pushing the pendulum once again to the Greek side. Rather, I aim to steer between what the most recent and focused studies have revealed to be two wrong tendencies. On the one hand, Winter's position that Paul's Corinth was "invariably Roman," irrespective of social circle or standing, must surely be rejected. However, neither can we say that the city was "publically Roman" and otherwise Greek,[110] as if Paul's Corinth was, as it were, a Greek city liveried over with a purple-hemmed toga. Indeed, the situation was much more complicated than either of these positions allows. In this regard, we should probably distinguish, as Millis does, between Corinth's public or higher strata character on the one hand and its private or lower strata character on the other, albeit with the realization that *these will not fall neatly into separate "Roman" and "Greek" compartments*. Millis rather proposes that although people of the lower strata were "more solidly Greek in outlook," those of the higher strata were also willing to "straddle the cultural divide," and as a result exhibited traits from both Greek and Roman culture[111] – bilingualism was only one example. Thus, as a "hybrid" city, Corinth could show "different faces in different circumstances and contexts."[112] Speaking on the topic of religion, Christine Thomas has agreed: "[T]here was no single position even among the privileged classes; the levels of discourse were complex and context-specific. Depending on the audience envisaged by the cultural text, elites could appear either more or less Greek."[113] Jorunn Økland has come to the same conclusion: because the city was a "multifaceted, multilayered society," it is impossible to say whether the religion of Roman Corinth was marked more by continuity or more by discontinuity with the earlier Greek city; probably this is not even a helpful distinction. Instead, when it comes to religion, we are compelled to ask *who* was worshipping particular deities, in *what language* they were doing so, and *what evidence* different groups have left for us to examine.[114] In this whole discussion, then, *context and particularity remain paramount.*

So was Paul's Corinth more "Greek" or more "Roman"? Clearly that depends on *who* and *what* is under consideration. If we are talking about the

219–47; and K. Galinsky, "The Augustan Empire: Unity and Diversity," in *Augustus: Introduction to the Life of an Emperor* (Cambridge: Cambridge University Press, 2012), 159–75.

[110] This is the conclusion of Wendel Willis in "Corinthusne deletus est?" *BZ* 35 (1991): 233–41.

[111] Millis, "The Social and Ethnic Origins of the Colonists," 32.

[112] *Ibid.*, 34.

[113] Thomas, "Greek Heritage in Roman Corinth and Ephesos," in *Corinth in Context*, 146.

[114] J. Økland, "Ceres, Κόρη, and Cultural Complexity," in *Corinth in Context*, 229.

Corinthian "elite," that *may*, on *some* issues, tilt the balance toward the "Roman" side. However, we would need to make several qualifications. As for the Corinthian church, we have seen that, barring the question of Erastus, there were probably no upper elites. Below that level, the church contained perhaps only a handful of prosperous up-and-comers. Moreover, if Corinthian elites tended to "straddle" the Greek-Roman divide, even a *few* Erasti would not constitute proof that, as one important article has put it, "the Corinthian church had a *distinctly* 'Roman' character";[115] it would indicate only a mixed-culture character at best. And then what of the middling and lower-class majority? Finally, there is the question of what issue one is talking about: is one talking, for example, about the Corinthians' embrace of such values as *dignitas*, *severitas*, and *virtus* – "Roman" virtues – or about their philosophical perspectives – a "Greek" pursuit? At all events, we shall not resolve the, apparently confused, Greek-versus-Roman Corinth question here. Suffice it to say that the divisions in the Corinthian church, to whatever extent they might have been engendered by secular "Roman" values, were surely influenced by "Greek" ones as well, not least if philosophy had anything to do with it.

An educated "elite"?

We now return to the issue of social status in the Corinthian church. We have identified eight Corinthians who likely belonged to the economic middling group of their social milieu. Longenecker places five of these in what he calls the "ES4" bracket, the socioeconomic tier consisting of those who possessed a moderate (ES4b) to high (ES4a) surplus of funds. These included Erastus, Gaius, Stephanus, Crispus, and Phoebe, with Erastus falling at the higher end, at ES4a. Friesen, in his early analysis (2004), had placed Gaius and Erastus at his basically equivalent PS4 level, although he also identified Chloe, Priscilla, and Aquila as potential candidates.

Because wealth and education usually went hand in hand, we are bound to ask what implications the socioeconomic level of these individuals might have had for their exposure to philosophy, a significant if less popular focus of learning in Greco-Roman education. To this end, we look next at questions related to wealth and literacy in the ancient world, before moving to an examination of the various contexts in which philosophy itself was encountered, and of what level of acquaintance each of these contexts might have afforded.

115 Adams and Horrell, *Christianity at Corinth*, 6; emphasis added.

Literate education

Apart from adaptations demanded by the context, available resources, and needs of the students, education across the Greco-Roman world followed a remarkably uniform progression. At the primary level, the student learned to copy and read letters, syllables, and words. At the next level, he (rarely she) progressed to technical analysis of "canonical" authors. Finally, the best, and most fortunate, students culminated their training by studying in a school of rhetoric and, if they were inclined, in the school of a philosopher.

In mid-sized cities, teachers were available at both the primary and secondary levels. Primary instruction could be acquired through public schools, through tutors outside the home (Suetonius, *Gramm.* 17; Pliny, *Ep.* 3.3.3; Quintilian, *Inst.* 1.2) or – in elite households – from the parents themselves.[116] For advanced education, one would have needed to travel to one of the great urban centers, such as Rome, Alexandria, or Athens.

Despite the wide availability of primary instruction, the vast majority of the population lacked even basic skills in literacy. Of those who did receive instruction, attrition was high as students progressed through the primary and secondary levels, and only a miniscule proportion reached the rhetorical stage.[117] Peasants were seldom among the literate, and still less slaves. Poorer artisans fared no better, although some artisans seemed to have been prosperous enough to receive at least basic training in literacy; sometimes they are even found among the "gymnasial" class (discussed later in the chapter).[118] In Rome we still have traces of graffiti written by artisans of various kinds, including fullers, weavers, pastry cooks, perfumers, and even a lowly repairer of a shoemakers' tools.[119] As for women, a fair number achieved a high level of mastery in written composition, but these were the exceptions. Women rarely received a basic literary education and never had access to higher, rhetorical training.[120] All said, the total percentage of literate individuals in the Greco-Roman world is unlikely to have exceeded 15 percent, even if in urban centers

[116] W. V. Harris, *Ancient Literacy* (Cambridge, MA: Harvard University Press, 1989), 233; R. Cribiore, *Gymnastics of the Mind: Greek Education in Hellenistic and Roman Egypt* (Princeton, NJ: Princeton University Press, 2001), 105.

[117] A conclusion that Morgan (*Literate Education in the Hellenistic and Roman Worlds*, 69, 201) deduces from the comparatively low number of papyri that include rhetorical exercises.

[118] Harris, *Ancient Literacy*, 277, 330.

[119] Harris (*Ancient Literacy*, 264), citing *CIL* IV 1711; 1768–9, 2184, 4100, 4102–4, 4106–7, 4109, 4112–13, 4115, 4117–18, 4120; and 8258–9.

[120] On women in education according to the papyri, see Cribiore, *Gymnastics of the Mind*, 180–6.

such as Rome that percentage would have been substantially higher.[121] This group was confined mostly to men of the upper and middle classes, but it would have included some women and the occasional poor artisan, peasant, or slave. As such, literacy would have been achieved by most within Longenecker's ES1 to ES4 categories, some within ES5, but very few at the lower end of the scale.

The conduits of philosophy

At the primary and secondary levels of education, philosophy received little attention.[122] Occasionally students encountered the philosophers in their interaction with gnomic sayings (γνωμαί/*sententiae*), which they regularly copied and paraphrased in school exercises, but even here non-philosophical authors were more prevalent.[123] Despite a de-emphasis on philosophy at the lower levels of education, however, philosophy remained a powerful force in first-century society, not only guiding politics and ethics among elites but also shaping the everyday outlook of ordinary citizens. Its influence was everywhere. Grammatical theory, encountered beginning at the lower levels of education, imitated Stoic cosmology: as a linguistic microcosm of the universe, words had to be ordered in a way that reflected "conformity with nature"; there was a natural or "right" way of adjoining words just as there was a natural order to the universe.[124] Moreover, training in Epicurean philosophy could be completed by those without even a secondary education. Apart from school contexts, philosophy was disseminated to the masses in a number of ways. We have inscriptions that placard lengthy philosophical

[121] Harris, *Ancient Literacy*, 175–84, who, as to estimations of the ancient literate population, is still taken to have "put paid" to this line of inquiry (so W. A. Johnson, "Introduction," in *Ancient Literacies* [Oxford: Oxford University Press, 2009], 8).

[122] See Morgan's analysis (*Literate Education in the Hellenistic and Roman Worlds*, 50, 312–18) based on the papyri.

[123] However, Diogenes the Cynic appears with some frequency. For a tabulation of authors cited in gnomic sayings, see Morgan, *Literate Education in the Hellenistic Worlds*, 122–3. On the other hand, ancient literary tractates on education often cite Cicero's philosophical prose (e.g., Quintilian, *Inst.* 1.8.6; 10.1.81–4, 131; Macrobius, *Sat.* 3.14; Pliny, *Ep.* 2.14.2; Suetonius, *Gramm.* 16), and various literary sources include philosophers in their lists of recommended reading (e.g., Cicero, *De or.* 1.52ff; 3.39; Quintilian, *Inst.* 10.1.27ff).

[124] For a discussion of Stoic influence on grammar, see Long, "Roman Philosophy," 191–2; and Morgan, *Literate Education in the Hellenistic and Roman Worlds*, 169–74; on Stoic influence on Theon's *progymnasmata*, see G. Reichel, *Quaestiones Progymnasmaticae*, PhD dissertation, University of Leipzig (1909), 23–30; on Stoic adaptations to antecedent rhetorical theory, see J. R. Butts, "The Progymnasmata of Theon: A New Text with Translation and Commentary," PhD dissertation, Claremont Graduate School (1986), 6–7.

messages, obviously aimed at reaching as many people as possible with their salutary messages;[125] however, these would have spoken only to literates, or to illiterates to whom someone had been kind enough to relay the messages. Most conspicuous of all were the wandering "street preachers" who were ready to chasten whatever passersby would welcome their reproaches. Such were typically of the Cynic variety, austere vagabonds who eschewed conventional education and institutions.[126] But undoubtedly there were peddlers of all the philosophies. In major centers such as Athens, itinerants were constantly coming and going, and philosophers of all stripes were prepared to discuss their ideas in the open marketplace or on the Acropolis, as they were doing upon Paul's visit to the city (Acts 17:16–33).

For philosophy to have had a conscious, far-reaching, and coherent impact on the individual, however, one would most probably have needed more formal exposure. A person with basic literacy and enough leisure might have devoted himself (or herself) to independent study by taking in hand one of the handbooks, or "epitomes," of philosophy, which summarized the key doctrines of the various philosophical schools. Extant epitomes are preserved in Arius Didymus, Stobaeus, and Diogenes Laertius.

But the most exhaustive exposure to philosophy came by studying in the school of a philosopher after completion of secondary school or higher rhetorical education.[127] In earlier days, all the philosophical schools were stationed in Athens, each with its own σχόλαρχος, or "head." The havoc wreaked on Athens by Sulla in the Mithridatic Wars of 88–86 BC, however, precipitated the end of Athens' tenure at the center of the philosophical world. From that point, philosophy became decentralized, and small, local philosophical groups representing respective schools began to crop up throughout the Greco-Roman world.[128] In these schools, students began by learning a few general ideas about the history of philosophy and an outline of the beliefs of the schools, then moved on to general reading of their doctrines, and finally to studying and analyzing a particular school's classic or "canonical" writings.[129]

[125] Harris, *Ancient Literacy*, 219–20.

[126] For such individuals, see Dio Chrysostom, *Or.* 32, Lucian's *Peregrinus*, and the Cynic Epistles.

[127] F. H. Colson and G. H. Whitaker (*Philo, in Ten Volumes*, Loeb Classical Library [Cambridge: Cambridge University Press, 1968], 4:452) note that Philo provides extensive discussion of the Stoic view that the Encyclia (the liberal arts and sciences encountered at the early stages of education) was merely preparation for study in philosophy.

[128] D. Sedley, "The School, from Zeno to Arius Didymus," in *Cambridge Companion to the Stoics* (Cambridge: Cambridge University Press, 2002), 24–8.

[129] Marrou, *A History of Ancient Education*, 208.

It could be expected that any member of the elite would have had a basic acquaintance with the major schools. But the Stoic perspective dominated. Indeed, Roman patricians were naturally drawn to the Stoic system, and for obvious reasons: it envisaged the world as governed by a universal "natural law" and humanity as comprising a single "world community" – an ideal thought to have been fulfilled in the Empire. Stoic ideas pervaded the writings of the late republic and early empire, even the writings of "non-philosophical" writers like Vergil and Horace.[130] Many of the most distinguished Roman statesmen of this period were Stoics: Cato and Seneca the Younger, Helvidius Priscus, Arulenus Rusticus, and even the emperor Marcus Aurelius.[131] Frequently, Greek Stoics rose to eminence in the government: both Athenodorus and Arius Didymus were appointed governors under Augustus. Further examples abound.

From ancient literature and epigraphy we have evidence of established philosophical schools and teachers all over the Mediterranean world. Occasionally permanent schools were set up in gymnasia, as was the school of Zenodotus the Stoic (*IG* II^2 1006). Several ancient inscriptions refer to the "successors of the doctrines of Zeno," the founding Stoic, or else plainly designate teachers as Stoics.[132] An inscription of particular interest to us, dated between 50 and 100 AD, honors a *Corinthian* Stoic named Lucius Peticius Propas (Λούκιον Πετίκιον Πρόπαντα, φιλόσοφον Στωϊκὸν Κορίνθιον; *IvO* 453). This perhaps places Lucius as head of a Stoic school in Corinth at precisely the time of the Corinthian correspondence.

A less rigorous but almost equally selective alternative to studying in an established philosophical school was to study in a gymnasium, a Greek-based institution of higher learning (mentioned previously in connection with the Erastus inscriptions) in which students received a formal, if somewhat superficial, acquaintance with the major philosophies of the day. For several reasons, this venue deserves more detailed treatment.

Gymnasium education

Development of the gymnasium

Although the study of rhetoric dominated instruction at most levels of Greco-Roman education, subsequent to "secondary" or "tertiary" training

[130] Gill, "The School in the Roman Imperial Period," in *Cambridge Companion to the Stoics*, 56.

[131] P. A. Brunt, "Stoicism and the Principate," *Papers of the British School at Rome* 43 (1975): 7–35.

[132] M. N. Tod ("Sidelights on Greek Philosophers," *JHS* 77 [1957]: 132–41) lists several.

many also went on to receive instruction in philosophy. Privileged Greeks undertook training in the gymnasium. This institution had arisen in the Classical period for purposes of military training. In Athens, all male citizens in their eighteenth year – the so-called ἔφηβοι ("pubescent boys," "ephebes") – registered in the gymnasium ἐφηβεία ("ephebate") for a two-year period of military and physical training. With the rise of the Greek philosophical schools in the fourth century BC, however, training became more intellectually focused, and study in rhetoric and philosophy ultimately supplanted physical training in importance.[133] The Hellenistic period concretized the form of instruction, and rhetoric and philosophy became the chief ingredients of training.[134] From the beginning of the third century BC, every major philosophical school could be found in the gymnasium.[135] By 119/118 BC, ephebic training in Athens had ceased to be compulsory for citizens, and foreigners were admitted to join.[136] From the second century BC on, the practice of using itinerant lecturers rather than permanent professors became conventional, doubtless for reasons of economy and convenience.[137] These lecturers might have been any of the itinerant philosophers, rhetors, or other experts who happened to be in the city at the time.[138]

The virtual disappearance of the gymnasium's military purpose coincided with several other important changes in the character of the institution. Socially speaking, from the early third century BC on, the gymnasium took on great significance as a definer of status. It became essentially an association for the "budding elite."[139] Membership was selective, and in some places depended on Greek hereditary requirements on both sides of

[133] N. M. Kennell ("The Greek Ephebate in the Roman Period," *The International Journal of the History of Sport* [2009]: 332; cf. 333–4) observes that during the Roman period military training in the gymnasium is virtually unknown, save in the gymnasium at Athens.

[134] On philosophers in the gymnasium, see C. A. Forbes, "Expanded Uses of the Greek Gymnasium," *CP* 40 (1945): 34–6; O. Tzachou-Alexandri, "The Gymnasium: An Institution for Athletics and Education," in *Mind and Body* (Athens: Greek Ministry of Culture, 1989), 37; Dutch, *The Educated Elite in 1 Corinthians*, 301, 302; as well as *IG* II^2 1006,19,64; Quintilian, *Inst.* 12.2.8; and Cicero, *De or.* 2.21.

[135] Forbes, "Expanded Uses of the Greek Gymnasium," 32–42.

[136] O. W. Reinmuth, "The Ephebate and Citizenship in Attica," *TAPA* 79 (1948): 211–31.

[137] We have only one philosopher on record as a permanent professor; on this score, see Tzachou-Alexandri ("The Gymnasium: An Institution for Athletics and Education," 37), who cites *IG*^{2} II 1006, lines 19, 64.

[138] Forbes ("Expanded Uses of the Greek Gymnasium," 35) observes that these lecturers were "as varied as those of the modern lecture platform."

[139] J. T. Townsend, "Ancient Education in the Time of the Early Roman Empire," in S. Benko and J. J. O'Rourke (eds.), *The Catacombs and the Colosseum* (Valley Forge: Judson, 1971), 150.

the family.[140] Yet, we also have evidence for gymnasium-educated Jews: Philo of Alexandria is a well-known example.[141] Members who had completed ephebic training formed similar, equally selective associations, which enjoyed the same benefits as the ephebes. Among these associations were the νεοί ("young men"), the γερόντες ("old men"), and the "old boys from the gymnasium" (ἀπὸ γυμνασίου, ἐκ τοῦ γυμνασίου), who were, in essence, simply "alumni."[142] Moreover, members were usually expected to foot their own expenses, which could include the cost of lectures, uniforms, oil (for exercise), and other accoutrements[143] – expenses beyond the means of most people but probably affordable to those with a moderate surplus of funds.

Along with a reduction of the length of ephebic training from two years to one came a reduction in the seriousness of the institution's intellectual component. With only a year of exposure, one can imagine that the general cultural level was "not very high."[144] Even apart from the brevity of the program, its members seem not always to have taken the intellectual element altogether too seriously, as we find attested in Cicero, among others:

> Even in the present day, although the sages may be in occupation of all the gymnastic schools, yet their audiences would rather listen to the discus than to the Master, and the moment its clink is heard, *they all desert the lecturer, in the middle of an oration upon the most sublime and weighty topics*, in order to anoint themselves for athletic exercises; so definitely do *they place the most trifling amusement before that which the philosophers describe as the most solid advantage*.
>
> (Cicero, *De or.* 2.21 [Sutton and Rackham, LCL]; emphasis added; cf. Epictetus, *Diatr.* 2.16.26–39, esp. 29)

140 For evidence of hereditary requirements in Roman Egypt, see J. Whitehorne, "The Ephebate and the Gymnasial Class in Roman Egypt," in *Status Declarations in Roman Egypt* 19 (New Haven: The American Society, 1982), 171–84.

141 Scholarship is virtually unanimous in the case of Philo; on his education, see especially D. Runia, *Philo of Alexandria and the Timaeus of Plato* (Leiden: Brill, 1986), 32–36; for other Jews, see Dutch, *The Educated Elite*, 147–64; and especially A. Kerkeslager, "Maintaining Jewish Identity in the Greek Gymnasium: A Jewish 'Load' in CPJ 3.519," *JSJ* 28 (1997), 12–33.

142 So Joyal (*Greek and Roman Education*, 143), citing SEG 8.694. Graduates tended to keep up with each other for life; so N. M. Kennell, *The Gymnasium of Virtue: Education and Culture in Ancient Sparta*, Studies in the History of Greece and Rome (Chapel Hill: University of North Carolina Press, 1995), 43.

143 So Jones (*The Greek City*, 150), who cites inscriptional evidence.

144 Marrou, *A History of Education in Antiquity*, 189; though as he points out (186–8), the training was not exactly "popular"-level either.

In short, ephebic training had become relatively superficial.

Finally, it should be said that the ephebate of the Hellenistic period showed a steady decline in numbers, ultimately leveling off at only a fraction of what it had been during the Classical period. In Athens, the nearly 600 ephebes on the register in the late fourth century BC dwindled within the next two centuries to about 150, where it more or less remained throughout the next few centuries.

All the same, the gymnasium continued well into the Roman period, even in Roman *municipia* and colonies. As already noted, although Corinth had been reestablished as a Roman colony in the first century BC, this ultimately did little to hinder continuing Greek influence, particularly within the realm of education. Indeed, we have firm archaeological evidence that there was a "new gymnasium" in Roman Corinth, constructed as early as the middle of the first century AD.[145] This dating is corroborated by an inscription that refers to "gymnasium victories," which can be dated to AD 55 on the basis of the ἀγωνοθήτης named in the same inscription.[146] We also have an inscription referring to a "gymnasiarch" official (γυμνασίαρχος), apparently also dating to the second half of the first century.[147] Possibly – if Epictetus' passing remark is any indication (*Diatr.* 3.1.34) – by the close of the first century, Corinth had an official ephebate as well.[148]

While it is true that Corinth's political institutions took Roman form (i.e., administration by *aediles* and *duoviri*),[149] it should be mentioned here that such a structure was not, in the Roman period, intrinsically incompatible with a functional gymnasium. Under Roman rule the gymnasium became increasingly severed from state oversight, so that it became a largely private institution.[150] Indeed, Corinth was not the only

[145] For the evidence, see J. Wiseman, "Excavations at Corinth, The Gymnasium Area, 1965," *Hesperia* 36 (1967): 13–41; "Excavations at Corinth, The Gymnasium Area, 1966," *Hesp* 36 (1967): 402–28; "Excavations at Corinth, The Gymnasium Area, 1967–1968," *Hesperia* 38 (1969): 64–106; "The Gymnasium Area at Corinth, 1969–1970," *Hesperia* 41 (1972): 1–42. For its location, see Wiseman, "Corinth and Rome I," 442fig11.

[146] See discussion in Dutch, *The Educated Elite in 1 Corinthians*, 133.

[147] Wiseman, "The Gymnasium Area at Corinth, 1969–1970," 20.

[148] A possibility to which N. M. Kennell gives credence, in *Ephebeia: A Register of Greek Cities with Citizen Training Systems in the Hellenistic and Roman Periods*, Nikephoros Beihefte 12 (Hildes-heim, Weidmann, 2006), 42.

[149] For the inscriptional evidence, see A. West, *Corinth,* Vol. VIII, part II, *Latin Inscriptions, 1896–1926* (Cambridge, MA: Harvard University Press, 1931); and J. H. Kent, *Corinth,* Vol. VIII, part III, *The Inscriptions 1926–1950* (Princeton, NJ: American School of Classical Studies at Athens, 1966).

[150] See A. H. M. Jones, *Cities of the Eastern Provinces* (New York: Oxford University Press, 1937), 312; Marrou, *A History of Ancient Education*, 388n25; M. Hengel, *Judaism*

"Roman" city to continue using gymnasia and electing related officials subsequent to Roman colonization or enfranchisement. This was also the case in Sinope and Pisidian Antioch in Asia Minor, and Naples and Tarentum in southern Italy. In fact, Pisidian Antioch could claim an elected gymnasiarch official, and Naples an official ephebate.[151] Moreover, Roman citizens are found frequently in the ephebic lists.[152] Even in Rome itself, Greek athletics and the gymnasium were embraced far earlier than has usually been appreciated.[153] In sum, while it is possible that the Corinthian gymnasium (present by AD 55?) had not been constructed by the time of the Corinthian correspondence (AD 55/56?), neither can its existence at that time be ruled out.[154]

Moreover, several other cities within just a few miles of Corinth contained gymnasia as well. These included Argos, Epidauros, Megara, Sicyon, and – most famously of all – Athens, where we found the two

and Hellenism: Studies in Their Encounter in Palestine during the Early Hellenistic Period (London: SCM, 1974), 1:66n63; Kennell, *Ephebeia*, xiv; and Kennell, "The Greek Ephebate in the Roman Period," 325, 326.

151 Sinope: Strabo, *Geogr.* 12.3.11 – Pisidian Antioch: *JRS* 1916: 106.6; 1924:198.32 – Naples: Strabo, *Geogr.* 5.4.7; *I.Napoli* I.33; SEG 33.755; *IvO* 56; Suetonius, *Aug.* 98.3; cf. 92.2 – Tarentum: Strabo, *Geogr.* 6.3.1; cf. 6.1.2. Possibly Rhegium's old gymnasium remained operative as well: cf. *IG* XIV 616 and *CIL* X 16. And we should not forget "Nero's gymnasium" in Rome, although there is some discrepancy in the primary sources as to the label: some refer to it as a *thermae* (Jerome, *Chron.* 63), some as a γυμνάσιον/*gymnasium* (Dio, *Or.* 61.21.1; Tacitus, *Ann.* 14.47.3; Philostratus, *Vit. Apoll.* 4.42), and others as both (Suetonius, *Nero* 12.3). For an overview of the secondary literature related to Nero's gymnasium, see G. G. Fagan, *Bathing in Public in the Roman World* (Ann Arbor: University of Michigan Press, 2002), 110n21.

152 A. S. Chankowski, *L'Éphébie hellénistique: Étude d'une institution civique dans les cités grecques des îles de la Mer Égée et de l'Asie Mineure* (Culture et cité, 4 ; Paris: De Boccard, 2010), 278.

153 In spite of the squeamishness toward Greek athletics expressed in some literary sources (e.g., Plautus, *Amph.* 1011; *Epid.* 197–8; *Bacch.* 66–7; Varro, *Rust.* 2.pref.2). On this see especially Z. Newby, *Greek Athletics in the Roman World* (Oxford: Oxford University Press, 2005), 21–44, 229–71; and Fagan, *Bathing in Public in the Roman World*, 214–215n80.

154 Murphy O'Connor (*St. Paul's Corinth*, 96) notes that, according to *Pseudo-Julian*, Roman Corinth was using its taxes "not to furnish gymnastic or musical contests" but "to buy bears and panthers for hunting shows which they often exhibit in their theaters" (Pseudo-Julian, *On Behalf of the Argives* 408a–409d; translated in Murphy-O'Connor, *St. Paul's Corinth*, 96). From this he concludes that Corinth "did not continue the tradition of 'gymnastic contests or musical contests' but opted for 'a foreign spectacle' (409b)." To the contrary, however, the document does *not* state that the city no longer held gymnastic contests, only that this is not what the preponderance of public funds was being used for. In any case, we have evidence that in the Roman period gymnasium activities were substantially defrayed by the gymnasiarch himself (see, e.g., the literature cited in n. 150 to this chapter). Moreover, hunting exhibitions and gymnastic competitions were certainly not mutually exclusive, as Plutarch (*Pomp.* 52.5) evinces.

Erasti discussed earlier.[155] We shall consider the Athenian ephebate at some length in the subsections that follow.

The gymnasium and 1 Corinthians

A recent study by Robert Dutch has identified several passages in 1 Corinthians in which Paul's language echoes gymnasium instruction, most of them involving either athletic images or reference to gymnasium personnel.[156] These include: a possible reference to a gymnasium instructor (1:20), language of nursing and nature (3:1–4), certain agricultural metaphors (3:5–9), Paul as "father" (4:6, 21), removing the marks of circumcision (7:18–24), and boxing imagery (9:24–27). Based on these texts, in conjunction with archaeological and literary evidence of a gymnasium in Corinth, Dutch infers that the Corinthian church must have included some among what he calls the gymnasium-educated "elite." As such, Paul is found correcting the Corinthians by fashioning his discourse in the familiar speech of the gymnasium. Dutch is successful in demonstrating that many of these references have school-related connotations, though it must be said that few of them really evoke a *distinctive* gymnasium context. He is most convincing in his interpretation of 7:18–24, where Paul speaks of removing the marks of circumcision. As Dutch points out, the gymnasium, with its regular display of nude athletes, provides the most plausible context in which such a practice would have been an issue. Clear documentation reveals that Jews sometimes braved reversal of their circumcision in order to compete there.[157]

While I agree with Dutch that Corinth indeed *could* have contained a gymnasium by the time Paul wrote 1 Corinthians (AD 55/56?), given the fact that most of our evidence falls squarely in the latter half of the first century, I do not have full confidence in this possibility. Even so, gymnasia were ubiquitous, and in Paul's day several cities near Corinth could

[155] By the early Roman era, gymnasia had been established in some 200 cities across the Mediterranean world. For an exhaustive overview of the spread of gymnasia between the fifth and first centuries BC, see J. Delorme, *Gymnasion: Etude sur les monuments consacrés a l'education en gréce*, Bibliothéque des écoles Françaises d'Athénes et de Rome (Paris: Editions E. de Boccard, 1960). For the Hellenistic and Roman periods, see N. M. Kennell, *Ephebeia: A Register of Greek Cities with Citizen Training Systems in the Hellenistic and Roman Periods*, Nikephoros Beihefte 12 (Hildes-heim, Weidmann, 2006); Chankowski, *L'Éphébie hellénistique*, 143–233.

[156] R. Dutch, *The Educated Elite in 1 Corinthians: Education and Community Conflict in Graeco-Roman Context*, JSNTSup 271 (London: T & T Clark International, 2005).

[157] *Ibid.*, 295–7. Cf. 1 Macc 1:15; Josephus, *Ant.* 12.5.1; *Apion* 2.13.137; Philo, *Spec. Leg.* 1.2; Martial, *Epigr.* 7.82.

claim them. Dutch's insight into the relevance of the gymnasium may therefore still provide a fruitful avenue for inquiry. We shall, however, have to move beyond his work in at least two important ways: (1) by employing our more recent insights on ancient economy, which will in turn allow further precision regarding the meaning and identity of the "elite"; and (2) by considering the prospect that the gymnasium was an important source of *philosophical* knowledge for certain Corinthian church members.

Social status and gymnasium education

We have already noted that the Corinthian church may not have included anyone from the highest echelons of society, or what Longenecker calls ES1–3. But might people *below* this level have studied in the "elite" gymnasium? If we consider ephebic class sizes in relation to overall city population, we can be certain that a great number in fact did. The ephebate in Athens, which is thought to have been the model for the other Hellenistic cities and therefore "typical" of the ephebate across the Greco-Roman world,[158] affords us with enough information to formulate the basis for a calculation. To be sure, we shall have to work with ballpark figures. Yet, as we shall see, these figures will be well sufficient for our point to stand, even on a conservative estimate.

Although we are left with no census data for the population of Athens in the Roman era, estimates based on demographic trends and comparison with analogous cities make it most probable that, in the first century AD, it contained a total city population (citizens, foreigners, slaves, and all) in the range of 30,000 to 50,000 people.[159] For argumentative purposes, we

[158] So Chankowski, *L'Éphébie hellénistique*, 227–33, echoing Marrou, *A History of Education in Antiquity*, 105.

[159] In fact, Donald Engels (*Roman Corinth: An Alternative Model for the Classical City* [Chicago: University of Chicago Press, 1990], 79) informs us that only *two* classical cities have left us census information providing a city population: Apamea and Alexandria. Although in the fourth century BC Athens could have boasted perhaps as many as 20,000 (E. Ruschenbusch, "Doch noch einmal die Bürgerzahl Athens im 4.Jh.v.Chr.," *ZPE* 72 [1988]: 139–40) or 30,000 *citizens* (M. H. Hansen, *Three Studies in Athenian Demography* [Copenhagen: Kgl. Danske Videnskabernes Selskab, 1988]), we know that its population decreased substantially throughout the Hellenistic period (C. Mosse, *Athens in Decline, 404–86 BC* [Boston: Routledge, 1973]; also E. Spentzou, "Athens," in N. Wilson [ed.], *Encyclopedia of Ancient Greece* [New York: Routledge, 2006], 113). Once it leveled off again at the beginning of the first century AD, it remained stable throughout the next 200 years (J. Day, *An Economic History of Athens under Roman Domination* [New York: Anro, 1973], 279). For lack of census data or other exact measures during this period, some have avoided making numerical judgments (e.g., Day, *An Economic History of Athens under Roman Domination*, 271). Others, however, have sought estimates from what is available:

shall choose to err on the higher end and proffer somewhere between 40,000 and 50,000 people. Out of these, some 1.82 percent – judging from mortality studies[160] – would have been eighteen years of age and therefore eligible to enter the gymnasium ephebate. Therefore, at any given time (assuming a stable first-century population), first-century Athens would have contained somewhere between 728 (1.82 percent of 40,000) and 910 (1.82 percent of 50,000) individuals of ephebic age.

Now, out of these, what percentage actually *did* receive an ephebic education? Our extant figures for the Roman period are as shown in Table 9.

e.g., J. C. Russell (*Late Ancient and Medieval Population* [American Philosophical Society, 1958], 77, 78), who estimates a total population of 28,000 in the middle of the third century AD – though numbers were still recovering in the wake of the epidemics that had swept through Greece around the turn of the same century; also R. Stark ("Christianizing the Urban Empire: An Analysis Based on 22 Greco-Roman Cities," *Sociological Analysis* 52 [1991]: 77–88, esp. 78), who places the population at 30,000 around AD 100. One may also approximate the population of first-century Athens by comparison with Corinth, for which Engels (*Roman Corinth*, 79–84, 179–81), among others, has carried out a more meticulous analysis. Engels notes that when Aristides (*For Poseidon* 23) addressed Corinth around the middle of the second century AD, he could speak of it as the largest city in Greece, apparently without rousing the contempt of his listeners. Based on the probable geographical extent of economic and commercial activity, and the density of the population in Roman Corinth, Engels estimates a *second*-century population between 52,500 and 87,000 – the largest population in the city's ancient history. Furthermore, given that the city apparently outgrew its water supply during the reign of Hadrian, and at least 56,000 could have been supported on the new system constructed thereafter, Engels concludes that Corinth's population during the first quarter of the second century AD must have increased beyond 56,000. While Engels's figures have not gone unquestioned, they deviate little from figures proposed more recently: Rinse Willet's ("Whirlwind of Numbers: Demographic Experiments for Roman Corinth," *Ancient Society* 42 [2012]: 127–58, esp. 151) recent synthesis of earlier studies estimates a total Corinthian population of 30,000–50,000 people during the Roman era – which, if anything, might even compel us to *lower* our figures for Athens. Hence, if the population of Athens remained stable throughout the first and second centuries AD, and it could not have closely rivaled Corinth in the mid-second century, then in the first century it can hardly have had a population larger than 50,000.

[160] I have used the Coale-Demeny West Model of A. J. Coale, P. G. Demeny, and B. Vaughan, *Regional Model Life Tables and Stable Populations* (New York and London, 1983). Although the model has received some criticism (i.e., W. Scheidel, "Roman Age Structure: Evidence and Models," *JRS* 91 [2001]: 1–26; and *Debating Roman Demography* [Leiden: Brill, 2001]), the recent and informative study from Tim H. Parkin (*Old Age in the Roman World: A Cultural and Social History* [Baltimore: Johns Hopkins University Press, 2002]) continues to endorse it. Parkin explains that, as a "stationary population model," the Coale-Demeny West Model assumes that birth and death rates remain "constant over an indefinite period and are equal (the growth rate is zero), and the population is closed, that is there is no effect from migration, and any short term fluctuations as a result of such factors as plague, war, and famine are smoothed out over the long term" (48); figures apply equally to either sex (328n46). Parkin affirms that the revisions made to Coale-Demeny in light of the criticisms of Scheidel have made "little difference" in the figures. Thus, Parkin affirms that the present model is sufficiently accurate with regard to generalized population over time: we simply "do not have sufficient evidence to fit any ancient population with more precision" (328n46).

Table 9. *The Athenian ephebate, 119 BC–AD 200*

Source	Date	Total # ephebes
IG II^2 1008	119/8 BC	141 (17 foreigners 124 Athenians)
IG II^2 1009	117/6 BC	174 (12 foreigners, 162 Athenians)
IG II^2 1011	107/6 BC	140 (24 foreigners, 116 Athenians)
IG II^2 1028	102/1 BC	138 (36 foreigners, 102 Athenians)
IG II^2 1039	83–73 BC	110 (5 foreigners, 105 Athenians)
IG II^2 1043	38/7 BC	119 (66 foreigners, 53 Athenians)
IG II^2 1963	AD 13/12	130
IG II^2 1969, 1970	AD 45/6	102
IG II^2 1973	AD 41–54	96
IG II^2 1996	AD 92/3	231 (151 foreigners, 80 Athenians)
IG II^2 2017	AD 97/8	72 (12 foreigners, 60 Athenians)
IG II^2 2024	AD 111/2	100 (79 foreigners, 21 Athenians)
IG II^2 2026	AD 116/7	52 (4 foreigners, 48 Athenians)
IG II^2 2065	AD 150/1	77 (7 foreigners, 70 Athenians)
IG II^2 2086	AD 163/4	136 (41 foreigners, 95 Athenians)
IG II^2 2097	AD 169/70	234 (154 foreigners, 80 Athenians)
IG II^2 2103	AD 172/3	215 (109 foreigners, 106 Athenians)
IG II^2 2130	AD 192/3	124 (39 foreigners, 85 Athenians)
IG II^2 2128	AD 200	198 (104 foreigners, 94 Athenians)

As is evident, numbers shifted slightly from century to century. But the average number of *total* ephebes per year (Athenians + foreigners) seems to have remained fairly consistent. If we separate the data roughly by century, the averages are as follows:

119/8 BC–AD 1: 137 ephebes
AD 13/12–100: 114 ephebes
AD 101–200: 141 ephebes

The same can be said for the average number of *Athenian* ephebes per year (where this information can be determined):

119/8 BC– AD 1: 95 Athenian ephebes
AD 13/12–100: 70 Athenian ephebes
AD 101–200: 74 Athenian ephebes

In both the first and third periods, Athenians comprised more than half of the ephebes (69 percent in the first period and more than 52 percent in the third). This means that, even if Athenians were gradually giving way to foreigners in terms of total numbers, we can still assume that Athenians in the second period comprised more than half of the ephebes (about 60 percent would be commensurate – 68.5 out of 114), as indeed the two figures we do have from the middle period indicate (i.e., at an average of 70 Athenians per class). Therefore, while the number of Athenians in comparison with foreigners does shift some from one period to the next, for our purposes that shift is negligible: we are safe in saying that the Athenian ephebate in the first century averaged about seventy Athenian citizens per entering class.

While "foreign" ephebes were not Athenian citizens, it has generally been assumed by specialists that Athens was their primary place of residence.[161] We may therefore conclude that a fair number of them would have remained in Athens upon completion of the ephebate. Even so, to simplify things, and to make our case still more probable, let us omit foreigners and treat only these seventy Athenian citizens who entered the ephebate each year: if the urban center of first-century Athens contained an overall population of 40,000 individuals, and thus 728 of these were of ephebic age, then some 9.6 percent of Athenian eighteen-year-olds entered the ephebate each year. If it contained a population as large as 50,000 individuals, and thus 910 individuals of ephebic age, then that number would be somewhat lower, at 7.7 percent.

Admittedly, it would be too much to assume that every Athenian ephebe remained in Athens for the remainder of his life. But Athenian emigrants would have been offset to some extent by those foreigners who decided to remain after completing the ephebate, as well as by the arrival of ephebate-educated immigrants from other cities. We should also bear in mind that our mortality figures do not vary by socioeconomic class, and the wealthy are likely to have survived longer than the "average" person. We may therefore safely conclude that ephebate-educated eighteen-year-olds in Athens amounted, at the very least, to 7–8 percent of the eighteen-year-old urban population, and may well have comprised as much as 9–10 percent. Given that urban economy, and not that of the surrounding rural areas, has been the concern of Friesen's (2004) poverty scale and Longenecker's (2009; 2010) economy scales, we can make nearly a direct comparison between these ephebate figures and the PS/ES economy

[161] M. J. Osborne, and S. G. Byrne, *The Foreign Residents of Athens* (Paris: Peeters, 1996), xxix.

brackets: if 7–10 percent of eighteen-year-old Athenians entered the ephebate each year, it is apparent that far more than the elite 3 percent must have received an ephebic education.[162] Indeed, we are safely spilling over into Longenecker's "ES4" bracket.

Even if we rejected the *urban* economy scales of Longenecker (2009; 2010) and Friesen (2004), and relied solely on the Friesen and Scheidel's (2009) model, which considers the *overall* distribution of wealth rather than that of *urban* territory alone, still our point would obtain. The aggregate population of settlements and towns surrounding Athens cannot have amounted to more than 20,000.[163] We would then have a total population of 60,000–70,000 people in all the Corinthia (city with its hinterlands) and thus an eighteen-year-old population between 1,092 and 1,274, leaving us still with somewhere between 5.5 percent and 6.4 percent of eighteen-year-olds in or around Athens who were receiving an ephebic education, and therefore a large number of ephebes who belonged, not to the highest elite group, but to the upper-middling/middling group of the population (ES4–5). This range of membership is born out by inscriptional evidence, where we do find the occasional artisan attested as members of the gymnasial class.[164]

What might all this mean for gymnasium education in Roman Corinth? While we *do* have some evidence for a gymnasium and affiliated officials in first-century Corinth, as we have seen, we have no direct evidence for an official ephebate, at least not beyond a couple of doubtful hints.[165] Official ephebate or not, however, gymnasium education was always selective, being open almost exclusively to the "upper classes." Therefore, whether one received an official ephebate education in Corinth (less likely), a gymnasium education in Corinth apart from an official ephebate (possible),

[162] Another way of getting at the desired figure is to compare the aggregate number of ephebes in the city – that is, the sum total from *all* graduating classes – with the overall population. Thus, adjusting for mortality in accordance with the Coale-Demeny West Model, we would have seventy eighteen-year-old ephebes, sixty-nine nineteen-year-olds who *had been* ephebes, sixty-eight twenty-year-olds who *had been* ephebes, and so on. All together, these would amount to 5–6% of the city's population, depending on whether we settle with 40,000 or 50,000 as our starting figure. Of course, this percentage is somewhat lower than the 7–10% figure calculated earlier because it does not account for those still under the age of eighteen who belong to wealthy households and eventually *will* enter the ephebate.

[163] Engels (*Roman Corinth*, 84) estimates 20,000 for the areas surrounding the larger city of Roman Corinth. Willet ("Whirlwind of Numbers," 150) estimates an urban-rural population ratio of 4:1 for Roman Corinth, which would yield an addition of only some 10,000 people.

[164] Harris, *Ancient Literacy*, 276–7.

[165] Epictetus, *Diatr.* 3.1.34, mentioned by Kennell, *Ephebeia*, 42; cf. *1 Clem.* 3:1.

or a gymnasium education in either form through a gymnasium nearby (more likely), the implications would have been the same; such a one was among the privileged, generally at least among the top 10 percent of society. Here again the question whether our Erastus was the same man as the Athenian ephebe presents itself as a real possibility.

In sum, we have good reason to believe that, for cities like Athens, upwards of 7–10 percent of the urban population (or about 6 percent of the city's combined urban-plus-hinterland population) had gone or would go through the gymnasium. Our working figure for the Athenian population would need to be impossibly higher – indeed, 100,000–150,000 – for ephebes to have been drawn only from the top 3 percent of urban society. Hence, even though we have relied on a rough estimate for our starting Athenian population, we easily remain within sufficient range for our case to stand.

Finally, it should be said that, if our 7–10 percent figure seems high, it is surely because our expectations about gymnasium privileges have been conditioned by the older and economically imprecise "elite-versus-non-elite" way of talking about ancient society. It is now apparent that, if a gymnasium education was considered "elite," this could not have meant that it was limited to the top 1–3 percent of society. It must have included a large portion of ES4a people, in addition to ES4b and ES5 members who rubbed elbows with the right people. All of this confirms the possibility that certain Corinthian church members were within reach of a credentialed philosophical education. Whether such an education was completed in Corinth, Athens, or elsewhere,[166] this could easily have included individuals like Gaius, Stephanus, or – still most tantalizingly of all – Erastus.[167]

Church relations

Relations with outsiders

We have seen so far that the denizens of first-century Corinth would have been influenced to a considerable extent by Greek culture and

[166] E.g., Argos, Epidauros, Megara, Sicyon, or Athens, which were all in close vicinity to Corinth.

[167] While there is evidence in Roman Egypt that some girls participated in the gymnasia, they were the exceptions; e.g., *P.Corn.* I.18; *P.Oxy.* XLIII.3136; cf. Plutarch, *Pomp.* 55.1. Occasionally we find female gymnasiarchs, but these appear late in the Roman period; so Kennell, "The Greek Ephebate in the Roman Period," 329. The role of women in church assemblies is a different issue: cf. M. Y. Macdonald and J. H. Tulloch, *A Woman's Place: House Churches in Earliest Christianity* (Minneapolis: Fortress, 2006), cf. 1–16, 144–63.

philosophical currents – not just Roman influences – and that some within the Corinthian church likely had a formal philosophical education within reach. It remains for us to ask how Paul's converts to Christianity could ever have justified adopting pagan philosophy even where it may blatantly have contradicted his Christian message.

The situation in the Corinthian church seems to have been born out of a dynamic process involving several integrally related factors, including – but not reducible to – good relations with outsiders, a lack of deterrents to conversion, and a high tolerance for theological pluralism.[168] It is difficult to say what came first. Probably when Paul first arrived in Corinth, the Corinthians found aspects of his message amenable to their current ways of thinking. Interpreting Christianity in terms of mainstream/pagan categories of thought, they then went on with business as usual, leaving theological and ethical boundaries insufficiently defined and remaining fully integrated into their old social networks. As a result, connected outsiders perceived few deterrents to conversion, and the church in turn attracted further individuals who would retain the mentality of their secular acculturation after joining the community. In that way, a kind of pluralistic outlook would continue to thrive within the church. Such an outlook would continue to perpetuate both good relations with outsiders and a deterrent-free invitation to join the community, and the effect would be paid back in turn. The Corinthians would then have seen no problem embracing Christianity while also drawing heavily from elements of Greek philosophy.

The Corinthian assembly

One more aspect of the Corinthian church's social setting needs to be addressed – the configuration of its assemblies. The issues involved here include the venues used for church meetings, the total size of the Corinthian church, and the models on which its meetings were based.

It has long been held that church gatherings took place in private homes. In 1983, Jerome Murphy-O'Connor attempted to shed new light on these gatherings with the publication of a short chapter entitled "House-churches and the Eucharist."[169] The essay called attention to a first-century villa discovered near Corinth, at Anaploga. As a "typical"

[168] For similar discussions, see Barclay, "Thessalonica and Corinth," 49–74; and J. Walters, "Civic Identity in Roman Corinth and Its Impact on Early Christians," in *Urban Religion in Roman Corinth*, 415–16.

[169] J. Murphy-O'Connor, *St. Paul's Corinth*, Good News Studies 6 (Wilmington: Michael Glazier, 1983), 153–60; (Collegeville: Liturgical, 2002), 178–85.

house,[170] this villa included among its features a *triclinium* or "dining room" measuring approximately 5.5 × 7.5 meters, and an atrium of approximately 5 × 6 meters. Based on comparisons with similar houses, Murphy-O'Connor concluded that an average triclinium in a private villa would have measured about 36 sq. meters, and an average atrium about 55 sq. meters. Perhaps such was the house of Gaius, presumably one of the wealthier members of the Christian community at Corinth (Rom 16:23)? If so, his home could have accommodated about nine individuals in the triclinium and some thirty to forty in the atrium – about forty to fifty individuals in all.[171]

But if this was the size of a "typical" Corinthian villa, could it have accommodated the whole Corinthian church? Murphy-O'Connor observes that we can calculate a minimum estimate of the church's size based on the information afforded from Acts and the Pauline epistles. If we omit Chloe (as Murphy-O'Connor does), sixteen individuals are named.[172] We may then add spouses and baptized household members, including children, servants/slaves, and relations. In all, the church will then have contained a bare *minimum* of forty to fifty individuals.[173] As Murphy-O'Connor observes, ordinarily the church probably met in different homes, in subgroups (Rom 16:5; 1 Cor 16:19; cf. Col 4:15; Phlm 2), and only occasionally came together as a "whole" church (Rom 16:23), at which times a relatively sizeable house would have been necessary to accommodate everyone.[174]

More recently, scholars have begun to consider alternative meeting spaces. In 2004, two important articles were published on the issue. David Balch made a case that meetings were more likely held in small apartment blocks.[175] David Horrell, on the other hand, was less restrictive, arguing

[170] Murphy-O'Connor, *St. Paul's Corinth* (1983), 155.

[171] *Ibid.*, 156. This figure was later disputed by Carolyn Osiek and David Balch (*Families in the New Testament World: Households and House Churches* [Louisville: Westminster John Knox, 1997]), who argued for a considerably larger number (pp. 201–2).

[172] Priscilla and Aquila (Acts 18:2), Titius Justus (Acts 18:7), Crispus (Acts 18:8; 1 Cor 1:14), Sosthenes (Acts 18:17), Gaius (1 Cor 1:14; Rom 16:21–4), Stephanus (1 Cor 1:16; 16:17); Apollos (1 Cor 16:12), Fortunatus (1 Cor 16:17), Achaicus (1 Cor 16:17), Lucius, Jason, Sosipater, Tertius, Erastus (Rom 16:21–4), and Quartus (Rom 16:21–4).

[173] Murphy-O'Connor. *St. Paul's Corinth* (1983), 155; (2002), 182.

[174] *Ibid.*, 156; (2002), 183. Horsley (*1 Corinthians*, 30) argues from 1 Cor 11:18; 14:23; cf. 10:20; Rom 16:23 that multiple house churches must have existed. On this basis Craig Steven de Vos (*Church and Community Conflicts: The Relationships of the Thessalonian, Corinthian, and Philippian Churches with Their Wider Civic Communities*, SBLDS 168 [Atlanta: Scholars, 1999], 203–5) estimates as many as 100 Corinthian Christians. Hays (*1 Corinthians*, 7) estimates 150–200.

[175] D. L. Balch, "Rich Pompeiian Houses, Shops for Rent, and the Huge Apartment Building in Herculaneum as Typical Spaces for Pauline House Churches," *JSNT* 27 (2004): 28.

that early churches probably met in a variety of venues, including not only country villas, peasant homes, and smart town apartments, but also rooms behind or over shops, and even "ramshackle and temporary dwellings of the destitute."[176] Helpful as these developments have been, however, Peter Oakes's 2009 monograph has confirmed that Murphy-O'Connor's original scenario remains plausible, regarding both the house setting and the number of people that such settings might have accommodated.[177]

The meetings themselves have been likened to those of other contemporary groups. Years ago Meeks compared early church assemblies with four other ancient models: the household, the voluntary association, the synagogue, and – of most interest to us – philosophical schools.[178] He concluded that although all offer close analogies, "none of the four models ... captures the whole of the Pauline *ekklesia*."[179] Comparison with philosophical schools has subsequently been taken up by others.[180] Yet Meeks's conclusion continues to be affirmed: no model offers a perfect analogy to church meetings. In a recent reconsideration of Meeks's work, however, Edward Adams has offered a judicious contribution in distinguishing between *perceptions* of these meetings by outside observers and the meetings as they were conceived by the insiders themselves. Perhaps more importantly, he distinguishes also between Paul's *ideal* for these communities and the reality that the Corinthians embodied.[181]

176 D. Horrell, "Domestic Space and Christian Meetings at Corinth: Imagining New Contexts and the Buildings East of the Theatre," *NTS* 50 (2004): 366. In any case, it is doubted whether Murphy-O'Connor's Corinthian villa can be said to be "typical," for we know too little about urban Corinth to make any kind of informed comparison. For this discussion, see D. N. Schowalter, "Seeking Shelter in Roman Corinth: Archaeology and The Placement of Paul's Communities," in *Corinth in Context*, 327–41.

177 See Oakes, *Reading Romans in Pompeii*, 81, where he explores the possibility of house churches of about 40 people. Though B. S. Billings ("From House Church to Tenement Church: Domestic Space and the Development of Early Urban Christianity – The Example of Ephesus," *JTS* 62 [2011], 541–69) argues that tenement blocks woud have provided better accommodation.

178 Meeks, *First Urban Christians*, 75–84.

179 *Ibid.*, 84.

180 L. Alexander, "Paul and the Hellenistic Schools: The Evidence of Galen," in *Paul in His Hellenistic Context*, 60–83; and "IPSE DIXIT: Citation of Authority in Paul and in the Jewish and Hellenistic Schools," in T. Engberg-Pedersen (ed.), *Paul beyond the Judaism-Hellenism Divide* (Louisville: Westminster John Knox, 2001), 103–27; C. Glad, *Paul and Philodemus: Adaptability in Epicurean and Early Christian Psychagogy* (Leiden; New York: Brill, 1995); and S. Stowers, "Does Pauline Christianity Resemble a Hellenistic Philosophy?" in *Paul beyond the Judaism-Hellenism Divide*, 81–102.

181 E. Adams, "First-Century Models for Paul's Churches: Selected Scholarly Developments since Meeks," in T. Still and D. Horrell (eds.), *After the First Urban Christians* (Edinburgh: T & T Clark, 2009), 77.

In the end, much of what we know about early church assemblies remains speculative. It can be said on the basis of our socioeconomic data, however, that five or six individuals of moderate wealth within a church of fifty-plus members does not sound disproportionate, especially in the wealthy city of Corinth. According to our assessment of ancient education, that some of these may have had some formal acquaintance with philosophy appears to be a reasonable possibility. The upshot is that some within their midst may indeed, against Paul's better wishes, have viewed their group as a kind of philosophical school, the gospel as a sort of philosophy, and their teachers as purveyors of its wisdom.

Conclusions

Any reconstruction of 1 Corinthians must be informed by the social circumstances of first-century Corinth. This chapter has addressed several aspects of the Corinthian social context with an eye to our thesis that Stoic philosophy was a major driving force in the church's divisions.

In considering the religio-cultural mores of first-century Corinth, I have agreed with the consensus that the church, while containing a Jewish contingent, was primarily of Gentile orientation and that their problems were essentially of a Gentile nature. Yet I have also attempted to redress misleading cultural characterizations of the city as "thoroughly" or "invariably" Roman, "Roman rather than Greek," or "geographically in Greece, culturally in Rome," and of the Corinthian church as "distinctly Roman." For too long have such assertions served, intentionally or not, to sideline Greek philosophy from the discussion. Indeed, based on the consistent conclusions of recent classical examinations of the city, it has been shown that Paul's Corinth, although a Roman colony, was not "simply Roman" but was rather a unique Roman-Greek amalgam comprised of a highly Greek populace, and an aristocracy that was quite willing to "straddle the cultural divide."

The question of social standing in the Corinthian church has also been a major concern in this chapter. Although disagreeing in the exact details, Friesen and Longenecker have both confirmed that the church was beset to some degree by social stratification, with the majority of its members falling around, at, or below subsistence level, and a minority (albeit, most think, an influential one) perhaps at the PS/ES4 level, possessing a moderate (to high) surplus of funds. It was noted that individuals at the ES4 level of society would usually have been literate and could have perused philosophical handbooks on their own; but many individuals at this level would also have obtained formal philosophical training in a gymnasium. If Dutch's conclusions are valid – namely that Paul employs gymnasium imagery throughout the letter as a way of chastening those educated there – then the gymnasium may also provide a plausible context in which certain Corinthians could have received philosophical training. While philosophy diffused itself throughout the various echelons of society in a variety of ways – street preachers, books, inscriptions, as well as local schools of philosophy, which we have found even in Corinth itself (cf. *IvO* 453) – as we shall see in Chapter 5, the gymnasium may have provided just the level of philosophical instruction the wise Corinthians seem to have had.

Erastus remains an elusive figure. If he is not to be identified with the aedile of *Corinth VIII* 232, still Goodrich's recent work on the nature of the office of οἰκονόμος gives us strong reasons to see him as a man of exceptional status among early Christians. We have added to the discussion here by drawing attention to the thin distribution of relevant Erastus references from the ancient world. Strikingly, beside *Corinth VIII* 232 we have evidence of only *two* Erasti at all in first-century Greece, both of them associated with the Athenian gymnasium and both appearing precisely in the middle years of the century, just prior to the Corinthian correspondence. The appearance of the name there may only tempt us. But it creates no strain on the imagination to suppose that one of these two elite young men standing on the brink of a political career might have gone on after his time in the gymnasium in the 40s to be οἰκονόμος in the nearby city of Corinth.

All said, it has become apparent that the social conditions both of first-century Corinth and of the Corinthian church itself provided more than a suitable environment to allow for the infiltration of Stoic philosophy into the church's midst. Whether that did in fact happen, and a form of Stoic "wisdom" took center stage in the church's divisions, is the subject of Chapter 5.

5

THE "WISE MAN" AMONG THE CORINTHIANS

With each of the foregoing chapters, we have been pursuing a reassessment of the current consensus on the question of the Corinthians' divisive "wisdom." Having contended in Chapter 2 that the regnant, rhetorical thesis provides an unsatisfactory explanation for the evidence, working from the distillation of the Corinthians' views identified in Chapter 3, and the social-historical data of Chapter 4, we can now develop our constructive contribution: the Corinthians' wisdom is best understood as a *Christian* adaptation of *Stoic* philosophy, conceived, as we shall see, in response to a Pauline message that to a philosophically educated audience must have struck a familiar chord.

It will be imperative that the present argument not be evaluated apart from the work undertaken in the first four chapters. Moreover, it cannot be overemphasized that the present thesis, like any other, will rely to some extent on an argument from *coherence*. While some of the arguments can be regarded, independently, as secure fixtures, others will provide mutual support for each other or rest partly on the foundation of the former. But when *all* the data is taken together – a full examination of the letter, a balanced consideration of the social context, and a careful treatment of counter theses – it should become evident that the Stoic thesis provides more than a viable alternative to theses advanced in recent years. Indeed, if a Stoic explanation has not yet received the attention it deserves, we shall see that it is not for a want of evidence.

The present chapter will proceed as follows. After traversing a brief history of the Stoic school and an overview of its extant literary sources, we shall then move to an analysis of 1 Corinthians and its Corinthian language under the five topical domains identified in Chapter 3: wisdom/ the wise man, status distinctions, freedom and indifferents (treated together), and "dualism."

Because of the danger of distortion presented by selective treatment of the letter, the present chapter must take a more comprehensive approach. Accordingly the Stoic hypothesis is tested on the letter *as a whole* – every major section – as we move through our five topics. The goal is not to be reductive. Stoic connections will not *always* leap off the page. Some material may reveal that Stoic connections remain only a possibility, or that Stoicism provides only some supporting justification for the Corinthians' behavior or views without necessarily constituting the chief driving force. On occasion I indulge in speculation. Yet, less clear examples ought to be clarified by the clearer ones, and for the greater part of the material, Stoic connections will prove to be quite conspicuous, and essential to the issues at stake. More importantly, I hope to show that the Stoic explanation cuts across the *whole* of the letter, providing a unifying and compelling explanation for all of the letter's *dominating* topics and for the Corinthian language and slogans that appear in connection with them.

Stoicism

History of the school

In Paul's day, Stoicism was already several hundred years old.[1] The great Socrates, who died in 399 BC, had taught Antisthenes, who had taught Crates of Thebes, who in turn taught the famous Cynic Diogenes of Sinope, master of the founding Stoic Zeno (335–263 BC).[2] With Socrates as a common fountainhead, Stoicism naturally drew from a variety of the schools he had inspired. It drew heavily from Cynicism and Platonism, and to a lesser extent from Aristotelianism.[3] Subsequent to Zeno and his immediate successor, Cleanthes, these various streams of influence were synthesized under the school's third scholarch, Chrysippus. Stoicism as it was formulated under Chrysippus became the authoritative and "more or less standard" version of Zeno's philosophy.[4] Although Cynic influence

[1] For the history of the school, see A. A. Long and D. N. Sedley, *The Hellenistic Philosophers* (Cambridge: Cambridge University Press, 1987), 1:1–9; D. N. Sedley, "The School, from Zeno to Arius Didymus," in *Cambridge Companion to the Stoics* (Cambridge: Cambridge University Press, 2002), 7–32; D. N. Sedley, "Introduction," in *The Cambridge Companion to Greek and Roman Philosophy* (Cambridge: Cambridge University Press, 2003), 1–19; J. Brunschwig and D. Sedley, "Hellenistic Philosophy," in *The Cambridge Companion to Greek and Roman Philosophy*, 151–83; C. Gill, "The School in the Roman Imperial Period," in *Cambridge Companion to the Stoics*, 33–58; and B. Inwood and L. P. Gerson, *The Stoics Reader: Selected Writings and Testimonia* (Indianapolis: Hackett, 2008), x–xv.

[2] Antisthenes (ca. mid-fifth–mid-fourth century BC); Crates of Thebes (ca. 368/365–288/285 BC); Diogenes of Sinope (ca. 412/403–ca. 324/321 BC).

[3] So Inwood and Gerson, *The Stoics Reader*, xi.

[4] As Inwood (*The Stoics Reader*, xii) puts it.

did not disappear,[5] its ethical extremism and raffish defiance of conventional values became appreciably muted.

In Stoicism, school loyalty therefore meant loyalty to Zeno – or rather, Zeno as interpreted through Chrysippus. For several generations after Chrysippus, Zeno's authority was upheld by an unbroken succession of scholarchs: Diogenes of Babylon, Antipater, and finally Panaetius, the last scholarch before Athens witnessed its demise under the onslaught of Sulla's army in 88/89 BC. In the period that followed, Stoic teachers established schools in various localities, of which the Rhodian school of Posidonius, student of Panaetius, was most notable. It was Posidonius who had taught philosophy to the great Roman orator Cicero (*Nat. d.* 1.6; cf. 2.88; *Fin.* 1.6; *Tusc.* 2.61), who himself committed much of his master's thought to writing. From Posidonius through the second century AD, many eminent Stoic teachers left their marks – the Tarsians Zeno and Antipater, along with the famous Epictetus, and others – but none wielding the weight of authority commanded by the early scholarchs.[6] Chrysippus, without dispute the most important thinker in the history of the school, continued to represent the standard of Stoic orthodoxy. Indeed, centuries later, Epictetus was still able to equate "being a Stoic teacher" with "expounding Chrysippus" (*Diatr.* 1.4.6–9; 1.17.13–18).

Despite the essential stability of the Stoic system, Stoic thinkers were not afraid to add to, or even revise, the doctrines of their founders. Thus it becomes important to distinguish several phases in the school's history. The customary divisions are "Early Stoicism" (from Zeno through Chrysippus), "Middle Stoicism" (Panaetius and Posidonius), and "Imperial" or "Roman Stoicism" (epitomized in Seneca, Epictetus, and Marcus Aurelius).[7] Middle Stoicism marked somewhat of a departure from early Stoicism in the area of psychology, as Panaetius, and then more definitively Posidonius, sought to integrate Stoic and Platonic ideas on the nature of the soul. These endeavors were symptomatic of the philosophical climate of the day, which exhibited a growing tendency toward "eclecticism." Following upon the demise of the major schools' headquarters in Athens in 88 BC, Platonism on the one hand – which was still alive in the form of the "Fourth Academy" – and Stoicism on the other grew increasingly closer together, ending with the virtual disappearance of Stoicism and the rise of Neo-Platonism around AD 200. In the

[5] See, e.g., Long and Sedley, *The Hellenistic Philosophers*, §58–59, 67A–H.

[6] See, e.g., Tod, "Sidelights on Greek Philosophers," 140; Gill, "The School in the Roman Imperial Period," 34–6; Sedley, "The School, from Zeno to Arius Didymus," 30.

[7] However, Sedley ("The School, from Zeno to Arius Didymus," 7) divides it into five.

intervening period, Stoicism survived in two different forms: one in the shape of what is often called "popular philosophy" – a nebulous entity that drew together features common to several philosophical schools but that had Stoicism as its dominating ingredient – the other in the form of "Roman Stoicism," which remained a distinctive school. Like the Stoics of the Middle period, however, Roman Stoics were not afraid to deviate from earlier teachings. Seneca, for instance, showed readiness to deviate from Stoic teachings (*Ot.* 3.1), or to criticize (*Ep.* 90.7; *Nat.* 7.22.1) or revise them (*Ep.* 33.7–8; 64.7); he was also avowedly influenced by other philosophical systems (*Ep.* 58.6; 108.13, 22; *Nat.* 3.27.3; 5.20 7.30.1–2). Nonetheless, Stoics of the "Middle" and "Roman" phases both remained staunchly devoted to the essential teachings of their school. Claims of deviation notwithstanding, Posidonius was "invariably reported in the ancient world as a Stoic without qualification,"[8] identified himself as an interpreter of Stoicism rather than an innovator, and, by common consensus, remained fundamentally orthodox.[9] What is true of Posidonius was true of "Middle Stoicism" generally – it was marked more by continuity than change.[10] So it was also with Roman Stoicism. Seneca, although an occasional dissenter and mildly eclectic, was a self-identified Stoic (*Ep.* 33.4; *Ben.* 2.17.3; 4.8.1; 5.12.3; cf. *Vit. beat.* 3.2) and maintained orthodox Stoic positions on nearly all the major issues. As others have demonstrated, perhaps the only exception to his orthodoxy was in the area of psychology – where he followed Posidonius.[11] Thus, as in Middle Stoicism, Roman Stoicism did offer partial innovations, as well as new ways of expressing old ideas, but on the whole it remained entirely within the early Stoic framework.[12]

Sources

Such development in the history of Stoicism has some bearing on our use of the sources. Because Stoicism was essentially conservative, the views of the earliest Stoic thinkers continued to be retained in the school's later phases. We need only exercise caution, then, in matters where we find later Stoics explicitly parting ways with their predecessors, or where we

[8] See I. G. Kidd, *Posidonius, Volume 3: The Translation of the Fragments* (Cambridge University Press, 1999), and ancient testimonia cited on p. 61.

[9] Cf. Kidd, *Posidonius*, 3:1–29; *OCD*, 1232.

[10] As stated in Inwood and Gerson, *A Stoic Reader*, vii; see also Sedley, "The School, from Zeno to Arius Didymus," 22–4.

[11] J. M. Rist, "Seneca and Stoic Orthodoxy," *ANRW* 2.36:3.

[12] Gill, "The School in the Roman Imperial Period," 33–58.

have substantial evidence for development over time. Here only one such area proves of much consequence, and that, as suggested earlier, is in the matter of the relation between body and soul. Beginning with the Middle Stoics, later Stoics in effect abandoned the earlier monistic perspective of Zeno and Chrysippus and, for reasons tied with ethics, substituted something that looked closer to a Platonic dualism;[13] this outlook was retained among the Roman Stoics active in Paul's day.

We must also distinguish between two different *kinds* of sources. There are, on the one hand, writers such as Seneca and Marcus Aurelius, who, in addition to preserving memoirs from earlier thinkers, write *as* Stoics and therefore also as representatives of *contemporary* Stoicism. On the other hand, we have writers that aim simply to collect and preserve earlier philosophical thought, without necessarily endorsing the views as their own. Such are the "doxographies" instantiated in Cicero and Plutarch, and the "epitomes" of Stobaeus, Arius Didymus, and Diogenes Laertius. Because these sources preserve almost exclusively earlier views (Diogenes Laertius, for instance, names no Stoic later than the second century), they too serve as useful guides to traditional Stoicism. Beside the doxographies and epitomes, we have also the fragments of the early Stoics preserved in later writers. A wealth of these have been collected in the multivolume sets *Stoicorum Veterum Fragmenta* (*SVF*) and Long and Sedley's *Hellenistic Philosophers* (LS), to which I make reference throughout.

1 Corinthians and Stoicism

Addressees

Before presenting my case that Stoicism had infiltrated the ranks of the Corinthian church, we need briefly to address the question of the letter's addressees. In the light of our previous chapter, Theissen's suggestion that the letter targeted a small but influential minority[14] from among the "upper classes" probably stands in need of qualification. On the one hand, we have noted potential problems with such language as "the upper classes." Moreover, it must be noted that Paul explicitly *addresses* the whole community (1:2 – "To the church of God that is in Corinth, to those

[13] See A. A. Long, "Carneades and the Stoic Telos," *Phronesis* 12 (1967): 59–90; Long, "Roman Philosophy," in *The Cambridge Companion to Greek and Roman Philosophy*, 207.

[14] E.g., G. Theissen, "Social Stratification in the Corinthian Community," in *The Social Setting of Pauline Christianity*, 72; and "Social Conflicts in the Corinthian Correspondence," 377.

who are sanctified in Christ Jesus, called to be saints, together with all those who in every place call on the name of our Lord Jesus Christ, both their Lord and ours").[15] Yet this is not to say that Paul intended to *blame* the whole community – at least not in equal measure. Indeed, it is this that seems to have captured Theissen's attention. "Some" have become arrogant (4:18), "some" have denied the resurrection of the dead (15:12). Likewise *some* apparently think of themselves as "spiritual," "perfect," and "knowledgeable," against a separate class of those who are "unspiritual," "immature," and "weak" (chs. 8, 10; 12–14). Paul himself champions the perspective of the "weak" throughout chapters 8–10, implicating the (so-called) "strong" in chapter 10; and he pleads on behalf of the "have-nots" in 11:17–34. Moreover, many of the problems in the letter seem either to imply, if not require, a more privileged contingent as the culprits (candidates include 6:1–11; chs. 8, 10; 11:17–34).[16] Thus, since Theissen, interpreters have argued, with great success, that the culpable "wise men" are to be identified with certain ones among the "wealthier" (though I do not say, "upper class") members of the church.

If Theissen has set us on the right path, we will need to resist any temptation to swing from the distinct-parties view of Baur and earlier scholarship to the conclusion that the group or groups Paul addressed shared *no* cohesiveness whatsoever. Moreover, if interpreters have been right that certain "red threads" extend through all the major issues in the letter, we might then reasonably assume the presence of a consistent perspective, from perhaps a single group (which we must avoid multiplying without due cause), however loosely they might have united themselves. I should only like to make two caveats. First, if it can be said that the "wise" had adopted a two-tier view of Christian believers – the wise and the foolish, the perfect and the immature, the knowledgeable and the weak – this need not imply that they thought of the church as being comprised of two distinct "parties." Second, the "wisdom" espoused by the dominant minority may also have percolated down to some who were not a part of their immediate circle.[17] Social relations in Roman society, knit together as they were in a complex web of patron-client connections, were too complex to allow for such clear-cut social or economic boundaries. Thus, if the "wise" were generally among the "wealthy," exceptions could be expected.

[15] E.g., Collins (*1 Corinthians*, 16) and Fitzmyer (*1 Corinthians*, 52).

[16] For an overview, see Dunn, *1 Corinthians*, 43–65.

[17] Demonstration of this point in the light of first-century social dynamics will have to be taken up in future studies.

Analysis

Wisdom and the wise man

Interpreters have long agreed that the chief source of the church's divisions was their professed "wisdom," or σοφία. Not only is this subject discussed first in the letter, but it is discussed at greater length than any other topic, and in intimate connection with the dissentiousness broached in 1:10–12. Despite the almost endless variety of ways in which this wisdom has been interpreted, the external and internal evidence, I believe, combine to make a compelling case that some form of Stoic wisdom provided the framework for the Corinthians' understanding of wisdom. Here we continue our examination of "wisdom" and "wise man" language begun in Chapter 2.

Σοφός. Although lexical usage of σοφία varied widely across antiquity, several stages in the development of the concept can be distinguished.[18] Prior to Socrates, the term was used predominantly to denote practical skill, whether in the arts, politics, or some other matter of life experience. Beginning with Socrates and his earliest followers, the term's semantic center drifted from the realm of the practical to that of the theoretical. Hence, its earlier reference to practical, and especially mundane matters, began giving way to concerns related to speculative knowledge, or contemplation of things "divine."[19] A third stage in the history of the concept was reached with the Hellenistic philosophical schools, which united the practical and the theoretical in their notion of the "wise man" (ὁ σοφός). The Stoic definition of wisdom encapsulated the new ideal: wisdom was "knowledge of things both divine *and* human" (θείων τε καὶ ἀνθρωπίνων ἐπιστήμη, *SVF* 2.35–36; cf. Cicero, *Off.* 1.153). As shown in Chapter 2, by the first century, "wisdom" was practically a synonym for "philosophy" and apparently carried little if any technical association with "rhetoric."

Accordingly, it was the Stoics who earned pride of place in developing the idea of the "wise man," or ὁ σοφός.[20] For the Stoics, the σοφός was the one who had both the theoretical knowledge and the practical

[18] For a summary of this movement, see F. Volpi, "Wisdom," *Brill's New Pauly: Antiquity* (electronic version); and U. Wilckens, "Σοφία, σοφός, σοφίζω," *TDNT* 7:467.

[19] As evinced both from literary sources and the papyri; cf. Chantraine, *Dictionnaire étymologique de la langue grecque*, 1031; MM 582.

[20] For the various conceptions of the wise man and the Stoics' important role in their development, see G. B. Kerferd, "The Sage in Hellenistic Philosophical Literature," in J. G. Gammie and L. G. Perdue (eds.), *The Sage in Israel and Ancient Near East* (Winona Lake: Eisenbrauns, 1990), 320–8; and B. Fiore, "The Sage in Select Hellenistic and Roman Literary Genres," in *The Sage in Israel and Ancient Near East*, 329–42.

know-how to exercise consistent virtue (*SVF* 1.216; 1.235; 1.548; D. L. 7.121–6; Cicero, *Mur.* 29–31), in which consisted happiness (D. L. 7.89/ *SVF* 3.39), the end or τέλος of human existence. Thus, while all had access to wisdom by means of their share in the all-infusing divine Logos (Cicero, *Nat. d.* 2.23–25, 28–30; *Off.* 1.107, 110–11, 114–17), only the σοφός consistently made use of his reasoning faculties so as actually to attain it. Other people were merely "inferior" (φαῦλοι; *SVF* 3.657–84).

The technical connotation of σοφός in 1 Corinthians has seldom been commented on. In most of its occurrences, the term is used with reference to a *class* of people (with the generic article in 1:19, 27; 3:19, 20; generic but anarthrous in 1:20). Of its ten occurrences in 1 Corinthians, arguably every occurrence except one is substantive: 3:10 is the single exception, where it is applied attributively to Paul, and with a different meaning ("wise" in his application of a τέχνη or "practical skill"). Even where σοφός is clearly substantive and masculine (e.g., 1:19, 20, 27; 3:19, 20; 6:5), its technical force has unfortunately been obscured in modern translations, where the term has usually been rendered either "the wise" (e.g., NAS, NIV, and NRSV on 1:19; 3:19, 20; cf. 1:26), or with the less elegant expression, "the one who is wise" (NRSV on 1:20).[21]

Several pieces of evidence, however, point to the Stoic understanding of the term, at least as the starting point for Paul's discussion. The external evidence is not without significance. Not only was Stoicism the most dominant of the philosophies in the first century, especially among the wealthier classes, but the *Stoic* "wise man" was far and away the best known. The Stoics in fact boasted that they had exclusive right to the title (e.g., Cicero, *Fin.* 3.75; Lucian, *Vit. auct.* 20). Evidence actually suggests that the Stoic definition served as the galvanizing force for development of the concept in the other philosophical schools, which seem to have defined their wise man *against* that of the Stoics.[22] In some ways, then, the Stoic meaning can be seen as almost the default sense of the term.

Yet the Stoic meaning is also suggested by the evidence of 1 Corinthians itself. We have already noted that Paul characterizes the Corinthians'

[21] In this case, the attempt to be gender inclusive has unfortunately obscured the technical meaning of the word. To be sure, in the ancient world women too could be considered "wise" (see H. Harich-Schwarzbauer, "Women Philosophers," *Brill's New Pauly: Antiquity* [electronic version]), but σοφός itself, like many attributes that indicated the ideals of human virtue, was gendered in the masculine because it was thought to be a properly masculine trait. To capture this historical sense of the term, classical scholars therefore rightly continue to persist in rendering σοφός "wise man" when it seems to carry the philosophical meaning. For one recent work that has made such a case, see Inwood and Gerson, *A Stoic Reader*, ix.

[22] So G. B. Kerferd, "The Sage in Hellenistic Philosophical Literature," in *The Sage in Israel and Ancient Near East*, esp. 320–2.

wisdom as a Greek and not a Jewish pursuit (1:22), and many of the letter's problems are, only with difficulty, explained on the hypothesis of Hellenistic-Jewish origins.[23] Conversely, Paul consistently paints the Corinthian wise in the colors of the Stoic wise man.

The Stoics had defined their wise man with a series of statements known as "paradoxes" (παράδοξα), so called because these statements, if taken literally, seemed "astonishing" (lit. "contrary to belief"). These typically followed the form "Only the wise man is *x*…, Only the wise man is *y*…, etc." Most often they listed a whole series of predicates in a single description. For example:

> The *wise man* alone is *ruler*, alone *master*, alone *king*, alone *leader*, alone *free*. (*SVF* 3.613)

> He [the *wise man*] will most rightly be called *king* … *master* … *rich*. Rightly will he be said to *own all things* … ; rightly will he be called *beautiful* … and alone *free*. (*Fin*. 3.75)

Commentators have long noted that Paul's words in 4:8 put the language of the paradoxes in the Corinthians' mouths: "Are you already *rich* (ἐπλουτήσατε; cf. 1:5)? Are you already *kings* (ἐβασιλεύσατε)?"[24] It should be noted here that to take "rich" and "kings" as references to the sophists, as Bruce Winter does, is not the most natural reading; indeed, in so doing he is compelled to list "leaders" rather than "kings" as the parallel.[25] Moreover, that the *Stoics* had so described their wise man is well known, as we find attested in the fragments:

> only the *wise man* is … *rich* [πλούσιος] and *king* [βασιλεύς].
> (cf. *SVF* 3.655; cf. Cicero, *Fin*. 3.75; *Mur*. 61)

Paul continues to strike a Stoic note throughout chapters 1–4, in many cases calling to the fore ideas that also figure prominently throughout the letter. He continues the language of the paradoxes to characterize the wise in 4:10:

> you are … *prudent* [φρόνιμοι] … *strong* [ἰσχυροί] … *held in honor* [ἔνδοξοι].
> (cf. *SVF:* 3.655; *SVF* 1.216; *SVF* 3.603; 3.567)

In 10:15 he repeats φρόνιμος, stating tongue in cheek that he speaks "as to prudent men." He uses still further predicates from the paradoxes in 1:26

[23] See Fee, *The First Epistle to the Corinthians*, 14.

[24] As far back as Lightfoot, *Notes on the Epistles of St. Paul*, 200; and Weiss, *Der erste Korintherbrief*, 157–9.

[25] Winter, *Philo and Paul among the Sophists*, 138, 187–95, esp. 190, 193, 199.

(δυνατοί, *SVF* 3.364; εὐγενεῖς, *SVF* 3.594)[26] and 2:6 (τέλειοις, *SVF* 1.566; ἀρχόντων, *SVF* 3.364). *If* 2:1–5 ("not with wisdom of word") can indeed be taken antithetically to the Corinthians' own position, it is surely worth noting that the Stoic wise man was also said to be "eloquent" (ῥητορικός) – that is, because he was convincing in argument (D. L. 7.122/*SVF* 3.612). Nearly the whole letter bespeaks an obsession with "freedom," a noteworthy value in the paradoxes and in Stoic thought generally (e.g., *SVF* 3.599).

Finally, Paul's *repeated*, if theologically qualified, assertion to the Corinthians in 3:21, 22 – "all things belong to you" – provides an important Stoic resonance because it corresponds precisely with the Stoic paradox – "all things belong to the wise man" – at the level of both syntax and vocabulary: Corinthian σοφοί as the implied referent + the copulative verb εἶναι (or Latin *esse*) + a Greek genitive of possession (or Latin dative of possession):

> πάντα ὑμῶν [σοφῶν] ἐστιν [all things are yours] (1 Cor 3:21)
>
> πάντα σοφῶν ἐστιν [all things are the wise man's] (*SVF* 3.590)

This passage, however ("whether Paul, or Apollos, or Peter, all things belong to you"), is equally important because it distinctly echoes the "party slogans" of 1:12 – perhaps one of our first direct clues that the divisions may have a Stoic connection.[27] Compare:

> ἐγὼ μέν εἰμι Παύλου, ἐγὼ δὲ Ἀπολλῶ, ἐγὼ δὲ Κηφᾶ [I am of Paul, I of Apollos, I of Cephas] (1 Cor 1:12)
>
> εἴτε Παῦλος εἴτε Ἀπολλῶς εἴτε Κηφᾶ . . . πάντα ὑμῶν ἐστιν [Whether Paul or Apollos or Cephas . . . all things are yours] (1 Cor 3:21–22)

In sum, the point to underline here is not just that a number of Stoic-referring predicates are *present* in these verses – for some are unremarkable in themselves – but that they are so *numerous*, that they are topically if not even verbally *repeated* throughout the letter, that they are *clustered together* in a fashion redolent of the Stoic paradoxes (esp. 1:26; 4:8–10), and that they are in every case clustered around *wisdom* language, often even the "*wise man*" explicitly (e.g., 1:26; 3:19–23). If the Corinthians

[26] Although 1:26 has similarities with Jer 9:24 and 1 Kgs 2:10, it matches neither verbatim.

[27] As Lightfoot (*Notes on the Epistles of St. Paul*, 195) and Weiss (*Der erste Korintherbrief*, 89–91) noted long ago.

were *not* thinking of themselves as Stoic wise men, then, still we could not escape the conclusion that Paul must, for some reason, have been trying to cast them as such:

1. Wise man (σοφός)
2. Of noble birth (εὐγενής)
3. Powerful (δύνατος)
4. Perfect (τέλειος)
5. Ruler (ἄρχων)
6. All things belong to (πάντα γὰρ ὑμῶν ἐστιν)
7. Rich (πλουτεῖν)
8. King (βασιλεύειν)
9. Prudent (φρόνιμος)
10. Strong (ἰσχυρός)
11. Held in honor (ἔνδοξος)
12. Free/freedom (cf. ἐλευθερος, ἐξουσία)
13. [Persuasive in speech (πειθοῖς σοφίας λόγοις)]

Γνῶσις. Outside the first four chapters of the letter, we find not σοφία/σοφός but its companion γνῶσις. Conceptual overlap between the terms suggests that they are here interrelated.

Prior to the first century, γνῶσις apparently carried no religious connotations. It was rather the umbrella term for "knowledge," "recognition," or "acquaintance" generally (LSJ). For Plato, γνῶσις, in its various forms, involved seeing things "as they really are" (Plato, *Resp*. 5.476Dff; 5.477Aff; 9.581B). To see things as such was to see the "good" (Plato, *Resp*. 5.476C, D), as the φιλόσοφος or "lover of wisdom" saw things. Plato had also coined the term γνωστικός for reference to that which gave speculative knowledge, in distinction from merely practical knowledge (*Pol*. 258E). It is worth pointing out that, if the Corinthians' "knowledge" was conceived to be at all like Plato's, this would then clearly place their wisdom/knowledge in the "philosophical" sphere, rather than – as Pogoloff has tried to do in connecting it with rhetoric – the "practical" sphere.

In broader philosophical usage, both σοφία and γνῶσις can be found as the genus beneath which more specific types of knowledge fall. Σοφία, for instance, was defined as the highest form of knowledge, and that which encompassed knowledge in all its lower forms (e.g., ἐπιστήμη and νοῦς in Aristotle, *Eth. nic*. 6.7.3, 5). Aristotle (*An. post*. 2.99b-100b) reveals that γνῶσις could be used similarly, namely as a general term encompassing each of the more specific forms of knowledge, including perception (αἴσθησις), memory (μνήμη), experience (ἐμπειρία), and – in its highest form – scientific knowledge (ἐπιστήμη).[28] For the Stoics, "lack of knowledge" was ἀγνοία (*SVF* 3.548), which we find as the antithesis of γνῶσις in 1 Corinthians (cf. 8:1; 10:1; 12:1). The Stoics, as we have already seen, defined *wisdom* as "*knowledge* of things divine and human" (*SVF* 2.35). While this is "knowledge" as ἐπιστήμη, it is to be observed that ἐπιστήμη was in turn defined as the "γνῶσις of first principles" (*SVF* 2.949).[29] Seneca retains the Greek definition of wisdom, rendering ἐπιστήμη with the Latin *scientia* (Seneca, *Ep*. 89.5), just as the Vulgate renders γνῶσις throughout 1 Corinthians: the Corinthians, for instance, "have *scientiam*" (8:1). The upshot is that, in both Stoic and broader philosophical usage, γνῶσις in its various forms was understood to be *that in which σοφία* consisted. That the Corinthians then elevated γνῶσις to a religious level is almost certain. But we shall revisit this point later in the chapter.

Λόγος. Related, but subservient, to σοφία and γνῶσις in 1 Corinthians is λόγος. This term is invariably connected with one of the other terms, or a cognate, when it means anything more specialized than simply "speaking" (cf. with σοφία in 1:17; 2:1, 4, 13; 12:8; in contrast to μωρία in 1:18; with γνῶσις/γινώσκω in 1:5; 4:19, 20). Σοφία and γνῶσις, by contrast, occur dozens of times each in their various cognate forms (σοφία, σόφος; and γνῶσις, γινώσκω, οἶδα, ἀγνωσία, ἀγνοέω), and quite often independently.

These observations, together with the Stoic "wise man" connections illustrated earlier, could point toward a different meaning for λόγος than "speech," "rhetoric," or "eloquence": if λόγος was indeed a Corinthian catchword as σοφία and γνῶσις were, the Corinthians may have understood it not as the faculty of speech per se, but as that human capacity in which were combined both "word" *and* its rational content – "reason." Like Stoics, they see themselves as sharers in divine reason through the Λόγος, which was said to infuse the cosmos (cf. D. L. 7.134; *SVF* 1.87). It was, moreover, by sharing in the Λόγος that the Stoic wise man was considered infallible in "argument" (λόγος; D. L. 7.47). So understood, Paul's disavowal of σοφία λόγου or "wisdom of word" (with λόγος in the singular, one will notice; cf. 1:17; 2:1, 4, 5, 13) might have been heard first and foremost as a repudiation of a certain kind of *rational argumentation* – or "wisdom of *argumentation*" – in favor of a wisdom that relied on the power of the Holy Spirit alone (2:4–5).

[28] For more on Greek usage, see R. Bultmann, "γινώσκω, γνῶσις, ἐπιγινώσκω, ἐπίγνωσις," *TDNT* 1:689–92.

[29] And it is worth pointing out that Plato sometimes uses γνῶσις absolutely, and thus in the same sense as ἐπιστήμη; e.g., *Resp*. 6.508E.

Of course, this is not to say that the Corinthians had no conception of the Spirit (they did), nor that Paul had no use for rational argumentation (he did). It is to say that, according to Paul, they had misunderstood what it meant to be *truly* "spiritual." But now we have got ahead of ourselves.

Status distinctions

In addition to styling themselves "wise men," the culpable Corinthians also touted a number of spiritual status distinctions meant to set them apart from their putative inferiors: they were "knowledgeable" (cf. 8:1–13) over against the "weak" (ἀσθενής), "perfect" (τέλειος) over against the "immature" (νήπιος), and "spiritual" (πνευμάτικος) over against the "unspiritual" (ψύχικος). I treat these contrasts in order.

The "knowledgeable" vs. the "weak." The issue of the so-called "strong" versus the "weak" in 1 Corinthians 8, 10 has received abundant attention since Theissen's socioeconomic explanation nearly forty years ago.[30] According to Theissen, the "strong" in these chapters are the wealthy; the "weak" are the poor. Convincing as exegetes have found this interpretation, however, I believe we need to take another look at how its terms have been defined. In my view, "strong" (to use Theissen's term, "starken") and "weak" should *not*, in their present Pauline context, be taken as socioeconomic *references*. Indeed, the context does not actually tell us that the first group is "strong," but rather that they claim to have "knowledge" (8:1; cf. 8:7, 10, 11). Second, the "weak" are identified as such not on the basis of any socioeconomic data – there is nothing of the kind here – but rather clearly on the basis of their approach to the *noetic* issue of *conscience* and its predilections in *judgment* (8:7, 9–13).

Still, Anthony Thiselton, struggling to encapsulate both dimensions of "weakness" in a single term, translates ἀσθενής as "insecure," investing it with double duty as a socioeconomic *and* a prudential descriptor.[31] This, I would argue, is to confuse *general characteristics* with *specific semantic reference*, however. No doubt, we could also predicate of Paul's "weak" people "political disenfranchisement," "low repute," and "feeble bodies," but we need not grope about to find a word nebulous enough to embrace the term's full range of semantic possibilities. Moreover, to say that theological judgments are often embedded in socio-economic matrices may be true, but it is not at all the point. No matter how the trait *originates*,

[30] G. Theissen, "Die Starken und Schwachen in Korinth: Soziologische Analyse eines theologischen Streits," *EvTh* 35 (1975): 155–72.
[31] Thiselton, *First Epistle to the Corinthians*, 644.

something more specific is here being *referred to* by the term, and that, quite plainly, is that these people are weak in "conscience" (8:7). Thus, we are better advised to construe "weak" and – if we must continue to use the term – "strong" as *noetic* categories, predicated of certain people who *happen also* to be "wealthier" and "poorer" respectively. My preference in the light of the text, however, would be to label these, not the "strong" and the "weak," but rather the "*knowledgeable*" and the "weak": οἱ ἔχοντες γνῶσιν and οἱ ἀσθενεῖς (cf. 8:10–11; 1:25, 27). The first group claims, on the basis of its knowledge (8:1), that it has the freedom to eat idol-meat (εἰδωλόθυτα). Those who defect from this knowledge they denigrate as "weak."

"Knowledge" and "weakness" figure prominently in Stoic ideas on moral judgment. The Stoics believed that ignorance (ἀγνοία) and consequent poor judgment resulted from "weakness" (ἀσθένεια) in the soul (*SVF* 3.177; 3.473; 3.548). When one exercised "weak assent" (ἀσθενῆς συγκατάθεσις) to a sense impression received (Stobaeus 2.111.18–112.8/*SVF* 3.548; cf. *SVF* 3.378; 3.473), it led to false judgments (*SVF* 1.67; 3.177; Plutarch, *Mor.* 1122c; Cicero, *Tusc.* 4.15; Epictetus, *Diatr.* 2.15.20). What one wanted was knowledge that was "secure and unchangeable" – which was achieved by "reason," or λόγος (Stobaeus 2.73.16–74.3/*SVF* 3.112). Disobedience to reason – or "weakness" – constituted surrender to the "passions" (*SVF* 3.378, 389; cf. Posidonius, *fr.* 163, 164). The passion of "distress" (λύπη), for instance, was considered "an irrational contraction, or a fresh opinion that something bad is present" (LS 65B [Long and Sedley 411]) or – alternatively defined – "a shrinking at what is thought to be something to avoid" (LS 65D [Long and Sedley, 412]). "Fear" (φόβος) they defined as "an irrational shrinking [aversion] or avoidance of an expected danger" (LS 65B [Long and Sedley, 412]) or the regarding of a thing "that need not be shunned as though it ought to be shunned" (Cicero, *Tusc.* 4.26 [King, LCL]). Because fear was usually experienced when one was in a "weak" frame of mind (Seneca, *Ep.* 50.9), the Stoics advised people not to expose themselves to things by which they were easily seduced (Seneca, *Ep.* 116.5).

It is in this light that the Corinthian contrast is to be understood.[32] The wise have distinguished between (1) the person who was "weak" because of inadequate exercise of reason and (2) the person who was *knowledgeable* and therefore capable of appropriately discerning what to choose and

[32] Abraham Malherbe too understands the problem in this way, in "Determinism and Free Will in Paul: The Argument of 1 Cor 8 and 9," in *Paul in His Hellenistic Context*, 231–55.

avoid. The "knowledgeable" ostensibly obeyed reason in recognizing that idol-meat presented no grounds for fear or distress. Thus they unwaveringly assented to the impulse to eat. The "weak," on the other hand, wrongly shrunk from what seemed to them necessary to avoid.

The Corinthian slogan in 8:1, then, implicitly sets the two groups apart from each other. Such a conclusion obtains regardless which formulation of the slogan we prefer – that is, whether (1) the culpable Corinthians assert, "We know that *we* all have knowledge, [but the *weak* do not]"; or (2) they have said, "We know that *we* have knowledge," and Paul has qualified the assertion by adding "all" to their "we."[33]

Context lends the Stoic interpretation further support, for Paul here tempers the Corinthian perspective with additional Stoic considerations: all things may be "permissible," but all *good* things should also be, as the Stoics say, "beneficial" (συμφέρει, 10:23a; cf. Arius Didymus 5d/*SVF* 3.86; 11h/*SVF* 3.208; Epictetus, *Diatr.* 2.22.27; cf. 1.28.5; 2.26.2; 2.22.19; 4.7.9).[34] Thus, for the sake of one's brethren, one need, like the Stoic, exercise "self-control" (ἐγκρατεύω, 1 Cor 9:25; cf. *SVF* 3.274–5). To Stoics, then, Paul responds as a Stoic.

To be sure, non-Stoics talked about "weakness" as well. Stanley Stowers for instance notes, after providing copious examples from the Stoics, two further texts in which weakness is discussed. *On Frank Criticism*, an Epicurean text composed by Philodemus of Gadara in the first century BC, maintains that constructive criticism is insufficient to heal the "weak" of their erroneous beliefs and practices (59.1–11). In the same vein, Plutarch makes mention of those who abandon philosophy on account of their weakness, exhibiting as they do no firmness in the face of reproof (*Mor.* 46E–F). From these texts Stowers concludes that "'[t]he weak' and 'weakness'" were "established concepts in Greco-Roman society."[35]

Be that as it may, it should be noted that these non-Stoic texts scarcely approximate the notion of "weakness" found in the Stoics, whether in importance or in their technical conceptualization. It was the Stoics who made the concept central to their ethical system and, more importantly,

[33] With the first option, preferred by Conzelmann (*1 Corinthians*, 140), πάντες must be understood as being qualified by the verb's embedded subject, "we." The second option is preferred by Garland (*1 Corinthians*, 366). Both interpretations, however, understand the situation in precisely the same way: those who possess knowledge believe that others in the church – namely the "weak" – do not.

[34] It was Stoic philosophy that had lent the term to the art of rhetoric, where it is often found in deliberative speeches.

[35] Stowers, "Paul on the Use and Abuse of Reason," in *Greeks, Romans, and Christians*, 282.

the Stoic system in which we find a formulation corresponding precisely with what we find in 1 Corinthians 8: from the perspective of the "knowledgeable," the "weak" have assented to false judgment by shunning what they need not shun.[36]

The "perfect" vs. the "immature." At several points in the letter a related distinction is made – that between the τέλειος and the νήπιος person (cf. 2:6–16; 3:1–3; 13:10–11; cf. 14:20). We have already noted that Paul appropriates these, among other Corinthian terms, in 2:6–16; 3:1–3. Paul plays on the distinction again in 14:20 (cf. 13:10–11), retaining the contrast but reversing the Corinthians' status claim: "do not be children [νηπιάζετε] in your thinking; rather, be infants in evil, but in thinking be adults [τέλειοι]" (NRSV).[37]

Analogous to the distinction made between the "wise" and the "inferior" person, νήπιος-τέλειος is a distinctively Stoic contrast. Since Lightfoot, commentators have asserted that Pythagoras had made this distinction, but none of them cite any ancient sources. The apparent error has been perpetuated in commentaries ever since.[38] Moffatt merely states that "the metaphor was common among the Stoics ever since the days of Pythagoras" – apparently (if surprisingly) unaware that Pythagoras predated the Stoics by some 200 years.[39] Prior to the Corinthian correspondence, the metaphorical distinction is limited entirely to philosophical writers.[40] We find it among the old Stoics, and otherwise only in Philo of Alexandria, who had obviously co-opted it from the philosophical school. In the Stoic fragments, the distinction appears exactly as we have it in 1 Corinthians – the "*perfect*" (τέλειος) versus the "*immature*" (νήπιος) person (*SVF* 3.519) – right alongside the characteristic Stoic opposition between the "excellent" (σπουδαῖος) and "inferior" (φαῦλος) person.

For the philosophers, the τέλειος, or "perfect," person was the one who had attained the τέλος of human existence. The Stoic wise man was said

[36] This is one area in which the Stoics seem to have drawn from Aristotle; see, e.g., Aristotle, *Eth. nic.* 7.7.8.

[37] Cf. 13:10–11 – "[10] but when the perfect [τέλειον] comes, the partial will come to an end. [11] When I was a child, I spoke like a child [νήπιος], I thought like a child [νήπιος], I reasoned like a child [νήπιος]; when I became an adult, I put an end to childish ways [τὰ τοῦ νηπίου]" (NRSV).

[38] In addition to the quotation from Moffatt, see also Robertson and Plummer, *First Epistle to the Corinthians*, 36.

[39] Moffatt, *The First Epistle of Paul to the Corinthians*, 28, 36; cf. Lightfoot, *Notes on the Epistles of St. Paul*, 173; Robertson and Plummer, *First Epistle to the Corinthians*, 36.

[40] Pseudo-Aristotle, *Probl.* 901b, 25; Philo, *Migr.* 1.46; *Agr.* 1.9; 9.6; *Somn.* 2.10; *Post.* 1.152; *Sobr.* 1.9; cf. Epictetus, *Diatr.* 2.16.39; Seneca, *Ep.* 4.2. In the NT: Heb 5:11–14. It appears in a literal sense in some medical texts: Hippocrates, *Artic.* 33.91; Plutarch, *fr.* 136.13; Soranus, *Gynaeciorum libri iv*, 2.36.1.3; 2.56.2.1.

to be "perfect" in judgment because of his unerring use of reason (Sextus Empiricus, *Math.* 7.151–7). Thus, it was said: "The wise man (ὁ σοφός) does everything well. ... In their [the Stoics'] opinion the doctrine that the wise man does everything well is a consequence of accomplishing everything in accordance with right reason and in accordance with virtue" (Stobaeus 2.66/*SVF* 3.560 [Long and Sedley 380]). By contrast, the νήπιος was the "immature" person, the one who had perhaps made headway but still far fell short of the goal (Epictetus, *Diatr.* 3.24.53; cf. 1.4.18–32; *Ench.* 51).

The Corinthian wise apparently believed they had reached the superior state. Paul repeats their τέλειος language several times (2:6–16; 3:1–3; 13:10–11; cf. 14:20), but in each case also uses it to bring them down to size, either adding that they are *not* in fact perfect or else listing "knowledge" as one of those things that comes short of the actual quality of perfection. We find a striking case in point in 8:2, where after quoting the Corinthian claim that they "have knowledge" (8:1), he rejoins that they "do not yet know in the way they ought to." To aspiring philosophers Paul speaks, allusively, as one himself – he is Socrates, reminding his students that true wisdom is in *knowing that you do not yet know* (cf. Socrates in Plato, *Resp.* 354C; *Charm.* 175A–B; *Lys.* 222D–E; *Prot.* 361A–B; Epictetus, *Ench.* 46.2; see also 1 Cor 3:18).

The "spiritual" vs. the "unspiritual." The third Corinthian distinction was that between the πνευμάτικος ("spiritual") and the ψύχικος ("unspiritual") person, which first emerges in Paul's reappropriation of Corinthian terminology in 2:13–15. Interpretation has been stymied here by the fact that no known literature prior to the Corinthian correspondence bears witness to such a direct contrast.[41] Although the exact terminology is absent, Richard Horsley surmises that it could stem from within the Hellenistic-Jewish wisdom tradition epitomized in the Wisdom of Solomon and Philo of Alexandria, where we find frequent distinctions between two types of humanity: the "heavenly" and the "earthly," the "immortal" and the "mortal," the "perfect" and the "immature," and so on. Πνευμάτικος and ψύχικος would then draw an analogous distinction, with each term indicating a respective religious status.[42]

While Horsley's theory offers a plausible contribution to the discussion, I wish to offer what I think may be a likelier alternative. Most would agree that the πνευμάτικος-ψύχικος distinction, as a pair, has *not* been

[41] So Horsley, "Pneumatikos vs. Psychikos," 269–70, 271; "How Can Some of You Say That There Is No Resurrection of the Dead?," 229.

[42] Horsley, "Pneumatikos vs. Psychikos," 280.

borrowed wholesale from some contemporary system of thought (hence the reason we do not find the exact contrast in comparative literature) but is a genuinely *new* development. But if it does not issue from Philo's brand of Judaism, then what other possibilities are at hand? I submit that Stoicism provides all the raw elements for the Corinthian distinction, including *even* the terminology for both items in the pair.

Πνευμάτικος itself emerges as a specialized term in Stoic circles. Athenaeus of Attaleia had founded a medical school that went by the name Πνευμάτικοι (LS 55F). Athenaeus had been a disciple of the famous Stoic Posidonius, and his "Pneumatist" school was said to have followed the teachings of the canonical Stoic Chrysippus (Galen, *De diff. puls.* 3.641.15–642.7).

The Πνευμάτικοι derived their name from their Stoic cosmology. The Stoics maintained that the cosmos consisted of four elements, two of them active and two passive. The active elements, air and fire, blended with each other through and through to create hot "breath," or πνεύμα (LS 47F-I). Πνεύμα acted as the sustaining cause of the universe by pervading the passive elements, earth and water. Πνεύμα, however, passed through objects at varying levels of tension (LS 47M-Q). It passed through lifeless things like logs and stones at the level of "tenor" (ἕξις), providing them with mere material coherence. Through plants it passed as "physical" (φύσικός) breath, nurturing them as living things. Through irrational animals it passed as "psychic" (ψυχικός) breath, giving them the powers of impression and impulse. Only through human beings did it pass at the level of reason or "rational soul" (λόγικη ψυχή or νοῦς). It was this high tension of πνεύμα that gave humans their capacity for *wisdom*.

If, as interpreters agree, the πνευμάτικος-ψύχικος distinction was a Corinthian coinage, clearly it did not originate in a vacuum. In this regard, the question must be asked: Do we have any better framework for explaining its origins than the πνεύμα-infusion model just presented? To my mind, this model provides a perfectly plausible explanation, and one that assumes only minimal development on the part of the Corinthians: the wise were πνευμάτικοι, fully "rational" human beings filled with πνεύμα at its highest level; beneath them were the ψύχικοι, inferior types who thought merely at the level of "psychic" breath, like the irrational beasts. If 2:15 reflects the Corinthian position – "the spiritual man [πνευμάτικος] judges all things but he himself is judged by no one" – this scheme would fit its meaning well.

The context lends this Stoic-influenced interpretation further credence. As interpreters have widely agreed, vv. 10–16 are rife with

Corinthian terminology, which Paul has apparently hijacked and turned to his own purposes.[43] Here he makes several statements apparently intended to evoke Stoic cosmology: (1) In a manner of speaking, the Stoics too believed that the "the Spirit searches out all things" (1 Cor 2:10).[44] In this vein, Seneca remarked that "we should live ... and think ... as if there were someone who could look into our inmost souls; ... Nothing is shut off from the sight of God. He is witness of our souls" (*Ep.* 83.1; cf. 41.2). (2) Πνεῦμα was said to infuse the entire cosmos, constituting what the Stoics called a "world soul" (LS 44C; 46E–F; 47C; 54A, B). Against such a view, Paul here reminds the Corinthians that they "have received not the *spirit of the world*, but the *Spirit that is from God*" (2:12). (3) For the Stoic, the νοῦς was the "mind" of the individual infused with divine πνεῦμα at the level of "reason" (Philo, *Imm.* 35–36/*SVF* 2.458). Paul, however, rounds off this section with a pithy corrective: "*we* have the mind (νοῦν) of *Christ*" (2:16).

It would be a mistake to dismiss Stoic resonance in this passage on the basis that Paul might have made *conceptually* similar statements elsewhere. We must give weight to the fact that these Stoic resonances occur in strikingly dense configuration, each, for Paul, rare or anomalous in its present form, and in a passage already widely noted for its uncharacteristic vocabulary.[45]

All of this, I think, provides evidence that Stoic cosmology likely served as the starting point for the Corinthians' πνευμάτικος-ψύχικος distinction: it provided them with both the necessary conceptual categories *and* their terminology. The Corinthian *innovation* was in pitting πνευμάτικος and ψύχικος against each other as two kinds of *Christians*, possessed of different levels of "spiritual" or intellectual achievement. Helping give shape to this distinction were the two other status contrasts, which we have seen were made explicitly in Stoicism – that between the "perfect" and "immature" person and that between the "knowledgeable" and the "weak." Each of these three contrasts simply filtered Pauline teaching through Stoic categories.

[43] As he will do again in 15:44–7 (πνευμάτικος-ψύχικος), in his discussion of the resurrection body.

[44] This is a rather uncommon expression in Paul. Its likeness appears otherwise only in Rom 8:27 – a reference subsequent to 1 Corinthians.

[45] I may also mention Paul's use of the philosophic principle "like is known by like" in 2:10. On this, see B. E. Gärtner, "The Pauline and Johannine Idea of 'To Know God' against the Hellenistic Background," *NTS* 14 (1967/68): 215–21.

Freedom and indifferents

The Corinthians perhaps had no watchword more sacred to them than "freedom." Finding expression in a wide variety of terms,[46] the topic can be traced through almost every issue in the letter. Appeals to freedom have been made with regard to both sexual misconduct (chs. 5–6, esp. 6:12, 13) and sexual abstinence (ch. 7, esp. 7:4); it lingers behind the issue of eating idol-meat (chs. 8, 10; esp. 8:9) and Paul's lengthy response on what godly freedom ought to look like (ch. 9); and it has contributed to the problems of individualism that plague the practice of the Lord's Supper (11:17–34) and the church's assemblies for worship (11:2–16; chs. 12, 14).

Always an essential value to the Greek mind,[47] the notion of freedom had been uniquely developed by the Hellenistic philosophical schools. When Greek democracy crumbled in the wake of Alexander the Great, philosophers turned from the autonomy of the polis to that of the individual. From that point, nowhere was individual freedom heralded more loudly – and in a way, quietly – than it was in Stoicism. Should freedom survive, it would have to assert itself not out in the public sphere, but from deep within the heart of the individual.

The Stoics maintained that freedom belonged exclusively to the wise man. It was another of their paradoxes that he alone was free, while even kings were "slaves":

> The wise man alone is free (ἐλεύθερον) and bad men are slaves, freedom (ἐλευθερίαν) being power (ἐξουσία) of independent action, whereas slavery is privation of the same. . . . Moreover, according to them [the Stoics] not only are the wise (σοφούς) free, they are also kings (βασιλέας); kingship being irresponsible rule [i.e., rule that is answerable to no one], which none but the wise can maintain. (D. L. 7.121–2 [Hicks, LCL]/*SVF* 3.544)

Because of the wise man's exceptional grasp of wisdom, he was said to live by whatever law he pleased (Seneca, *Ben.* 2.18.4). He was "his own master" (Seneca, *Brev. vit.* 5.3). Freedom was thus the "right to live as you wish" (Epictetus, *Diatr.* 2.1.23; cf. 1.12.9; 1.17.28; 2.16.37; 4.1.1; Philo, *Prob.* 59–60; Cicero, *Parod.* 5.2).

[46] I.e., ἔξεστιν, ἐξουσία, ἐξουσιάζω, ἐλεύθερος, ἐλευθερία.

[47] For an overview from the late classical to the Roman period, see D. Sviatoslav, *The Greek Slogan of Freedom and Early Roman Politics in Greece* (Oxford: Oxford University Press, 2011).

The point for the Stoics, however, was that the wise man was free with regard to *moral judgment*, that his judgment could be compelled to the contrary by no one. In this regard, Epictetus explains how one could so steel himself even before the might of a tyrant:

> Take my paltry body, take my property, take my reputation, take those who are about me. If I persuade any to lay claim to these things, let some man truly accuse me. 'Yes, but I wish to control your judgments also.' *And who has given you this authority? How can you have the power to overcome another's judgment?* (*Diatr.* 1.29.9–10; [Oldfather, LCL]; emphasis added; cf. 4.1.156–8)

Maintaining personal autonomy of judgment was paramount.

In part, Stoic freedom was grounded in the Stoics' understanding of what constituted good and evil. For the Stoics – as also for the Cynics – these matters were limited to the sphere of "moral choice" (προαίρεσις), and excluded so-called external and physical goods such as health, wealth, and pleasure, as well as their opposites: disease, poverty, and pain. Epictetus explains: "No man is master of another's moral purpose; and: In its sphere alone are to be found one's good and evil. It follows, therefore, that no one has power either to procure me good, or to involve me in evil, but I myself alone have authority over myself in these matters" (*Diatr.* 4.12.8–9 [Oldfather, LCL]).

This class of things that fell "between good and evil" they called "indifferents" (ἀδιάφορα, *SVF* 3.70). Although the Stoics typically differentiated between "preferable" (e.g., health) and "non-preferable" (e.g., sickness) indifferents, this distinction was not always retained. The Stoic Aristo, for example, treated everything that was not virtue or vice with complete indifference, "recognizing no distinction whatsoever in things indifferent" (D. L. 7.160). Moreover, there is good evidence to suggest that Stoic indifferents were commonly interpreted in this way, even among the educated (e.g., Lucian, *Symp.* 47; D. L. 7.36; Cicero, *Fin.* 4.78).

Of course, one can find something like "indifferents" outside the Stoics and Cynics. Aristotle speaks of things that are merely "productive" of good or evil, but not good or evil in themselves (*Top.* 6.9). Plato can speak of health, strength, beauty, and even certain virtues as sometimes profitable (ὠφέλιμα) and sometimes harmful (βλάβερα) (Plato, *Meno* 87E–88E). He notes that certain things can be good if used rightly, evil if used wrongly, but neither good nor evil (οὔτε κακὸν οὔτε ἀγαθόν) if left entirely alone (*Euthyd.* 280E). He also mentions "intermediate things" (τὰ μεταξύ) such as sitting, walking, running, or inanimate objects like sticks or stones (*Gorg*. 467E–468B). This last example is similar to one of the *two* ways in which the Stoics thought about indifferents (see D. L. 7.104–5/*SVF* 3.119); they mention, for instance, "the number of hairs on one's head, or stretching or contracting a finger" – things which activate neither impulse nor repulsion of ethical action. Yet, this sort of indifference was not the kind for which the Stoics were most known. They were concerned rather with that kind of indifferent that activated impulse or repulsion of ethical action and thus had bearing on one's happiness: life, health, and wealth and their opposites – death, disease, and poverty.

Ultimately, the non-Stoic examples of "indifference" provide poor comparanda for the Stoic doctrine. No doubt, most human beings have a place for things "neither good nor evil" – or indeed, things "amoral." Nothing we find in Plato or Aristotle approximates the Stoic doctrine of indifferents in technicality or importance, nor do they articulate specialized or standardized vocabulary for this class of things. It was the early Stoic Aristo who had coined the term "ἀδιάφορα" to denote those things intermediate between good and evil (cf. D. L. 6.105; 7.37) – although in this the Cynics followed him as well. As the doctrine was subsequently developed under Chrysippus, it became central to the Stoic ethical system, and a doctrine that the Academics not only refused to accept but to which they found themselves vociferously opposed.[48] Put simply, when one thought of "indifferents," one thought first of the Stoics.

Although Stoic "freedom" was meant to be applied to virtuous living, it is easy to see how the notion might have been abused. Freedom often degenerates into license, as the philosophers had long known.[49] Such seems to have been the case in 1 Corinthians, in which several issues seem best explained in terms of a Stoic-like assertion of freedom.

Sexual immorality (5:1–13; 6:12–20). Although Paul leaves us little information regarding the sexually immoral man who had taken his "father's wife" as his own (5:1–13), abuse of the Stoic doctrine of freedom would explain the scenario well.[50] Paul resumes the discussion in 6:12–20, where we find the Corinthian appeal, "all things are permissible

[48] See Long and Sedley, *The Hellenistic Philosophers*, 1:401–10.

[49] The philosophers' understanding of freedom had a long history of abuse in the broader public; e.g., Aristotle, *Pol.* 1317 11; Plato, *Resp.* 557B (on the "democratic man"); *Areop.* 20; Dio Chrysostom, *Or.* 14.4–8.

[50] I should mention that Pascuzzi (*Ethics, Ecclesiology, and Church Discipline*) has made an argument similar to the one made here: 5:1–13 was influenced by the Stoic view that incest was morally indifferent. Paul Hartog's response ("'Not Even Among the Pagans' [1 Cor. 5:1]: Paul and Seneca on Incest," in D. E. Aune and J. Fotopoulos (eds.), *The New Testament and Early Christian Literature in Greco-Roman Context: Studies in Honor of David E. Aune*, NovTSup 122 [Leiden; Boston: Brill, 2006], 51–64) that both Musonius

for me" (πάντα μοι ἔξεστιν, 6:12a), followed by his own Stoic-sounding repartee, "but not all things are *beneficial* [συμφέρει]."

The Corinthian appeal shares obvious connections with what has just been sketched. To begin, the assertion "all things are permissible for me" (πάντα μοι ἔξεστιν) finds almost verbatim parallel in the Stoics. In a discourse widely regarded as Stoic in origin,[51] Dio Chrysostom defines "freedom" as "the knowledge of what is allowable [ἔξεστιν] and what is forbidden" (*Or.*14.18). Still closer to our text is the following passage from Diogenes Laertius, which includes the same terminology, but also in connection with the "wise man":

> [A]ll things belong [πάντα εἶναι] to the wise men [τῶν σοφῶν]. For the law has given to them all-complete authority [παντελῆ ἐξουσίαν]. (D. L. 7.125)

The reasoning behind this was that, if the wise man's use of reason had reached complete "conformity with the law of nature" or, as it were, conformity with the will of God, then all that was God's was the wise man's, including complete authority for autonomous action.

We find a relatively close parallel in Cynic material: "All things belong to the gods. The gods are friends to the wise, and friends share all property in common; therefore all things are the property of the wise" (D. L. 6.72 [Hicks, LCL]; cf. Crates, *Epistle 27;* Diogenes, *Epistle 10*, 2–7). Yet the Cynic is here making a claim about ownership of the world rather than about autonomous action. We therefore lack any mention of "authority" (i.e., ἐξουσίαν, or related language) as we find in our Stoic passages. Partial parallels can be found elsewhere, although most of these either lack mention of the "wise man" or were themselves obviously influenced by Stoicism.[52]

In 1 Cor 6:12a, the unnamed man had probably made the appeal himself ("all things are permissible *for me*"). But the community seems

Rufus and Seneca dissented from this view is important, though not at all insurmountable. That there were two known dissenters, as Hartog argues, to this otherwise orthodox Stoic position is hardly enough to undermine the force of Pascuzzi's argument, which is that orthodox Stoics *did* justify incest on the basis that it was indifferent, and that certain Corinthian Christians seem to have done the same by using a *Stoic* slogan.

[51] So J.W. Cohoon in *Dio Chrysostom, Orations*, in J.W. Cohoon (trans.), Loeb Classical Library 339 (Cambridge, MA: Harvard University Press, 1977), 2:123.

[52] Winter (*After Paul Left Corinth*, 2001) draws attention to literature involving the coincidence of πάντα and ἔξεστιν, arguing that permissibility in "all things" was "the prerogative of those who possessed power" and was part of the "intellectual intercourse" of "educated people" (pp. 81–2, 85). That is not to say, however, that people did not declare this right *on the basis of* a Stoic conceptualization of freedom, as those in many of Winter's closer examples likely do (e.g., Dio, *Or.* 14). Will Deming ("The Unity of 1 Corinthians 5–6," *JBL* 119 [1996]: 289–312) focuses on political parallels, although most of these, as it happens, come from the philosophers. Of course, we cannot ignore that the assertion of 6:12

to have consented, for Paul indicates that they have *refused to judge* the man and are rather "puffed up." This is a puzzling attitude for them to assume given that taking one's father's wife was illegal in both Jewish and Roman law.[53] It must be asked: What could have stimulated such an uppity response – that is, not simply refusing to judge, but actually *boasting* about it? I am hesitant to accept Chow's explanation, who maintains it was because the man was a patron in the community.[54] Indeed, under that hypothesis, we might expect some conniving from the community – a wink or turning of a blind eye so as not to offend one so economically advantageous – and we *might* even expect them to boast *about having a patron*, but why should we expect them to boast, as seems to be the case, either about the man's *behavior itself* or their own *failure to judge* – that is, not *in spite of* but *because of* the community's moral failure?[55] This boasting seems only to be explicable if the community[56] felt some greater ethical principle had been served by allowing the man to "do as he wished." Specifically: the blameworthy individuals are proud because they have realized the important Stoic contention that they "do not have power to overcome another's *judgment*" (Epictetus, *Diatr.* 1.29.9–10). Like the Stoic wise man who has "all-complete authority" (παντελῆ ἐξουσίαν), some person, or several influential people within the Corinthian church, have boasted that "all things are permissible" (πάντα ἔξεστιν) as a way of justifying the man's behavior. Sleep with his father's wife if he will: that is a matter for his personal judgment. Paul, however, reminds them that Stoic freedom had its limits: the act must be "beneficial" (συμφέρει, 6:12b), and here it clearly is not. Ironically, Paul sounds the better Stoic.

Admittedly, indiscriminate sexual behavior could be seen as a Cynic feature as well,[57] for a stream of Cynicism tended toward complete

may partially overlap with several realms of discourse. But the intended resonances can only be determined by comparing the wider *range* of conceptual interactions evoked across the letter as a *whole*.

[53] So Conzelmann, *1 Corinthians*, 96; see also Collins, *1 Corinthians*, 209, for evidence.

[54] Chow, *Patronage and Power*, 130–40; cf. M. Goulder, "Libertines? (1 Cor 5–6)," *NovT* 41 (1999): 347–8; and Winter, *After Paul Left Corinth*, 44–57.

[55] If they are grieved *in spite of* the man's sin, the parallel in thought is lost: "You are puffed up (*in spite of* the situation), but you should rather be grieved (*because of* the situation)." But the alternative translation allows for the parallel to remain intact: "You are puffed up (*because of* the situation), but you should rather be grieved (*because of* it)."

[56] That is not to say that the *whole church* exhibited this attitude, but rather the minority which is thought by most to have been disproportionately influential within the church.

[57] This connection is mentioned by J. Dupont, *Gnosis: la connaissance religieuse dans les epitres de Saint Paul* (Louvain, 1949), 304. Downing (*Cynics, Paul, and the Pauline Churches*) assumes that the Cynic view in particular, and not that of the Stoics or any other group, explains the problem in this passage (pp. 89–93).

indifference in such matters. We should not forget, however, that the earliest Stoics had drawn upon Cynic teaching on this very point, and thereupon incorporated these ideas into their own system. Under Cynic influence Zeno had not only said that it was permissible to lie with a prostitute (*SVF* 3.755–6), but he had also advocated "a community of wives with free choice of partners" (D. L. 7.131 [Hicks, LCL]; cf. 7.33; Sextus Empiricus, *Pyr.* 3.201–9). Likewise, Chrysippus – the Stoic par excellence – is said to have permitted nothing less than "marriage with mothers and daughters and sons" (*SVF* 3.744; cf. 3.743, 745–6, 653)! Would it then have been at all incredible if, in this case, some within the Corinthian church thought of Paul's Christian community as a realization of Zeno's community ideal?

Abstinence (7:1–40). It has proved difficult for interpreters to reconcile the apparently "ascetic" sexual views of chapter 7 ("It is good for a man not to touch a woman," 7:1)[58] with the apparently dissolute sexual outlook reflected in chapters 5 and 6 ("all things are permissible for me," 6:12a).[59] Some interpreters have sought to reconcile the tension by suggesting that certain philosophical schools, for example, Epicureanism[60] or Cynicism,[61] left room for both positions. The same, however, could be said for Stoicism. On the one hand, marriage and child-bearing were "according to nature" (Stobaeus 2.109.10–110.4/*SVF* 3.686) and were desirable insofar as they facilitated virtue and service to society (Musonius Rufus, *Diatr.* 13a; 14; Cicero, *Fin.* 3.62–8).[62] Yet these things were also relegated to the category of things "indifferent" because they fell outside the realm of moral choice (Epictetus, *Diatr.* 4.5.6). Some Stoics even advocated a form of abstinence. Musonius Rufus, for instance, believed that sexual intercourse was justified "only when it occurs in marriage and is indulged in for the purpose of begetting children, since that is lawful, but unjust and unlawful when it is mere pleasure-seeking, *even in marriage*" (*Diatr.* 12 [Lutz 87]; emphasis added; cf. D. L. 7.110–17). Seneca, who followed Panaetius on the matter, saw marriage as a mere distraction:

[58] To "touch a woman" (ἅπτειν) always refers to sexual intercourse in ancient Greek literature; so Fee, *First Epistle to the Corinthians*, 275.

[59] For a relatively recent attempt and a history of solutions, see Goulder, "Libertines?," 334–48.

[60] Tomlin, "Christians and Epicureans in 1 Corinthians," 62–4.

[61] Downing, *Cynics, Paul, and the Pauline Churches*, 107–13.

[62] For this reason Will Deming (*Paul on Marriage and Celibacy: The Hellenistic Background of 1 Corinthians 7* [Grand Rapids: Eerdmans, 2004]) argues that Paul has taken the Stoic perspective over against the purely ascetic – or "Cynic" – one. As shown here, however, Stoics could be equally ascetic.

> I think Panaetius [the Stoic] gave a charming answer to the youth who asked whether the wise man would fall in love: "As to the wise man, we shall see, What concerns you and me, who are still a great distance from the wise man, is to ensure that we do not fall into a state of affairs which is disturbed, powerless, subservient to another and worthless to oneself."
> (*Ep*. 116.5/Panaetius, *fr*. 114 [Long and Sedley 423])

In the same vein, ἔρως, or erotic love, was classed among the "passions," those irrational impulses that constituted, or at least precipitated, false judgments (Stobaeus 2.90,19–91.9/*SVF* 3.394; Arius Didymus 10b/*SVF* 2.91); the only acceptable form of ἔρως was friendship (LS 67D; Arius Didymus 5b9/*SVF* 3.717; cf. 1.263).

Clearly, any of this is enough to account for ascetic-leaning Stoics. But if the problem reflected in 1 Corinthians 7:1 was in fact grounded in Stoic views, this would make it difficult to see the "wise" in Corinth as a single, clearly defined group, for the slogan of 6:12 apparently reflects a directly conflicting outlook (although this is a difficulty with which any thesis must reckon). It is possible that both positions could have issued from among the educated: indeed, the "ascetic" and "libertine" positions make a common appeal to *freedom*, which could be wielded for whatever purposes one wished. But it is equally possible that the assertion of "freedom" had percolated from the educated down to the lower ranks of the church, where it was seized upon for somewhat different purposes.

Interestingly, Paul's rejoinder in 7:4 links the issue with freedom explicitly: "[T]he wife does not have authority (ἐξουσιάζει) over her own body, but the husband does; likewise the husband does not have authority (ἐξουσιάζει) over his own body, but the wife does." Paul's rhetoric is carefully chosen here, for it again mimics a Stoic viewpoint: as the Stoics said, spouses should not "deprive each other" because they hold "everything in common up to their own bodies, or rather even up to their very souls" (Stobaeus, *Anth*. 4.67.24 [Ramelli 77]; cf. Musonius Rufus, *Diatr*. 13a; D. L. 7.87).[63] Paul again beats the Corinthians at their own game.[64]

Freedom and eating meat sacrificed to idols (8:1–11:1). Corinthian freedom with respect to sex found parallel in their outlook on food (chs. 8,

[63] In the NT, this notion is found otherwise only in Eph 5:28 (albeit with less striking verbal similarities), a passage long noted for its connections with the *haustafeln* of philosophical literature; for which see J. P. Hering, *The Colossian and Ephesian* Haustafeln *in Theological Context* (New York: Peter Lang, 2007), 9–59.

[64] Worth mentioning also are the resonances between Paul's position in 7:7–8, 28–35 and Seneca, *Ep*. 53.9 72.3–4 116.5.

10). Apparently they applied the same slogan to this topic: "all things are permissible" (10:23a). They also claim that "[f]ood will not bring us close to God. We are no worse off if we do not eat, and no better off if we do" (8:8), and that "an idol is nothing (οὐδέν)" (8:4). And of course all of this is grounded in their view that they, unlike the "weak," "have knowledge" (8:1).

We have already commented on the role played by knowledge in the judgments of the Stoic wise man. Knowledge and judgment were explicitly linked in the Stoic definition of "judgment" as "the awareness and recognition (γνῶσιν) of right things" (Arius Didymus 11m). It fits the facts to assume that this was also the principle seized upon by the wise Corinthians in their consumption of idol-meat: equipped with knowledge, they have judged it right to eat, again explicitly as an exercise of personal "rights." That they saw this as a matter of personal rights is suggested by Paul's remark regarding "that very 'freedom' *of yours* (ἡ ἐξουσία ὑμῶν αὕτη," 8:9).

Their judgment, however, is also rooted in a sort of indifference toward food. On this topic the early Stoics had expressed a shockingly liberal perspective. Chrysippus, for instance, had taught, "if the flesh [of one's dead parents] is edible, people should use it" (Sextus Empiricus, *Pyr.* 3.247–8 [Long and Sedley 431]; cf. *SVF* 3.747–50). He also noted that "eating certain food" had been "discredited without reason" (Plutarch, *Mor.* 1044F/*SVF* 3.753 [Long and Sedley 430]). This freedom was justified on the grounds that dietary matters fell under the category of "things indifferent": these things were outside the realm of moral choice.

The Stoic perspective on the gods – and "idols" – was more complicated. Some ancient sources say that the Stoic would perform sacrifices and build temples (D. L. 7.119). Many, however, demurred: "It is a doctrine of Zeno *not* to build temples of the gods; for a temple not worth much is also not sacred, and nothing made by builders or workmen is worth much" (Plutarch, *Mor.* 1034B/*SVF* 1.264 [LS 430]; my italics; cf. D. L. 7.33). Seneca expressed an even harsher opinion, as seen in his lost book *Against Superstitions*, fragments of which have been preserved by St. Augustine. There he denounces graven images in a fashion redolent of the Old Testament prophets: "They [people] dedicate images representing sacred, immortal, inviolable beings in base, inert matter; they give them the shapes of men, of wild beasts, or of fishes; . . . And they give the name of divinities to those images, though they would be classed as monsters if they suddenly came to life" (Augustine, *Civ.* 6.10 [Bettenson 248]). Accordingly, he maintained that popular cultic rituals were not acceptable to the gods. If the wise man must conform to them, it was only because they were ordered by law, not because the gods were pleased with them. Indeed, the civil cult was "a matter of custom, having little connection with truth" (Bettenson 250).

Despite their frequent use of the plural "gods," however, the Stoics – like most philosophers – were essentially monotheistic. They believed that though he/she/it had many names, there was only one God: "[T]hey call him Zeus [*Dia*] as the cause [*di' hon*] of all things; Zēn in so far as he is responsible for, or pervades, life [*zēn*]; Athena because his commanding-faculty stretches into the aether; Hera because it stretches into the air; ... [etc.]" (D. L. 7.147/*SVF* 2.1021 [Long and Sedley 323]).[65] In this regard, it is not without interest that the apparent Christian creed of 1 Cor 8:6 actually takes a *Stoic* formula as its point of departure, even if it has been transformed for use in a Christian context: "[F]or us there is one God, the Father, from whom are all things and for whom we exist, and one Lord, Jesus Christ, through whom are all things and through whom we exist" (NRSV).[66] A formulation strikingly similar to this is evident, among other places, in the Diogenes Laertius passage just cited (7.147). Marcus Aurelius, however, makes the resemblance more formally obvious. Note in the following text, the reference to "all things" + a series of prepositional relations + the relation of these "things" in all of these ways to "God":

> from you [God] are all things, in you are all things, and to you are all things. (*Med.* 4.23)

> for us there is one God, the Father, from whom are all things and for whom we exist, and one Lord, Jesus Christ, through whom are all things and through whom we exist. (1 Cor 8:6)

For all that, the wise Corinthians could easily have viewed Jewish-Christian monotheism and Stoic theism as being essentially compatible.

One can only wonder, then, whether Stoicism does not again shed light on the Corinthians' views: the wise have judged it right to eat *idol-meat* because they were *indifferent* toward both *idols* and *meat*. They claim, with perfectly balanced indifference, "We are no worse off if we do not eat, and no better off if we do" (8:8): food was neither advantageous nor disadvantageous. But aside from what food what *was* in itself (i.e., material and indifferent), it also made no difference to them whether it

[65] See also Cleanthes' *Hymn to Zeus* (*SVF* 1.537); D. L. 7.135–6/*SVF* 1.102; and Seneca, *Ben.* 4.7–8.

[66] For a compendium of literature and parallels on this passage, see Stowers, "Paul on the Use and Abuse of Reason," 276; and Thiselton, *First Epistle to the Corinthians*, 635.

had been *sacrificed* to an idol, for to them "an idol is *nothing* (οὐδέν)" (8:4). Though a Jew or an Epicurean would have shared this sentiment (e.g., Epistle of Jeremiah; Cicero, *Nat. d.* 1.123, respectively), what should strike us is the recognizably Stoic way it is expressed here. For the Stoics, all that is outside the realm of moral purpose – everything indifferent – was to be considered "nothing." Like the slogan of 1 Cor 8:4, the Stoic mantra was typically expressed with the copulative plus οὐδέν (Paul himself uses this formula in 7:19 –"circumcision is *nothing* [οὐδέν]" – and nowhere else in his letters).[67] Sextus Empiricus provides one of countless examples: "When parents die, we should use the simplest methods of burial, as though the body, like the nails or teeth or hair, *were nothing* (οὐδέν)" (*Pyr.* 3.247–8/LS 67G [Long and Sedley 431]; cf. D. L. 10.124–5; Epictetus, *Diatr.* 1.4.27; 1.9.13; 3.8.2; 3.16.15; *Ench.* 1.5; 32.2).

Paul, however, expostulates against this exercise of "freedom." With it the Corinthians have served "their own" interest (τὸ ἑαυτοῦ) rather than the "other's" (τὸ τοῦ ἑτέρου; 10:24, 33; cf. 13:5). Far from being "beneficial" (συμφέρον) to the whole (10:23b), such exercise has precipitated the destruction of the brothers and sisters who are "weak" in conscience, for whom Christ died (8:11).

Against their individualism, Paul lays forth in chapter 9 what he thinks a proper exercise of freedom ought to look like, drawing heavily from Greek philosophical topoi in the process.[68] To be sure, he speaks of this discourse as a "defense" (ἀπολογία; 9:3); but to see it *primarily* as a "defense of his apostleship," addressing a major bone of contention in the Corinthian church, seems to miss the point, and as Thiselton has observed, puts too much stock in partition theories (which suggest that 1 Corinthians 9 does not belong here) and in passé studies on early apostolic conflicts (which suggest Paul was at major loggerheads with the Twelve).[69] That this passage is first and foremost a call to *imitation* is in fact explicitly indicated by the coda of 11:1 ("be imitators of me"). As such, Paul presents his own conduct as an *example* of how one's "rights" (ἐξουσία, 9:4–6, 12) ought to be voluntarily *surrendered* in the interest and service of the Other. Thus, if the Stoics' paradox was that "only the wise man is free," the Christian's is this: the one who is free in Christ is really a slave, of both Christ and his/her

[67] Although a similar expression appears in Gal 6:15.

[68] Malherbe, "Determinism and Free Will in Paul," esp. 243–55.

[69] Thiselton, *First Epistle to the Corinthians*, 666–73. As Thiselton convincingly argues, Paul strives to establish his apostolic credentials not because they had been doubted, but because he needs to show, for the sake of present argument, that *he had "rights" to renounce in the first place*.

brethren (9:19–23). Paul illustrates with the image of an athletic ἀγῶν or "contest," a metaphor commonplace among the philosophers.[70] Like an athlete in complete "self-control" (ἐγκρατεύειν), he abuses and "enslaves" (δουλαγογῶ) his body for the sake of a greater prize (9:24–27). Only by limiting his personal rights, he insists, will he become a sharer in the Gospel's blessings.

Head-covering and gender deportment (11:2–16; 14:34–36). With the question of head-covering in 11:2–16, again the issue of freedom crops up.[71] Here social mores have been violated with regard to head-covering in public worship. Paul addresses both men and women, possibly because both had flouted custom. The general motivation seems to have been the same as in the preceding chapters: the culprits vaunt the freedom to do as they alone see right.

Paul leaves us at least one clue that this was in fact the case when he again calls the notion of ἐξουσία to the fore: whatever is meant when he says that women should have a "sign of authority (ἐξουσία) on their heads" (11:10), surely he is alluding to the earlier individualism of 6:12 (ἔξεστιν), chapter 7 (ἐξουσίαζω), and chapters 8 and 10 (ἐξουσία). In this case, freedom relates to the question of conventional gender deportment. This may also be the issue in 14:34–6, where the issue is whether women should speak out in church. We shall have to revisit both of these issues later in the chapter.

Practices surrounding the Lord's Supper (11:17–34). A strong individualism also besets the church in its gatherings for the Lord's Supper (11:17–34). It has been reported that there are "divisions" at these meetings (σχίσματα; 11:18), and Paul complains that "when the time comes to eat, each of you goes ahead with your own supper, and one goes hungry and another becomes drunk" (11:21). Since Weiss's commentary more than a century ago, it has been noted that socioeconomic causes were probably involved.[72] Theissen developed the idea by arguing that portion sizes may have been decided on the basis of wealth and social clout (e.g., Pliny, *Ep.* 2.6; Martial, *Epigr.* 3.60).[73] Murphy-O'Connor contributed further by bringing the size of the "typical" villa into the discussion: only a select few would have been privileged to eat in the triclinium, given its

[70] For parallels, see Fee, *First Epistle to the Corinthians*, 434n2; and Thiselton, *First Epistle to the Corinthians*, 712.

[71] Fee, *First Epistle to the Corinthians*, 497–8, 510–12, 518; Thiselton, *First Epistle to the Corinthians*, 829, 839.

[72] Weiss, *Der erste Korintherbrief*, 103.

[73] Theissen, "Social Integration and Sacramental Activity, 1 Cor 11:17–34," esp. 153–63.

prohibitively small size.[74] The rest of the church – those of less consequence in the community – would be forced to dine in the atrium.

But might Stoic influences in the church (to indulge in some speculation here) shed further light on their divisions' underlying causes? Despite Stoic concern for a cosmos in which all pieces functioned in perfect harmony with each another, Stoicism exhibited a heavy bent toward individualism, most of all in the Roman era. This was because their wise man was said to be "self-sufficient" (Seneca, *Ep.* 9.13). In this regard, Epictetus remarks that wise men "rely on nothing but themselves" (*Diatr.* 1.9.8–9); rather, the wise man "looks for all his help or harm from himself" (*Ench.* 48.1). In the same vein, Musonius Rufus noted that "what one can get from himself it is superfluous and foolish as well to get from someone else" (Musonius Rufus, *fr.* 45 [Lutz 141]; cf. *Diatr.* 11). Seneca stated that the wise man ought to imitate Jupiter, who at the final dissolution of the cosmos will "retire into himself and give himself over to his own thoughts" (Seneca, *Ep.* 9.16). It was told that the Stoic Stilbo had stated, with almost Jupiter-like self-sufficiency, that he had "lost nothing" when his city had burned to the ground – and his wife and children with it (Seneca, *Ep.* 9.18). When Stoicism did speak of community, it was conceived in highly exclusive terms. They had always said to avoid the influence of the "rabble" (Seneca, *Ep.* 14.9; 18.4; 25.6–7; 29.11; 31.1; 36.2; *Vit. beat.* 1.5; *Tranq.* 7.4). Friendship, rather, existed only between the wise (Arius Didymus 11m/*SVF* 3.630; cf. 11i/*SVF* 3.626; D. L. 7.124). Zeno reportedly stated that "all who are not virtuous are foes, enemies, slaves and estranged from one another (D. L. 7.32–33/LS 67B).[75] Of course, traditionally Stoicism had tried to reconcile the exclusivity-cosmopolitanism dialectic with recourse to their (paradoxical) theory of οἰκειώσις, which maintained that the interests of the individual and the interests of the whole ought to converge;[76] but this was a theory difficult to sustain beneath the pressures of imperial life. Emphasizing their ethical autonomy against the tyrant's powers of coercion, Roman Stoics gravitated more heavily to the side of the individual. Perhaps, for the self-styled "wise men" in Corinth, this translated into a

[74] Murphy-O'Connor, *St. Paul's Corinth* (1983), 153–60; (2002), 178–85. However, our deepened insights into early Christian meeting places in recent years makes the thesis more hypothetical than was once thought.

[75] For development in the Stoic idea of the city, see M. Schofield, *The Stoic Idea of the City* (Cambridge: Cambridge University Press, 1991).

[76] For the full theory, see T. Engberg-Pedersen, *The Stoic Theory of Oikeiosis: Moral Development and Social Interaction in Early Stoic Philosophy*, Studies in Hellenistic Civilization 2 (Aarhus: Aarhus University Press, 1990).

kind of group-exclusivity? They were the superior inner circle, the rest were second-class Christians – or in Stoic terms – the "weak," "immature," and "unspiritual."

Spiritual gifts and the order of worship (chs. 12–14). Chapters 12–14 are integrally connected with the problems that precede. Thiselton observes that the threefold repetition of "knowledge" in 12:1–3 makes it clear that Paul is taking on those πνευμάτικοι who claim they have γνῶσις.[77] Now, just as freedom played a role in the issue of "knowledge" in chapters 8, 10, so does it play a role in the issue of spiritual gifts in chapters 12–14. Worship services are roiled by a din of competing tongues-speakers and fusillades of prophecies (14:27–33). This cacophony of "disorder" (14:33) arises from the church's rampant individualism. Each person is wont to say "I have no need of you" (12:21) – perhaps not unlike the wise man who "relies on no one but himself." But Paul again appeals to them in Stoic terms: they are to be driven not by their sense of personal freedom, but by a sense of "benefit" (συμφέρον; 12:7). This benefit must be measured in terms of its consequences on the whole. He illustrates with a metaphor from the human body, a metaphor that, despite adaptations to suit his Christology, is clearly borrowed from the Stoics.[78] Compare the following passages from Paul and the Stoic Hierocles (to my knowledge, hereto uncompared in the secondary literature), noting especially their common usage of similes and conditionals:

> [12] For just as the body is one and has many members, and all the members of the body, though many, are one body, so it is with Christ. [13] For in the one Spirit we were all baptized into one body – Jews or Greeks, slaves or free – and we were all made to drink of one Spirit. [14] Indeed, the body does not consist of one member but of many. [15] If the foot would say, "Because I am not a hand, I do not belong to the body," that would not make it any less a part of the body. [16] And if the ear would say, "Because I am not an eye, I do not belong to the body," that would not make it any less a part of the body. [17] If the whole body were an eye,

[77] Thiselton, *First Epistle to the Corinthians*, 916–17.

[78] Vague similarities in rabbinic literature notwithstanding, Stoic examples are by far the closest in form, as is reflected in the example presented here. For conceptual parallels in rabbinic literature, see W. D. Davies, *Paul and Rabbinic Judaism: Some Rabbinic Elements in Pauline Theology* (Philadelphia: Fortress, 1948), 53–7. For other examples in the Pauline corpus: Rom 12:4-5; 1 Cor 1:10–17; Eph 4:4–6; Col 1:18, 24; 2:19 although the idea is fully developed only in 1 Corinthians and, later, Romans. For further comparison between Paul and Stoicism on this score, see M. Lee, *Paul, the Stoics, and the Body of Christ*, SNTSMS 137 (Cambridge: Cambridge University Press, 2006).

> where would the hearing be? If the whole body were hearing, where would the sense of smell be? . . . [21] The eye cannot say to the hand, "I have no need of you," nor again the head to the feet, "I have no need of you." . . . [26] If one member suffers, all suffer together with it; if one member is honored, all rejoice together with it. (1 Cor 12:12–17, 21, 26, NRSV; cf. 10:17)

> [O]ne's brothers are parts of oneself, just as my eyes are parts of me and so too my legs and hands and the rest. . . . Just as eyes and hands, accordingly, if each should obtain its own soul and mind, would respect the other parts in every possible way for the sake of their declared communality, since they are not even able to perform their own function well without the presence of the other parts, so too we, who are human beings and confess to having a soul, should not omit any effort in behaving toward our brothers as one ought.
> (Hierocles/Stobaeus, *Anth.* 4.84.20 [Ramelli 89])

If the Corinthians were *over*emphasizing Stoic individualism, Paul is clever here to balance their perspective with the Stoic body metaphor: with it he affirms that the ambit of one's concern must stretch beyond the sphere of the self or one's inner circle so as to compass the wider community.

"Dualism"

The Corinthian attitude of freedom and indifference toward food and sex cannot be viewed apart from their anthropology and cosmology. Here Stoicism again rears its head.

Although the early Stoics had conceived of the body in monistic terms, a gradual drift toward dualism had taken place by the time of the Roman Stoics.[79] The old Stoics had maintained that even the soul is a "body," for that which is incorporeal "does not even make contact with a body" – whereas the soul does (*SVF* 1.518 [Long and Sedley 272]). Posidonius and the Middle Stoics, however, moved Stoic anthropology in a decidedly Platonist direction (to which it was already close),[80] so that by the

[79] For more on dualism and its connection with the views of the wise Corinthians see, e.g., J. R. Asher, *Polarity and Change in 1 Corinthians 15: A Study of Metaphysics, Rhetoric and Resurrection* (Tübingen: Mohr Siebeck, 2000); and Garcilazo, *The Corinthian Dissenters and the Stoics*, 51–63.

[80] See A. A. Long, "Soul and Body in Stoicism," *Phronesis* 27 (1982): 34–6.

time of Seneca and Epictetus it looked more like dualism than like the monism of the early Stoics.[81]

Of course, the old Stoics had unwittingly left berth for the new position: death, Chrysippus had said, is merely "the separation of the soul from the body" (*SVF* 2.790). By the time of Seneca, the distance between soul and body simply widened, largely so as to sustain the possibility of ethical autonomy, undetermined by bodily or other external matters.[82] In that regard, Seneca tells us that the body is a "heavy and earthly prison" (*gravi terrenoque*; *Ep*.102.22), or an "inn" in which one dwells only for a short time (*hospitium*; *Ep*.120.14). It is also described as a "chain" that manacles one's freedom (*Ep*. 65.21). Thus the body was of only the meanest significance. Epictetus regularly refers to it with the pejorative σωμάτιον, or "paltry body" (cf. *corpusculum*, Seneca, *Ep*. 41.4), frequently including it in his mantra "My paltry body is nothing to me" (*Diatr*. 3.22.21; cf. 3.22.24, 40–4 [Oldfather, LCL]). Marcus Aurelius reports that Epictetus used to say, "You are a little soul, carrying around a corpse (νεκρόν)" (Epictetus, *fr*. 26). For Epictetus, the body was the mere "husk" (κέλυφος; Epictetus, *Diatr*. 1.23.1), the soul was the self (*Diatr*. 1.29.9–10, 18; 2.13.13, 16). He illustrates by way of Socrates, who had said, "Anytus and Meletus can kill me, but they cannot hurt me" (*Diatr*. 1.29.18). He urges others to adopt the same thinking:

> When the tyrant threatens and summons me, I answer "Whom are you threatening?" If he says, "I will put you in chains," I reply, "He is threatening my hands and my feet." If he says, "I will behead you," I answer, "He is threatening my neck." If he says, "I will throw you into prison," I say, "He is threatening my whole paltry body"; … Does he, then, threaten *you* [σοὶ] at all? – If I feel that all this is nothing to *me* [ἐμοὶ] – not at all.
>
> (*Diatr*. 1.29.5–7 [Oldfather, LCL]; emphasis added; cf. 4.7.31–2)

The soul, on the other hand, was "sacred and eternal" (Seneca, *Helv*. 11.7). It was the divine part of the person, the "holy spirit" (*sacer spiritus*) of God dwelling within (Seneca, *Ep*. 41.1; cf. *Ep*. 31.11; Epictetus, *Diatr*. 1.14.6–17; 2.8.9–29). Thus Seneca said that mortal existence was a "prelude to the longer and better life" and death the termination of the

[81] See N. T. Pratt, *Seneca's Dramas* (Chapel Hill: University of North Carolina Press, 1982), 58–61.

[82] Long spells this out in "Soul and Body in Stoicism."

body but not of the soul (*Ep.* 102.23).[83] He also speaks of the soul's "release" (*emissus*) from the body at death, upon which it looks down on human affairs while enjoying a nearer vision of things divine (*Pol.* 9.2, 3). Accordingly, in his *Consolation of Marcia*, he says of the woman's deceased son:

> Only the image of your son – and a very imperfect likeness it was – has perished; he himself is eternal and has reached now a far better state, stripped of all outward encumbrances and left simply himself. This vesture of the body which we see, bones and sinews and the skin that covers us, this face and the hands that serve us and the rest of our human wrapping – these are but chains and darkness to our souls. By these things the soul is crushed and strangled and stained and imprisoned in error, is kept far from its true and natural sphere. It constantly struggles against this weight of the flesh in the effort to avoid being dragged back and sunk; it ever strives to rise to that place from which it once descended. There eternal peace awaits it when it has passed from earth's dull motley to the vision of all that is pure and bright.
>
> (*Cons. Marc.* 25.4 [Basore, LCL]; cf. *Ep.* 79.12; 86.1)

Just as the soul would survive death, so also would it survive the great conflagration at the end of the age (*SVF* 2.809), although all matter would be destroyed. In the conflagration, the elements would be resolved into their primordial state: "all things" (πάντα) would be in Zeus, and Zeus in all (*SVF* 2.596–632; cf. Seneca, *Ep.* 9.16).[84]

Because the body stood outside the sphere of moral choice, the Stoics reckoned its affairs among the indifferents. Musonius Rufus expressed indifference toward sundry matters in this regard: food (*Diatr.* 18–19), clothing (*Diatr.* 20), and shelter (*Diatr.* 19). But death also was included. The Stoics said that it was "no evil [οὐ κακόν]," and scorned it no less than would an Epicurean. Thus, Epictetus intones: "Are not these things indifferent – indeed, nothing – to us [οὐδὲν πρὸς ἡμᾶς]? And is not death [θάνατος] no evil [οὐ κακόν]?" (*Diatr.* 1.9.13 [Oldfather, LCL]; cf. 3.8.1–2).[85] Seneca's view is comparable: "Death is helpful to

[83] For Seneca's views on life after death, see J. N. Sevenster, *Paul and Seneca* (Leiden: Brill, 1961), 224–9.

[84] Although two or three Stoics along the way are said to have doubted the conflagration: so Philo, *Indestr.*, 76–7.

[85] "It is nothing to us [οὐδὲν ἐστὶν πρὸς ἡμᾶς]" is one of his usual ways of referring to the indifferents, including death (1.4.27; cf. 3.8.2; *Ench.* 1.5).

many ... sets many free from tortures, want, ailments, sufferings, and weariness. We are in the power of nothing when once we have death in our power!" (*Ep*. 91.21).

Not unlike the Roman Stoics, the Corinthian wise seem to have relegated dietary and bodily matters to a lower plane of existence. Their denigration of the physical shows through clearly in their justification of lax sexual conduct (5:1–13 6:12–20), their support of liberal dietary practices (6:13; chs. 8, 10; 11:17–34), possibly in their views on gender and marriage (ch. 7; 11:2–16; 14:34–6), and most definitely in their denial of a bodily resurrection (15:12–58).

Sexual immorality (5:1–13; 6:12–20). As to the problems in 5:1–13/ 6:12–20, clearly certain ones had placed too low a premium on the body. They say "all things are permissible" (evidently including sex with one's father's wife) because bodily matters were regarded as being irrelevant. That this was their viewpoint is evident from their two supporting slogans – "Food is meant for the stomach and the stomach for food, and God will destroy both one and the other" (6:13a), and "every wrong which one commits is outside the body" (6:18) – both declaring the body irrelevant in moral matters. We have already seen the verbal ties connecting 6:12a with Stoicism. But a compelling case can also be made for the other two slogans.

It is a rarely noted point that the terminology used for "sin/wrong" in 6:18 is virtually anomalous in Paul, but common coin in the Stoics.[86] Beside its occurrence here, ἁμάρτημα appears in only *one* other instance in Paul (Rom 3:28), and then in only one further passage in the entire NT (Mark 3:28, 29). By contrast, Paul's usual term for "sin" – ἁμαρτία – appears nearly fifty times in his major epistles alone. These numbers mirror the Stoic sources. Ἁμαρτία is virtually nonexistent in the Stoics. Rather, it is ἁμάρτημα that acts as the technical term for a "wrong act" (cf. verb: ἁμαρτανεῖν), in contrast to κατορθώμα, or a "right act" (Arius Didymus 11e/*SVF* 3.501). A ἁμάρτημα was said to be an act performed "contrary to reason" (Arius Didymus 11a/*SVF* 3.500). Epictetus describes it as "a kind of ignorance" (ταύτην ἄγνοιαν; *Diatr*. 2.24.20). Thus, it was a blunder committed not in the body, but in the mind.

As in 6:12b, 7:4, and 12:12–30, Paul once again sallies back with countering Stoic responses, first in 6:18c, and then again in 6:19c. His statement in 6:18c – "he who commits fornication sins against his own body" – is found almost verbatim in the Stoics: "everyone who sins, sins

[86] In my encounters, it has been noted only by Stowers, "Paul on the Use and Abuse of Reason," 60.

against himself" (*SVF* 3.289).[87] Then, in 6:19c (cf. 7:23), he subverts the Corinthian position with another turn of Stoic doctrine: the "body is not your own" (οὐκ ἑαυτῶν). This exact expression is found frequently in the Stoics, with slightly different meaning (Epictetus, *Diatr.* 3.20.1; 3.22.21, 34, 40–4; 4.1.66, 78, 87, 104, 158; 4.7.17, 31–32; *Ench.* 1.1; Seneca, *Ep.* 120.18–19). The Stoics had several closely related reasons for the assertion: because one's body was merely a mélange of the cosmos's supply of material elements (LS 62K) and was thus only a part of a larger whole (D. L. 7.87); because the self was located not in the body but in the soul (Epictetus, *Diatr.* 1.19.9; 1.29.5–7, 22–9); because the body was a sort of temple of God (Seneca, *Ep.* 41.1; *Ep.* 31.11; Epictetus, *Diatr.* 1.14.6–17; 2.8.9–29); and especially because the body resided outside the individual's own control, liable as it was to disease, lameness, and most of all the whims of "tyrants" (cf. Epictetus, *Diatr.* 4.7.17; *Ench.* 1.9). What *did* belong to the individual was the power of moral judgment. The wise Corinthians, however, have taken this principle to mean that "every wrong committed is outside the body" – that is, every wrong occurs strictly in the intellectual sphere and bodily matters can, for all intents and purposes, be bracketed out. Paul of course would have agreed that each individual was part of a larger body, that the soul was almost a "divine" part of the person, and that external goods lay largely outside one's control. But what he could not have agreed with was the conclusion that the body is on those counts morally irrelevant. Rather, it is "the temple of the Holy Spirit" (6:19; cf. 3:16; 9:26), bought at a price and defiled to one's own peril.

Eating meat sacrificed to idols (8:1–13; 10:1–11:1). A "dualistic" devaluation of the physical would also help explain indiscriminate consumption of idol-meat (chs. 8, 10). The culprits can say, "We are no worse off if we do not eat, and no better off if we do" (8:8), because food belongs to a lower plane of existence.

The slogan of 6:13a features the same attitude: "Food is meant for the stomach and the stomach for food, and God will destroy both one and the other." We find a comparable Greek equivalent in Musonius Rufus, arguing that food is meant for nourishment and nothing more: "[T]he throat was designed to be a passage for food ... and the stomach was made for the same purpose as the root was created in plants" (*Diatr.* 18b, 8–10 [Lutz 119]). But we find a closer parallel in a Posidonian fragment preserved by Seneca: he notes that while man's first business is virtue, to

[87] As R. M. Grant ("Hellenistic Elements in 1 Corinthians," in *Early Christian Origins* [Chicago: Quadrangle Books, 1961], 64) observes.

this is joined the "useless and fleeting flesh, *fitted only for the reception of food* [*receptandis tantum cibis habilis*]" (Posidonius, *fr.* 184/Seneca, *Ep.* 92.10). This text lacks the proverbial rhythm of the Corinthian slogan, and Seneca of course paraphrases in Latin, but it agrees perfectly in sense:

> τὰ βρώματα τῇ κοιλίᾳ καὶ ἡ κοιλία τοῖς βρώμασιν [food is for the stomach and the stomach for food] (1 Cor 6:13a)
>
> *caro, receptandis tantum cibis habilis* [flesh, fitted only for the reception of food] (Posidonius, *fr.* 184/Seneca, *Ep.* 92.10)

With this, 11:17–34 again comes to mind. Could the wise Corinthians be regarding food – the elements of the Supper – with the "indifference" they think is due merely physical things? To Paul's dismay, they show no greater discrimination here than they showed toward idol-meat in chapters 8, 10:

> 29 For all who eat and drink without discerning the body, eat and drink judgment against themselves. 30 For this reason many of you are weak and ill, and some have died. 31 But if we judged ourselves, we would not be judged. 32 But when we are judged by the Lord, we are disciplined so that we may not be condemned along with the world. (11:29–32, NRSV)

Marriage and gender (7:1–40; 11:2–16; 14:34–6). The Corinthians' "dualistic" mentality may also have led them along to their bizarre views on marriage and gender, as seen in chapter 7; 11:2–16; and 14:34–6.Often these texts have been explained in terms of an exaggerated or "over-realized" eschatology, espoused perhaps by a feminist party in the church.[88] Whatever the full value of this hypothesis might be, the suggestion does seem to hit around the truth of the matter: certain Corinthians have focused so narrowly on the "spiritual" dimension that they have forgotten the constraints of ordinary terrestrial existence, and some forego sexual unions (ch. 7), and perhaps others conventional gender distinctions (11:2–16; 14:34–6).

Verses 11:2–16 and 14:34–6 recall discussions related to gender in philosophical contexts. Stoicism exhibited a strong egalitarian tendency while at the same time maintaining gender distinctions thought to have been given by "nature" (φύσις), including that of *hair length.* Stoics were

[88] Cf. Moffatt, *The First Epistle of Paul to the Corinthians*, 78; Fee, *First Epistle to the Corinthians*, 270, 290; and the history of scholarship in Thiselton, *First Epistle to the Corinthians*, 521–5.

therefore among the few who encouraged women as well as men to study philosophy[89] – after all, women too had been endowed with reason (Musonius Rufus, *Diatr.* 3; 4).[90] The Stoic Cleanthes had written a treatise entitled *On the Thesis That Virtue Is the Same in Man and in Woman* (D. L. 7.175). And Zeno, as part of his utopian vision, had even enjoined that "men and women wear the same dress" (D. L. 7.33).

Yet, Stoics also emphasized that "nature" had given clues to the genders as to their differences. Though not unknown among the other philosophies (e.g., Heraclitus, *fr.* 1.8, 9; Plato, *Leg.* 10.888E-889C; *Crit.* 389B, C; *Phaedr.* 87E, 270C; cf. D. L. 6.71), the concept of "nature" played a distinctive role in Stoicism in that it was thought to provide the paradigm on which all ethical decisions should be based (LS 58). Indeed, only for Stoics and Cynics was the *telos* of human existence specifically to live "according to nature (κάτα φύσιν)" (LS 63). As the Stoics maintained, "There is no other or more appropriate way of approaching the theory of good and bad things or the virtues or happiness than from universal nature (φύσεως) and from the administration of the world" (Plutarch, *Mor.* 1035C-D/*SVF* 3.68 [Long and Sedley 368–9]). In this regard, Epictetus remarks:

> Can anything be more useless than the *hairs* on a chin? Well, what then? *Has not nature* (φύσις) used even these in the most suitable way possible? Has she not by these means distinguished between the male and the female? ... [I]n the case of women, just as nature has mingled in their voice a certain softer note, so likewise she [nature] has taken the hair from their chins. (Epictetus, *Diatr.* 1.16.9–14; emphasis added)

Similarly, Musonius Rufus advised that men "cut the hair from the head for the same reason that we prune a vine," but said to leave the eyebrows, eyelashes, and beard as nature (φύσις) had provided them (*Diatr.* 21.1–7 [Lutz 129]).

It comports entirely with the facts of the situation to assume that some Stoic-influenced Corinthians had been overdrawn toward a kind of absolute egalitarianism, as seemingly advocated by Zeno (e.g., to "wear the same dress"), while forgetting Stoic teachers' qualification regarding what is "according to nature" (κατὰ φύσιν). Yet, Paul has not forgotten

[89] Cf. Harich-Schwarzbauer, "Women Philosophers," *Brill's New Pauly: Antiquity* (electronic version).

[90] Although the Cynics did as well: Crates, *Epistle 28*; Crates, *Epistle 29*, 14–17; Crates, *Epistle 32*, 9–11; Diogenes, *Epistle 3*; Diogenes, *Epistle* 43.

it. In 11:14 he quips with a rhetorical question that looks much like the remark just cited from Epictetus:

> Does not even *nature* [φύσις] teach you that any man who wears his hair long dishonors himself? (1 Cor 11:14)
>
> Has not nature [φύσις] used even these [the hairs on the chin] in the most suitable way possible? (Epictetus, *Diatr.* 1.16.9–14)

Here the rhetorical-question formulation betrays that φύσις is summoned to meet an audience that Paul obviously expected to have thought in those terms.[91]

Denial of a general resurrection (15:12–58). Since the publication of Karl Barth's *Resurrection of the Dead* nearly a century ago, interpreters almost without exception have agreed that the denial of the resurrection reflected in 1 Corinthians 15 serves as the climax of and key to the epistle.[92] According to Wayne Meeks, it is the *communis opinio* of interpreters that that this chapter bears an integral relation with all the other issues in the letter.[93] It is explicitly anticipated in 6:14, and it is the logical consequence of the bodily devaluation that features from chapters 5 through 14.

It can be no accident that Paul treats last the issue in which the most is at stake. Indeed, for Paul it is one thing to adopt a dualism that sits light to the sacrificial status of meat, one thing to degrade the body with illicit sexual unions, but it is entirely another to deny what he avers to be the very core and essence of the Christian hope, that awaiting those who are in Christ is a post-mortem existence that is incorruptible and eternal – and also bodily (15:12–58).

As for what "some" in Corinth meant when they said "there is no resurrection of the dead" (15:12), the options are four: (1) they believed that the resurrection had already happened; (2) they have denied post-mortem existence of any kind; (3) they have denied a *bodily* resurrection; or (4) they held to some combination of these.[94]

[91] Which the syntax does not demand in Gal 4:7–9; 2:14–16; Rom 2:14–15; 2:27; 11:21, 24.

[92] See, e.g., K. Barth, *Resurrection of the Dead* (New York: Fleming H. Revell, 1933), 6; Conzelmann, *1 Corinthians*, 93; Fee, *First Epistle to the Corinthians*, 713, 716; for exceptions, see Thiselton, *First Epistle to the Corinthians*, 1171.

[93] Meeks, *First Urban Christians*, 121.

[94] For a summary of these four views and their adherents, see: B. Spörlein, *Die Leugnung der Auferstehung: Eine historisch-kritische Untersuchung zu 1 Kor 15* (Regensburg: Putstet, 1971), 1–19; M. C. de Boer, *The Defeat of Death: Apocalyptic Eschatology in 1 Corinthians 15 and Romans 5*, JSNTSup 22 (Sheffield: Sheffield Academic, 1988), 96–7; Schrage, *Der erste Brief an die Korinther*, 1:38–63; 2:385–6; Thiselton, *First Epistle to the Corinthians*, 1172–3, 1216.

The first option is a hangover of the old Gnostic thesis. After wide acceptance in German scholarship of the mid-twentieth century, it had been popularized for the English-speaking world with the translation of Ernst Käsemann's programmatic essay "Zum Thema der urchristlichen Apokalyptik."[95] According to Käsemann, "eschatological enthusiasm" (*eschatologischer Enthusiasmus*) is "the root of all that has gone wrong in Corinth." "[T]he dominant group in Corinth believed themselves to have reached the goal of salvation already – in the shape of baptism," and "the earthly body has been degraded to an insubstantial veil."[96] Accordingly, in 4:8 Paul indicates that the Corinthians are "*already* rich ... *already* kings," as if they *now* reign in the eschatological kingdom that in reality still waits in the offing. Because in 2 Tim 2:8 what seems to be a similar expression of "over-realized eschatology" generates a belief that "the resurrection has already happened," proponents of Käsemann's view assumed that the same situation has obtained in Corinth: when some say "there is no resurrection of the dead," they mean *not* that there will be no resurrection *after death*, but that it has *happened already* in the believer's present experience.

Over the last quarter-century, however, studies have increasingly concluded that this interpretation is flawed – and this conclusion we can now

[95] *ZTK* 59 (1962): 257–84, esp. 272–3; ET, "On the Subject of Primitive Christian Apocalyptic," in *New Testament Questions of Today* (Philadelphia: Fortress, 1969), 108–37. Before Käsemann, the thesis could be found in R. Bultmann, *Theologie des Neuen Testaments* (Tübingen: Mohr, 1953), 168; H. von Soden, "Sakrament und Ethik bei Paulus: Zur Frage der literarischen und theologischen Einheitlichkeit von 1 Kor 8–10," in *Urchristentum und Geschichte: Gesammelte Aufsatze und Vortrage* (Tübingen: Mohr, 1951), 1:259–60 – after Käsemann, in Barrett, *First Epistle to the Corinthians*, 109, 347–8; Lietzmann, *An die Korinther 1 und 2*, 19; L. Schotroff, *Der Glaubende und die feindliche Welt*, WMANT 37 (Neukirchener, 1970), 185–6; H. Koester, "Gnomai Diaphoi: The Origin and Nature of Diversification in the History of Early Christianity," in H. Koester (ed.), *Trajectories through Early Christianity* (Philadelphia: Fortress, 1971), 148–52; Bruce, *1 and 2 Corinthians*, 49–50; J. M. Robinson, "Kerygma and History in the New Testament," in *Trajectories through Early Christianity*, 30–40; H. R. Balz, *Christus in Korinth: Eine Einführung in den ersten Korintherbrief* (Kassel: J. G. Oncken, 1970), 48; Conzelmann, *1 Corinthians*, 88; E. Fasher, *Der erste Brief an die Korinther*, HTKNT 7:1 (Berlin: Evangelische Verlangsanstalt, 1975), 148; A. Thiselton, "Realized Eschatology at Corinth," *NTS* 24 (1978): 510–26; reaffirmed but qualified in Thiselton, *The First Epistle to the Corinthians*, esp. 40; Meeks, *First Urban Christians*, 178–9; Fee, *First Epistle to the Corinthians* 12; Senft, *La Premiere Epitre aux Corinthiens*, 67; Schrage, *Der erste Brief an die Korinther*, 57; Witherington, *Conflict and Community at Corinth*, 139–40; C. M. Tuckett, "The Corinthians Who Say 'There Is No Resurrection of the Dead' (1 Cor 15,12)," in R. Bieringer (ed.), *The Corinthian Correspondence*, BETL 125 (Leuven: Leuven University Press, 1996), 247–75; J. P. Sampley, "The First Letter to the Corinthians," *NIB* 10 (2002): 980–1; and Talbert, *Reading Corinthians*, 21.

[96] *New Testament Questions of Today*, 125–6.

call a consensus.[97] It has been shown, first, that 4:8 emphasizes not so much eschatology as ethics.[98] Second, eschatological language throughout the letter is Paul's own formulation rather than that of the Corinthians – for this is how Paul always preaches.[99] Third, 1 Cor 15:12 itself includes *no temporal reference*. The upshot is that 2 Timothy cannot be retrojected onto the Corinthian controversy. We have no clear evidence that the Corinthians believed the resurrection had "already happened."

Neither should it be maintained, however, that the Corinthians rejected post-mortem existence altogether, as if they had accepted either a "Cynic" (Downing) or an "Epicurean" (Tomlin) view that the present life was the only one.[100] In the first place, it should be said that Cynicism had nothing like an "orthodox" position on such questions; physics, which included matters of "psychology," was hardly a concern for the Cynics (D. L. 6.103). Moreover, Cynicism was a "way of life," not so much a distinct school with a canonical set of doctrines safeguarded by successive scholarchs. Thus, just as philosophers of all stamps could have Cynic leanings, so could self-identified Cynics assume the views of any of the major schools. This is why the Cynic Epistles can depict Heraclitus, Socrates, and Plato all as "Cynic," and the epistles themselves can affirm the view that death is the "separation of the soul from the body" and "the soul is immortal" (Diogenes, *Epistle 39*, 1–6; *Epistle 14*, 25–7; cf. Socratics, *Epistle* 25).

While the Epicurean view may have greater appeal, still some insurmountable obstacles stand against it. First, the Corinthian dissenters *do*

[97] Beginning with D. J. Doughty, "The Presence and Future of Salvation in Corinth," *ZNW* 66 (1975): 61–90, and growing in support from there: Horsley, "How Can Some of you Say That There Is No Resurrection of the Dead? Spiritual Elitism in Corinth," 204, 222; Fee, *First Epistle to the Corinthians*, 339; Horsley, *1 Corinthians*, 201, 217; D. W. Kuck, *Judgment and Community Conflict: Paul's Use of Apocalyptic Judgment Language in 1 Corinthians 3:5–4:5*, NovTSup 66 (Leiden: Brill, 1992), 16–25, 216–19; Paige, "Stoicism, *Eleutheria* and Community at Corinth," in *Worship, Theology and Ministry in the Early Church* (Sheffield, Eng.: JSOT), 184, 187; Barclay, "Thessalonica and Corinth: Social Contrasts," *JSNT* 47 (1992): 64; Litfin, *Paul's Theology of Proclamation*, 169, 222; Martin, *Corinthian Body*,106; Hays, *First Corinthians*, 8, 70, 71; Tomlin, "Christians and Epicureans in 1 Corinthians," 57; Hays, "Conversion of the Imagination," 396, 407, 409; Asher, *Polarity and Change in 1 Corinthians 15*, 39–41; and Garland, *1 Corinthians*, 14, 138, 699.

[98] See especially Doughty, "The Presence and Future of Salvation in Corinth"; and Kuck, *Judgment and Community Conflict*, 16–25, 216–19.

[99] See Barclay, "Thessalonica and Corinth."

[100] That the Corinthians have taken a distinctively Cynic perspective: Downing, *Cynics, Paul, and the Pauline Churches*, 105, 246 – that their perspective is Epicurean: Robertson and Plummer, *First Epistle of St. Paul to the Corinthians*, 346; and Tomlin, "Christians and Epicureans in 1 Corinthians."

seem to hold some belief in post-mortem existence, whereas the Epicureans rejected it entirely. Though a notoriously difficult text, Paul's reference to "those baptized on behalf of/for the sake of/over the dead [οἱ βαπτιζόμενοι ὑπὲρ τῶν νεκρῶν]" in 15:29 can be narrowed down to only a handful of plausible interpretations, all of them involving some post-mortem belief on the part of the Corinthians.[101] Second, the *reductio ad absurdum* mantra of the Corinthian's position in 15:32 – "Let us eat and drink, for tomorrow may die" – need hardly be taken as an indication that they *themselves* espoused an Epicurean view of the afterlife. This and other such statements of futility (e.g., 15:19 – "If in this life only we have hope in Christ, we are to be pitied more than all people") articulate not the Corinthians' actual position, but rather what Paul says is the *logical consequence* of it, which they seem not to have followed through to its end. Paul suggests: if there is no resurrection of the dead, then Christ was not raised, and if Christ was not raised, then each person is still dead in sin.[102] Third, the questions of Paul's interlocutor in v. 35 – "*How* are the dead raised? With *what kind* of body do they come?" – reveal that the real issue, as he understands their objections, is how a *bodily* resurrection can be *possible*. Paul then spends some twenty verses making his case (vv. 36–54).[103] Therefore, unless the "some" of 15:12 contained a discrete subgroup within it, with a separate list of objections to the resurrection (or unless we accept the unprovable and unproductive hypothesis that Paul has misunderstood the Corinthians),[104] we can only conclude that the dissenters *did* believe in immortality, but that it was an immortality that appertained strictly to the soul.

In recent decades this view has emerged as the dominant one.[105] Jeffrey Asher has persuasively shown that the Corinthians of 15:12, like the

[101] See Thiselton, *First Epistle to the Corinthians*, 1240ff.

[102] Asher (*Polarity and Change*, 2, 30–90) has agreed. Moreover, although seemingly consistent with Epicurean sentiment, the slogan itself is a verbatim quotation from LXX Isa 22:13.

[103] Answering first with a rebuke that calls to mind his first four chapters: "you fool!" (ἄφρων).

[104] Bultmann (*Theology of the New Testament*, in K. Grobel, trans. [New York: Scribner, 1951], 1:169) and Schmithals (*Gnosticism in Corinth*, 156) have argued that Paul misunderstood. But as J. Holleman (*Resurrection and Parousia: A Traditio-Historical Study of Paul's Eschatology in 1 Corinthians 15*, NovTSupp 84 [Leiden: Brill, 1996], 36) has insightfully responded, "If one supposes that Paul misrepresents the Corinthian opinion it becomes impossible to know the Corinthian point of view at all."

[105] E.g., Grosheide, *First Epistle to the Corinthians*, 363, 380; Allo, *Premiere Epitre aux Corinthiens*, 402; Fee, *First Epistle to the Corinthians*, 715, 741, 775, 779; Martin, *Corinthian Body*, 106, 122; Garland, *1 Corinthians*, 678, 699; Keener, *1–2 Corinthians*, 132; Barnett, *The Corinthian Question*, 111; and a host of further literature, cited by Thiselton, *First Epistle to the Corinthians*, 1174–5.

contemporary philosophical schools, had adopted a cosmology that prohibited the physical from ascending into the higher, and discrete, celestial realm. For the Corinthians, this "cosmic polarity" rendered a *bodily* resurrection simply impossible.[106] Thus Paul aimed in 1 Corinthians 15 to offer a solution the dissenters could accept without requiring that they abandon their presuppositions: cosmic polarity and bodily resurrection were compatible, so long as the resurrection body was understood to be a *transformed* body.

Needless to say, this would not limit the Corinthian viewpoint to a Stoic one. Belief in some kind of body-soul dualism and the immortality of the soul was shared not only by a number of philosophical schools,[107] but had common currency also at the popular levels, even if it was not maintained universally. Even so, Paul appears to give the conversation a Stoic turn. If some in Corinth did in fact take the perspective that only the soul survived death, and that in the final conflagration *all would be in Zeus and Zeus in all* (*SVF* 2.596–632; 3.302), then Paul's final words in 15:28 present them with a direct, and momentous, challenge: not *Zeus*, but *God*, will be "all in all" (πάντα ἐν πᾶσιν; cf. *SVF* 2.596–632; 3.302).[108]

Litigation (1 Cor 6:1–11)

The single remaining issue in the letter is the problem of litigation (6:1–11). The socioeconomic dimension of the issue – who was litigating against whom, whom the justice system was likely to favor, and so forth – has been explored extensively in previous studies.[109] While the question of *why* litigation was going on in the church is perhaps unanswerable, in the light of what we have seen, it may be worth recounting what Stoicism had to say on the issue.

Cleanthes is said to have written a book called *On Litigation* (D. L. 7.175), although it is now lost. We find brief treatment of the subject elsewhere. Arius Didymus remarks that "the man with good sense does not forgive anyone. For it is characteristic of the same person both to forgive someone and to believe that he did not do wrong through his own

[106] Asher, *Polarity and Change in 1 Corinthians*, 15.

[107] For more on the philosophers and cosmic polarity, see Asher, *Polarity and Change in 1 Cor 15*, 119–45.

[108] An expression that appears elsewhere in the NT only in Eph 1:23 and Col 3:11.

[109] Two articles treating the issue include: B. Winter, "Civil Litigation in Secular Corinth and the Church: The Forensic Background to 1 Cor 6:1–8," *NTS* 37 (1991): 559–72; and A. Mitchell, "Rich and Poor in the Courts of Corinth: Litigiousness and Status in 1 Cor 6:1–11," *NTS* 39 (1993): 562–86. One can find a good summary of recent scholarship in Garland, *1 Corinthians*, 197–200.

fault, when all do wrong through their own evil. Accordingly it is rightly said that he does not forgive those who are doing wrong." Arius then applies the principle to the matter of litigation:

> They say that the good man is not tolerant, since the tolerant can be begged off the punishment in accord with what is due, and that it is the mark of the same man to be tolerant and to assume that the punishments set out by law for the unjust are too harsh and to consider that the lawmaker apportions punishments contrary to what is due. (Arius Didymus 11d/*SVF* 3.640)

The idea as it is presented here is grounded in the belief that "the law is worthwhile" for the law is "correct reasoning."

Diogenes Laertius reports a similar view, although he also gives a further clue as to the justification – tolerance is an attribute of the "weak" mind:

> [T]hey [wise men] do no hurt to others or to themselves. At the same time they are not pitiful and make no allowance for anyone; *they never relax the penalties fixed by the laws*, since indulgence and pity and even equitable consideration are *marks of a weak mind*. (7.123 [Hicks, LCL]; emphasis added).

None of these data, I acknowledge, require that we see Stoic teaching as *the* reason why the Corinthians were litigating against each other. But it is evident that their actions could easily have found justification there. As we have seen, the wise in Corinth were indeed loath to be "of a weak mind" (cf. 1 Cor 8), and Arius Didymus and Diogenes Laertius, probably drawing from Cleanthes, both recommended litigation when laws were broken.[110] Moreover, it is interesting that Paul twice[111] brings philosophy into the picture at this point, asking in 6:5 and 6:7, respectively:

> Is there no 'wise man' among you who can judge between his brothers? (6:5)

> Why not rather be wronged [ἀδικεῖσθε]? Why not rather be defrauded? (6:7)

[110] The Corinthians may have exploited such Stoic ideology to justify their actions, but it can probably not have been Stoicism *alone* that generated their lawsuits. After all, they *were* apparently willing to forgive when it came to the adulterous man (5:1–13/6:12–20). Thus, social stratification must have played a part as well: they could wink at the sins of their confreres, but when they were wronged by an inferior, it was off to court with him.

[111] In addition, the μὴ πλανᾶσθε ("do not be deceived") formula in 6:9 is a characteristic of Stoic diatribe (e.g., Epictetus, *Diatr.* 4.6.23; cf. 2.20.7). See Garland (*1 Corinthians*, 211) for further literature on this point.

Verse 6:5 again suggests that some of the Corinthians fancied themselves "wise men." Verse 6:7 then quotes a principle that had been a commonplace among the philosophers since Plato. The Stoic Musonius Rufus, a near contemporary of Paul, provides us with a close parallel: the wise man, he says, ought to be disposed "to look upon doing a wrong [τὸ μὲν ἀδικεῖν] as worse than suffering one [τοῦ ἀδικεῖσθαι] . . . and to regard being worsted as better than gaining an unjust advantage" (*Diatr.* 3 [Lutz 41]; cf. *Diatr.* 10).[112] Is it any accident that Paul responds to the litigation issue by bringing to mind the equanimity requisite of the philosopher–wise man? Once again, it seems, we find Paul devising a philosophical *tour de force* against aspiring Christian philosophers.

Conclusion

In closing, let us recall what was stated about this chapter's procedure at the outset. We were to test the Stoic hypothesis, not on some preselected set of passages, nor on a single unit alone (e.g., 1 Corinthians 1–4), but on the whole gamut of issues presented *across the letter*. What has been sacrificed in such a broad-stroke analysis is depth. Moreover, it has meant that much of the present examination has been only experimental. Consequently, I do not pretend to have given a definitive treatment of every issue, nor do I mean to imply that Stoic influence was, in *every* instance in which it might be presumed, *necessarily* present. While on some issues Stoic influence has been shown to come clearly to the fore, on other issues I have allowed myself to speculate, in some cases going a bit beyond the evidence. All of this, however, has been undertaken with the conviction that parallels in perspective and thought can be justifiably established only on the basis of larger *patterns of correspondence*, characterized by *multiple points of contact* and *consistency of perspective* across the "total" range of evidence. Put differently, the system of reference must be determined by the total field of conceptual interactions that are at play.

Where then have we found the most convincing points of contact? Certain individuals, we must conclude, have styled themselves "wise men" and have described themselves with the language of the Stoic paradoxes in doing so (1:26; 2:6; 3:21–2; 4:8–10); they have exploited a Stoic slogan of freedom (6:12a/10:23a) in justifying their autonomy in a

[112] This concept is similar to one of the main ideas of Plato's *Republic*, and is also found, e.g., in Plato, *Gorg.* 469C; 408B; 509C; Aristotle, *Eth. nic.* 5.11.7–8; *Rhet.* 1.7.22; Philo, *Jos.* 20; Seneca, *Ep.* 95.52; cf. *SVF* 3.567–81.

variety of behaviors (6:12–20; chs. 8, 10); and – in a manner redolent of the Stoic understanding of "knowledge and weakness" – boasted knowledge to discern their freedom to undertake actions from which those of an allegedly "weak" mind have scrupled to avoid (chs. 8, 10). These Stoic ties, which extend across the great majority of the letter, have often been noted by other interpreters and should invite little disagreement.

Yet, if less clear material ought to be understood in the light of the clearer material, a strong case can be made that Stoic influence reached still farther. Moved by 1 Corinthians 1–4 to suspect Stoic undercurrents, we find that much sense can be made of further topics in the letter if we extend the Stoic explanation. In fact, two of the three status distinctions made by the agitators belonged most properly to Stoicism: that between the "perfect" (τέλειος) and the "immature" (νήπιος), and that between the "knowledgeable" (cf. γνῶσις) and the "weak" (ἀσθενῆς). This fact lends significant credibility to the supposition that the distinction between the "spiritual" (πνευμάτικος) and the "unspiritual" (ψύχικος) person might, as demonstrated, have been a development from within Stoicism as well. Likely, Stoicism was also the nearest impetus for the agitators' obsession with freedom, operative not only in those texts where the Corinthians are said to have asserted their "rights" (ch. 7; 11:2–16; 11:17–34; and chs. 12, 14) but also in their views on sex and diet, which they used a known Stoic slogan to justify (6:23a; 10:23a). Moreover, a notion of "indifference" toward the physical order seems unmistakeable in the slogans of 6:13, 18 8:8, and the problems related to them, even if the Corinthians did not put as fine a point on the doctrine as the Stoics did. Presumably, this perspective led into a kind of "dualism," so that food and bodily matters became morally irrelevant (6:12a, 18a; 8:8), and the notion of a bodily resurrection no longer appeared tenable (15:12–58). Should it be objected that some of these perspectives might find an equally adequate explanation in terms of some other ancient system of thought, it must be asked why, then, it is so consistently *Stoic language* – in the case of *every* Corinthian catchword and in *at least four* of their slogans (cf. 6:12a, 13a, 18a; 8:4) – that the Corinthians used to articulate those views.

The remaining issues have required greater speculation. Was Stoicism's egalitarian or spiritualizing inclination really responsible for "gender effacement" problems (cf. 11:2–16; 14:34–6)? Did the Stoic philosopher's disinclination to appear "soft" on wrongdoers help encourage litigation (6:1–11)? Were divisions at church meetings fostered by Stoic individualism, or by the formation of an exclusive "community of the wise" (11:17–34)? Perhaps not. Yet, in the light of what we have seen elsewhere in the letter, such explanations would not seem to put any real strain on the evidence.

A final clarification is in order regarding the use of disagreeing Stoic sources. Have I not emphasized Stoic *individualism* where this thing suited my purposes (10:14–22; 11:17–34), but Stoic *cosmopolitanism* where that seemed more expedient (chs. 12, 14)? Or *individual freedom* where this was more relevant (e.g., 6:12a/10:23a; 10:24, 33; 12:21), but a concern for *community benefit* where that seemed more to the point (e.g., 6:12b/10:23b; 12:7)? The astute reader will already have recognized the solution. The Stoic system teetered on a fine balance between individual and cosmopolitan concerns: in 1 Corinthians, the *Corinthians* had seized upon Stoic assertions of individual autonomy and freedom, and *Paul* on Stoicism's broader cosmopolitan vision. As the Corinthians leaned heavily to one side, Paul sought to counter them from the other. A similar strategy appears in several other issues discussed (cf. 6:18b vs. 6:18c; and comments on 6:7; 7:4; 11:14): when one Stoic tenet seemed to support the Corinthian position, Paul, using weapons from the Corinthians' own arsenal, found another that undermined it.

These last observations force the question of just *how* Stoic the Corinthian wise really were. Even if Stoicism served as the point of departure for many of the agitators' views, did Stoicism penetrate to the deep structure of their beliefs? Or was its influence only skin-deep? Might the Corinthians have been influenced by other systems as well? How might the present thesis be reconciled with alternative accounts of the Corinthian situation? It is to these questions that we now turn.

6

LOOSE ENDS

Having presented a case for Stoic influence in the Corinthian church, it remains to address how the Stoic thesis might dovetail with other currents in Corinthian studies. In this chapter, I first address the question of what role Paul and Apollos might have played in the formation of divisions in the church. Had "parties" formed in their names? Had they done something, wittingly or unwittingly, to bring this on? Had they been heard in Stoic terms? Next, it is asked whether the Stoic thesis provides a sufficient trajectory to explain the new exigencies seen in 2 Corinthians. Finally, I address each of the major alternative reconstructions of the letter that have been advanced throughout the last century, and the question of how the present thesis relates with them.

The question of Apollos

How does one reconcile the Stoic thesis with Paul's reference to church "parties" in 1:10–12? Long ago Baur had reduced Paul's four putative parties to two: one of Peter, the other of Paul.[1] As discussed in Chapter 2, however, it is now widely agreed that we have not four, nor even two, distinct "parties," each with its own champion and unique theology, but rather an "artificial" depiction, devised by Paul, of a church divided.[2]

Many, however, continue to literalize Paul's representation of the issue. For proponents of the rhetorical thesis, some are indeed "of Paul" and others "of Apollos," in accordance as each has been estimated for his rhetorical success. Although personally the two may have walked

[1] F.C. Baur, "Die Christuspartei in der korinthischen Gemeinde, der Gegensatz des paulinishcen und petrinischen Christentums in der ältesten Kirche, der Apostel Petrus in Rom," *Tübinger Zeitschrift für Theologie* 4 (1831): 61–206; and "The Epistles to the Corinthians," in *Paulus, der Apostle Jesu Christi* (Stuttgart: Becker & Muller, 1866), 268–320.

[2] For a summary of the current consensus, see Garland, *1 Corinthians*, 50–1.

together heart and hand, they are thought to have become unwitting champions of distinct opposing factions.[3]

Yet we have already discussed the extent to which this interpretation depends on information not found in 1 Corinthians. A rhetorical competition has been imagined largely on the basis that Paul is said to be "contemptible in speech" in 2 Corinthians (10:10) and Apollos is said to be "learned" in Acts (18:24). Otherwise, this hypothesis depends – so it seems to me – on a questionable interpretation of Paul's discussion of Apollos in 1 Corinthians 3–4. Upon closer investigation, one finds that this passage actually gives no mention of conflict between the two men, nor any clue that "rhetoric" was an issue. Moreover, the moment we remove the lens conferred on us by recent scholarship, it becomes clear that this passage need not suggest the conclusion that factions had been formed in their names. Rather, a controversy over "rhetoric" has been found here not because it is plainly described, but because we have been conditioned in recent years to see it. I hope to offer here a more Ockham-like reading of the passage, one which I think assumes less but makes equally good sense of the situation.

To begin, Paul gives every indication that he and Apollos were amicable: they are "one" (3:8); they perform complementary tasks (3:6–7), and are "fellow-workers" of God (3:9). In closing the letter, he calls Apollos a "brother," and affirms that he has "begged" him to return to Corinth (16:12) – an action difficult to fathom on the hypothesis that Apollos was responsible for the church's split.

But the real crux of the Apollos material comes in 4:6. Here, after presenting a metaphorical portrait of his harmonious relationship with Apollos in 3:5–4:5, Paul states: "I have applied (μετεσχημάτισα) all these things (ταῦτα) to Apollos and myself for your benefit, brothers and sisters" (NRSV). Debate has centered on the meaning of μετασχημάτισα.[4] In contemporary sources, the verb seems to have invariably meant "to change the appearance [of something into that of something else]"; accordingly: Ταῦτα . . . μετεσχημάτισα εἰς ἐμαυτὸν καὶ Ἀπολλῶν = "change the appearance of [acc. noun] into (εἰς) [acc. noun]." Compare the Latin, "change [acc. noun] into (*in*) [acc. noun]" (e.g., "change these circumstances into opposite things" [*sortem in contraria mutet*], Ovid, *Met.* 3.329; "Acis

[3] E.g., Pogoloff, *Logos and Sophia*, 196; Litfin, *Paul's Theology of Proclamation*, 228–9; Witherington, *Conflict and Community at Corinth*, 83, 86–130, 74n9, 124; Kremer, *Der erste Brief an die Korinther*, 32.

[4] However, the summaries of BDAG 641–2; Thiselton, *The First Epistle to the Corinthians*, 348–50; and Mihaila, *The Paul-Apollos Relationship*, 200–12 seem difficult to reconcile with one another.

having been changed into a river" [*Acis* ... in amnem versus], 13.896–7; "bodies changed into shapes that are not to be believed" [*in non credendos corpora versa modos*], Ovid, *Trist.* 2.63–64). The question, however, is whether the change here is from one *form of speech* to another or from one *class of people* to another. That is, does Paul mean that he has taken what was more or less the "*reality*" of the situation (i.e., "these things," Ταῦτα) and transformed it into the agricultural and architectural *metaphors* used instead (3:5–4:5)? Or does he mean that he has exchanged one set of names, to whom the material of 3:5–4:5 properly applied (i.e., the Corinthian culprits), to another set of names, to whom, strictly speaking, it did not (i.e., Paul and Apollos), possibly as a way of saving face for the true culprits?

The first interpretation runs aground at εἰς ἐμαυτὸν καὶ Ἀπολλῶν. Indeed, if "these things" have been transformed into *metaphors*, we are then either required to take the verb to mean something like "transfer" – an anomalous usage – or we are left wondering in what intelligible sense "these things" have been transformed "into Paul and Apollos" at all. The second interpretation, however, makes good sense of εἰς ἐμαυτὸν καὶ Ἀπολλῶν, and in fact corresponds perfectly with the ordinary usage of μετασχηματίζω: Paul has changed *what is relevant to one group of people* to *what is relevant to the names Paul and Apollos*.

This interpretation also finds ancient precedent. John Chrysostom had said regarding 1:10–12 that "the Corinthians were not actually calling on the name of Paul himself or Peter or Apollos." Rather, Paul was using "hyperbole," making his words "less offensive by not naming those who were dividing the church but concealing them, as if by masks, under the names of the apostles." According to Chrysostom, μετεσχημάτισα thus indicates that Paul's presentation aimed to "mask" the true culprits under the names "Paul" and "Apollos" so as to save the troublemakers their dignity.[5] Similar to Chrysostom's views are those of Ambrosiaster and Photius, along with a host of modern exegetes.[6]

Thus, while there may have been no *personal* conflict between Paul and Apollos, Paul's use of "allusion" (covert or not) reveals that there *was*

[5] J. L. Kovacs, *1 Corinthians*, The Church's Bible 53 (Grand Rapids: Eerdmans, 2005), 19, cf. 74.

[6] Ambrosiaster and Photius in Kovacs, *1 Corinthians*, 21, 75; also Robertson-Plummer, *Corinthians*, 80–1; Collins, *1 Corinthians*, 176; Winter, *Philo and Paul among the Sophists*, 196–201; Lindemann, *Der erste Korintherbrief*, 38–9; Talbert, *Reading Corinthians*, 20; C. C. Caragounis, *The Development of Greek and the New Testament* (Grand Rapids: Baker Academic, 2006), 562n279; Mihaila, *The Paul-Apollos Relationship*, 348–51; cf. B. Fiore, "'Covert Allusion' in 1 Cor 1–4," *CBQ* 47 (1985): 85–102.

conflict among *others* in the community. Yet, this conflict may *or may not* have revolved around the two names of "Paul" and "Apollos." Indeed, the use of μετασχημάτισα quite naturally suggests that their names had nothing to do with any personal feud at all. Rather, Paul offers only an *object lesson* in which he and Apollos are presented as a picture of perfect concord,[7] a picture he hopes the Corinthians will emulate. And in short, his insistence that his relationship with Apollos is amicable comes *not* because the Corinthians have formed parties named after them (an assumption driven by mirror-reading), but because he wishes to present their relationship as *an example of Christians in harmony*. Such an interpretation falls in step with the recent consensus that the church was embroiled in factionalism, and that certain circles or cliques had formed, but it reveals that we need not see "Paul" and "Apollos" as the real dividing line. *That* line has been drawn, not from the evidence of 1 Corinthians 3–4, but by connecting extraneous points *A* and *B* – 2 Corinthians 10:10 and Acts 18:24.

The role of Paul

Apparently eighteen months in Corinth was not long enough. No sooner had Paul set sail for Ephesus than problems of "wisdom" began brewing in the new church. Hurd believed it was something he had said – or indeed, many things he had said. It was Paul who had said "all things are permissible," Paul who had said "it is good for a man not to touch a women," Paul who had said that "we all have knowledge," that "food is for the belly, and the belly for food," and all the rest. The Corinthians simply repeated it. While few have been convinced by Hurd's thesis, he did raise a crucial question for reconstruction of Paul's epistles: What responsibility did Paul himself have for the peculiar ways in which his converts interpreted his message?

We have learned over the years that Paul's thought was not cut from a single cloth.[8] It was rather a complex weave of the diverse backdrops that made up his world – those Jewish, Greco-Roman, and "Christian." If the majority interpretation is right, probably Paul received a literary education in the Greek schools in Tarsus up through the secondary level (though some think he went higher), before culminating his education

[7] So also Caragounis, *The Development of Greek and the New Testament*, 562n279.

[8] By the time of W. D. Davies (*Paul and Rabbinic Judaism*, 1948), it was generally accepted that no hard-and-fast distinction can be made between Judaism and Hellenism. Martin Hengel later provided the definitive word in *Judaism and Hellenism* (SCM, 1974).

in Jerusalem as a Pharisee (cf. Acts 22:3), and then turning to Christ some years later.[9] His early schooling would have entailed some formal training in rhetoric[10] but little, if any, in philosophy. On the other hand, a man of letters such as himself, who may well have spent some time *reading* philosophy, and who was well traveled and active on the streets and in the forums of many of the major cities across the Greco-Roman world, can hardly have escaped acquaintance with the major trends. Tarsus, for instance, where he is said to have returned after his conversion (Acts 9:30), was a major ganglion of learning in those days, not least in the area of philosophy.[11]

His life experience in the Greco-Roman world shows through clearly in his letters. He was obviously familiar with topoi from a number of philosophical traditions – Socratic, Epicurean, Cynic, and Stoic included.[12] But the Stoic comparison has been the order of the day. Marriage, "freedom," the "law," "indifferents," and more – in all of

[9] Brown (*An Introduction to the New Testament*, 423–5 [cf. 69, 84, 426]) dubs this the "majority position." For further examples of this position, see S. E. Johnson, "Tarsus and the Apostle Paul," *Lexington Theological Quarterly* 15 (1980): 105–13; T. Lim, "Not in Persuasive Words of Wisdom," 137–49; and Murphy-O'Connor (*Paul*, 46, 48), who says Paul received at least some rhetorical education in Tarsus. Ronald Hock ("Paul and Greco-Roman Education," in *Paul in the Greco-Roman World*, in J. P. Sampley [ed.] [Continuum, 2003]) says Paul received a "full and thorough" Greek education (p. 198).

[10] On Paul's literary abilities see: R. Bultmann, *Der Stil der paulinischen Predigt und die Kynischstoische Diatribe* (Göttingen: Vandenhoeck & Ruprecht, 1910); F. Danker, "Paul's Debt to the *De Corona* of Demosthenes: A Study of Rhetorical Techniques in Second Corinthians," in D. F. Watson (ed.), *Persuasive Artistry: Studies in New Testament Rhetoric in Honor of George A. Kennedy*, JSNTSup 50 (Sheffield: Sheffield Academic, 1991), 262–80; S. K. Stowers, "Romans 7:7–25 as a Speech-in-Character (προσοποιία)," in *Paul in His Hellenistic Context*, 180–202; G. Holland, "Paul's Use of Irony as a Rhetorical Technique," in S. E. Porter and T. H. Olbricht (eds.), *The Rhetorical Analysis of Scripture*, JSNTSup 146 (Sheffield: Sheffield Academic, 1997), 234–48; G. Rowe, "Style," in S. E. Porter (ed.), *Handbook of Classical Rhetoric* (Leiden: Brill, 1997), esp. 124–50; Collins, *1 Corinthians*, 6–8; J. P. Sampley and P. Lamp, *Paul and Rhetoric* (New York: T & T Clark, 2010).

[11] We know of several eminent Stoics associated with Tarsus around his day – for instance, Zeno, Antipater, and Athenodorous; so Sedley, "The School, from Zeno to Arius Didymus," 30–31.

[12] See for example: H. D. Betz, *Der Apostel Paulus und die sokratische Tradition: Eine Exegetische Untersuchung zu seiner Apologie 2 Korinther 10–13*, BHT 45 (Tübingen: Möhr, 1972); Malherbe, "Graeco-Roman Religion and Philosophy and the New Testament," in E. J. Epp and G. W. McRae (eds.), *The New Testament and Its Modern Interpreters* (Philadelphia: Fortress, 1989), 8; A. Malherbe, *Paul and the Popular Philosophers* (Minneapolis: Fortress, 1989); N. W. de Witt, *St Paul and Epicurus* (Minneapolis: University of Minneapolis Press, 1954); R. B. Ward, "Musonius and Paul on Marriage," *NTS* 36 (1990): 281–9; C. E. Glad, *Paul and Philodemus: Adaptability in Epicurean and Early Christian Psychagogy*; T. Engberg-Pedersen, "Paul, Virtues, and Vices," in *Paul in the Greco-Roman World*, 608–34.

these things Paul bears some likeness to the Stoics.[13] Moreover, his use of "Stoic" rhetoric and metaphors has been the center of attention in several monographs and essays.[14] No doubt certain studies have pressed the comparison too far, but at least a partial resemblance can now be taken as scholarly "gospel."

The present examination of Paul's response in 1 Corinthians has confirmed that he was no stranger to the philosophical traditions, least of all Stoicism. It has been shown that he often counters the Corinthians' positions with recognizably Stoic terminology (6:5; 7:19; 11:14; 15:28; cf. 8:6) and arguments (6:7; 7:4; 6:12b/10:23b; 6:18b; 6:19c; 12:12–30; cf. 3:22–3), in many cases by providing the Stoic counterpoint needed to balance the Corinthians' otherwise Stoical excesses (e.g., what is "permissible" should also be "beneficial"; freedom has its limitations; the individual part must consider also the whole body; etc.). We would be remiss to pass over the significance of this language. Indeed, not only do most of these examples reflect discursive oddities in Paul; they generally also reflect a *verbal form* that is not adequately paralleled in Jewish literature. In the generally accepted Pauline letters, we find nothing outside 1 Corinthians formally resembling the statements, "Why not rather be wronged [ἀδικεῖσθε]? Why not rather be defrauded? But you both wrong and defraud" (6:7); "he who commits fornication sins against his own body" (6:18b); "your body is not your own" (6:19c; cf. Eph 5:28); or "the wife does not have authority over her own body, but the husband does ...." (7:4; cf. Eph 5:28). Granted, these examples are not all *conceptually* unique. Verse 6:7, for instance, reflects a principle of non-retaliation that is central to the teachings of Jesus (Matt 5:38–42) and not

[13] On marriage: Deming, *Paul on Marriage and Celibacy*; freedom: L. E. Galloway, *Freedom in the Gospel: Paul's Exemplum in 1 Corinthians 9 in Conversation with the Discourses of Epictetus and Philo* (Leuven: Peeters, 2004); law: N. Huttunen, "Stoic Law in Paul?" in T. Rasimus, T. Engberg-Pedersen, I. Dunderberg (eds.), *Stoicism in Early Christianity* (Peabody, MA: Hendrickson, 2010), 39–58; indifferents: Deming, "Paul and Indifferent Things." Engberg-Pedersen has convinced few with his suggestion that Paul was almost every inch the Stoic: see *Paul and the Stoics;* and *Cosmology and the Self in the Apostle Paul* (Oxford: Oxford University Press, 2010); cf. R. M. Thorsteinsson, "Stoicism as a Key to Pauline Ethics in Romans," in *Stoicism in Early Christianity*, 15–38. For an older but still definitive comparison between Paul and Seneca, see J. N. Sevenster, *Paul and Seneca* (Leiden: Brill, 1961).

[14] Paul's use of hardship lists: J. T. Fitzgerald, *Cracks in an Earthen Vessel: An Examination of the Catalogues of Hardships in the Corinthian Correspondence*, SBLDS 99 (Atlanta: Scholars, 1988); use of Stoic metaphors: R. Garrison, *The Graeco-Roman Context of Early Christian Literature* (Sheffield: Sheffield Academic, 1997); M. V. Lee, *Paul, the Stoics, and the Body of Christ*, SNTSMS 137 (Cambridge: Cambridge University Press, 2006); comparison of various terms and topics: Grant, "Hellenistic Elements in 1 Corinthians"; D. A. de Silva, "Paul and the Stoa: A Comparison," *JETS* 38 (1995): 549–64.

uncommon elsewhere in Paul (Rom 12:17–21), and the spirit of 7:4 might be adumbrated to some extent in OT material such as Exod 21:10. But it is surely significant that the precise *form* in which these texts are put here is recognizably that of the philosophers.

Other examples commend a philosophical form as well. The Stoic ethical term συμφέρει ("beneficial") is found only in the Corinthian correspondence, twice in direct response to Stoic slogans (e.g., 1 Cor 6:12b/10:23b). The expression "all in all" appears otherwise in the NT only in Eph 1:23 and Col 3:11. The body metaphor (12:12–30) is elaborated elsewhere only in Romans (12:4-5). And uses of σοφός ("wise man") and φύσις ("nature") are not only rare in Paul, but are in this letter clearly integrated to meet the occasion, as seen both by his leading rhetorical questions – "is there no *wise man* present to judge among you?" (6:5); "does not *nature* teach you that ... ?" (11:14) – and by his insinuation of the "wise man" into OT citations, where no text type seems to have actually included it – "He catches the wise man in his craftiness" (3:19//Job 5:13); "The Lord knows the thoughts of the wise man, that they are futile" (3:20//Ps 93:11). With all this we have hit only the tip of the iceberg. Further examples abound, although they are not always so unique.[15] The upshot is that, even if Paul's "Stoic" rhetoric cannot be limited to 1 Corinthians,[16] nowhere does he seem to employ it so heavily, so distinctly, and so *directly* in response to what are clearly the views of his "opponents" as he does in 1 Corinthians. What is more, not *one* of these examples occurs *in any Pauline letter prior to 1 Corinthians*.

I am aware that these claims call up a vexing set of hermeneutical questions, which we can only begin to answer here. In the first place, it must be asked: Was Paul's audience able to distinguish when he was speaking simply as a Hellenistic Jew who happened to use arguments that bore *incidental* similarities to Greek philosophy, from when he was making a conscious *effort* to exploit specifically Greek forms of discourse so as to be most persuasive to *them*, who were a predominantly Greek-minded audience? Second, are *we ourselves* able to make such distinctions in his speech?

To the first question we shall have to answer, No, in many cases they could not. Judging from the many analyses of Pauline thought that have appeared over the decades, it must be confessed that Paul exhibits striking Stoic affinities in many areas of his theology. When we consider his

[15] For a fairly lengthy list of terms and concepts, see Grant, "Hellenistic Elements in 1 Corinthians"; and de Silva, "Paul and the Stoa: A Comparison."

[16] See especially Engberg-Pedersen, *Paul and the Stoics*.

emphasis on an indwelling "Spirit" (πνεῦμα), the "law" (νόμος), "nature" (φύσις), "freedom" (ἐλεύθερος, ἐξουσία), "perfection" (τέλος, τέλειος, τελειόω), the "word" (λόγος), and the intellect (νοῦς, διαλογισμός, φρονέω) – all of which figure prominently both in his other letters and in Stoicism – it is easy to see how a Greek-minded audience, upon first hearing (or hearing of) his message, might have pulled it through the grid of Stoic discourse.

How then can *we* discern when Paul is "Greek" by accident and when he is Greek by design, if at times even his first auditors could not? We can hardly know more about the auditors' world than they knew themselves. And yet, might we know more about *Paul's message* than some of them did? Indeed, we should consider the strong possibility that the culprits in Corinth converted late in Paul's residency, or even *after* he departed. Could they not then have been misinformed about his message? I wonder, moreover, which of us – we or the Corinthian agitators – has examined 1 Corinthians, and a large body of Paul's writings, more minutely? Assuming (actually, with some confidence) that the palm would go to the modern exegete, I suggest that we would then have at least two anchors from which to begin sorting out the various voices in the Corinthian conversation:

1. We can build on the premise that Paul, although positively *not* a Stoic philosopher, did in many ways *sound* like one. Thus, it would be surprising indeed if some of his first auditors, especially in a city like Corinth, had *not* heard him as such.
2. Our second anchor, which we have been at pains to identify in this study, is the historical situation at the moment just prior to the composition of 1 Corinthians. I have argued, based principally on the material quoted from the Corinthians and on the dominating topical components of the letter, that a form of Stoicism must have been a leading irritant of the church's divisions.

With these two levels of the correspondence as hermeneutical anchors – Paul's Stoic-sounding message and the Corinthians' Stoic interpretation of it – we are then equipped with some relatively secure baselines for disaggregating the rhetorical layers of the letter. Thus, I imagine the course of events running as follows.

First, Paul takes up residence in Corinth, preaching his Gospel of Jesus Christ to open ears. Perhaps only a single soul, with Gentile background and some philosophical acquaintance, construes Paul's message – because of obvious similarities – in terms of Stoic philosophy, either having first heard him late in his residence or having been relayed his message just after he had departed. The recipient's limited knowledge of Pauline Christianity puts him in mind of the Stoic philosophy with which he is more familiar. An important figure in the community, this person then begins (unsystematically) to develop a kind of Christian philosophy – now Christianizing Stoicism, now Stoicizing Christianity – and from there infecting his circle of intimates and perhaps a few of his protégés with his way of thinking. Paul catches wind of these perversions and responds in kind, now consciously as a "Stoic" to "Stoics," and following his usual practice of abstaining from naming opponents. Exercising his "all things to all men" principle (1 Cor 9:19–23), he further avails himself of Stoic discourse, adding to his stock of Stoic commonplaces fresh terminology (6:5; 15:28) and axioms (3:22–3; 6:7; 6:12b/10:23b; 6:18b; 6:19c; 7:4), as needed for the situation, though sublimating that material to accord with his core Christian convictions.

The Divisions and 2 Corinthians

Crucial to the task of reconstructing the history of the Corinthian correspondence is the question of how the events following the composition of 1 Corinthians transpired to bring about 2 Corinthians 1–9 and 10–13. "Sophistic" connections have been said to cut across the two canonical letters, particularly at the point of supposed overlap between 1 Corinthians 1–4 and 2 Corinthians 10–13.[17] Could similar claims be made for the Stoic thesis presented here?

This is a question that, up to this point, I have deliberately aimed to avoid – for several reasons. In part these reasons have been methodological. I have made it my goal to follow the principle, widely upheld since Dahl, that we avoid bringing evidence from other NT literature into the discussion until we have first dealt with the evidence from the letter under consideration. As we have seen, recent failure to do so has considerably distorted interpretations of "wisdom" in 1 Corinthians, giving us a rhetorical/sophistic explanation that, upon closer investigation, must now be considered alien to the full breadth of the most pertinent evidence. I have tried to offer a corrective in that regard. Moreover, we should reflect on whether reconstructions of 2 Corinthians have not sometimes been liable to the same excesses of mirror-reading as have reconstructions of the letter(s)'s earlier counterpart. Admittedly, Paul does, in 2 Corinthians, seem to take precautions to distinguish himself from the "sophists" – as

[17] This is spelled out most fully in Winter, *Philo and Paul among the Sophists*.

when he says he is not a "peddler of the word of God" (2 Cor 2:17) – but then, abnegation of sophistic attributes is not limited to the Corinthian letters. This is an issue to which he seems everywhere to have been sensitive (cf. 1 Thess 1:5; 2:1–12; Gal 1:10). Such denials may therefore have had less to do with the precise historical occasion than they did with a general concern for reputation – perhaps in both canonical letters.

Were we pressed to demonstrate continuity across the Corinthian correspondence, however, some ponderable connections could be noted. Lack of Stoic "slogans" notwithstanding, it is noteworthy that much of the peculiar vocabulary of 1 Corinthians resurfaces. 2 Corinthians includes one of only two further instances of σοφία among the major Pauline epistles, and the *only* other instance where he speaks of wisdom *negatively* (2 Cor 1:12; cf. Rom 11:33); several cognates pertaining to being "rich," all of them rare or unique for Paul (πλουτίζω appears only in 1 Cor 1:5; 2 Cor 6:10; 9:11; πλουτέω only in 1 Cor 4:8 and 2 Cor 8:9; and πλούσιος, within the major Pauline epistles, only in 2 Cor 8:9); appeal to "benefit" (συμφέρει/σύμφορος), a Stoic-oriented concept that appears often, and only, in the Corinthian correspondence (1 Cor 6:12; 7:35; 10:23; 10:33; 12:7; 2 Cor 8:10; 12:1); several further instances of γνῶσις (2 Cor 2:14; 4:6; 6:6; 8:7; 10:5; 11:6), once conjoined with λόγος (11:6); the body as the "temple of God" image (6:16), used almost exclusively in the Corinthian correspondence (cf. Eph 2:19–22); ἐλευθερία (3:17); and – highly rare in the NT – the technical Stoic term φαῦλος (5:10).

All the same, the dominating view over the years has been that the circumstances of 1 Corinthians on the one hand and those reflected in 2 Corinthians on the other do *not* show significant continuity, and the problems in the latter have been fomented by a *new* group which, between letters, has infiltrated the community from the outside.[18] Winter's attempt to find a common denominator in his suggestion that sophism might have taken center stage in both 1 Corinthians 1–4, 9 and 2 Corinthians 10–13 can now be doubted, if my earlier assessment about the former has been on target. Otherwise, arguments that 1 and 2 Corinthians share opponents have been largely discredited as contrivances of Baur-like thinkers who

[18] That the opponents are the same – Judaizers: in Baur, "Die Christuspartei in der korinthischen Gemeinde, der Gegensatz des paulinishcen und petrinischen Christentums in der ältesten Kirche, der Apostel Petrus in Rom"; Gnostics: in W. Schmithals, *Gnosticism in Corinth: An Investigation of the Letters to the Corinthians*, John E. Steely (trans.) (Nashville: Abingdon, 1971). That the opponents are different – D. Georgi, *The Opponents of Paul in Second Corinthians: A Study of Religious Propaganda in Late Antiquity* (Philadelphia: Fortress, 1986); C.K. Barrett, "Paul's Opponents in 2 Corinthians," *NTS* 17 (1971): 1–54. Winter (*Philo and Paul among the Sophists*, 243) calls the view that the opponents are different the "common view."

imagine a single group of people hounding Paul and his converts now in one city, now in another.[19] The upshot is that, whatever the problems were in 2 Corinthians, they seem *not* to be essentially like those of the previous letter, even if some flotsam has drifted over. But, as the whole of 1 Corinthians has already been treated, this is an issue that the present work will have to defer.

Alternative theses

Any viable thesis should be able to counter or absorb the claims of its competition. But the superior thesis will be the one that can provide the *best* explanation for the *greatest part* of the evidence. It thus remains for us to show how the Stoic thesis relates with those other major interpretations that have figured in the history of scholarship. Can other theses explain some of the data better than the present one? Could the same be said, *mutatis mutandis*, for the present thesis? Is the Stoic thesis mutually exclusive of the others, or does it have the valence to absorb their explanatory potential without compromising its own distinctiveness? It is to these questions that we now turn.

Over-realized eschatology

According to proponents of the "over-realized eschatology" thesis, the Corinthians believed that the eschatological kingdom had already been consummated: on account of baptism, "already" they were "kings" over all, "perfect" in "knowledge," fully "spiritual," and in total possession of the resurrection experience. As such, they had developed, not a full-blown but a sort of "incipient" or "primitive Gnosticism."

Perhaps this interpretation may still be regarded as viable – as far as it goes. Part of its appeal is that it does not say much that is distinctive. It takes what was true of the Gnostic thesis and frees it from any single system of thought. It is a module that, with certain modifications, can be fitted with any number of theses, including a Stoic one.

Some, of course, have argued that the Corinthian perspective, if characterized by a Greek philosophical outlook, cannot have reflected an *over-realized* eschatology, but rather must be said to have reflected *no*

[19] Murphy-O'Connor's hypothesis (*Paul*, 302, 303ff; 2004: 176ff) represents a variation: the "spirit people" carry over from 1 to 2 Corinthians, although in the latter they make common cause with a new group from the outside – the Judaizers.

eschatology at all.[20] The Corinthians, they say, had no category for future blessings, only present ones. As an aside, it may be debated whether philosophers in general had no category for future blessings. But here the apparent contradiction in terms has a different source of confusion. The confusion is that the very label, *over-realized* eschatology, is itself oxymoronic. It is like an "over-sized small" or an "over-cooked medium-rare." The moment eschatology is over-realized, does it not then cease to be eschatology? Consequently, any supposed difference between "no eschatology" and "over-realized eschatology" is difficult to put one's finger on. Probably the contradiction is more in name than in fact: in neither case does the adherent take conscious thought of future blessings.

All, however, would agree on this point: the Corinthians exhibited "spiritualizing"[21] tendencies that manifested themselves in claims to exceptional wisdom, knowledge, perfection, and more. This fact, by itself, could be taken in any number of directions. But, based on a fresh view of the evidence, my own perspective has been this: the Corinthians conceived of themselves as Stoic "wise men," and yet also as *Christian* "wise men" who have attained exceptional spiritual status. For the wise Corinthians, this combination seemed to present no contradiction.

Hellenistic Judaism

Others have said that the Corinthians' wisdom was a form of Philonism, an Alexandrian brand of Hellenistic Judaism that integrated Jewish monotheism and Greek philosophy. Richard Horsley tirelessly promoted this view in a series of articles in the 1970s and 1980s, and has continued as its champion in more recent years.[22]

Horsley finds in Philo and the Wisdom of Solomon many of the same parallels found here: the Corinthians are "wise," "powerful," "nobly

[20] Horsley, *1 Corinthians*, 201, 217; Garland, *1 Corinthians*, 14, 138, 699; Kuck, *Judgment and Community Conflict*, 16–25, 217–18; Paige, "Stoicism, *Eleutheria* and Community at Corinth," 184, 187; Barclay, "Thessalonica and Corinth," 64; Martin, *Corinthian Body*, 106; Hays, "Conversion of the Imagination," 408–9; Asher, *Polarity and Change in 1 Corinthians 15*, 39–41.

[21] A term that Fee (*1 Corinthians*, 790) prefers as well.

[22] Horsley, "Pneumatikos vs. Psychikos"; "Wisdom of Words and Words of Wisdom in Corinth," *CBQ* 39 (1977): 224–39; "How Can Some of You Say That There Is No Resurrection of the Dead?"; "Consciousness and Freedom among the Corinthians (1 Cor 8–10)," 574–89; "Gnosis in Corinth," 32–51; as well as his commentary, *1 Corinthians*, 33–36; and his collection of essays, *Wisdom and Spiritual Transcendence at Corinth*; cf. J. A. Davis, *Wisdom and Spirit: An Investigation of 1 Cor 1:18–3:20 against the Background of Jewish Sapiential Traditions in the Greco-Roman Period* (University Press of America, 1984).

born," "wealthy," and "kings"; through possession of divine "Sophia," they are "perfect," "spiritual," and "strong," and thus superior to those whom they call "immature," "unspiritual," and "weak"; and their anthropological dualism has caused them to denigrate the body and deny the possibility of a bodily resurrection. The bearer of these views into the Corinthian church, says Horsley, had been none other than the Alexandrian Jew Apollos.

Despite the similarities of Horsley's thesis to the present one, some insuperable difficulties for his thesis emerge in the differences. First, as should now be apparent, Horsley's thesis attributes to Apollos an unbelievable level of responsibility in the church's divisions, making him out to be a *conscious* conduit of what Paul takes to be an insidious and divisive form of spiritual elitism, even while Paul, far from *rebuking* the man, goes out of his way to demonstrate their concord (3:4–4:6) and urges him to *return* to Corinth (16:12).[23] Second, while we know that the Corinthian church included a substantial population of Jews, Paul seems to characterize the majority as having had a Gentile or pagan background (5:1ff; ch. 10; 12:2). Third – and dealing the most serious blow against Horsley's thesis – Paul explicitly refers to wisdom, *not* as a Jewish pursuit, but as a Greek one (1:22). This statement cannot be dismissed as a mere "piece of rhetoric." "Rhetoric" of course may convey falsehoods, but they are either falsehoods on the surface only – such as in the case of irony – or they are actual falsehoods that the speaker wishes nonetheless to be *taken as true* by the audience. Clearly Paul is *presenting* Corinthian "wisdom" *as a Greek pursuit.* Fourth, and of equal importance, it should be noted that the parallels Horsley adduces – not some, but *all* of them – occur precisely at those points where Hellenistic Judaism had in fact drawn from *Stoicism.*[24] Even more, where his parallels are merely conceptual and not terminological – such as with πνευμάτικος-ψύχικος – we have found these in Stoicism as well, and there also with the terms themselves. With that, it should also be asked whether Horsley's thesis adequately explains what was *new* in Corinth. To my mind, the Corinthians have not swallowed a particular philosophy wholesale, but have rather *combined* it with their Christianity, leaving parts still recognizable from each body of thought but *transforming* those parts to form a whole that did not look *exactly* like either one.

[23] Barclay ("Thessalonica and Corinth," 65n29) makes the same point.

[24] This, in many cases, by Horsley's own admission: e.g., Horsley, "Consciousness and Freedom among the Corinthians (1 Cor 8–10)," 585; Horsley, "How Can Some of You Say That There Is No Resurrection of the Dead?," 206, 210, 226.

Other philosophies

Reviving an old, if less popular, thesis,[25] Graham Tomlin has submitted that much of the letter can be elucidated by Epicureanism. He contends that Epicureanism explains the libertine slogans of 6:12a/10:23a on the one hand and the asceticism of chapter 7 on the other, the Corinthians' derogatory view toward idols (8:4), their exclusiveness (11:17–34), and their denial of a general resurrection (15:12). Again, most of the parallels work conceptually, but the problem is that Tomlin demonstrates nothing approximating close *verbal* parallels – neither with the Corinthians' catchwords and phrases nor with their slogans. Moreover, the Epicurean explanation is almost certainly wrong in the case of 15:12, for we have already seen that the Corinthians did have some conception of immortality, but that it simply did not involve the body. Epicureanism, by contrast, maintained that human beings – indeed, all living things – were entirely material in make-up, with body and soul both being composed of "atoms," which merely dissolved at death.[26] While Epicureanism, then, may show some *conceptual overlap* with the Corinthians' positions, it fits far less perfectly (and exhaustively) with their views than does Stoicism.

A more robust explanation, I believe, has been offered in Cynicism. Admittedly, the Cynics had their own "wise man," who was said to be "free" even if a slave (Anacharsis, *Epistle 6*, 2; Diogenes, *Epistle 29*, 14–17; Heraclitus, *Epistle 9*, 28–30), who possessed everything though nothing (Crates, *Epistle 7*, 8; Socratics, *Epistle 22*, 105; Crates, *Epistle 27;* Diogenes, *Epistle 10*, 2–7; D. L. 6.37, 72), who believed that virtue was complete for happiness (Crates, *Epistle 3*, 16–17; D. L. 6.10) and everything else was a matter of indifference (Crates, *Epistle 29*, 10–11; D. L. 6.105), and who believed that all people were "citizens of the world" (Heraclitus, *Epistle 9*, 20; Heraclitus, *Epistle 9*, 10–14), and that one should resist the "crowd" and popular "opinion" (Crates, *Epistle 12*, 20–1; Crates, *Epistle 35*, 19–21; Diogenes, *Epistle 7*, 5–7; Diogenes, *Epistle 10*, 28–30) and live "according to nature" (Diogenes, *Epistle 10*, 25; Diogenes, *Epistle 25*, 17–20; Diogenes, *Epistle 39*, 7–8). All of these things they held more or less in common with the Stoics. Thus, we should not be surprised if the Corinthians in many respects exhibited what might be called "Cynic" tendencies.

Gerald Downing, however, has gone well beyond the evidence in maintaining that the Corinthians were *simply* Cynic, and *not* Stoic. He

[25] It is mentioned in connection with 1 Cor 15:12 as far back as Robertson and Plummer, *First Epistle of St. Paul to the Corinthians*, 346.
[26] See Long and Sedley, *The Hellenistic Philosophers*, 1:25–78.

argues that no Stoic would ever claim to be "rich" or "king," for that was a status reserved only for the wise man, and according to the Stoics – says Downing – one has never existed. Cynicism, on the other hand, was a "fast track" to virtue.[27] Moreover, the slogans of 6:12a/10:23a can be explained only in terms of Cynic indiscrimination in matters of diet and sex.[28] Finally, in chapter 15, Paul is addressing people "for whom this physical life is the only one (1 Cor 15:19), there is no other to come, whether by resurrection or by immortality (15:12)" – which for Downing can only mean he is addressing Cynics.[29]

While Downing is right to differentiate between Cynicism and Stoicism – which have too often been conflated[30] – he overstates the extent to which the Corinthians *themselves*, those probably only moderately advanced in philosophical knowledge, and clearly wont to *mingle* their philosophy with their Christianity, would have shown scrupulous concern for the difference between *less* and *more* acceptable Stoic views. In that regard we have already discussed how deeply indebted Zeno was to his Cynic master and how he had incorporated Cynic indifference on matters of food and sex into early Stoicism, views that were later defended by the canonical Stoic, Chrysippus. All of this is evident in the sources (*SVF* 3.743–56). It *is* true that these unseemly doctrines seem to have been a source of some embarrassment for later Stoics, but that does not mean that they ceased to be read, written, or taught *as Stoic views*. Rather, as the sources note, teachers were simply *hesitant* to teach these doctrines until students had "first proved themselves to be genuine philosophers" (*Strom.* 5.9.59.2/*SVF* 1.43 [Long and Sedley 430]).[31] But "genuine philosophers" the Corinthians were not. Why, then, after hearing that one could be made "perfect" through Christ, should they *not* have claimed to be "wise men," though it had been debated whether any – or at any rate, many – wise men had ever existed?[32] (As an aside, it might be asked whether Paul's question in 1:20 – "where is the wise man?" – is not in fact an acknowledgement of the Stoic debate over whether any wise man had yet existed). And yes, Cynicism was considered a "fast track to

[27] Downing, *Cynics, Paul, and the Pauline Churches*, 88–89.

[28] *Ibid.*, 89–93.

[29] *Ibid.*, cf. 246.

[30] As Malherbe laments in *Cynic Epistles*, 2; and *Paul and the Popular Philosophers*, 5, 11–24.

[31] Admittedly, Athenodorus the Stoic had expunged some passages from Zeno's *Republic* that were said to be "disapproved," but these were then summarily replaced (D. L. 7.34).

[32] See *SVF* 3.658; Sextus Empiricus, *Prof.* 9.133–6/LS 54D; Cicero, *Luc.* 145; Seneca, *Ep.* 42.1; Lucian, *Herm.* 76–77.

virtue,"[33] but that is precisely the reason *Stoics* gave for saying, repeatedly, that the Stoic wise man will "*play the Cynic*" (D. L. 7.121; Arius Didymus 11s/*SVF* 3.638). Moreover, we have already noted the inappropriateness of casting Cynicism as a distinct philosophical "school," complete with its own canon, set of orthodox teachings, and succession of scholarchs. Adherents of any number of schools could take on a Cynic lifestyle, most of all their cousins, the Stoics. Among other things, this means that a "Cynic"-minded person need not have denied an afterlife, as Downing suggests they would.

The preceding observations do force the question, however, whether the Corinthians have not simply adopted what has been called "popular philosophy."[34] The answer to that question turns largely on how that is defined. Is their "philosophy" a sort of diluted agglomeration of philosophical commonplaces, now so rarefied that its constituent sources are unrecognizable to its holders? Is it the sort of "average" philosophy of the day, the dominant cultural outlook, taken for granted by virtue of its formative influence in lower school curricula and the perspectives of the established elite? Or does it draw nearer to something like formal training, perhaps acquired by the Corinthians through fraternization with local schools of philosophy, gathered in the homes of the well-to-do, as Dale Martin imagines when speaking of "popular philosophy"?[35] The literature has seemed to show no consistency in this regard.

What gives me greater pause about the "popular philosophy" view, however, is the fact that it seems to be grounded in the only partially informed observation that, at certain points, *multiple* schools of thought seem simultaneously to provide suitable comparanda to what we find in 1 Corinthians. Indeed, it does not follow from these coincidences that we are dealing with "popular philosophy," for there was a deal great of overlap even among opposing systems, which remained distinctive schools all the same. For this reason, our task here has been to examine the "total" evidence of the letter in search of *patterns* of correspondences, which when viewed together have been hoped to yield a more accurate composite picture. What we have found is that the Corinthians' perspective fits remarkably well within a Stoic framework

[33] See Crates, *Epistle 13*, 10–11; Crates, *Epistle 16*; Crates, *Epistle 21*, 24–6; Diogenes, *Epistle 9*, 9–11; Diogenes, *Epistle 30*; Diogenes, *Epistle 44*, 9–10.

[34] For this view, cf. Collins, *1 Corinthians*, 97–8; Garland, *1 Corinthians*, 66; Thiselton, *The First Epistle to the Corinthians*, 166; Talbert, *Reading Corinthians*, 10; Adams and Horrell, *Christianity at Corinth*, 22; Keener, *1–2 Corinthians*, 5.

[35] Martin, *Corinthian Body*, 72–3.

throughout. They tout not simply "freedom," but freedom as "*wise* men," who are "rich," "kings," "perfect," and the rest, for whom "all things are permissible," in matters both sexual and dietary; those who lack this "knowledge" they denigrate as "immature," "weak" and "unspiritual," as if the latter were unreasoning creatures. All the major topical domains in the letter belong to Stoicism, the majority of them most properly so – the wise man, a strong emphasis on freedom, an appeal to indifference, a kind of anthropological and cosmological "dualism," and several contrasting spiritual or intellectual status indicators. Not only so, but almost all of the major terms and slogans that can be attributed to the Corinthians closely resemble the *actual language* of Stoicism. Conversely, much about their perspective would seem to *contradict* other philosophies of the day, as their belief in the afterlife did the Epicurean perspective on death; and *none* of their language finds parallel in another philosophy when it does not also in Stoicism. In a word: while some other philosophy may resemble the Corinthians' views and language on *this point or that*, only the Stoic system provides an explanation *across the board*.

But might the consistency of their "Stoic" perspective owe simply to the dominating role of Stoicism in that eclectic body of thought known as "popular philosophy"? And would there not be only a fine line between the Stoic-influenced popular philosophy associated with itinerant preachers of that day and the Christian-adapted "Stoic" system of the wise Corinthians? I admit, this would not be an impossible conclusion to draw. Yet, the appeal of the popular philosophy option as it has been presented in the past is, I think, now mitigated by at least two crucial factors that have emerged from this study: (1) despite shortcomings on the fine points, a *consistency* in the Corinthians' Stoic stance, as seen in a *cluster* or *pattern* of Stoic motifs, expressed in terms of recognizably Stoic *language*; and (2) the fact that a number of the Corinthians were – judging from the most precise means of analysis now available – economically positioned to have received some measure of *formal* philosophical training.

To my mind, formal training becomes the most crucial criterion for determining how the Corinthians themselves would have "named" their influences. In this regard, I think we would be remiss to disregard something like Martin's scenario, in which a few upwardly mobile Christians might have had fringe contact with local philosophical schools. We have already noted evidence of local Stoic teachers (*IvO* 453). But if we also give credence to the possibility that some, or even just *one* (Erastus?), had received a *gymnasium* education – which indeed seems to have been within reach – this would have provided precisely the level of philosophical instruction the Corinthian wise seem to have had. Attending lectures in the gymnasium, perhaps regularly, would certainly have been enough to advance them beyond the philosophical proficiency of the common person. True, they had (apparently) failed to apprehend what it meant to be a perfect "wise man," whom the philosophers held to be the embodiment of virtue; while touting the tags of the philosophers (e.g., 6:12a/10:23a), they failed to grasp the proper meaning. Even so, two points should be made in response. First, in the light of what we have seen about the cursory nature of gymnasium education, the use of itinerant philosophical lecturers in lieu of permanent teachers, and the often flippant attitude of the students, we should hardly be surprised if a gymnasium-educated Corinthian fell short of the philosophical ideal (after all, even the "true philosophers" failed to practice what they preached; e.g., Seneca, *Vit. beat.* 18.1; 20.1). Such a one would have reached a level of philosophical aptitude surpassing a repertoire of a few catchphrases void of any real meaning, and profound enough to have informed actual behavior and character, but would no doubt have been considered misguided from the perspective of a purist (he would have just enough knowledge to be dangerous). Second, we should not forget about the "Christian" ingredient in the Corinthians' views. In this regard, perhaps their leap to "wise man" status and "perfect" knowledge was *less* a consequence of an imprecise acquaintance with Stoicism than it was a conscious *adaptation* made in the light of their new status in Christ – indeed, in their minds, not a mistaken aberration from Stoicism, but a deliberate *development* or *transformation* of it?

That said, one final point should be clarified. Despite my contention that the Corinthian "wise men" have developed their views in keeping with Stoic discourse, obviously it was not Stoic philosophy *tout court*. Rather, the wise Corinthians have filtered Paul's *Christian message* through *Stoic categories*, whereupon they developed, informally and unsystematically, what may be called either a "Stoicized Christianity" or a "Christianized Stoicism." Yet, is this not simply "syncretism," that meld of Greco-Roman philosophical or religious elements with primitive Christianity to produce what is neither the one thing nor the other? In bygone days one might have said so, but in more recent times syncretism has come to be differently understood. Abraham Malherbe explains:

> Such an [i.e., the old] understanding of the matter is increasingly seen to be inadequate .... For instance, syncretism is no longer regarded as a process of homogenization in which contributing

> elements lose their individuality. On the contrary, engagement may very well lead to an accentuation of uniqueness.[36]

Thus understood, Corinthian "wisdom" could consist of both recognizably Stoic and recognizably Christian elements without our having to construe it as an amorphous kind of "syncretism."

Socioeconomic perspectives

Despite shifting focus to the philosophical dimensions of the church's problems, I have had no intention of underplaying socioeconomic factors. What I have emphasized is that socioeconomic and philosophical explanations should not, as they have sometimes been, be seen as mutually exclusive alternatives. Instead of posing false dichotomies, we ought to ask how the social position of some within the Corinthian church might even have *abetted* them in their attraction to Stoicism. Indeed, it must be reiterated that, in the first century, Stoicism was one of only two major players in the philosophical game (the second being Epicureanism), and of these was by far the greater attraction to those within society's upper crust.[37] Elites were drawn to Stoicism because it seemed to articulate a vision that was already being fulfilled in the Roman Empire: a single world community, established by God's providence and governed by a common law grounded in universal reason. As such, Stoicism provided a worldview that legitimated the established order and the sense of "*Romanitas*" that was the heartbeat of elite culture in the colonies. For this reason, it would have been almost the de facto philosophy for any social up-and-comer and, indeed, the natural choice for anyone with upwardly mobile aspirations. This squares with the situation in Paul's church precisely.

Rhetoric

Ample space has already been given to the question of rhetorical "wisdom" in Corinth (Chapter 2). I need only reiterate here that the evidence for that thesis is far weaker than has been thought in the past.

[36] Malherbe, *Paul and the Popular Philosophers*, 5; cf. Malherbe, "Graeco-Roman Religion and Philosophy and the New Testament," 6.

[37] See Long, "Roman Philosophy," in *The Cambridge Companion to Greek and Roman Philosophy*; and Greg Woolf's notice in LinkedIn's "The Poor, the Powerful, and Early Christianity" group, contributing to the discussion "Galinsky's Taxonomy for Ancient Anxiety Relief," posted on February 2, 2012; last consulted February 25, 2013.

Methodologically, the rhetorical thesis depends heavily on a more dangerous form of mirror-reading in assuming that what Paul forswears for himself (1:17; 2:1, 4) must on all counts be acceptable to his opponents, *and the center of the controversy to boot.* Of course, it may be that Paul, in the midst of condemning the philosophical wisdom of the Corinthians, *also* repudiated specifically the "wisdom" of rhetoric, or eloquence, in the denials of 1:17; 2:1, 4, 13. However, it would not for that reason follow that *rhetorical* wisdom then took front and center among the issues in the church. Rather, our examination of the evidence has led us to the conclusion that these denials would reveal, not the main bone of contention, but rather a *broadened* application of God's condemnation of one sort of human wisdom (the Stoic influence at play on this particular occasion) so as to embrace also dangerous human wisdom in all its forms (including the "wisdom" of eloquence). Thus, far from serving as an index for determining the central Corinthian issue, these denials would reflect merely a tangential, and – based on other texts, familiar (e.g., 1 Thess 1:5) – corollary of *Paul's response*.

Conclusion

In addressing the underlying causes for the church's divisions, we have looked at every major issue in 1 Corinthians, with especial attention to the Corinthians' catchwords, phrases, and slogans, along with the common threads found among their problems. This fuller examination of the evidence has led us to a conclusion that, though partially entertained in the past, has never received complete enough treatment to command wide acceptance: the divisive "wisdom" of the Corinthians, *as wisdom*, consisted of *Paul's gospel teaching filtered through the lens of Stoic philosophy* – and perhaps nothing more.

As noted in the previous chapter, much of my examination has been experimental, and perhaps not every connection drawn will be convincing to all. What must be underlined, however, is the arresting *consistency* with which Stoic language and notions appear in connection with the Corinthians' views *across the letter*. Indeed, all of the Corinthians' catchwords are endemic to or distinctive of the Stoic system (σοφός, σοφία, γνῶσις, λόγος, ἐξουσία, τέλειος vs. νήπιος, πνεύματικος vs. ψύχικος, "knowledgeable" vs. ἀσθενῆς); as many as four of their slogans verbally echo known Stoic sayings (6:12; 6:13; 6:18; 8:4); and the rest convey conceptually ideas that were uniquely emphasized in Stoicism: freedom, "indifferents," and a kind of anthropological or cosmological "dualism" (7:1; 8:1; 8:8; 15:12). Our thesis is further strengthened by the fact that

Paul frequently deploys arguments that are recognizably Stoic in form, anomalous within his known writings, and often peculiarly adapted to meet the occasion. Simply put, the Stoic thesis has the unique advantage of offering an explanation for a set of matters that recur across the letter, rather than explaining only the first four chapters, or only a few carefully selected verses.

Objections could be made. Admittedly, the "wise men" of Corinth were not particularly *good* Stoics, as Paul seems to have been aware. If they were aiming at Stoic indifference, egalitarianism, individualism, freedom, and progress toward "perfection," they had overshot them all. It is perhaps just such an observation that has led scholars like Conzelmann to dismiss the Corinthians' Stoic language merely as a "terminological starting point."[38] No doubt, this is the same mentality that has led scholars to the repeated conclusion that, while Paul often sounds like a Stoic, he (in so many words) "means something different by it."[39] But while such observations capture an element of truth, they also reflect an inadequate appreciation for the ways in which discourses can be seized upon, reused, and adapted in new discursive contexts, *without radically dissociating the words from their original system of reference*. In Paul's case, *retaining* Stoic associations was a critical part of his rhetorical strategy: he shared common ground with his interlocutors inasmuch as his argumentation continued to give off resonances of his opponents' discourse of choice, even as the related ideas were modified in new ways. Indeed, his attempt to "speak the language" of his interlocutors provides the best explanation for why he has chosen *Stoic* discourse to begin with, when other options were ready to hand.

Moreover, what I have argued here is *not* that the wise Corinthians were professional Stoic philosophers, committed wholeheartedly to the unadulterated teachings of Chrysippus, but that they were Pauline *Christians* who had taken Stoic discourse as their interpretive point of departure. Much of the Stoic content remained – indeed, ideas are not easily divorced from the particular terms that serve as their vehicles – but that content was also revised in the process of dialectical interaction with Paul's teaching.

Such a construal also obviates any objections related to the fact that the Corinthians used, with religious connotations, terminology that apparently had no such connotations previously, namely πνευμάτικος, ψύχικος, and γνῶσις. Although already familiar in Stoicism, these

[38] Conzelmann, *1 Corinthians*, 109.

[39] Cf. Lightfoot, *Notes on the Epistles of St. Paul*, 195, 200; Fee, *First Epistle to the Corinthians*, 110n53; 602n12; Schrage, *Der erste Brief an die Korinther*, 339.

concepts were not borrowed from that system whole, but were developed by the Corinthians in ways that were partially *new*.

The final objection is likely to be that several systems of thought seem to have co-potential to explain what was going on in Corinth. The terminology is indistinctive and ambiguous, it is said. We must think of the Corinthians' wisdom as nonspecific, a mere collection of popular topoi blended from any number of systems of thought. Such an objection, however, fails to appreciate the complexity of the relationship that exists between con-temporary ideological systems. At any period in time, competing systems are bound to share certain points of contact. Indeed, it is this common ground that makes dialogue between the adherents of those systems a communicative possibility at all. For a fuller appreciation of correspondence, then, we must look beyond discrete cross-sections of parallelism to *larger patterns of thought*: the system that best explains the evidence is the system that explains the *greatest part* of the evidence. In that regard, whatever value other systems of thought have been said to bring to the study of 1 Corinthians, none of these systems has provided the kind consistent pattern of correspondence the Stoic thesis has. As we now know, Gnostic parallels need no longer be brought into the discussion.[40] Epicureanism provides little verbal parallel to the Corinthians' language and seems blatantly to contradict their view on the (im)mortal soul. Platonism is a nonstarter because of its low contemporary popularity and inferior explanatory power with respect to precise Corinthian language and the full range of topics at hand. The over-realized eschatology thesis has been increasingly regarded as overstated, probably misnamed, and notoriously unspecific. To my mind, the Hellenistic Jewish and Cynic theses continue to be the best alternatives to the one presented here. Yet, beside being directly contradicted by Paul's association of wisdom with the *Greeks* in 1:22, the Hellenistic Jewish thesis surrenders all of its explanatory potential to the source from which Hellenistic Judaism had expropriated its parallel language – Stoicism itself. What then remains is the Cynic thesis, which I have argued need hardly be seen as an *independent* alternative. Indeed, Cynicism was not a unique philosophical *school* as distinct from the others. Malherbe concisely summarizes the Cynic self-definition:

> What made a Cynic was his dress and conduct, self-sufficiency, harsh behavior toward what appeared as excesses, and a practical ethical idealism, but not a detailed arrangement of a system

[40] Though some still do, e.g., Fee, *First Epistle to the Corinthians*, 252.

> resting on Socratic-Antisthenic principles. The result was that Cynicism was compatible with views that shared its ethical demands even if they were at cross purposes with its fundamentally different teaching in other matters.[41]

This means, first of all, that Cynicism *alone*, divorced from the official doctrines of the schools, is probably insufficient to explain issues like, say, the Corinthians' views on death, or their understanding of "knowledge" and "weakness." In this regard, Malherbe's definition also sounds a cautionary note against any who would attempt to drive a wedge between Cynicism and Stoicism. Although not identical, the two did share a close genetic relationship, which proves to be of some consequence for the analysis presented here: obviously the sort of Stoicism assumed in the Corinthian church inclined toward some of Stoicism's more Cynic-oriented traditions.

All told, the challenge presented on these pages has been that partial overlap in terms of the *parts* does not cancel out the distinctiveness of the image *as a whole*. Although Stoicism may not be evident in *every* problem in the letter, and it may overlap with other systems of thought in *certain* respects, I have contended that when we compare *all* the *dominating* topics and identifiable Corinthian language *across the whole* of the letter, and through the proper lens of social history, we discover a total assemblage that looks more distinctly like a development of Stoic wisdom than anything else.

Let us not forget here the time-tested adage that we all know and live by: unless traded for something with greater explanatory power, the simpler explanation is always the best. Indeed, it *may* be that other philosophical influences were at work, but at this point we must ask whether they are at all necessary. As has been shown, what we have in 1 Corinthians is a sort of wisdom that certain wealthier Corinthians are in fact likely to have been interested in and had access to in first-century Roman Corinth, that fits with the prevailing first-century meaning of the term "wise man" and his Stoic description, that consistently parallels the Corinthians' language and outlook, that explains Paul's often unique choice of counter-rhetoric, *and* that provides a unifying explanation for the wisdom-discourse of chapters 1–4 on the one hand and the various topics of 5–15 on the other.[42] As it is, then, I fail to see why the matter

[41] Malherbe, *Paul and the Popular Philosophers*, 12.

[42] With the permission of the *Journal of Theological Studies*, this sentence has been revised from Tim Brookins, "The Wise Corinthians: Their Stoic Education and Outlook," *JTS* 62 (2011): 51–76, esp. 52. Where changes have been made, the present form should be preferred.

would need to be complicated by the imposition of additional philosophical influences. In a word: if Stoicism provided the terms in which Paul's preaching was understood by some in Corinth, it was then but a short step to *any* of the language or positions that can be attributed to them; nothing that cannot be accounted for as innovations made right within this Pauline church.

7

CONCLUSION

Previous examinations of the wisdom debated in 1 Corinthians have focused sharply on chapters 1–4, and especially the unit found in 2:1–5. Valuable as such focused examinations have been, however, the fruit of wider investigation should now be evident. We have seen from the *pattern* of the Corinthians' language and of the problems that extend throughout the whole of the letter that the "wise man" among the Corinthians was not – as recent studies have had it – the "sophist" so much as he was the "Stoic." The divisions in the church were fomented primarily by a small group of Stoic-thinking and relatively wealthy Christians, who, after Paul left Corinth, had translated his gospel message into Stoic categories and denigrated the inferior majority.

Many of the reasons why this thesis has not received the attention it deserves have become evident along the way. As we have a seen, a major reason has been the wide disillusionment with literary parallels that overcame the guild in the mid-twentieth century. When the bathwater of Gnosticism was, rightly, thrown out, the embryo of a Stoic thesis unfortunately went with it. Of course, there remain those who have compared the Corinthians with Hellenistic-Jewish wise men, Epicureans, Stoics, or Cynics, but these are theses that the dominating discourse of present scholarship have been wont to discard. Particular religious or philosophical systems are said to be too specific. At best we can speak of a popular trend consisting of multiple philosophical influences. Enlightened as such statements are meant to sound, however, we have seen that they reflect only a partial grasp of the evidence. The positions of the Corinthians may seem to reflect "multiple" philosophical influences because there was overlap in the doctrines and discourses of the philosophical schools *themselves*. Partial overlap, however, owing to common philosophical heritage, hardly vitiates holistic distinctiveness. Stoicism did not cease to be a distinctive school of philosophy because it shared with the Academic school a similar view on the virtues, and with the Epicureans similar views on the senses, and with both a common stock of language, a concern for the good life, and much, much more. Likewise, the Corinthian perspective did not cease to be peculiarly "Stoic" (if also "Christian") simply because it shared some measure of overlap with other systems of thought. The upshot of our examination has been that, while semblances of the other philosophies appear here or there, only Stoicism clearly rears its head, both conceptually and verbally, *from the beginning of the letter to the end.* Unless it can be shown that some other system has the potential to explain the evidence to an equal extent, and in an equally satisfactory fashion, the appeal to (limited) overlap must be regarded simply as a red herring. As it is, I have argued that nothing additional to Stoicism and Pauline teaching is necessary to explain the culprits' "philosophy." What may, however, need further consideration is the nature of the processes involved in the innovative *mixing* of Christian and Stoic elements undertaken by the Corinthians, and in particular how more recent and adequate understandings of "syncretism" might explain the peculiar social-symbolical ways in which the church made those innovations.

A second reason for neglect of the Stoic thesis has been, ironically, an infelicitous shift in methodology. Trading one imperfect method for another, many interpreters have moved from putting excessive (and often anachronistic) focus on literary parallels, to mirror-reading from Paul's own assertions. Our return to literary parallels here, though now within proper social and chronological context, has led to some startling differences with recent conclusions because it has meant essentially a paradigm shift in what texts are used as the basis for reconstruction. Indeed, whereas the rhetorical thesis mirror-read its conclusions from Paul's statements in texts like 2:1–5 (his alleged repudiation of "rhetoric"), 4:5 (his defense against those who have purportedly "judged" his standing as an orator), and chapter 9 (his "defense" as in 4:5), I have tried to focus on the language and problems more securely linked with the *Corinthians themselves.* At many points this has led to a total reversal in how the letter is understood: 2:1–5, 4:5, ch. 9, and the like, for example, probably say much less about the Corinthians than they do about *Paul* (cf. 1 Cor 2:3–5; 1 Thess 1:5; 2:1–10). Conversely, when we turn our eyes to the texts that most directly reflect the Corinthians' views, we see nothing of rhetoric and everything of philosophy.

A series of false dichotomies has also served the oversight. Recent books have told us – in these exact words – that the Corinthians' wisdom was that of "rhetoric, *not* philosophy," that their divisions were "social, *not* theological or philosophical," and that their city was "Roman, *not*

Greek." All of these dichotomies have been found either ill-defined, overstated, or simply untrue. As we have seen, all have unfortunately *also* served to sideline philosophy from the discussion.

We have further been told that, because ancient students were not introduced to philosophy at the lower stages of literate education, which were focused almost exclusively on rhetoric, Pauline church members would not have had any serious acquaintance with it. However, our present assessment of the Corinthian church in the light of the most recent studies on ancient economy counsels that this conclusion be qualified. This church contained several individuals who were higher up on the social ladder, perhaps at the level of Longenecker's "ES4" bracket. These could easily have studied philosophy from the epitomes in circulation, as they almost certainly would have been literate. I have also shown, however, that many at this level, and perhaps even some below, would have had access to a so-called elite education in the gymnasium. Following this trail has led us to some tantalizing "Erastus evidence" that has not previously been brought into the discussion: outside the NT and the now disputed *Corinth VIII* 232, the only two Erasti known at all in first-century Greece were both gymnasium affiliates. Whether one of these went on to be οἰκονόμος in Paul's Corinth we may never know, but the extreme rarity of the name and the otherwise unlikely coincidence in chronology, location, and social station make it difficult not to give some credence to the possibility.

Perhaps a less obvious reason for the oversight has been the way in which the rhetoric-philosophy dynamic has played out in the history of the Church and in western history generally. The Church quickly took up Plato's mantle in railing against rhetoric as "mere eloquence,"[1] in favor of wisdom's true *content* – philosophy. By St. Augustine's day, and then on through the Medieval tradition, Christianity was in fact a *philosophy* and the Christian believer the true "lover of wisdom," or *philosopher*.[2] Although Augustine believed that rhetoric too might be pressed into the gospel's service,[3] this did not stop Plato's characterization of rhetoric as flashy in form and vacant in content from enduring throughout most of western history, in ecclesiastical and secular contexts alike.[4] In that

[1] See, for example, Theodoret of Cyrus on 1 Cor 1:17: "preaching is a gift given to a few, and it must not be confused with *mere eloquence*, which is purely superficial" (Kovacs, *The Church's Bible*, 12; emphasis added).

[2] See *Civ*. 19.

[3] On the usefulness of rhetoric, see St. Augustine's *De Doctrina Christiana*.

[4] For a survey on the relationship between rhetoric and philosophy in western history, see S. Ijsseling, *Rhetoric and Philosophy in Conflict*, 41–136.

regard, having now looked more carefully and exhaustively at the evidence of 1 Corinthians, we might ask whether the rhetorical interpretation has not been influenced more by our deep-rooted suspicion of sophistry and traditional sympathies with philosophy than it has by the actual evidence at hand: the haughty purveyor of claptrap seems far more deserving of our arrows than does our solemn, truth-telling ally, the philosopher.

A final reason for the oversight has been that most treatments of 1 Corinthians have been deplorably (if somewhat understandably) parochial in focus. This has meant not only that the merely *partial* treatment of the evidence from those advocating the rhetorical thesis has been found convincing enough, but also that the Stoic thesis itself has never received a full and detailed exposition. But no longer can we be content to build an entire reconstruction off of the shaky foundation of chapters 1–4, or worse, 2:1–5. Here I have tried to draw all the evidence together for the first time, evincing both the Stoic undercurrents that seem to have been at work in all the letter's dominating topics *and* the plausibility of the Stoic thesis vis-à-vis the social background of the Corinthian church. The cumulative weight of the evidence has mounted more than a formidable alternative to the previously regnant rhetorical thesis.

In closing, it should be said that several issues we have touched upon demand further attention. The question of Stoicism in Paul's thought continues to loom large. The fact that the Corinthians could hear him in Stoic terms is in itself evidence of resemblance. And then for him to posture as a Stoic in response – what should we say to these things? Is it mere "formal similarity"? Or should this prompt us to jettison the notion that there is any "intrinsic difference" between Paul and the Stoics altogether, as Engberg-Pedersen has argued?[5] Probably a more balanced treatment awaits. The present analysis supports the conclusion that Paul was rather a man of many worlds, capable of shifting between them as the rhetorical situation demanded, in the process exploiting discourses that supplied premises acceptable to his audiences, evoking familiar associations, retaining serviceable linkages in thought but emptying the source language of its original content where more subversive purposes were found necessary, and never abandoning his core, and essentially distinctive, Jewish-Christian convictions.

These conclusions also demand a fresh consideration for the contours of the Corinthian correspondence, and especially the relationship between 1 and 2 Corinthians. If past consensus has been right that the two letters

[5] Engberg-Pedersen, *Paul and the Stoics*, 11.

(or three, if 2 Corinthians is composite) are prompted by rather different occasions, the present argument gives us now further reason to rethink the extent to which "sophistic" concerns cut across them: the immediate controversy in which the church was embroiled and Paul's concern for his own public perception should probably not be conflated.

The time may also be ripe to begin rethinking the way in which "theological" or "philosophical" theses on the one hand and "socioeconomic" ones on the other, far from standing in irreconcilable opposition to each other, actually *work together* in explaining the letter's exigencies. In the past, each of these aspects has been explored independently. But they are not mutually exclusive. Perhaps Stoicism was attractive to certain upwardly mobile Corinthians for some of the same reasons it was attractive to Roman elites – because (beside appearing compatible with their Christianity) it justified the social and political status quo, served as the badge of their sophistication, helped enhance their honor, or the like? Whatever the reasons, ideology rarely acts alone in governing behavior, and the deeper complexities of the Corinthian exigencies will have to receive further reflection. [6]

Still further avenues could be explored: one might ask what part the Corinthian correspondence played in shaping Paul's theology, take up further reappraisal of the state of methodology in Corinthian studies, or reconsider rhetorical approaches to Paul in the light of the critical role played by the "*occasion*" in *informing* his rhetoric of choice.[7] For now, however, I hope only to have set the winds of change in motion on the question of the Corinthians' wisdom. If the present examination of the evidence has been on target, acceptance of the rhetorical thesis should begin to flag and the windfall should go to philosophy. But judgment on these matters shall have to be left to the wise.

[6] In this way, the present thesis is not mutually exclusive of recent social-historical inquiries such as those of R. Dutch, *The Educated Elite in 1 Corinthians* (2005); M. T. Finney, *Honour and Conflict in the Ancient World*, LNTS 460 (London: T & T Clark, 2011); and others.

[7] Our turn to rhetorical analysis of the NT as a way out of the problems associated with getting "behind" the text, then, brings us right back behind the text, for we cannot understand what Paul "means" without understanding how his words interplay with the meaning intended by his dialogue partners.

BIBLIOGRAPHY

Adams, Edward. "First-Century Models for Paul's Churches: Selected Scholarly Developments Since Meeks." Pp. 60–78 in *After the First Urban Christians*. Edited by Todd Still and David Horrell. Edinburgh: T & T Clark, 2009.

Adams, Edward and David Horrell. "Introduction." Pp. 1–50 in *Christianity at Corinth: The Quest for the Pauline Church*. Louisville: Westminster John Knox, 2004.

Adkins, A. W. H. "Review of Burkhard Gladigow's *Sophia und Kosmos: Untersuchungen zur Frühgeschichte von σοφός und σοφίη*." *The Classical Review*, New Series 21 (1971): 391–3.

Alcock, Susan E. *Graecia Capta: The Landscapes of Roman Greece*. Cambridge: Cambridge University Press, 1993.

Alexander, Loveday. "IPSE DIXIT: Citation of Authority in Paul and in the Jewish and Hellenistic Schools." Pp. 103–27 in *Paul beyond the Judaism-Hellenism Divide*. Edited by Troels Engberg-Pedersen. Louisville: Westminster John Knox, 2001.

"Paul and the Hellenistic Schools: The Evidence of Galen." Pp. 60–83 in *Paul in His Hellenistic Context*. Edited by Troels Engberg-Pedersen. London: T & T Clark, 1995; London: Continuum, 2004.

Allo, E. B. *Première épître aux Corinthiens*. 2d ed. Paris: Gabalda, 1956.

Anderson, R. Dean. *Rhetorical Theory and Paul*. Contributions to Biblical Exegesis and Theology 18. Leuven: Peeters, 1999.

von Arnim, Hans. *Stoicorum Veterum Fragmenta*. 4 vols. Leipzig: Eubner, 1924.

Asher, J. R. *Polarity and Change in 1 Corinthians 15: A Study of Metaphysics, Rhetoric and Resurrection*. Tübingen: Mohr Siebeck, 2000.

Baird, William. "'One against the Other': Intra-Church Conflict in 1 Corinthians." Pp. 116–36 in *The Conversation Continues: Studies in Paul and John in Honor of J. Louis Martyn*. Edited by Robert T. Fortna and Beverly R. Gaventa. Nashville: Abingdon, 1990.

Balch, David L. "Rich Pompeiian Houses, Shops for Rent, and the Huge Apartment Building in Herculaneum as Typical Spaces for Pauline House Churches." *Journal for the Study of the New Testament* 27 (2004): 27–46.

Balz, Horst Robert. *Christus in Korinth: Eine Einführung in den ersten Korintherbrief*. Kassel: J. G. Oncken, 1970.

Barclay, John M. "Mirror-Reading a Polemical Letter: Galatians as a Test Case." *Journal for the Study of the New Testament* 31 (1987): 73–93.

"Poverty in Pauline Studies: A Response to Stephen Friesen." *Journal for the Study of the New Testament* 26 (2004): 363–6.

Barnett, Paul W. *The Corinthian Question: Why Did the Church Oppose Paul?* Nottingham: Apollos, 2011.

Barrett, C. K. *A Commentary on the First Epistle to the Corinthians*. London: Adam and Charles Black, 1971.

"Paul's Opponents in 2 Corinthians." *New Testament Studies* 17 (1971): 1–54.

Barth, Karl. *Resurrection of the Dead*. New York: Fleming H. Revell, 1933.

Baur, F. C. "Die Christusparti in der korinthischen Gemeinde, der Gegensatz des paulinischen und petrinischen Christentums in der altesten Kirche, der Apostel Petrus in Rom." *Tübinger Zeitschrift für Theologie* 4 (1831): 61–206.

"The Epistles to the Corinthians." Pp. 268–320 in *Paulus, der Apostle Jesu Christi*. Stuttgart: Becker & Muller, 1866.

Betz, Hans Dieter. *Der Apostel Paulus und die sokratische Tradition: Eine Exegetische Untersuchung zu seiner Apologie 2 Korinther 10–13*. Beiträge zur historischen Theologie 45. Tübingen: Möhr, 1972.

Galatians: A Commentary on Paul's Letter to the Churches in Galatia. Philadelphia: Fortress, 1979.

"The Problem of Rhetoric and Theology According to the Apostle Paul." Pp. 16–48 in *L'Apotre Paul in Personalité, Style et Conception du Ministère*. Edited by A. Vanhoye. Bibliotheca ephemeridum theologicarum lovaniensium 73. Leuven: Leuven University Press, 1986.

Billings, Bradly S. "From House Church to Tenement Church: Domestic Space and the Development of Early Urban Christianity – The Example of Ephesus." *Journal of Theological Studies* 62 (2011): 541–69.

de Boer, M. C. *The Defeat of Death: Apocalyptic Eschatology in 1 Corinthians 15 and Romans 5*. Journal for the Study of the New Testament, Supplement Series 22. Sheffield: Sheffield Academic, 1988.

Bousset, Wilhelm. *Kyrios Christos: A History of the Belief in Christ from the Beginnings of Christianity to Irenaeus*. Translated by John E. Steely. Nashville: Abingdon, 1970.

Bowersock, G. W. *Augustus and the Greek World*. Oxford: Clarendon, 1965.

Branick, V. P. "Source and Redaction Analysis of 1 Corinthians 1–3." *Journal of Biblical Literature* 101 (1982): 251–69.

Bray, Gerald Lewis. *1–2 Corinthians*. Ancient Christian Commentary on Scripture: New Testament. Downers Grove: InterVarsity, 1999.

Brookins, Timothy. "Rhetoric and Philosophy in the First Century: Their Relation with Respect to 1 Corinthians 1–4." *Neotestamentica* 44 (2010): 233–52.

"The Wise Corinthians: Their Stoic Education and Outlook." *Journal of Theological Studies* 62 (2011): 51–76.

Brown, Raymond. *An Introduction to the New Testament*. The Anchor Yale Bible Reference Library. New Haven; London: Yale University Press, 1997.

Bruce, F. F. "'To the Hebrews' or 'To the Essenes.'" *New Testament Studies* 9 (1963): 217–52.

Brunschwig, Jacques and David Sedley. "Hellenistic Philosophy." Pp. 151–83 in *The Cambridge Companion to Greek and Roman Philosophy*. Edited by David N. Sedley. Cambridge: Cambridge University Press, 2003.

Brunt, P. A. "Stoicism and the Principate." *Papers of the British School at Rome* 43 (1975): 7–35.

Bullmore, Michael. *St. Paul's Theology of Rhetorical Style: An Examination of 1 Corinthians 2:1–5 in the Light of First-Century Rhetorical Criticism.* San Francisco: International Scholars Publications, 1995.

Bultmann, Rudolf. *Der Stil der paulinischen Predigt und die Kynischstoische Diatribe.* Göttingen: Vandenhoeck and Ruprecht, 1910.

The History of the Synoptic Tradition. Translated by John Marsh. Oxford: Basil Blackwell, 1968.

Theology of the New Testament. Translated by K. Grobel. New York: Scribner, 1951.

Burkert, Walter. "Platon oder Pythagoras? Zum Ursprung des Wortes 'Philosophie.'" *Hermes* 88 (1969): 159–77.

Butts, James R. "The Progymnasmata of Theon: A New Text with Translation and Commentary." Ph.D. dissertation, Claremont Graduate School, 1986.

Cadbury, H. J. "Erastus of Corinth." *Journal of Biblical Literature* 50 (1931): 42–58.

Campbell, Douglas. *The Deliverance of God: An Apocalyptic Re-Reading of Justification in Paul.* Grand Rapids: Eerdmans, 2009.

Canceth, Hubert and Helmuth Schneider. *Brill's New Pauly: Encyclopedia of the Ancient World: Antiquity.* 10 vols. Leiden; Boston: Brill, 2002–2010.

Caragounis, Chrys C. *The Development of Greek and the New Testament: Morphology, Syntax, Phonology, and Textual Transmission.* Grand Rapids: Baker Academic, 2006.

Chandler, Clive. *Philodemus on Rhetoric: Translation and Exegetical Essays.* London: Routledge, 2006.

Chankowski, Andrzej S. *L'Éphébie hellénistique: Étude d'une institution civique dans les cités grecques des îles de la Mer Égée et de l'Asie Mineure.* Culture et cité 4. Paris: De Boccard, 2010.

Chantraine, Pierre. *Dictionnaire étymologique de la langue grecque: Histoire des mots.* Paris: Klincksieck, 2000.

Chow, John. *Patronage and Power.* Journal for the Study of the New Testament: Supplement Series 75. Sheffield: JSOT, 1992.

Ciampa, Roy E. and Brian S. Rosner. *The First Letter to the Corinthians.* The Pillar New Testament Commentary. Grand Rapids, MI: Eerdmans, 2010.

Clarke, Andrew. *Secular and Christian Leadership in Corinth: A Socio-Historical and Exegetical Study of 1 Corinthians 1–6.* New York: Brill, 1993.

Coale, A. J., P. G. Demeny, and B. Vaughan, *Regional Model Life Tables and Stable Populations.* New York: Academic Press, 1983.

Cohoon, J. W. *Dio Chrysostom, Orations.* Vol. 2. Translated by J. W. Cohoon. Loeb Classical Library 339. Cambridge, MA: Harvard University Press, 1977.

Collins, Raymond. *1 Corinthians.* Sacra Pagina 7. Collegeville, MN: Liturgical, 1999.

Colson, F. H. and G. H. Whitaker. *Philo.* Vol. 4. Loeb Classical Library. Cambridge: Cambridge University Press, 1968.

Conzelmann, Hans. *1 Corinthians: A Commentary on the First Epistle to the Corinthians.* Hermeneia. Philadelphia: Fortress, 1975.

Coppens, J. "Les analogies qumrâniennes de l'Épître aux Hébreux." *La nouvelle revue théologique* 84 (1961): 128–41.

Cosgrove, Charles H. *The Cross and the Spirit: A Study in the Argument and Theology of Galatians*. Macon, GA: Mercer University Press, 1988.

Cribiore, Raffaella. *Gymnastics of the Mind: Greek Education in Hellenistic and Roman Egypt*. Princeton, NJ: Princeton University Press, 2001.

Dahl, Nils. "Paul and the Church at Corinth According to 1 Corinthians 1:10–4:21." Pp. 40–61 in *Studies in Paul: Theology for the Early Christian Mission*. Minneapolis, MN: Augsburg, 1977.

Danker, Frederick. "Paul's Debt to the *De Corona* of Demosthenes: A Study of Rhetorical Techniques in Second Corinthians." Pp. 262–80 in *Persuasive Artistry: Studies in New Testament Rhetoric in Honor of George A. Kennedy*. Journal for the Study of the New Testament: Supplement Series 50. Edited by D. F. Watson. Sheffield: Sheffield Academic, 1991.

Davies, W. D. *Paul and Rabbinic Judaism: Some Rabbinic Elements in Pauline Theology*. London: SPCK, 1948.

Davis, James A. *Wisdom and Spirit: An Investigation of 1 Cor 1:18–3:20 against the Background of Jewish Sapiential Traditions in the Greco-Roman Period*. Lanham, MD: University Press of America, 1984.

Day, John. *An Economic History of Athens under Roman Domination*. New York: Anro, 1973.

Deissmann, Gustav Adolph. *Light from the Ancient East: The New Testament Illustrated by Recently Discovered Texts of the Graeco-Roman World*. Translated by Lionel R. M. Strachan. 1927; repr. Peabody, MA: Hendrickson, 1995.

Delorme, J. *Gymnasion: Etude sur les monuments consacrés a l'education en gréce. Bibliothéque des écoles Françaises d'Athénes et de Rome*. Paris: Editions E. de Boccard, 1960.

Deming, Will. "Paul and Indifferent Things." Pp. 384–94 in *Paul in the Greco-Roman World*. Edited by J. Paul Sampley. London: Continuum, 2003.

Paul on Marriage and Celibacy: The Hellenistic Background of 1 Corinthians 7. Grand Rapids, MI: Eerdmans, 2004.

"The Unity of 1 Corinthians 5–6." *Journal of Biblical Literature* 119 (1996): 289–312.

Dodd, C. H. *The Interpretation of the Fourth Gospel*. Cambridge: Cambridge University Press, 1968.

Doughty, Darrell. "The Presence and Future of Salvation in Corinth." *Zeitschrift für die neutestamentliche Wissenschaft und die Kunde der älteren Kirche* 66 (1975): 61–90.

Downing, F. Gerald. *Cynics, Paul, and the Pauline Churches*. London: Routledge, 1998.

Dunn, James. *1 Corinthians*. New Testament Guides. Sheffield: Sheffield Academic, 1995.

"1 Corinthians 15:45 – Last Adam, Life-Giving Spirit." Pp. 127–41 in *Christ and Spirit in the New Testament: Studies in Honour of Charles Francis Digby Moule*. Edited by B. Lindars and S. S. Smalley. Cambridge: Cambridge University Press, 1973.

"Reconstructions of Corinthian Christianity." Pp. 295–310 in *Christianity at Corinth: The Quest for the Pauline Church*. Edited by Edward Adams and David Horrell. Louisville, KY: Westminster John Knox, 2004.

Dupont, J. *Gnosis: la connaissance religieuse dans les epitres de Saint Paul*. Louvain: Gabalda, 1949.

Dutch, R. S. *The Educated Elite in 1 Corinthians: Education and Community Conflict in Graeco-Roman Context*. Journal for the Study of the New Testament: Supplement Series 271. New York: T & T Clark, 2005.

Engberg-Pedersen, Troels. *Cosmology and the Self in the Apostle Paul*. Oxford: Oxford University Press, 2010.

Paul and the Stoics. Edinburgh: T & T Clark, 2000.

"Paul, Virtues, and Vices." Pp. 608–34 in *Paul in the Greco-Roman World*. Edited by J. Paul Sampley. London: Continuum, 2003.

Engberg-Pedersen, Troels and M. D'Agostino. "Un Paolo stoico o un Epitteto paolino? Ripensare gli slogan in 1 Cor 6,12–20." *Rivista Biblica Italiana* 54 (2004): 41–75.

Engels, Donald. *Roman Corinth: An Alternative Model for the Classical City*. Chicago: University of Chicago Press, 1990.

Fagan, G. G. *Bathing in Public in the Roman World*. Ann Arbor: University of Michigan Press, 2002.

Fasher, E. *Der erste Brief an die Korinther*. Herders theologischer Kommentar zum Neuen Testament 7/1. Berlin: Evangelische Verlangsanstalt, 1975.

Fee, Gordon. *1 Corinthians*. New International Commentary on the New Testament. Grand Rapids, MI: Eerdmans, 1987.

Finney, Mark T. *Honour and Conflict in the Ancient World: 1 Corinthians in its Greco-Roman Social Setting*. Library of New Testament Studies 460. London: T & T Clark, 2011.

Fiore, Benjamin. "'Covert Allusion' in 1 Cor 1–4." *Catholic Biblical Quarterly* 47 (1985): 85–102.

"The Sage in Select Hellenistic and Roman Literary Genres." Pp. 329–42 in *The Sage in Israel and Ancient Near East*. Edited by John G. Gammie and Leo G. Perdue. Winona Lake, IN: Eisenbrauns, 1990.

Fitzgerald, John T. *Cracks in an Earthen Vessel: An Examination of the Catalogues of Hardships in the Corinthian Correspondence*. Society of Biblical Literature Dissertation Series 99. Atlanta, GA: Scholars, 1988.

Fitzgerald John T. and L. Michael White. "*Quod est comparandum*: The Problem of Parallels." Pp. 13–39 in *Early Christianity and Classical Culture*. Edited by J. T. Fitzgerald, T. H. Olbricht, and L. M. White. Leiden: Brill, 2003.

Fitzmyer, Joseph. *1 Corinthians: A New Translation with Introduction and Commentary*. New Haven, CT; London: Yale University Press, 2008.

Forbes, C. A. "Expanded Uses of the Greek Gymnasium." *Classical Philology* 40 (1945): 32–42.

Greek Physical Education. New York: The Century Company, 1929.

Fotopoulos, John. "Arguments Concerning Food Offered to Idols: Corinthian Quotations and Pauline Refutations in a Rhetorical Partitio (1 Corinthians 8:1–9)." *Catholic Biblical Quarterly* 67 (2005): 611–31.

Food Offered to Idols in Roman Corinth: A Socio-Rhetorical Reconsideration of 1 Cor 8:1–11:1. Wissenschaftliche Untersuchungen zum Neuen Testament 2:151. Tübingen: Mohr Siebeck, 2003.

Friesen, Steven. "Poverty in Pauline Studies: Beyond the So-Called New Consensus." *Journal for the Study of the New Testament* (2004): 323–61.

"The Wrong Erastus: Ideology, Archaeology, and Exegesis." Pp. 231–56 in *Corinth in Context: Comparative Studies on Religion and Society*. Edited by

Steven J. Friesen, Daniel N. Schowalter, and James C. Walters. Leiden: Brill, 2010.

Friesen, Steven and W. Scheidel. "The Size of the Economy and the Distribution of Income in the Roman Empire." *Journal of Roman Studies* 99 (2009): 61–91.

Funk, Robert. "Word and Word in 1 Cor 2:6–16." Pp. 275–303 in *Language, Hermeneutic, and Word of God*. New York: Harper & Row, 1966.

Galloway, Lincoln E. *Freedom in the Gospel: Paul's Exemplum in 1 Corinthians 9 in Conversation with the Discourses of Epictetus and Philo*. Leuven: Peeters, 2004.

Garcilazo, Albert V. *The Corinthian Dissenters and the Stoics*. New York: Peter Lang, 2007.

Gardner, P. D. *The Gifts of God and the Authentication of a Christian: An Exegetical Study of 1 Corinthians 8–11*. Lanham, Md.: University Press of America, 1994.

Garland, David E. *1 Corinthians*. Baker Exegetical Commentary on the New Testament 1. Grand Rapids: Baker Academic, 2003.

Georgi, Dieter. *The Opponents of Paul in Second Corinthians: A Study of Religious Propaganda in Late Antiquity*. Philadelphia: Fortress, 1986.

Gill, Christopher. "The School in the Roman Imperial Period." Pp. 33–53 in *Cambridge Companion to the Stoics*. Cambridge: Cambridge University Press, 2002.

Gill, David W. J. "Corinth: A Roman Colony in Achaea." *Biblische Zeitschrift* 37 (1993): 259–64.

"In Search of the Social Elite in Corinth." *Tyndale Bulletin* 44 (1993): 323–37.

Glad, Clarence. *Paul and Philodemus: Adaptability in Epicurean and Early Christian Psychagogy*. Leiden; New York: Brill, 1995.

Goodrich, John K. "Erastus of Corinth (Romans 16.23): Responding to Recent Proposals on his Rank, Status, and Faith." *New Testament Studies* 57 (2011): 583–93.

"Erastus, Quaestor of Corinth: The Administrative Rank of ὁ οἰκονόμος τῆς πόλεως (Rom 16:23) in an Achaean Colony." *New Testament Studies* 56 (2010): 90–115.

Paul as an Administrator of God in 1 Corinthians. Society of New Testament Studies Monograph Series 152. Cambridge: Cambridge University Press, 2012.

Goulder, Michael. "Libertines? (1 Cor 5–6)." *Novum Testamentum* 41 (1999): 334–48.

Paul and the Competing Mission in Corinth. Peabody, Mass.: Hendrickson, 2001.

"σοφία in Corinthians." *New Testament Studies* 37 (1991): 516–34.

Grant, Robert M. "Hellenistic Elements in 1 Corinthians." Pp. 60–66 in *Early Christian Origins*. Chicago: Quadrangle Books, 1961.

Paul in the Roman World: The Conflict at Corinth. Louisville, Ky.: Westminster John Knox, 2001.

"The Wisdom of the Corinthians." Pp. 51–55 in *The Joy of Study*. New York: Macmillan, 1951.

Grindheim, Sigurd. "Wisdom for the Perfect: Paul's Challenge for the Corinthian Church (2:6–16)." *Journal of Biblical Literature* 121 (2002): 689–709.

Grosheide, Frederick. *Commentary on the First Epistle to the Corinthians*. Grand Rapids: Eerdmans, 1953.

Gupta, Nijay K. "Mirror-Reading Moral Issues in Paul's Letters." *Journal for the Study of the New Testament* 34 (2012): 361–81.

Hall, David R. *The Unity of the Corinthian Correspondence*. London; New York: T & T Clark, 2003.

Hansen, Mogens Herman. *Three Studies in Athenian Demography*. Copenhagen: Kgl. Danske Videnskabernes Selskab, 1988.

Harris, William V. *Ancient Literacy*. Cambridge: Harvard University Press, 1989.

Hartog, Paul. "'Not Even Among the Pagans' (1 Cor. 5:1): Paul and Seneca on Incest." Pp. 51–64 in *The New Testament and Early Christian Literature in Greco-Roman Context: Studies in Honor of David E. Aune*. Edited by David E. Aune and John Fotopoulos. Novum Testamentum Supplements 122. Leiden; Boston: Brill, 2006.

Hays, Richard. *1 Corinthians*. Louisville, Ky.: John Knox Press, 1997.

"Conversion of the Imagination." *New Testament Studies* 45 (1999): 391–412.

Heinrici, C. *Der erste Brief an die Korinther*. Kritisch-exegetischer Kommentar über das Neue Testament 5:6. Göttingen: Vandenhoeck & Ruprecht, 1896.

Henderson, Ian. "The Second Sophistic and Non-Elite Speakers." Pp. 23–35 in *Perceptions of the Second Sophistic and Its Times – Regards sur la Seconde Sophistique et son époque*. Edited by Thomas Schmidt and Pascale Fleury. Toronto: University of Toronto Press, 2011.

Hengel, Martin. *Judaism and Hellenism: Studies in Their Encounter in Palestine during the Early Hellenistic Period*. London: SCM, 1974.

The Pre-Christian Paul. London: SCM; Philadelphia: Trinity Press International, 1994.

Hering, James P. *The Colossian and Ephesian Haustafeln in Theological Context*. New York: Peter Lang, 2007.

The First Epistle of Saint Paul to the Corinthians. London: Epworth, 1962.

Hiigel, John. *Leadership in 1 Corinthians: A Case Study in Paul's Ecclesiology*. Studies in the Bible and Early Christianity 57. Lewiston, N.Y.: E. Mellen, 2003.

Hitchman, Richard and Fabienne Marchand. "Two Ephebic Inscriptions: IG II2 1973A and 1973B." *Zeitschrift für Papyrologie und Epigraphik* 148 (2004): 165–76.

Hock, Ronald F. "Cynics and Rhetoric." Pp. 755–774 in *Handbook of Classical Rhetoric*. Edited by Stanley Porter. Leiden: Brill, 2001.

"Paul and Greco-Roman Education." Pp. 198–227 in *Paul in the Greco-Roman World*. Edited by J. Paul Sampley. London: Continuum, 2003.

Holland, Glen. "Paul's Use of Irony as a Rhetorical Technique." Pp. 234–48 in *The Rhetorical Analysis of Scripture*. Edited by Stanley E. Porter and Thomas H. Olbricht. Journal for the Study of the New Testament: Supplement Series 146. Sheffield, Eng.: Sheffield Academic, 1997.

Holleman, J. *Resurrection and Parousia: A Traditio-Historical Study of Paul's Eschatology in 1 Corinthians 15*. Novum Testamentum Supplements 84. Leiden: Brill, 1996.

"Methods of Historical Reconstruction." Pp. 255–71 in *Christianity at Corinth: The Quest for the Pauline Church*. Edited by Edward Adams and David Horrell. Louisville: Westminster John Knox, 2004.

Holmberg, Brent. *Sociology and the New Testament: An Appraisal*. Minneapolis: Fortress, 1990.

Horrell, David. "Domestic Space and Christian Meetings at Corinth: Imagining New Contexts and the Buildings East of the Theatre." *New Testament Studies* 50 (2004): 349–69.

The Social Ethos of the Corinthian Correspondence: Interests and Ideology from 1 Corinthians to 1 Clement. Studies of the New Testament and Its World. Edinburgh: T & T Clark, 1996.

Horsley, G. H. R., ed. *New Documents Illustrating Early Christianity*. New Documents Illustrating Early Christianity Series. 9 vols. Ancient History Documentary Research Centre: Macquarie University, 1976–1987.

Horsley, Richard. *1 Corinthians*. Nashville: Abingdon, 1998.

"Consciousness and Freedom among the Corinthians (1 Cor 8–10)." *Catholic Biblical Quarterly* 40 (1978): 574–89.

"Gnosis in Corinth: 1 Cor 8:1–6." *New Testament Studies* 27 (1981): 32–51.

"How Can Some of You Say That There Is No Resurrection of the Dead?" *Novum Testamentum* 20 (1978): 203–31.

"Pneumatikos vs. Psychikos: Distinctions of Spiritual Status among the Corinthians." *Harvard Theological Review* 69 (1976): 269–288.

Wisdom and Spiritual Transcendence at Corinth: Studies in First Corinthians. Eugene, Oreg.: Cascade, 2008.

"Wisdom of Words and Words of Wisdom in Corinth." *Catholic Biblical Quarterly* 39 (1977): 224–239.

Hurd, J. C. *The Origin of 1 Corinthians*. New York: Seabury, 1965.

Huttunen, Niko. "Stoic Law in Paul?" Pp. 39–58 in *Stoicism in Early Christianity*. Edited by Tuomas Rasimus, Troels Engberg-Pedersen, and Ismo Dunderberg. Peabody, Mass.: Hendrickson, 2010.

Ijsseling, Samuel. *Rhetoric and Philosophy in Conflict: An Historical Survey*. Hague: M. Nijhoff, 1976.

Inwood, Brad and Lloyd P. Gerson. *The Stoics Reader: Selected Writings and Testimonia*. Indianapolis; Cambridge: Hackett, 2008.

Johnson, S. E. "Tarsus and the Apostle Paul." *Lexington Theological Quarterly* 15 (1980): 105–13.

Johnson, William A. "Introduction." Pp. 3–12 in *Ancient Literacies*. Oxford: Oxford University Press, 2009.

Jones, A. H. M. *Cities of the Eastern Provinces*. New York: Oxford University Press, 1937.

The Greek City: From Alexander to Justinian. Oxford: Clarendon, 1940.

Joyal, Mark, Iain McDougall, and J. C. Yardley, eds. *Greek and Roman Education: A Sourcebook*. Milton Park: Routledge, 2009.

Judge, E. A. *The Social Pattern of Christian Groups in the First Century*. London: Tyndale, 1960.

Käsemann, Ernst. "Zum Thema der urchirstlichen Apokalyptik." *Zeitschrift für Theologie und Kirche* 59 (1962): 257–84. ET, "On the Subject of Primitive Christian Apocalyptic." Pp. 108–37 in *New Testament Questions of Today*. Philadelphia: Fortress, 1969.

Katsari, Constantina and S. Mitchell. "The Roman Colonies of the Greek East: Questions of State and Civic Identity." *Athenaeum* 95 (2008): 219–47.

Keener, Craig. *1–2 Corinthians*. New Cambridge Bible Commentary. Cambridge: Cambridge University Press, 2005.

Kempthorne, R. "Incest and the Body of Christ: A Study of 1 Corinthians 6.12." *New Testament Studies* 14 (1967–1968): 568–74.

Kennedy, George. *Classical Rhetoric and Its Christian and Secular Tradition from Ancient to Modern Times*. Chapel Hill: University of North Carolina Press, 1999.

Kennell, Nigel M. *Ephebeia: A Register of Greek Cities with Citizen Training Systems in the Hellenistic and Roman Periods*. Nikephoros Beihefte 12. Hildes-heim: Weidmann, 2006.

"The Greek Ephebate in the Roman Period." *The International Journal of the History of Sport* (2009): 323–42.

The Gymnasium of Virtue: Education and Culture in Ancient Sparta. Studies in the History of Greece and Rome. Chapel Hill: University of North Carolina Press, 1995.

Kent, J. H. Corinth, Vol. VIII, part III, *The Inscriptions 1926–1950*. Princeton, N.J.: American School of Classical Studies at Athens, 1966.

Kerferd, George B. "The Sage in Hellenistic Philosophical Literature." Pp. 320–28 in *The Sage in Israel and Ancient Near East*. Edited by John G. Gammie and Leo G. Perdue. Winona Lake: Eisenbrauns, 1990.

Kerkeslager, A. "Maintaining Jewish Identity in the Greek Gymnasium: A Jewish 'Load' in CPJ 3.519." *Journal for the Study of Judaism in the Persian, Hellenistic, and Roman Periods* 28 (1997): 12–33.

Kidd, Ian G. *Posidonius, Volume 3: The Translation of the Fragments*. Cambridge: Cambridge University Press. 1999.

Kittel, G., and G. Friedrich, eds. *Theological Dictionary of the New Testament*. Translated by G. W. Bromiley. 10 vols. Grand Rapids: Eerdmans, 1964–1976.

Klutz, Todd E. "Re-Reading 1 Corinthians after Rethinking 'Gnosticism.'" *Journal for the Study of the New Testament* 26 (2003): 193–216.

Koester, Helmut. "Gnomai Diaphoi: The Origin and Nature of Diversification in the History of Early Christianity." Pp. 114–57 in *Trajectories through Early Christianity*. Edited by Helmut Koester. Philadelphia: Fortress, 1971.

"The Silence of the Apostle." Pp. 339–50 in *Urban Religion in Roman Corinth: Interdisciplinary Approaches*. Edited by Daniel N. Schowalter and Steven J. Friesen. Harvard Theological Studies 53. Cambridge: Harvard Theological Studies, 2005.

Kolarcik, Michael, S. J. "The Sage behind the Wisdom of Solomon." Pp. 245–57 in *Scribes, Sages, and Seers: The Sage in the Eastern Mediterranean World*. Edited by Leo Perdue. Göttingen: Vandenhoeck & Ruprecht, 2008.

Kovacs, Judith L. *1 Corinthians*. The Church's Bible 53. Downer's Grove, Ill.: InterVarsity, 1999.

Kremer, Jacob. *Der erste Brief an die Korinther*. Regensburg: F. Pustet, 1997.

Krentz, Edgar. "Logos or Sophia: The Pauline Use of the Ancient Dispute between Rhetoric and Philosophy." Pp. 277–90 in *Early Christianity and Classical Culture: Comparative Studies in Honor of Abraham J. Malherbe*. Edited by John T. Fitzgerald, Thomas H. Olbricht, and L. Michael White. Leiden: Brill, 2003.

Kuck, D. W. *Judgment and Community Conflict: Paul's Use of Apocalyptic Judgment Language in 1 Corinthians 3:5–4:5*. Novum Testamentum Supplements 66. Leiden: Brill, 1992.

Kwon, Oh-Young. "A Critical Review of Recent Scholarship on the Pauline Opposition and the Nature of its Wisdom (σοφια) in 1 Corinthians 1–4." *Currents in Biblical Research*, 8 (2010): 386–427.

Laird, Margaret L. "The Emperor in a Roman Town: The Base of the Augustales in the Forum at Corinth." Pp. 67–116 in *Corinth in Context: Comparative Studies on Religion and Society*. Novum Testamentum Supplements 134. Edited by Friesen, Steven J. and Daniel N. Schowalter, and James C. Walters. Leiden: Brill, 2010.

Lakey, Michael. *Image and Glory of God: 1 Corinthians 11:2–16 as a Case Study in Bible, Gender and Hermeneutics*. Library of New Testament Studies 418. London: T & T Clark, 2010.

Lampe, Peter. *Christians at Rome during the First Two Centuries*. London: Continuum, 2006.

Landvogt, Peter. *Epigraphische Untersuchungen über den ΟΙΚΟΝΟΜΟΣ: Ein Beitrag zum Hellenistischen Beamtenwesen*. Strassburg: M. Dumont Schauberg, 1908.

Lang, Friedrich. *Die Briefe an die Korinther*. Göttingen: Vandenhoeck & Ruprecht, 1994.

Lee, Michelle. *Paul, the Stoics, and the Body of Christ*. Society of New Testament Studies Monograph Series 137. Cambridge: Cambridge University Press, 2006.

Levison, John R. "Did the Spirit Inspire Rhetoric?" Pp. 25–40 in *Persuasive Artistry*. Edited by Duane F. Watson. Sheffield: Sheffield Academic, 1991.

Lietzmann, D. Hans. *An Die Korinther I, II*. Tübingen: Mohr, 1969.

Lightfoot, J. B. *Notes on the Epistles of St. Paul*. Edited by J. R. Harmer. Repr. Grand Rapids: Baker, 1980; first published: London: Macmillan, 1895.

Lim, Timothy. "Not in Persuasive Words of Wisdom, but in the Demonstration of the Spirit and Power (1 Cor 2:4)." *Novum Testamentum* 29 (1987): 137–49.

Lindemann, Andreas. *Der erste Korintherbrief*. Handbuch zum Neuen Testament. Tübingen: Mohr Siebeck, 2000.

Litfin, Duane. *St. Paul's Theology of Proclamation: 1 Corinthians 1–4 and Greco-Roman Rhetoric*. Society for New Testament Studies Monograph Series 79. Cambridge: Cambridge University Press, 1994.

Lomas, Kathryn. *Roman Italy, 338 BC-AD 200: A Sourcebook*. Psychology Press, 1996.

Long, A. A. "Carneades and the Stoic Telos." *Phronesis* 12 (1967): 59–90.

"Roman Philosophy." Pp. 184–210 in *The Cambridge Companion to Greek and Roman Philosophy*. Edited by David N. Sedley. Cambridge: Cambridge University Press, 2003.

"Soul and Body in Stoicism." *Phronesis* 27 (1982): 34–57.

Long A. A. and D. N. Sedley. *The Hellenistic Philosophers*. 2 vols. London: Cambridge University Press, 1987.

Longenecker, Bruce. "Exposing the Economic Middle: A Revised Economy Scale for the Study of Early Christianity." *Journal for the Study of the New Testament* 31 (2009): 243–78.

Remember the Poor: Paul, Poverty, and the Greco-Roman World. Grand Rapids: Eerdmans, 2010.

Lütgert, W. *Freiheitspredigt und Schwarmgeister in Korinth*. Göttingen: C. Bertelsman, 1908.

Lyons, George. *Pauline Autobiography*. Society of Biblical Literature Dissertation Series 73. Atlanta, Ga.: Scholars, 1985.

Macdonald, Margaret Y. and Janet H. Tulloch. *A Woman's Place: House Churches in Earliest Christianity*. Minneapolis: Fortress, 2006.

Malherbe, Abraham J. "Determinism and Free Will in Paul: The Argument of 1 Cor 8 and 9." Pp. 231–55 in *Paul in His Hellenistic Context*. Edited by Troels Engberg-Pedersen. London: T & T Clark, 1995; London: Continuum, 2004.

"'Gentle as a Nurse': The Cynic Background to 1 Thess II." *Novum Testamentum* 12 (1970): 203–17.

"Graeco-Roman Religion and Philosophy and the New Testament." Pp. 3–26 in *The New Testament and Its Modern Interpreters*. Edited by Eldon J. Epp and George W. McRae. Philadelphia: Fortress, 1989.

"Hellenistic Moralists and the New Testament." *ANRW* 2.26: 267–333. Part 2, *Principat*, 33.1. Edited by H. Temporini and W. Haase. New York: de Gruyter, 1989.

Paul and the Popular Philosophers. Minneapolis: Fortress, 1989.

Social Aspects of Early Christianity. Philadelphia: Fortress, 1983.

Malherbe, Abraham J., ed. *The Cynic Epistles: A Study Edition*. Missoula, Mont.: Scholars, 1977.

Marrou, Henri. *A History of Education in Antiquity*. New York: The New American Library, 1956.

Marshall, Peter. *Enmity in Corinth: Social Conventions in Paul's Relations with the Corinthians*. Wissenschaftliche Untersuchungen zum Neuen Testament 2:23. Tübingen: Mohr Siebeck, 1987.

Martin, Dale B. *Corinthian Body*. New Haven: Yale University Press, 1995.

Slavery as Salvation: The Metaphor of Slavery in Pauline Christainity. New Haven: Yale University, 1990.

Mason, H. J. *Greek Terms for Roman Institutions: A Lexicon and Analysis*. Toronto: Hakkert, 1974.

McLean, Bradley Hudson. *An Introduction to Greek Epigraphy of the Hellenistic and Roman Periods from Alexander the Great down to the Reign of Constantine (323 BC-AD 337)*. Ann Arbor: University of Michigan, 2002.

Meeks, Wayne. *The First Urban Christians*. New Haven: Yale University Press, 1983.

Meggitt, Justin. *Paul and Poverty*. Studies of the New Testament and its World. Edinburgh: T&T Clark, 1998.

Mihaila, Corin. *The Paul-Apollos Relationship and Paul's Stance toward Greco-Roman Rhetoric*. Library of New Testament Studies 402. New York: T & T Clark, 2009.

Millis, Benjamin. "The Social and Ethnic Origins of the Colonists in Early Roman Corinth." Pp. 13–36 in *Corinth in Context: Comparative Studies on Religion and Society*. Edited by Friesen, Steven J. and Daniel N. Schowalter, and James C. Walters. Leiden: Brill, 2010.

Mitchell, Alan. "Rich and Poor in the Courts of Corinth: Litigiousness and Status in 1 Cor 6:1–11." *New Testament Studies* 39 (1993): 562–86.

Mitchell, Margaret. "Concerning peri de in 1 Corinthians." *Novum Testamentum* 31 (1989): 229–56.

Paul and the Rhetoric of Reconciliation. Louisville, Ky.: Westminster John Knox, 1993.

Moffatt, J. *The First Epistle of Paul to the Corinthians*. London: Hodder & Stoughton, 1938.

Morgan, Teresa. *Literate Education in the Hellenistic and Roman World*. Cambridge: Cambridge University Press, 1999.

Morris, Leon. *The First Epistle of Paul to the Corinthians*. Tyndale New Testament Commentaries. London: Tyndale, 1958.

Mosse, Claude. *Athens in Decline, 404–86 BC*. Boston: Routledge, 1973.

Moule, C. F. D. *An Idiom Book of New Testament Greek*. Cambridge: Cambridge University Press, 1959.

Munck, Johannes. "Menigheden uden Partier." *Dansk Teologisk Tidsskrift* 15 (1952): 215–233. ET, "The Church without Factions: Studies in 1 Corinthians 1–4." Pp. 135–67 in *Paul and the Salvation of Mankind*. London: SCM, 1959.

Paulus und die Heilsgeschichte. Copenhagen: E. Muncksgard, 1954. ET, *Paul and the Salvation of Mankind*. London: SCM, 1959.

Murphy-O'Connor, Jerome. "Corinthian Slogans in 1 Cor. 6:12–20." *Catholic Biblical Quarterly* 40 (1978): 391–96.

"Food and Spiritual Gifts in 1 Cor. 8:8." *Catholic Biblical Quarterly* 41 (1979): 292–98.

Paul: A Critical Life. Oxford: Oxford University Press, 1996.

Paul: His Story. Oxford: Oxford University Press, 2004.

St. Paul's Corinth: Texts and Archaeology. Collegeville, Minn.: Liturgical, 2002.

Nanos, Mark D. *The Irony of Galatians: Paul's Letter in First-Century Context*. Augsburg: Fortress, 2002.

Nguyen, V. H. T. *Christian Identity in Corinth: A Comparative Study of 2 Corinthians, Epictetus, and Valerius Maximus*. Tübingen: Mohr Siebeck, 2008.

Oakes, Peter. "Constructing Poverty Scales for Graeco-Roman Society: A Response to Steven Friesen's 'Poverty in Pauline Studies.'" *Journal for the Study of the New Testament* 26 (2004): 367–71.

Reading Romans in Pompeii. Minneapolis: Fortress; London: SPCK, 2009.

Økland, Jorunn. "Ceres, Κορή, and Cultural Complexity: Divine Personality Definitions and Human Worshippers in Roman Corinth." Pp. 199–229 in *Corinth in Context: Comparative Studies on Religion and Society*. Novum Testamentum Supplements 134. Edited by Friesen, Steven J. and Daniel N. Schowalter, and James C. Walters. Leiden: Brill, 2010.

Omanson, Roger L. "Acknowledging Paul's Quotations." *Bible Translator* 43 (1992): 201–13.

Osborne, M. J. and S. G. Byrne. *The Foreign Residents of Athens*. Paris: Peeters, 1996.

Osiek, Carolyn and David Balch. *Families in the New Testament World: Households and House Churches*. Louisville, Ky.: Westminster John Knox, 1997.

Paige, Terrence. "Stoicism, Eleutheria, and Community at Corinth." Pp. 180–93 in *Worship, Theology and Ministry in the Early Church*. Edited by Michael J. Wilkins and Terrence Paige. Sheffield: JSOT, 1992.

Parkin, Tim H. *Old Age in the Roman World: A Cultural and Social History*. Baltimore: Johns Hopkins University Press, 2002.

Pascuzzi, Maria. *Ethics, Ecclesiology, and Church Discipline*. Rome: Editrice Pontificia Universita Gregoriana, 1997.

Pearson, B. A. "Hellenistic-Jewish Wisdom Speculation and Paul." Pp. 43–66 in *Aspects of Wisdom in Judaism and Early Christianity*. Edited by Robert L. Wilken. Notre Dame, Ind.: Notre Dame University Press, 1975.

Pneumatikos-Psychikos Terminology in 1 Corinthians. Missoula: Society of Biblical Literature for the Nag Hammadi Seminar, 1973.

Pogoloff, Stephen M. *Logos and Sophia: The Rhetorical Situation of 1 Corinthians*. Society of Biblical Literature Dissertation Series 134. Atlanta: Scholars, 1992.

Porter, Stanley E. "Paul of Tarsus and His Letters." Pp. 533–86 in *Handbook of Classical Rhetoric*. Edited by Stanley Porter. Leiden: Brill, 2001.

Pratt, Norman T. *Seneca's Dramas*. Chapel Hill, N.C.: University of North Carolina Press, 1982.

Reichel, Georg. *Quaestiones Progymnasmaticae*. Ph.D. diss., University of Leipzig, 1909.

Reinmuth, O. W. "The Ephebate and Citizenship in Attica." *Transactions and Proceedings of the American Philological Association* 79 (1948): 211–31.

Rist, J. M. "Seneca and Stoic Orthodoxy." *ANRW* 2.36: 1993–2012. Part 2, Principat, 33.1. Edited by H. Temporini and W. Haase. New York: de Gruyter, 1989.

Robertson, Archibald and Alfred Plummer. *A Critical and Exegetical Commentary on the First Epistle of St. Paul to the Corinthians*. International Critical Commentary. Edinburgh: T & T Clark, 1914.

Robinson, James M. "Kerygma and History in the New Testament." Pp. 20–70 in *Trajectories through Early Christianity*. Edited by Helmut Koester; Philadelphia: Fortress, 1971.

Rowe, Galen. "Style." Pp. 121–58 in *Handbook of Classical Rhetoric*. Edited by Stanley E. Porter. Leiden: Brill, 2001.

Runia, David. *Philo of Alexandria and the Timaeus of Plato*. Leiden: Brill, 1986.

Ruschenbusch, E. "Doch noch einmal die Bürgerzahl Athens im 4.Jh.v.Chr." *Zeitschrift für Papyrologie und Epigraphik* 72 (1988): 139–140.

Russell, J. C. *Late Ancient and Medieval Population*. American Philosophical Society, 1958.

Salmon, E. T. *Roman Colonization under the Republic*. Ithaca, N.Y.: Cornell University Press, 1970.

Sampley, J. Paul. "The First Letter to the Corinthians." *New Interpreter's Bible* 10 (2002): 771–1003.

Sampley, J. Paul and Peter Lamp. *Paul and Rhetoric*. New York: T & T Clark, 2010.

Sandbach, F. H. *Stoics*. New York: Norton, 1975.

Sandmel, Samuel. "Parallelomania." *Journal of Biblical Literature* 81 (1962): 1–13.

Scheidel, Walter. *Debating Roman Demography*. Leiden: Brill, 2001.

"Roman Age Structure: Evidence and Models." *Journal of Roman Studies* 91 (2001): 1–26.

"Stratification, Deprivation and Quality of Life." Pp. 40–59 in *Poverty in the Roman World*. Edited by M. Atkins and R. Osborne. Cambridge: Cambridge University Press, 2006.

Schenkeveld, Dirk M. "Philosophical Prose." Pp. 195–264 in *Handbook of Classical Rhetoric*. Edited by Stanley E. Porter. Leiden: Brill, 2001.

Schlier, Heinrich. "Kerygma und Sophia: zur neutestamentlichen Grundlegung des Dogmas." Pp. 206–32 in *Die Zeit der Kirche: Exegetische Aufsätze und Vorträge*. Freiburg: Herder, 1956.

Schmithals, Walter. *Die Gnosis in Korinth: eine Untersuchung zu den Korintherbriefen*. Göttingen: Vandenhoeck & Ruprecht, 1969. ET, *Gnosticism in Corinth: An Investigation of the Letters to the Corinthians*. Nashville: Abingdon, 1971.

"Die Korintherbrief als Briefsammlung." *Zeitschrift für die neutestamentliche Wissenschaft und die Kunde der älteren Kirche* 64 (1973): 263–88.

Schofield, Malcolm. *The Stoic Idea of the City*. Cambridge: Cambridge University Press, 1991.

Schowalter, Daniel N. "Seeking Shelter in Roman Corinth: Archaeology and The Placement of Paul's Communities." Pp. 327–42 in *Corinth in Context: Comparative Studies on Religion and Society*. Novum Testamentum Supplements 134. Edited by Friesen, Steven J. and Daniel N. Schowalter, and James C. Walters. Leiden; Boston: Brill, 2010.

Schrage, Wolfgang. *Der erste Brief an die Korinther*. 4 vols. Evangelisch-katholischer Kommentar zum Neuen Testament 7. Zürich; Düsseldorf: Benziger Verlag, 1991–2001.

Sedley, David. "Introduction." Pp. 1–19 in *The Cambridge Companion to Greek and Roman Philosophy*. Cambridge: Cambridge University Press, 2003.

"The School, from Zeno to Arius Didymus." Pp. 7–32 in *Cambridge Companion to the Stoics*. Cambridge: Cambridge University Press, 2002.

Senft, C. *La Première épître de Saint Paul aux Corinthiens*. Commentaire du Nouveau Testament. 2d ed. Geneva: Labor et Fides, 1990.

Sevenster, J. N. *Paul and Seneca*. Leiden: Brill, 1961.

de Silva, D. A. "Paul and the Stoa: A Comparison." *Journal of the Evangelical Theological Society* 38 (1995): 549–64.

Smith, J. E. "1 Corinthians 6:13–14: Isolating Slogans, Rethinking Soma, 'Correcting' Translations." Paper presented at the annual meeting of the Southwest Commission of Religious Studies. Irving, Tx. March 10, 2012.

"Slogans in 1 Corinthians." *Bibliotheca Sacra* 167 (2010): 68–88.

"The Roots of a 'Libertine' Slogan in 1 Corinthians 6:18." *Journal of Theological Studies* 59 (2008): 63–95.

Smyth, H. W. *Greek Grammar*. Cambridge, Mass.: Harvard University Press, 1956.

von Soden, H. "Sakrament und Ethik bei Paulus: Zur Frage der literarischen und theologischen Einheitlichkeit von 1 Kor 8–10." Pp. 239–75 in volume 1 of *Urchristentum und Geschichte: Gesammelte Aufsatze und Vortrage*. Tübingen: Mohr, 1951.

Spengel, L. *Rhetores Graeci*. Leipzig: Teubner, 1854; repr. 1966.

Spentzou, Efrossini. "Athens." Pp. 111–113 in *Encyclopedia of Ancient Greece*. Edited by Nigel Wilson. New York: Routledge, 2006.

Spörlein, B. *Die Leugnung der Auferstehung: Eine historisch-kritische Untersuchung zu 1 Kor 15*. Regensburg: Putstet, 1971.

Stanton, G. R. "Sophists and Philosophers: Problems of Classification." *American Journal of Philology* 94 (1975): 350–64.

Stark, Rodney. "Christianizing the Urban Empire: An Analysis Based on 22 Greco-Roman Cities." *Sociological Analysis* 52 (1991): 77–88.

Stowers, Stanley. "A 'Debate' over Freedom: I Corinthians 6:12–20." Pp. 59–71 in *Christian Teaching: Studies in Honor of Lemoine G. Lewis*. Edited by Everett Ferguson. Abilene, Tx.: Abilene Christian University, 1981.

"Does Pauline Christianity Resemble a Hellenistic Philosophy?" Pp. 81–102 in *Paul beyond the Judaism-Hellenism Divide*. Edited by Troels Engberg-Pedersen. Louisville: Westminster John Knox, 2001.

"Romans 7:7–25 as a Speech-in-Character (προσοποιία)." Pp. 180–202 in *Paul in His Hellenistic Context*. Edited by Troels Engberg-Pedersen. London: T & T Clark, 1995; London: Continuum, 2004.

Strecker, Georg and Udo Schnelle. *Neuer Wettstein: Texte zum Neuen Testament aus Griechentum und Hellenismus. Bd. 2. Texte zur Briefliteratur und zur Johannesapokalypse*. Berlin: Walter de Gruyter, 1996.

Sumney, Jerry L. *Identifying Paul's Opponents: Questions of Method in 2 Corinthians*. Sheffield, JSOT: 1990.

"Studying Paul's Opponents: Advances and Challenges." Pp. 40–58 in *Paul and His Opponents*. Edited by Stanley E. Porter. Leiden: Brill, 2005.

Sviatoslav, Dmitriev. *The Greek Slogan of Freedom and Early Roman Politics in Greece*. Oxford: Oxford University Press, 2011.

Taiwo, Moses. *Paul's Rhetoric in 1 Corinthians 10:29b-30*. Saarbrücken, Müller: 2008.

Talbert, Charles. *Reading Corinthians: A Literary and Theological Commentary*. Macon, Ga.: Smyth & Helwys, 2002.

Terrell, Patricia Elyse. *Paul's Parallels: An Echoes Synopsis*. New York: Continuum, 2009.

Theissen, Gerd. "Die Starken und Schwachen in Korinth: Soziologische Analyse eines theologischen Streits." *Evangelische Theologie* 35 (1975): 155–72.

"Social Conflicts in the Corinthian Correspondence: Further Remarks on J. J. Meggitt, Paul, Poverty and Survival." *Journal for the Study of the New Testament* (2003): 371–91.

"Social Integration and Sacramental Activity: An Analysis of 1 Cor. 11:17–34." Pp. 145–74 in *The Social Setting of Pauline Christianity*. Philadelphia: Fortress, 1982.

"Soziale Schichtung in der Korinthische Gemeinde: Ein Beitrag zur Soziologie des hellenistischen Urchristentums." *Zeitschrift für die neutestamentliche Wissenschaft und die Kunde der älteren Kirche* 65 (1974): 232–72.

The Social Setting of Pauline Christianity. Philadelphia: Fortress, 1982.

"The Social Structure of Pauline Communities: Some Critical Remarks on J. J. Meggitt *Paul, Poverty, and Survival*." *Journal for the Study of the New Testament* (2001): 65–84.

Thiselton, Anthony C. "Realized Eschatology at Corinth." *New Testament Studies* 24 (1978): 510–26.

The First Epistle to the Corinthians. New International Greek Testament Commentary 7. Grand Rapids: Eerdmans, 2000.

Thomas, Christine M. "Greek Heritage in Roman Corinth and Ephesos: Hybrid Identities and Strategies of Display in the Material Record of Traditional Mediterranean Religions." Pp. 117–49 in *Corinth in Context: Comparative Studies on Religion and Society*. Novum Testamentum Supplements 134.

Edited by Friesen, Steven J. and Daniel N. Schowalter, and James C. Walters. Leiden: Brill, 2010.

Thorsteinsson, Runar M. "Stoicism as a Key to Pauline Ethics in Romans." Pp. 15–38 in *Stoicism in Early Christianity*. Edited by Tuomas Rasimus, Troels Engberg-Pedersen, and Ismo Dunderberg. Peabody, Mass.: Hendrickson, 2010.

Thrall, M. E. *The First and Second Letters of Paul to the Corinthians*. Cambridge: Cambridge University Press, 1965.

Tod, Marcus N. "Sidelights on Greek Philosophers." *The Journal of Hellenic Studies* 77 (1957): 132–41.

Tomlin, Graham. "Christians and Epicureans in 1 Corinthians." *Journal for the Study of the New Testament* 68 (1997): 51–72.

Townsend, John T. "Ancient Education in the Time of the Early Roman Empire." Pp. 139–63 in *The Catacombs and the Colosseum*. Edited by J. Benko and S. O'Rourke. Valley Forge: Judson Press, 1971.

Tuckett, C. M. "The Corinthians Who Say 'There Is No Resurrection of the Dead' (1 Cor 15,12)." Pp. 247–75 in *The Corinthian Correspondence*. Edited by R. Bieringer. Bibliotheca ephemeridum theologicarum lovaniensium 125. Leuven: Leuven University Press, 1996.

Tzachou-Alexandri, O. "The Gymnasium: An Institution for Athletics and Education." Pp. 21–40 in *Mind and Body*. Athens: Greek Ministry of Culture, 1989.

Van Unnik, W. C. "The Meaning of 1 Corinthians 12:31." *Novum Testamentum* 35 (1993): 142–59.

de Vos, Craig Steven. *Church and Community Conflicts: The Relationships of the Thessalonian, Corinthian, and Philippian Churches with Their Wider Civic Communities*. Society of Biblical Literature Dissertation Series 168. Atlanta, Ga.: Scholars, 1999.

Walters, J. "Civic Identity in Roman Corinth and Its Impact on Early Christians." Pp. 397–417 in *Urban Religion in Roman Corinth: Interdisciplinary Approaches*. Edited by Daniel N. Schowalter and Steven J. Friesen. Harvard Theological Studies 53. Cambridge: Harvard Theological Studies, 2005.

Ward, R. B. "Musonius and Paul on Marriage." *New Testament Studies* 36 (1990): 281–9.

Weiss, Alexander. "Keine Quästoren in Korinth: zu Goodrichs (und Theissens) These über das Amt des Erastos (Röm 16.23)." *New Testament Studies* 56 (2010): 576–81.

Weiss, Johannes. *Der erste Korintherbrief*. Göttingen: Vandenhoeck & Ruprecht, 1910.

The History of Primitive Christianity. New York: K. W. Wilson-Enckson, 1937.

Welborn, L. L. *End to Enmity: Paul and the 'Wrongdoer' of 2 Corinthians*. Berlin: de Gruyter, 2011.

Politics and Rhetoric in the Corinthian Epistles. Macon, Ga.: Mercer University Press, 1997.

West, Allen. Corinth, Vol. VIII, part II, *Latin Inscriptions*, 1896–1926. Cambridge, Mass.: Harvard University Press, 1931.

Whitehorne, J. "The Ephebate and the Gymnasial Class in Roman Egypt." Pp. 171–84 in *Status Declarations in Roman Egypt* 19. New Haven: The American Society, 1982.

Wickkiser, Bronwen L. "Asklepios in Greek and Roman Corinth." Pp. 37–66 in *Corinth in Context: Comparative Studies on Religion and Society*. Novum Testamentum Supplements 134. Edited by Friesen, Steven J. and Daniel N. Schowalter, and James C. Walters. Leiden: Brill, 2010.

Willet, Rinse. "Whirlwind of Numbers: Demographic Experiments for Roman Corinth." *Ancient Society* 42 (2012): 127–58.

Willis, Wendel. "Corinthusne deletus est?" *Biblische Zeitschrift* 35 (1991): 233–41.

Winter, Bruce. *After Paul Left Corinth: The Influence of Secular Ethics and Social Change*. Grand Rapids: Eerdmans, 2001.

"Civil Litigation in Secular Corinth and the Church: the Forensic Background to 1 Cor 6:1–8." *New Testament Studies* 37 (1991): 559–72.

Philo and Paul among the Sophists: A Hellenistic Jewish and a Christian Response. Ph.D. diss., Macquarie University, 1988. Published in Cambridge: Cambridge University Press, 1997; 2d ed.; Grand Rapids: Eerdmans, 2002.

"Rhetoric." Pp. 820–22 in *The Dictionary of Paul and His Letters*. Edited by Gerald F. Hawthorne and Ralph P. Martin. Downers Grove: InterVarsity, 1993.

Wiseman, James. "Corinth and Rome I: 228 BC-AD 267." *ANRW* 7.1: 438–548. Part 2, Principat, 33.1. Edited by H. Temporini and W. Haase. New York: de Gruyter, 1989.

"Excavations at Corinth, The Gymnasium Area, 1965." *Hesperia* 36 (1967): 13–41.

"Excavations at Corinth, The Gymnasium Area, 1966." *Hesperia* 36 (1967): 402–28.

"Excavations at Corinth, The Gymnasium Area, 1967–1968." *Hesperia* 38 (1969): 64–106.

"The Gymnasium Area at Corinth, 1969–1970." *Hesperia* 41 (1972): 1–42.

Witherington, Ben. *Conflict and Community in Corinth: A Socio-Rhetorical Commentary on 1 and 2 Corinthians*. Grand Rapids: Eerdmans, 1995.

Jesus von Nazareth: Mythus oder Geschichte? Tübingen: J. C. B. Mohr, 1910.

de Witt, Norman Wentworth. *St. Paul and Epicurus*. Minneapolis: University of Minneapolis Press, 1954.

Wolff, Christian. *Der erste Brief des Paulus an die Korinther*. Leipzig: Evangelische Verlagsanstalt, 1996.

Woodhouse, S. C. *English-Greek Dictionary: A Vocabulary of the Attic Language*. London; New York: Routledge, 1998.

Yamauchi, Edwin M. *Pre-Christian Gnosticism*. Grand Rapids; London: Eerdmans, 1973.

"Pre-Christian Gnosticism Reconsidered a Decade Later." Pp. 187–249 in *Pre-Christian Gnosticism: A Survey of the Proposed Evidences*. Grand Rapids, Mich.: Baker Book House, 1983.

Yeo, Khiok-Khing. *Rhetorical Interaction in 1 Corinthians 8–10*. Biblical Interpretation Monograph Series 9. Leiden: Brill, 1995.

INDEX OF PASSAGES

Old Testament
1 Kings
  2.10, 162
Deuteronomy
  6.4, 89
  32.39, 89
Exodus
  21.10, 207
Genesis
  2.18, 87
Isaiah
  22.13, 195
  44.6, 89
Jeremiah
  9.24, 162
Job
  5.13, 35, 95, 207
Psalms
  93
    11, 35
  93.11, 95, 207

New Testament
1 Corinthians, 84–86
  1.10–12, 1, 55, 201, 203
  1.10–17, 184
  1.11, 46, 71, 81, 84, 118
  1.12, 90, 94, 162
  1.14, 149
  1.16, 109, 149
  1.16–17, 109
  1.17, 9, 10, 30, 41, 42, 43, 48, 51, 52, 59, 62, 65, 66, 96, 164, 220, 227
  1.17–2.16, 40
  1.17–2.5, 12, 47, 55
  1.17–25, 14
  1.17–31, 10
  1.18, 41, 164
  1.18–25, 12
  1.19, 35, 44, 160
  1.2, 157
  1.20, 35, 44, 47, 141, 160, 215
  1.22, 33, 44, 125, 160, 213
  1.25, 166
  1.25–27, 14
  1.26, 47, 59, 73, 76, 106, 160, 161, 162, 198
  1.27, 35, 44, 160, 166
  1.5, 96, 161, 164, 210
  2.1, 10, 30, 42, 43, 51, 62, 65, 96, 164, 220
  2.1–5, 10, 12, 44, 48, 59, 62, 68, 73, 78, 162, 225, 226, 228
  2.1–10, 226
  2.3, 14
  2.3–5, 45, 52, 226
  2.4, 10, 17, 30, 42, 43, 51, 62, 65, 96, 164, 220
  2.4–5, 44, 164
  2.5, 13, 10
  2.6, 162, 198
  2.6–16, 10, 12, 17, 77, 82, 94, 96–97, 102, 168
  2.10, 171
  2.12, 171
  2.13, 10, 30, 42, 51, 62, 65, 96, 164, 220
  2.13–15, 169
  2.15, 82, 91, 92, 93, 94, 100, 170
  2.16, 83, 84, 171
  2.17, 17
  3.1–3, 46, 77, 96–97, 168
  3.1–4, 141
  3.3, 46, 76
  3.4, 72, 90, 94
  3.4–4.6, 213
  3.5–4.5, 202
  3.5–9, 141
  3.6–7, 202
  3.7, 66
  3.8, 202
  3.9, 202
  3.10–11, 168

1 Corinthians (cont.)
3.16, 88, 189
3.18, 35, 72, 95, 98, 169
3.19, 10, 35, 44, 95, 160, 207
3.19–23, 162
3.20, 35, 44, 95, 160, 207
3.21–22, 162, 198
4, 228
4.1–5, 72
4.5, 46, 226
4.6, 141, 202
4.8, 59, 77, 84, 98, 100, 161, 193, 210
4.8–10, 47, 73, 106, 162, 198
4.10, 14, 76, 98
4.18, 158
4.19, 164
4.20, 164
4.21, 141
5, 197
5.1, 71, 84
5.1–13, 57, 102, 174–177, 188–189, 213
5.6, 88
5.7–8, 84
5.12–13, 83
5.13, 84
5–6, 172
6.1–11, 57, 125, 158, 196–198, 199
6.2, 88
6.3, 88
6.5, 35, 44, 95, 160, 197, 206, 207, 209
6.7, 197, 200, 206, 209
6.9, 88, 197
6.12, 72, 83–84, 91, 92, 93, 96, 100, 172, 178, 182, 210, 220
6.12–13, 90
6.12–18, 84
6.12–20, 57, 102, 125, 174–177, 188–189, 197, 199
6.12a, 86, 102, 175, 177, 188, 198, 214, 215, 218
6.12b, 83, 176, 188, 206, 209
6.13, 91, 92, 93, 100, 102, 172, 188, 199, 220
6.13a, 86, 188, 189, 190
6.14, 192
6.15, 88
6.16, 88
6.18, 91, 92, 93, 100, 188, 199, 220
6.18a, 102
6.18b, 85, 188, 206, 209
6.18b–c, 200
6.19, 84, 88, 189
6.19c, 188, 206, 209
6.23a, 199
7, 188, 199, 214
7.1, 71, 72, 81, 86, 88, 91, 93, 177, 178, 220
7.2, 87
7.4, 172, 178, 188, 200, 206, 209
7.6, 87
7.7, 87
7.7–8, 178
7.8, 86
7.1–40, 57, 177–178, 190
7.13–14, 85
7.18, 124
7.18–24, 141
7.19, 181, 206
7.23, 189
7.26, 86
7.28–35, 178
7.34, 84
7.35, 210
7.40, 83
8.1, 72, 82, 87, 88, 89, 91, 92, 93, 95, 100, 164, 165, 166, 167, 169, 179, 220
8.1–11.1, 178–182
8.1–13, 57, 83, 165, 189
8.2, 72, 88, 95, 98, 169
8.3–4, 72
8.4, 82, 89, 90, 91, 92, 93, 100, 179, 181, 199, 214, 220
8.6, 180, 206
8.7, 89, 125, 165
8.7–12, 14
8.8, 90, 91, 92, 93, 100, 102, 179, 180, 189, 199, 220
8.9, 96, 172, 179
8.9–13, 165
8.10, 165
8.10–11, 97, 166
8.11, 90, 165, 181
8.12–13, 90
8–10, 165, 188, 198
9, 172, 226
9.1–27, 57, 181–182
9.3, 72, 82, 181
9.13, 88
9.15–23, 56
9.19–23, 209
9.22, 14
9.24, 88
9.24–27, 141
9.25, 167
9.26, 189
9.27, 84

10, 84, 213
10.1–11.1, 57, 189–190
10.1, 164
10.2, 88
10.10, 62
10.13, 66
10.14, 90
10.14–22, 200
10.15, 161
10.17, 185
10.19–21, 90
10.20, 108, 149
10.23, 72, 90, 91, 92, 210
10.23a, 167, 179, 198, 199, 214, 215, 218
10.23b, 181, 206, 209
10.24, 181
10.26, 84
10.33, 181, 210
11.1, 82, 181
11.2–16, 57, 102, 172, 182, 188, 190, 199
11.10, 182
11.14, 192, 200, 206, 207
11.17–34, 56, 57, 73, 102, 107, 158, 172, 182–184, 188, 190, 199, 214
11.18, 71, 84, 108, 149, 182
11.21, 182
11.29–32, 190
12, 172
12.1, 88, 164
12.1–3, 184
12.2, 125, 213
12.7, 184, 200, 210
12.8, 88, 95, 96, 164
12.12–26, 185
12.12–30, 188, 206
12.21, 184, 200
12.22, 14, 56
12–14, 184–185, 199, 200
13.2, 88, 95
13.5, 181
13.8, 88, 95
13.10–11, 97, 168
14, 172
14.12, 83, 97
14.20, 97, 168
14.23, 108, 149
14.27–33, 184
14.34–36, 182, 188, 190, 199
14.37, 72, 83, 97, 98
15.12, 72, 82, 84, 90, 91, 92, 93, 100, 158, 192, 195, 214, 215, 220
15.12–58, 84, 188, 192–196, 199
15.1–58, 57
15.19, 195, 215
15.27, 84
15.28, 196
15.29, 195, 206, 209
15.32, 84, 195
15.33, 84
15.35, 195
15.36–54, 195
15.44, 97
15.44–47, 171
15.46, 97
16.9, 149
16.12, 149, 202, 213
16.15, 109
16.15–17, 109
16.17, 71, 119, 149
16.19, 109
1 Thessalonians
1.5, 45, 52, 210, 220, 226
2.1–12, 45, 52, 210
5.15, 207
5.23, 84
2 Corinthians
1.12, 210
2.14, 210
2.17, 210
2.1–7, 72
3.17, 210
4.6, 210
5.10, 210
6.6, 210
6.10, 210
6.12, 72
6.16, 210
6.17, 87
7.1, 84
7.2, 72
7.8–11, 72
8.7, 210
8.9, 210
8.10, 210
8.14, 106
9.11, 210
10.5, 210
10.10, 47, 202, 204
11.6, 210
12.1, 210
2 Timothy
2.8, 193
4.20, 118
Acts
17.16–33, 135
18.2, 149
18.2–3, 109
18.7, 149

Acts (cont.)
18.8, 109, 149
18.17, 149
18.18–19, 109
18.24, 47, 59, 62, 202, 204
19.22, 118
9.30, 205
Colossians
3.11, 196, 207
4.15, 149
Ephesians
1.23, 196, 207
2.19–22, 210
4.1–6, 184
5.28, 178, 206
Galatians
1.10, 45, 52, 210
2.14–16, 192
4.7–9, 192
6.1, 96
6.15, 181
Hebrews
5.11–14, 168
Jude
19, 97
Luke
6.20–21, 84
11.19, 83
Mark
3.28–29, 188
14.36, 83
Matthew
5.3–6, 84
5.38–42, 206
Philemon
2, 149
Philippians
2.1–4, 184
4.2–3, 184
Romans
2.14–15, 192
2.27, 192
3.28, 86, 188
5.1–6, 184
6.16, 88
8.27, 171
11.21, 192
11.24, 192
11.33, 210
12.17–21, 207
15.1–6, 207
16.1, 108
16.2, 108
16.5, 109, 149
16.21–24, 149
16.22, 119
16.23, 108, 109, 110, 118, 149

Apocrypha
1 Maccabees
1.15, 141

Apostolic Fathers
1 Clement
3.1, 146

Ancient Authors
Aelius Aristides
Or. 46.22–23, 106
Appian
Hist. rom. 2.1, 126
Punica 136, 125
Apuleius
Metam. 10.18, 126
Aristotle
An post. 2.99b–100b, 163
Eth. nic. 5.11.7–8, 198
Eth. nic. 6.7.3, 5, 163
Eth. nic. 7.7.8, 168
Pol. 1253a14, 40
Pol. 1317.11, 174
Rhet. 1.7.22, 198
Top. 6.9, 173
Arius Didymus
5b9, 178
5d, 167
10b, 178
11a, 188
11d, 197
11e, 188
11m, 179, 183
11s, 216
Augustine
Civ. 19, 227
Civ. 6.10, 179
Aulus Gellius
Noct. att. 16.13, 126
Cicero
De or. 1.47, 24
De or. 1.52, 134
De or. 2.21, 137, 138
De or. 3.5–58, 21
De or. 3.39, 134
De or. 3.49, 22
De or. 3.65–66, 23
De or. 3.72, 21
Fam. 15.16.3, 22
Fam. 17.3, 22

Fin. 1.6, 155
Fin. 3.3, 23
Fin. 3.62–68, 177
Fin. 3.75, 160, 161
Fin. 4.4, 23
Fin. 4.78, 173
Inv. 1.1, 22
Inv. 1.1–3, 34
Inv. 1.5, 22
Inv. 2.178, 22
Luc. 145, 215
Luc. 26, 44
Mur. 29–31, 160
Nat. d. 1.6, 155
Nat. d. 1.123, 181
Nat. d. 2.23–25, 28–30, 160
Nat. d. 2.88, 155
Off. 1.107–17, 160
Off. 1.153, 159
Off. 1.159, 35
Off. 2.5, 34
Off. 2.60, 35
Off. 3.29–93, 35
Off. 3.7, 35
Off. 3.72, 33
Off. 3.96, 33
Parod. 5.2, 172
Tusc. 1.1, 34
Tusc. 2.61, 155
Tusc. 4.15, 166
Tusc. 4.26, 166
Tusc. 4.3, 34
Tusc. 5.8, 34

Clement of Alexandria
Strom. 5.9.59.2, 215

Cynic Epistles
Anacharsis, *Epistle 6*, 2, 214
Crates, *Epistle 3*, 16–17, 214
Crates, *Epistle 7*, 8, 214
Crates, *Epistle 12*, 20–21, 214
Crates, *Epistle 13*, 10–11, 216
Crates, *Epistle 16*, 216
Crates, *Epistle 21*, 24–26, 216
Crates, *Epistle 27*, 175, 214
Crates, *Epistle 28*, 191
Crates, *Epistle 29*, 10–11, 214
Crates, *Epistle 29*, 14–17, 191
Crates, *Epistle 32*, 9–11, 191
Crates, *Epistle 35*, 19–21, 214
Diogenes, *Epistle 3*, 191
Diogenes, *Epistle 7*, 5–7, 214
Diogenes, *Epistle 9*, 9–11, 216
Diogenes, *Epistle 10*, 2–7, 175, 214
Diogenes, *Epistle 10*, 25, 214
Diogenes, *Epistle 10*, 28–30, 214
Diogenes, *Epistle 14*, 25–27, 194
Diogenes, *Epistle 25*, 17–20, 214
Diogenes, *Epistle 29*, 14–17, 214
Diogenes, *Epistle 30*, 216
Diogenes, *Epistle* 39, 1–6, 194
Diogenes, *Epistle 39*, 7–8, 214
Diogenes, *Epistle* 43, 191
Diogenes, *Epistle 44*, 9–10, 216
Heraclitus, *Epistle 9*, 10–14, 214
Heraclitus, *Epistle 9*, 20, 214
Heraclitus, *Epistle 9*, 28–30, 214
Socratics, *Epistle 22*, 105, 214
Socratics, *Epistle* 25, 194

Dio
Or. 7.123, 33
Or. 8.5–10, 106
Or. 10.32, 41
Or. 12.13, 20
Or. 13.11, 24
Or. 14.18, 175
Or. 14.4–8, 174
Or. 18.17, 20
Or. 22.4–5, 20
Or. 31.3, 24
Or. 31.8, 24
Or. 31.8–12, 24
Or. 32, 135
Or. 32.11.8, 42
Or. 32.18, 41, 45
Or. 32.2, 33
Or. 32.68, 24
Or. 33.14, 20
Or. 34.3, 24
Or. 37.8, 106
Or. 37.26, 129
Or. 4.32.2, 41
Or. 55.1–6, 46
Or. 61.21.1, 140
Or. 72.15, 33

Dio Cassius
43.50.3–5, 125

Diodorus
32.327.3, 125

Diogenes Laertius
1.121, 216
3.46, 115
6.10, 214
6.37–72, 214
6.71, 191
6.72, 175
6.103, 194
6.105, 174, 214

Diogenes Laertius (cont.)
7.175, 191, 196
7.32–33, 183
7.33, 177, 179
7.34, 215
7.36, 173
7.37, 174
7.44, 52, 79, 44
7.47, 164
7.48, 33
7.87, 178, 189
7.89, 160
7.104–5, 174
7.110–17, 177
7.119, 179
7.121–2, 172
7.121–6, 160
7.122, 162
7.123, 197
7.125, 175
7.131, 177
7.134, 164
7.135–6, 180
7.147, 180
7.160, 173
8.55, 46
9.63, 46
10.85, 45
7.124, 183
10.124–5, 181
Epictetus
Diatr. 1.1.13–18, 155
Diatr. 1.4.18–32, 169
Diatr. 1.4.27, 181, 187
Diatr. 1.4.6–9, 155
Diatr. 1.9.13, 181, 187
Diatr. 1.9.8–9, 183
Diatr. 1.12.9, 172
Diatr. 1.14.6–17, 186
Diatr. 1.16.9–14, 191, 192
Diatr. 1.17.28, 172
Diatr. 1.19.9, 189
Diatr. 1.21.1, 186
Diatr. 1.28.5, 167
Diatr. 1.29, 186
Diatr. 1.29.18, 186
Diatr. 1.29.5–29, 189
Diatr. 1.29.5–7, 186
Diatr. 1.29.9–10, 173, 176
Diatr. 2.1.23, 172
Diatr. 2.8.9–29, 186
Diatr. 2.13.13–16, 186
Diatr. 2.15.20, 166
Diatr. 2.16.26–39, 138
Diatr. 2.16.37, 172
Diatr. 2.16.39, 168
Diatr. 2.20.7, 197
Diatr. 2.22.19, 167
Diatr. 2.22.27, 167
Diatr. 2.23.46–7, 23
Diatr. 2.24.1–3, 23
Diatr. 2.24.20, 188
Diatr. 2.26.2, 167
Diatr. 3.1.34, 139, 146
Diatr. 3.7.34, 46
Diatr. 3.8.1–2, 187
Diatr. 3.8.2, 181, 187
Diatr. 3.16.15, 181
Diatr. 3.20.1, 189
Diatr. 3.22, 186
Diatr. 3.22.21, 186
Diatr. 3.22.21–44, 189
Diatr. 3.23, 23
Diatr. 3.24.53, 169
Diatr. 3.26.23, 24
Diatr. 4.1.1, 172
Diatr. 4.1.66–158, 189
Diatr. 4.12.8–9, 173
Diatr. 4.5.6, 177
Diatr. 4.6.23, 197
Diatr. 4.7.17, 189
Diatr. 4.7.17–32, 189
Diatr. 4.7.31–32, 186
Diatr. 4.7.9, 167
Ench. 1.1, 189
Ench. 1.5, 181, 187
Ench. 1.9, 189
Ench. 32.2, 181
Ench. 46.2, 169
Ench. 48.1, 183
Ench. 51, 169
fr. 26, 186
Florus
Epitome of Rom. Hist. 2.32, 126
Galen
De diff. puls. 3.641.15–642.7, 170
Heraclitus
fr. 1.8–9, 191
Hippocrates
Artic. 33.9, 168
Horace
Sat. 1.14.103–29, 21
Isocrates
Antid. 89, 23
Antid. 15.199–200, 22, 32
Nic. 5–9, 40
Jerome
Chron. 63, 140

John Chrysostom
- *Hom. 1 Cor.* 3.1, 91

Josephus
- *Ant.* 12.5.1, 141
- *Ant.* 18.11, 46
- *Apion* 2.13.137, 141
- *J.W.* 2.119, 46
- *Vit.* 1.10–12, 47
- *Vit.* 68, 106

LS
- 44C, 171
- 46E–F, 171
- 47C, 171
- 47F–I, 170
- 47M–Q, 170
- 54A, B, 171
- 58, 191
- 62K, 189
- 63, 191
- 65B, 166
- 65D, 166
- 67D, 178

Lucian
- *Bis acc.* 32, 22
- *Dem.* 48.6, 47
- *Eunuch.* 7, 25
- *Eunuch.* 13, 25, 44
- *Fug.* 10–11, 25
- *Fug.* 13, 25
- *Herm.* 14.7, 47
- *Herm.* 76–77, 215
- *Icar.* 29–30, 25
- *Iupp. conf.* 19, 25
- *Iupp. conf.* 27, 25
- *Iupp. conf.* 30, 25
- *Iupp. conf.* 32, 25
- *Men.* 4–5, 25
- *Par.* 31–37, 25
- *Par.* 43, 25
- *Par.* 56, 25
- *Peregr.* 15.17, 47
- *Symp.* 1, 47
- *Symp.* 47, 173
- *Vit. auct.* 20, 160

Lucretius
- *De Rer. Nat.* 1.635–44, 34
- *De Rer. Nat.* 5.7–21, 34

Macrobius
- *Sat.* 3.14, 134

Marcus Aurelius
- *Med.* 4.23, 180

Martial
- *Epigr.* 3.60, 182
- *Epigr.* 7.82, 141

Musonius Rufus
- *Diatr.* 3, 191
- *Diatr.* 3, 198
- *Diatr.* 4, 191
- *Diatr.* 5.26–37, 20
- *Diatr.* 6.7–10, 20
- *Diatr.* 12, 177
- *Diatr.* 13a, 177, 178
- *Diatr.* 17.14–16, 24
- *Diatr.* 14. *See*
- *fr.* 45, 183
- *Diatr.* 11, 183
- *Diatr.* 18–19, 187
- *Diatr.* 20, 187
- *Diatr.* 18b.8–10, 189
- *Diatr.* 7.33, 191
- *Diatr.* 21.1–7, 191
- *Diatr.* 10, 198

Ovid
- *Met.* 3.329, 202
- *Met.* 13.896–7, 203
- *Trist.* 2.63–64, 203

Parmenides
- *Nature* fr. 8.50, 41, 45

Pausanias
- *Descr.* 2.1.2, 125
- *Descr.* 2.2.2, 106

Philo
- *Agr.* 1.9, 168
- *Agr.* 9.6, 168
- *Cher.* 1.10, 41
- *Congr.* 1.79, 49
- *Contempl.* 4, 23
- *Dec.* 1.1, 42
- *Det.* 74, 23
- *Ebr.* 1.100, 42
- *Ebr.* 1.37, 42
- *Gig.* 1.48, 42
- *Her.* 246–7, 23
- *Imm.* 35–36, 171
- *Indestr.* 76–77, 187
- *Jos.* 20, 198
- *Jos.* 230, 20
- *Legat.* 281, 124
- *Migr.* 1.46, 168
- *Migr.* 1.201, 42
- *Mos.* 1.29, 283, 20
- *Mos.* 2.48, 66, 130, 140, 150, 20
- *Post.* 1.152, 168
- *Post.* 101, 41
- *Prob.* 59–60, 172
- *Q. G.* 3.33, 41
- *Sobr.* 1.9, 41, 168
- *Somn.* 2.10, 168

Philo (cont.)
Spec. Leg. 1.2, 141
Philodemus
Lib. 59.1–11, 167
Philostratus
Vit Apoll. 4.42, 140
Pindar
Paean. 122, 105
Plato
Areop. 20, 174
Charm. 175A–B, 169
Crit. 389B–C, 191
6.322–3, 115
Euthyd. 280E, 173
Gorg. 408B, 198
Gorg. 469C, 198
Gorg. 509C, 198
Leg. 839B, 41, 45
Leg. 888E–889C, 191
. 222D–E, 169
Meno 87E–88E, 173
Phaedr. 87E, 191
Phaedr. 88D, 41, 45
Phaedr. 245C, 33
Phaedr. 259e–261a, 40
Phaedr. 270C, 191
Prot. 343a, 32
Prot. 361A–B, 169
Resp. 354C, 169
Resp. 362A, 20
Resp. 411D, 41
Resp. 411D, 45
Resp. 476D, 163
Resp. 477A, 163
Resp. 485D, 24
Resp. 508E, 164
Resp. 521D, 20
Resp. 521D, 527B, 601B, 20
Resp. 557B, 174
Resp. 581B, 163
Thaet. 164D, 33
Symp. 215C–216C, 44
Plautus
Amph. 1011, 140
Bacch. 66–67, 140
Epid. 197–98, 140
Pliny
Ep. 2.6, 182
Ep. 2.14.2, 134
Ep. 3.3.3, 133
Ep. 3.6, 106
Ep. 5.8, 124
Nat. Hist. 34.1.6–8, 106
Plutarch
Caes. 52, 125
Caes. 57, 125
fr. 136.13, 168
Mor. 1034B, 179
Mor. 1035C–D, 191
Mor. 1044F, 179
Mor. 1122c, 166
Mor. 148D, 33
Mor. 46E–F, 167
Mor. 831a, 106
Mor. 999E, 41
Pomp. 52.5, 140
Pomp. 55.1, 147
Posidonius
fr. 163–4, 166
Pseudo-Aristotle
Probl. 901b, 168
Pseudo-Cicero
Rhet. Her. 1.1.1, 23
Pseudo-Julian
On Behalf of the Argives 408a–409d, 140
Quintilian
Inst. 1.pr.3, 34
Inst. 1.pr.9–20, 23, 38
Inst. 1.pr.13, 37
Inst. 1.pr.13, 17–19, 21
Inst. 1.pr.13–15, 23
Inst. 1.pr.14, 34
Inst. 1.pr.14–15, 21
Inst. 1.pr.17, 39
Inst. 1.1.4, 37
Inst. 1.2, 133
Inst. 1.8.6, 134
Inst. 1.9–27, 38
Inst. 1.10.5, 37
Inst. 1.10.6, 37
Inst. 1.10.8, 38
Inst. 1.10.15, 37
Inst. 1.10.24, 38
Inst. 2.4.17, 38
Inst. 2.14.1–3, 34
Inst. 2.15.24–31, 23
Inst. 2.15.33, 37
Inst. 2.15.34, 21
Inst. 2.17.27–28, 37
Inst. 2.20.2, 4, 40
Inst. 2.20.7, 40
Inst. 2.21.13, 21
Inst. 10.1.27, 134
Inst. 10.1.36, 21
Inst. 10.1.68, 37
Inst. 10.1.81–84, 134
Inst. 10.1.131, 134
Inst. 10.2.28, 38

Inst. 11.1.10, 37
Inst. 11.1.33, 21
Inst. 11.1.35, 37, 38
Inst. 12.1.18, 37
Inst. 12.1.24, 38
Inst. 12.1.39, 37
Inst. 12.1.4, 37
Inst. 12.2, 38
Inst. 12.2.1–23, 23
Inst. 12.2.29, 23
Inst. 12.2.5, 21
Inst. 12.2.6, 21
Inst. 12.2.7, 37, 59
Inst. 12.2.8, 34, 137
Inst. 12.3.12, 21
Inst. 12.6.7, 34, 37
Inst. 12.7.9, 37
Inst. 12.10.52, 23
Inst. 12.11.30, 23
Inst. 12.16.14–15, 23
Inst. 4.44.57, 23
Inst. 6.3.109, 37
Inst. 9.1.41, 38
Seneca
Ben. 2.17.3, 156
Ben. 2.18.4, 172
Ben. 4.7–8, 180
Ben. 4.8.1, 156
Ben. 5.12.3, 156
Brev. vit. 5.3, 172
Cons. Marc. 25.4, 187
Ep. 1.137–145, 24
Ep. 102.22, 186
Ep. 102.23, 187
Ep. 104.22, 24
Ep. 108.12, 20
Ep. 108.13, 156
Ep. 108.22, 156
Ep. 108.23, 24
Ep. 108.35–37, 20
Ep. 108.39, 20
Ep. 108.5–6, 23
Ep. 109, 36
Ep. 111.3, 33
Ep. 116.5, 166, 178
Ep. 120.14, 186
Ep. 120.18–19, 189
Ep. 14.9, 183
Ep. 18.4, 183
Ep. 2.75–76, 24
Ep. 20.2, 20
Ep. 25.6–7, 183
Ep. 29.11, 183
Ep. 3.59–61, 24
Ep. 3.70–73, 24
Ep. 31.1, 183
Ep. 31.11, 186
Ep. 33.4, 156
Ep. 33.7–8, 156
Ep. 36.2, 183
Ep. 4.2, 168
Ep. 41, 36
Ep. 41.1, 186
Ep. 41.2, 171
Ep. 41.4, 186
Ep. 42.1, 215
Ep. 45.5–6, 20
Ep. 45.8, 20
Ep. 48.5, 20
Ep. 50.9, 166
Ep. 52.14, 20
Ep. 53.9, 178
Ep. 58.6, 156
Ep. 64.7, 156
Ep. 65.21, 186
Ep. 72.3–4, 178
Ep. 75.3–5, 23
Ep. 75.4, 20
Ep. 75.7, 20
Ep. 79.12, 187
Ep. 79.9–10, 23
Ep. 83.1, 171
Ep. 86.1, 187
Ep. 88.4, 20
Ep. 88.42, 20
Ep. 88.42–43, 24
Ep. 89.4, 34
Ep. 89.4–6, 36
Ep. 89.5, 164
Ep. 89.6, 34
Ep. 9, 36
Ep. 9.13, 183
Ep. 9.16, 183, 187
Ep. 9.18, 183
Ep. 90.7, 156
Ep. 91.21, 188
Ep. 92.10, 190
Ep. 95.13, 20
Ep. 95.52, 198
Helv. 11.7, 186
Nat. 3.27.3, 156
Nat. 5.20, 156
Nat. 7.22.1, 156
Nat. 7.30.1–2, 156
Ot. 3.1, 156
Pol. 9.2–3, 187
Tranq. 7.4, 183
Vit. beat. 1.5, 183

Seneca (cont.)
Vit. beat. 3.2, 156
Vit. beat. 16.3, 36
Vit. beat. 18.1, 218
Vit. beat. 20.1, 218
Vit. beat. 24.4, 34
Sextus Empiricus
Math. 7.151–7, 169
Prof. 9.133–6, 215
Pyr. 2.135–43, 44
Pyr. 3.201–9, 177
Pyr. 3.247–8, 179, 181
Soranus
Gynaeciorum libri iv 2.36.1.3, 168
Gynaeciorum libri iv 2.56.2.1, 168
Stobaeus
2.111.18–112.8, 166
2.66, 169
2.73.16–74.3, 166
Anth. 4.67.24, 178
Anth. 4.84.20, 185
Strabo
Geogr. 12.3.11, 140
Geogr. 13.608, 115
Geogr. 17.3.15, 125
Geogr. 2.3.5, 44
Geogr. 5.4.7, 140
Geogr. 6.1.2, 140
Geogr. 6.3.1, 140
Geogr. 8.6.20, 105
Geogr. 8.6.23, 105, 125
Suetonius
Aug. 92.2, 140
Aug. 98.3, 140
Cal. 53.2, 24
Claud. 25.4, 124
Gramm. 16, 134
Gramm. 17, 133
Nero 12.3, 140
Nero 19, 129
SVF
1.216, 160, 161
1.235, 160
1.518, 185
1.537, 180
1.548, 160
1.566, 162
1.67, 166
1.87, 164
2.35–36, 159
2.596–632, 187, 196
2.790, 186
2.809, 187
2.949, 164
3.177, 166
3.274–5, 167
3.289, 189
3.302, 196
3.364, 162
3.378, 166
3.389, 166
3.394, 178
3.473, 166
3.519, 168
3.548, 166
3.560, 169
3.567, 161
3.567–81, 198
3.590, 162
3.594, 162
3.599, 162
3.603, 161
3.613, 161
3.653, 177
3.655, 161
3.657–84, 160
3.658, 215
3.686, 177
3.70, 173
3.743–56, 215
3.743–6, 177
3.747–50, 179
3.755–6, 177
Tacitus
Agr. 4, 34
Ann. 14.47.3, 140
Theon
Prog. 120, 23
Prog. 123.7, 9, 14, 20, 24, 37
Prog. 124.9, 37
Prog. 126.16, 37
Thucydides
1.13.2, 5, 105
Varro
Rust. 2.pref.2, 140

Papyri
P. Heid. Bi. 7 [IIa]), 114
P.Corn. I.18, 147
P.Oxy. XLIII.3136, 147

Inscriptions
AE (1984) 625, 114
CIG 1241, 115
CIG 1249, 114
CIG 2811, 111
CIL 4.4614, 115
CIL 4.4641, 115

CIL IV 1711, 133
CIL IV 1768–69, 133
CIL IV 2184, 133
CIL IV 4100, 133
CIL IV 4102–04, 133
CIL IV 4106–07, 133
CIL IV 4109, 133
CIL IV 4112–13, 133
CIL IV 4115, 133
CIL IV 4117–18, 133
CIL IV 4120, 133
CIL IV 8258–59, 133
CIL V 7232, 114
CIL VI 1300, 114
CIL VI 15031, 115
CIL VI 15325, 115
CIL VI 15439, 115
CIL VI 24452, 114
CIL VI 7513, 114
CIL X 16, 140
CIL X 527, 115
CIL X 6144, 115
CIL XIV 4562, 4, 114
CIL XVI 33, 115
Corinth VIII 232, 109, 116, 117, 152
I.Napoli I.33, 140
IAphrodMcCabe 275, 111
IG II^2 1006, 136, 137
IG II^2 1008, 144
IG II^2 1009, 144
IG II^2 1011, 144
IG II^2 1028, 144
IG II^2 1039, 144
IG II^2 1043, 144
IG II^2 1945, 115–117
IG II^2 1963, 144
IG II^2 1968, 115–117
IG II^2 1969, 1970, 144
IG II^2 1973, 144
IG II^2 1985, 115–117
IG II^2 1990, 115–117
IG II^2 2017, 144
IG II^2 2024, 144
IG II^2 2026, 144
IG II^2 2065, 144
IG II^2 2086, 144
IG II^2 2097, 144
IG II^2 2103, 144
IG II^2 2128, 144
IG II^2 2130, 144
IG II^{2}1996, 144
IG IV 1488, 114
IG XIV 616, 140
IGR 4.813, 112
IGRR 4.813, 111
ISmyrna 24.761, 111
ISmyrna 24.771, 111
ISmyrna 24.772, 111
IStratonikeia 22.1, 111
IvO 453, 136, 152, 217
IvO 56, 140
JRS (1916) 106.6, 140
JRS (1924) 198.32, 140
SEG 11.622, 115
SEG 1988, 214 no. 710, 112
SEG 24. 174 no. 496, 112
SEG 25.194 = IG II^2 2323, 221, 115
SEG 26.1044, 111
SEG 33.755, 140
SEG 8.694, 138
TAM 5.743, 111

INDEX OF MODERN AUTHORS

Adams, E., 3, 125, 127, 132, 150
Adkins, A. W. H., 35
Alcock, S., 106, 126
Alexander, L., 150
Allo, E., 10, 12, 195
Anderson, R. D., 8, 11, 32
Asher, J., 185, 194, 195, 196, 212

Baird, W., 66, 73, 125
Balch, D., 149
Balz, H., 193
Barclay, J., 51, 63, 67, 122, 148, 194, 212, 213
Barnett, P., 195
Barrett, C. K., 1, 11, 193, 210
Barth, K., 192
Baur, F. C., 1, 201, 210
Betz, H. D., 60, 65, 205
Billings, B., 150
Bowersock, G., 126
Branick, M. V. P., 1
Brookins, T., 73, 223
Brown, R., 205
Bruce, F. F., 65, 193
Brunschwig, J., 154
Brunt, P., 136
Bullmore, M., 11, 12, 16, 60
Bultmann, R., 164, 193, 195, 205
Burkert, W., 35
Butts, J., 134
Byrne, S., 145

Cadbury, H., 109
Campbell, D., 84
Caragounis, C., 204
Chandler, C., 22
Chankowski, A., 140, 141, 142
Chantraine, P., 25, 32, 159
Chow, J., 3, 73, 176
Ciampa, R. E., 1, 11, 75
Clarke, A., 2, 16, 67, 74, 106, 112, 125
Coale, A., 143
Cohoon, J., 175
Collins, R., 11, 63, 85, 158, 176, 203, 205
Colson, F., 135
Conzelmann, H., 11, 12, 63, 86, 167, 176, 193, 221
Coppens, J., 65
Cosgrove, C. H., 66, 69
Cribiore, R., 133

Dahl, N., 47, 69
Danker, F., 205
Davies, W., 184, 204
Davis, J., 2, 212
Day, J., 142
de Boer, M. C., 192
de Silva, D., 206, 207
de Vos, C., 149
de Witt, N., 205
Deissmann, G., 105
Delorme, J., 141
Demeny, P., 143
Deming, W., 84, 175, 177, 206
Dodd, C. H., 65
Doughty, D., 194
Downing, F., 58, 176, 177, 194, 215
Dunn, J. D. G., 6, 75, 107, 158
Dupont, J., 176
Dutch, R., 137, 138, 139, 141, 229

Edgar, E., 12
Engberg-Pedersen, T., 183, 205, 207, 228
Engels, D., 106, 142, 146

Fagan, G., 140
Fasher, E., 193
Fee, G., 1, 11, 12, 47, 86, 125, 161, 177, 182, 192, 193, 194, 195, 212, 221, 222

Finney, M. T., 1, 6, 16, 229
Fiore, B., 159
Fitzgerald, J., 65, 206
Fitzmyer, J., 11, 47, 124, 158
Forbes, C., 137
Friesen, S., 110, 113, 119, 120, 121, 122
Funk, R., 1, 10, 11

Galinsky, K., 131
Galloway, L., 206
Garcilazo, A., 5, 185
Gardner, P., 88
Garland, D., 11, 63, 67, 83, 85, 87, 118, 125, 127, 167, 194, 195, 196, 197, 201, 212
Garrison, R., 206
Gärtner, B., 171
Georgi, D., 210
Gerson, L., 154, 156, 159, 160
Gill, C., 136, 154, 156
Gill, D., 126
Glad, C., 150
Goodrich, J., 110, 111, 112, 113, 118
Gordon, F., 87
Goulder, M., 3, 176, 177
Grant, R., 4, 5, 47, 127, 189, 206, 207
Grindheim, S., 16
Grosheide, F., 1, 11, 12, 195
Gupta, N. K., 66

Hall, D., 72
Hansen, M., 142
Harich-Schwarzbauer, H., 160, 191
Harris, W., 133, 135
Hartog, P., 174
Hays, D., 67
Hays, R., 5, 11, 16, 58, 63, 85, 125, 149, 194, 212
Heinrici, C., 73
Henderson, I., 16
Hengel, M., 139, 204
Hering, J., 6, 12, 178
Hitchman, R., 115, 116
Hock, R., 205
Holland, G., 205
Holleman, J., 195
Holmberg, B., 75
Horrell, D., 3, 76, 106, 107, 119, 125, 127, 132, 150
Horsley, G., 111
Horsley, R., 2, 11, 12, 48, 72, 149, 169, 194, 212, 213
Hurd, J. C., 1
Huttunen, N., 206

Ijsseling, S., 20, 227
Inwood, B., 154, 156, 160

Johnson, S., 205
Jones, A. H. M., 125, 138, 139
Joyal, M., 138
Judge, E., 105, 108, 124

Käsemann, E., 193
Katsari, C., 130
Keener, C., 11, 17, 195
Kennell, N., 137, 138, 139, 141, 146, 147
Kent, J. H., 114, 139
Kerferd, G., 35, 160
Kerkeslager, A., 138
Kidd, I., 156
Kistemaker, S., 87
Koester, H., 193
Kolarcik, M., 35
Kovacs, J., 86, 203, 227
Kremer, J., 11, 202
Krentz, E., 11, 17, 18, 29
Kuck, D., 194, 212
Kwon, O. Y., 16, 31

Laird, M., 127
Lakey, M., 4
Lampe, P., 108
Landvogt, P., 111
Lang, F., 11, 12
Lee, M., 184, 206
Levison, J. R., 60
Lietzmann, D., 11, 193
Lightfoot, J. B., 4, 8, 9, 11, 12, 161, 162, 168, 221
Lim, T., 60, 205
Lindemann, A., 11, 12, 203
Litfin, Duane, 2, 12, 14–15, 18, 28, 29, 41, 46, 47, 48, 57, 58, 60, 63, 194, 202
Lomas, K., 129
Long, A., 129, 134, 154, 157, 174, 185, 214, 219
Longenecker, B., 108, 120, 121, 122
Lütgert, W., 2
Lyons, G., 65

Macdonald, M., 147
Malherbe, A. J., 5, 65, 66, 74, 105, 123, 166, 181, 205, 215, 219
Marchand, F., 115, 116
Marrou, H., 22, 25, 129, 135, 138, 139, 142
Marshall, P., 2, 124

Martin, D., 2, 16, 111, 194, 195, 212, 216
Mason, H., 111
McLean, B., 111, 112
Meeks, W., 8, 105, 107, 108, 112, 150, 192, 193
Meggitt, J., 105, 113–115, 118
Mihaila, C., 16, 30, 202
Millis, B., 128, 129, 131
Mitchell, A., 196
Mitchell, M., 6, 66, 81, 87
Mitchell, S., 130
Moffatt, J., 11, 12, 168, 190
Morgan, T., 129, 133, 134
Munck, J., 2, 15, 69
Murphy-O'Connor, J., 2, 106, 113, 119, 123, 125, 126, 140, 148, 149, 183, 205, 211

Nanos, M., 69
Newby, Z., 140
Nguyen, V., 16, 127

Oakes, P., 108, 121, 122, 123, 150
Økland, J., 131
Osborne, M., 145
Osiek, C., 149

Paige, T., 5, 194, 212
Pascuzzi, M., 5, 174
Pearson, B. A., 2
Plummer, A., 1, 10, 11, 168, 194, 203, 214
Pogoloff, Stephen, 1, 2, 17, 25, 28, 29, 30, 39, 40, 47, 60, 74, 202
Pratt, N., 186
Purcell, N., 130

Reichel, G., 134
Reinmuth, O., 137
Rist, J., 156
Robertson, A. T., 1, 10, 11, 168, 194, 203, 214
Robinson, J., 193
Rosner, B. S., 1, 11, 75
Rowe, G., 205
Runia, D., 138
Ruschenbusch, E., 142
Russell, J., 143

Salmon, E., 126, 129
Sampley, J., 193
Sandmel, S., 64
Scheidel, W., 120, 121, 143
Schenkeveld, D., 24
Schlier, H., 11
Schmithals, W., 2, 6, 11, 195, 210
Schofield, M., 183
Schotroff, L., 193
Schowalter, D., 150
Schrage, W., 11, 192, 193, 221
Sedley, D., 135, 154, 155, 174, 205, 214
Senft, C., 10, 12, 193
Sevenster, J., 187, 206
Smith, J. E., 72, 82, 85
Smyth, H. W., 83
Spengel, L., 37
Spentzou, E., 142
Spörlein, B., 192
Stanton, G. R., 25
Stark, R., 143
Stowers, S., 4, 150, 167, 180, 188, 205
Sumney, J., 65, 70
Sviatoslav, D., 172

Taiwo, M., 3
Talbert, C., 11, 63, 193, 203
Theissen, G., 3, 8, 73, 78, 105, 106, 107, 109, 110, 112, 113, 119, 122, 123, 157, 165, 182
Thiselton, A. C., 2, 11, 84, 86, 118, 127, 165, 180, 181, 184, 192, 193, 195, 202
Thomas, C., 127, 131
Thorsteinsson, R., 206
Tod, M., 136, 155
Tomlin, G., 58, 177, 194
Townsend, J., 137
Tuckett, C., 193
Tulloch, J., 147
Tzachou-Alexandri, O., 137

Van Unnik, W. C., 66
Vaughan, B., 143
Volpi, F., 159
von Soden, H., 193

Wallace, D., 30
Wallace-Hadrill, A., 130
Walters, J., 129, 148
Ward, R., 205
Weiss, A., 112
Weiss, J., 4, 6, 8, 9, 11, 161, 162, 182
Welborn, L., 9, 45, 60, 75, 111, 118, 123, 124
West, A., 139
Whitaker, G., 135
White, L. M., 65

Whitehorne, J., 138
Wickkiser, B., 128
Wilckens, U., 8, 159
Willet, R., 143, 146
Willis, W., 131
Winter, Bruce, 2, 15–16, 18, 26, 28, 30, 41, 44, 46, 47, 48, 49, 60, 126, 161, 175, 176, 196, 203, 209, 210
Wiseman, J., 124, 126, 139
Witherington, B., 11, 12, 16, 46, 63, 75, 85, 108, 193, 202
Wolff, C., 11, 30, 85
Woodhouse, S. C., 42
Woolf, G., 130, 219

Yamauchi, E. M., 3